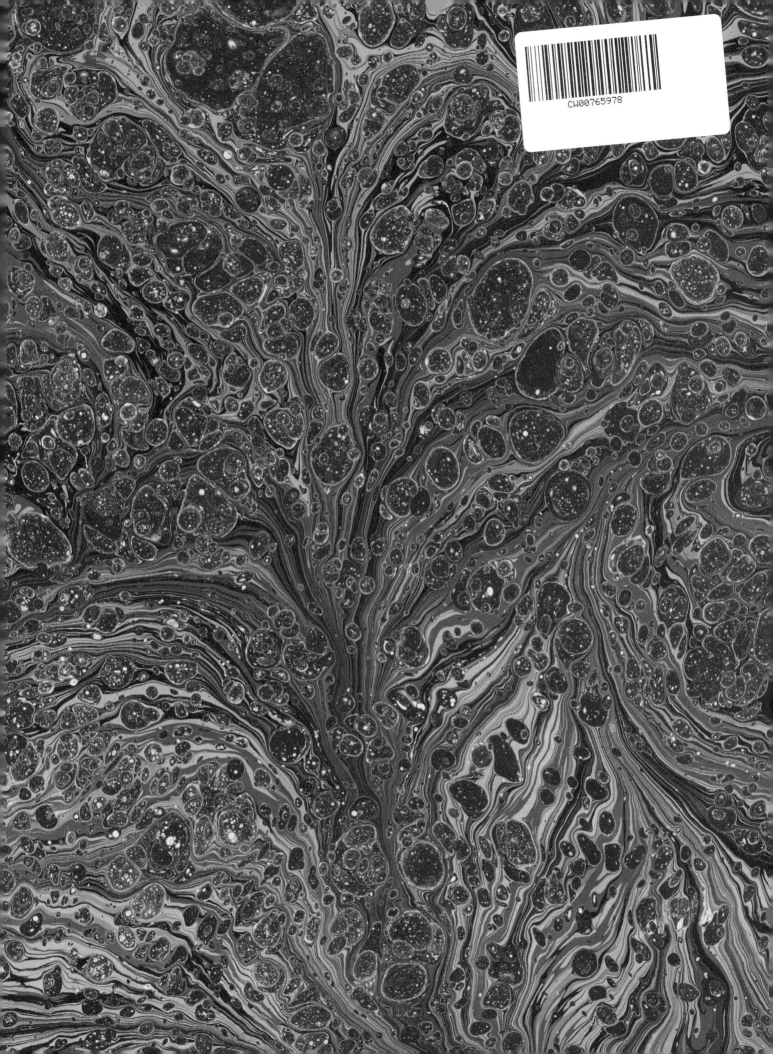

The Century Series

The Century Series:

The USAF Quest

for Air Supremacy

1950 - 1960

An Illusrated History

F-100 • F-101 • F-102
F-104 • F-105 • F-106

Ted Spitzmiller

Schiffer Military History
Atglen, PA

Bill McDonald USAF

Book Design by Stephanie Daugherty.

Copyright © 2011 by Ted Spitzmiller.
Library of Congress Control Number: 2011944778

Printed in China.
ISBN: 978-0-7643-4038-3

We are interested in hearing from authors with book ideas on related topics.

Published by Schiffer Publishing Ltd.
4880 Lower Valley Road
Atglen, PA 19310
Phone: (610) 593-1777
FAX: (610) 593-2002
E-mail: Info@schifferbooks.com.
Visit our web site at: www.schifferbooks.com
Please write for a free catalog.
This book may be purchased from the publisher.
Please include $5.00 postage.
Try your bookstore first.

In Europe, Schiffer books are distributed by:
Bushwood Books
6 Marksbury Avenue
Kew Gardens
Surrey TW9 4JF, England
Phone: 44 (0) 20 8392-8585
FAX: 44 (0) 20 8392-9876
E-mail: Info@bushwoodbooks.co.uk.
Visit our website at: www.bushwoodbooks.co.uk
Try your bookstore first.

CONTENTS

CONTENTS

This book is dedicated to those courageous young pilots and backseaters who flew the *Century Series Fighters*— gentlemen, thank you for your service!

ACKNOWLEDGMENTS

I am indebted to many *Century Series* pilots and others who combed their logbooks, diaries, and faded memories to help provide input for this book. It is impossible to credit in the order of their contribution, but let me first recognize Donn Byrnes (Colonel, USAF Ret.), a former fighter pilot and author who assisted in the organization of the manuscript over a period of several months and enlightened discussion over more than a few cups at Starbucks.

Jonathan Myer (Colonel USAF Ret.) was an incredible resource in reviewing and commenting on the entire content. His in-depth historical knowledge (and grammatical assistance) was critical to the formation of this book. He helped in researching and integrating the F-101 *Voodoo* chapter, which included: the F- and CF-101B/F interceptor, F-101A/C fighter-bomber, and RF-101A/C, G/H and B photo-reconnaissance variants. His interceptor teams comprised both U.S. and Canadian sources for North American air defense: George Coats, Lee Goettsche, Luke Graves, Neal Mishler, Frank Murray, Walt Pearson, Dudley Potter, Bob Reimers, and Jim Stumpf. Bill McDonald (ANG) covered U.S. air defense, while ADC museum historian Marty Isham verified facts for their units. Orv Malcomson led fellow-RCAF veterans Fraser Barnes, Dave Collings, Mike Dolan, Brian Drury, Don Ferguson, Russ Hellberg, Reg Howard, Tom Murray, Dave Peart, Allen Sundvall, and Gerry Walker in expanding the section on Canadian air defense operations. Bob Hanson and Dud Potter added detail for the F-101A/C nuclear strike operations, while Neal Mishler doubled for RF-101A/C operations. Photo-recce equipment data was provided for all the RF-101 versions by Chuck James (ANG), while author Doug Gordon (quoting Don Karges among many others in his shared works) addressed RF-101 operations in the Far East. Several of these contributors also provided photographs of their F-101s, both in flight and at rest, while all helped ensure accuracy of the several F-101 stories.

George Andre (Lt. Colonel USAF Ret.) supplied his extensive knowledge of several of the *Century Series*. Whenever I saw an email from George, I knew I was in for an informative and enjoyable read. Don Beck had the honor of earning the first "North Vietnam 100 Mission" patch and his insights on the recce missions were invaluable.

Edward T. Rock (Colonel, USAF Ret.), whose compilation of stories in *First In, Last Out: Stories by the Wild Weasels* prompted many email exchanges and chapter reviews. Lew Chesley (Colonel, USAF Ret.) handed over a good part of his library for my reference work, as well as his keen memory of *Wild Weasel* operations. My appreciation to Allen Lamb for his *Wild Weasel* input.

Ron Standerfer opened the archives of the Super Sabre Society's *Intake* magazine for me. Craig Coulter (Colonel, USAF Ret.) was always as close as the phone (or lunch) for answers to specific questions about his experiences with the F-100 and F-105.

W. Howard Plunkett (Lt. Colonel USAF Ret.) came to this project in its later stages and was very helpful in providing a number of critical changes, as well as allowing me to use material from his article "When the Thunderbirds Flew the Thunderchiefs" (Air Power History, Fall 2009).

Ron Darcey (F-102), and Lee Holcom and John Revak (F-100) made that extra effort to provide critical reviews.

Frank Fisher (Colonel, USAF Ret.) commanded the first F-100 fighter squadron to deploy across the Atlantic using aerial refueling. Frank has three MiGs, one probable and one damaged to his credit in Korea (about as close as you can come to being an Ace without being one). We had interesting phone interviews.

Mark Smith (Colonel, USAF Ret.) helped connect me to several important resources. I also enjoyed my phone interviews with Dudley Larsen (Lt. Colonel USAF Ret.), whose experiences in Cold Lake as an F-104 exchange pilot with the Canadian Air Force were highly illuminating. I was particularly appreciative of the details of flying the F-106 as provided by Daniel R. "Doc" Zoerb (Colonel, USAF Ret.) and William Rutledge (Brigadier General, USAF Ret.), as they offered an appreciation of the ADC intercept environment.

A last-minute contributor to the F-106 chapter was Mark Foxwell (Colonel, USAF Ret.), who, following prior "Six" assignments, was the last Commander of IWS, aka *USAF Interceptor Weapons School*, and here adds his many years of '106 expertise to that chapter.

Among the many others who contributed to this book are Stan Hood (Brigadier General, USAF Ret.), James C. Parham, Jr., and Ken Leudeke (Lt. Col. USAF Ret.), who gave interesting facets of flying the the F-104. Gerald Bjerke, Joe Revisky, and Bill Jowett provided contributions to the F-102. Thanks to Richard Stultz and Dennis Geesaman for their F-106 input, and to Jock Williams and Clay Keen.

Jack Morris provided chapter reviews, while Dave Straub shared his considerable expertise in assisting me with photo information.

Figure 00-00. A KC-136 refuels three F-106 *Delta Dart* Interceptors using the boom. Note that each has a pair of the "supersonic" wing tanks. USAF Photo.

The quotes from Frank "Pete" Everest are courtesy of *Aviation Magazine* (see the bibliography for the web link).

As with virtually anything committed to the written word, there will be mistakes, misunderstandings, and omissions for which I must take full responsibility. If there was any difficulty in putting this book together, it was having to truncate many of the narratives provided to avoid a multi-volume project. I sincerely thank these gentlemen for the honor of recording their participation as pilots and crew of the *Century Series Fighters*.

I am also appreciative of the research that so many authors performed in the publications listed in the bibliography, and to my daughter Susie Kritter and granddaughters Baylee Kritter, Crystal Spitzmiller, and Megan Spitzmiller for their assistance in the preparation of the manuscript. I would also like to recognize the quiet inspiration of yet another generation—my grandson, JJ Kritter.

Ted Spitzmiller

The U.S. Air Force's *Century Series* jet fighters (*not* "fighter-jets")—now categorized as "Generation Two" of the five-generation dynasty of jet-powered aircraft from the P-80 to the F-35—have a special mystique from their very name. Of the ten fighters addressed in this book, only six have operational histories; the other four "died early," or never were. For those who might grumble at the deliberate omission of the F-4 (né F-110) or the F-111, the author's choice is supported by no less than the editors of *Air Force magazine*: "*The F-4 and F-111 are not generally considered part of the Century Series.*" (Letters, June 2011 issue.)

For those who want to know quickly what this book is really about, scan the Table of Contents for indications of its structure and the many topics covered; they certainly go beyond just "fighters," however glamorous. A summary:

- The first five chapters cover key background topics, the *Century Series* "environment" as it were—from milestone concepts and technical prerequisites... to global politics and the wars and requirements they entailed... to various aspects of supersonic aircraft design, development, and testing against the dimly understood aerodynamics at the time... to the air-to-air weapons they were to carry as tools of their trade... to the "GCI" and then computer-driven air battle management systems that controlled our Gen-2 fighters' operations for some missions and areas... to the distinctive experiences of those of us who flew the "birds" and have lived long enough to talk about them here.

- The next ten chapters address, in numerical order, the ten fighters whose numbers comprise the *Century Series*, from the F-100 through the F-109. Six "lived" (like most of us); the others did not (like some of us)—but all share the politics of requirements and funding, the uncertainty and often chance that led to success or failure in their early years, the vision and genius behind their design, the randomness of business competition for a vacillating customer, and the skills and determination of those who tested the results.

As these chapters are in order of nomenclature, rather than historical sequence, time frames go back and forth, references may overlap, and facts and anecdotes are sometimes repetitive—but that's okay, because each aircraft chapter is self-contained and can stand on its own; the reader concerned with a specific aircraft won't have to pick pieces out of several chapters to get the story ... except that some of the general background in the first five chapters may be helpful as "common ground."

A second point is that not every topic within all the missions or activities of a given aircraft may be included. Sometimes this may be because no documentation or knowledgeable contributor turned up to address it, or perhaps because it's already treated thoroughly elsewhere. To paraphrase Defense Secretary Donald Rumsfeld from years ago, *You do the job with the forces you have.*

A third point is that, as my regular backseaters said when I was marveling at some prevailing error in Web articles, *There's an awful lot of [shi-erra] on the Internet.* And that's one thing we relics of the *Century Series* era may want to do during this third half of our lives: identify such errors and the rascals responsible and seek to "set the record straight"! For example, one of the myths that aroused universal rebuttal in this book is the oft-quoted theme that the SAGE automated system controllers could data-link their commands to interceptors' autopilots and thus fly them to intercept right from their blockhouse. We flyers all know that this was never so, but don't blame the controllers—they actually were our battle managers if WWIII had gone from Cold to Hot, but we pilots and aircrews did the final work. Blame instead the slippery souls who prefer a slick sexy story to the cooler complexity of the actual truth. These are the real facts of our lives and times, and we should try to keep them straight and true if we can. Once *we're* gone, who else will do it?

All of which leads to another discovery while researching certain facts: there are some genuine facts that simply haven't been recognized or documented—"dots" that haven't been "connected." The one we found for the F-101 chapter (e.g.) was what *really* happened to the Air Force's last F-101B—when it was retired in 1982. One serendipitous photograph... associated with an international group narrative that emerged in fragments... yielded the answer! Readers of this book may find, or may be encouraged to research, other such "facts" or bits of accepted "conventional wisdom" that turn out to be misleading... or simply wrong. So, once again, those who know from their own experience what *really* happened in this or that instance owe it to themselves and the rest of us to re-determine the truth! Leave the hype and horse-hockey to the war stories we might yet swap over a pitcher of some adult beverage—it's our true legacy that needs support.

Two strengths of this book:

- One is the various histories of how our *Century* fighters, fighter-bombers, and fighter-interceptors emerged (or not) from the clouds of uncertainty and frustration that accompanied their designs, development, and acquisition; how they could be designed to meet one requirement, but wind up being built for another, and how missions came and went, and aircraft were reconfigured accordingly. Such are the documented facts of their origination and employment. The names of company owners and key engineers are comprehensively recorded; they are the ones whose creative theories and energies drove the trial-and-error of methodical testing, were chastened by the scope and pacing of scientific discovery, and were constrained by the cycles of on-and-off government decisions, choices, and funding. Their varied competitive struggles are linked by the company interactions and outcomes that preface each *Century* fighter's chapter.

- The other strength is the author's inclusion of so many relevant, complementary— at times duplicative but reinforcing— first-person accounts by military flyers of the late 1950s into the 1970s of what it was like to operate the first supersonic fighters of their day: to "have been there" and "done that"—even if the "T-shirts" have long ago dissolved in sweat, JP-4, and battery acid. These are *not* "exploits" of the hand-waving "There I was…upside down at 40 thousand feet" variety, the kind that made my first unit commander's response be: "…*Why squadron commanders go gray.*…" Instead they are thoughtful, laconic, informal accounts of experiences with and critiques of their aircraft—not as exotic toys to be enjoyed by their "flyboys," but as complex *weapon systems* to be understood, mastered and applied within the spectrum of combat readiness through active conflict, as national decisions might require. These are the mature retrospectives of people whose choices, acquired skills and persistence enabled them to join the fraternity of those military aviators who flew the "fast jets." Their critiques of their airplanes' good and bad features are frank and illustrative, as each went through its own "growing pains": none of these fighters was perfect as fielded; all revealed flaws or limitations; and all needed fixes, modifications and successive upgrades to improve their safety, performance, and mission-specific capabilities—not only early on, but throughout their operational lives.

This book is indeed a collection of its *Century Series* fighters' stories, selective in places, but ranging from their well-documented developments as aircraft systems… to the subjective but representative accounts of their operations as U.S. war machines… by those who knew them best—the men who flew them, and loved them for what they were.

Jonathan Myer
(June, 2011)

United States Air Force fighter designations (which started with the Curtiss P-1 in 1923) reached the century mark with the design of the North American F-100 in 1952. This occurred at the very point where operational fighters had the potential to exceed the speed of sound in level flight. Fighter aircraft developed during the decade of the 1950s, with the designations F-100 through F-109, are referred to as the *Century Series*.

As the second generation of America's jet-powered combatants, they are remarkable for several reasons, besides being the first specifically designed to fly at supersonic speeds. They embodied the research gained from experimental craft such as the Bell X-1 (the first to break the seemingly impenetrable sound barrier). However, unlike research aircraft, they were exploring new dimensions of flight from an operational perspective, and their Mach busting excursions, usually measured in minutes ("dash" as opposed to "cruise"), were limited by the efficiency of the powerplants and airframes of the era. These aircraft had to perform, not just in predefined test conditions, but also in an expanded performance envelope encompassing high speeds at extreme altitudes, pulling heavy G-forces and firing weapons or releasing ordnance. Perhaps more importantly, these new high-performance fighters had to be capable of being flown by the average military pilot—some with not quite "*the right stuff.*"

Three *Century Series* aircraft (F-103, F-108 and F-109) never advanced beyond the design stage, as requirements, technology, and tactics moved at a rapid pace during that decade—the rising cost of developing such advanced aircraft had to be balanced against other defense needs. Only one was built and not put into production (F-107). The useful lives of those six aircraft that went into operational service were long and varied—one (the F-104) performed in its military role almost 50 years after the prototype first took to the air.

The result of this innovative decade of the 1950s was a stable of aircraft that forged new pathways through the sky. Even today, more than a half-century later, current production fighters barely surpass the speeds and altitudes at which these aircraft flew. However, today's fighters employ capabilities that *Century Series* pilots could only have dreamed. Even some *Century Series* design objectives were not realized within the development environment of the 1950s and required the advances in materials, propulsion, electronics and computing technology of the 1960s and beyond to ultimately allow them to reach their full potential. Thus, the *Century Series*

Figure 00-01. The principal experimental aircraft flown by NACA in the early 1950s that contributed to the wealth of knowledge that produced the Century Series. The Douglas X-3 (center) surrounded by the Bell X-1A (lower left), Douglas D-558, Convair XF-92A, Bell X-5, Douglas D-558-2, and Northrop X-4. NASA Photo.

Figure 00-02. First four Century Series fighters at Edwards AFB. F-104 (foreground), F-100, F-102, and the F-101. USAF photo.

story is one that moves past their initial introduction and to the operational period in the war in Southeast Asia. It was here that some decisions made a decade earlier would come to haunt and hinder the pilots who had to fight that war from the cockpit.

In describing the various aspects of the *Century Series*, some readers may find it helpful to review a brief history of the genealogy of the fighter (Chapter

Figure 00-03. First four Century Series Fighters. North American F-100A Super Sabre (bottom), Lockheed F-104 Starfighter (left), McDonnell F-101 Voodoo (top), and Convair F-102 Delta Dagger (right). USAF Photo.

One), the geopolitical nature of the Cold War (Chapter Two), and a fundamental understanding of fighter design considerations (Chapter Three) and the weapons carried (Chapter Four). The various attributes of the fighter pilot of the era (Chapter Five) introduce a brief biography of several who are subsequently quoted at various times in the remainder of the book.

On 18 September 1962 the Department of Defense, under the direction of its Secretary, Robert McNamara, instituted the unification of military aircraft designations using the USAF system as a model. An attempt was made to fit existing Navy designations still on the books as operational with the numbering scheme that started over from "1". Thus, the initial set from F-1 (the North American FJ *Fury*) to F-11 (Grumman F-11-F *Tiger*) were drawn from these. Air Force fighter designations, which at that time had progressed to the General Dynamics F-111, were retained, except that the McDonnell F-110 assumed its Navy-derived name as the F-4.

Some fighters that carried a century designation are not included in this book. The McDonnell F-110 (which became the tri-service F-4) was first developed as a Navy interceptor, and therefore has been omitted. The General Dynamics F-111, which represented a new third generation that was "more bomber than fighter" of the 1960s-70s era, is likewise absent. The Lockheed F-117 *Nighthawk* stealth tactical attack plane, whose use of the *Century Series* designation was an attempt to mask the project for security considerations, is also beyond the scope of this book. The numbers between the F-111 and the F-117 were apparently used as cover designations for Soviet fighters clandestinely brought into the United States for test and evaluation.

The air power lessons of World War II, coupled with the strategies of nuclear warfare as the Cold War evolved, deeply affected the design, roles and tactics of the *Century Series Fighters*. The rapid advances made in electronics and the increasing power of the newer engines made the post-war period one of extensive prototype research and development. This is the story of the *Century Series Fighters*; a chronicle of the men and machines and the ideas that set the standard for a half-century of fighter development.

The Fighter is Born

The development of combat aircraft generically called fighters has progressed through a wide variety of demands over the years. Introduced during the First World War, aircraft armed with one or two light machine guns went out like knights on horseback to take command of their domain. Their primary task was to deny the enemy the ability to perform airborne reconnaissance operations.

The Wright brothers invented the airplane only a decade before the Great War—the "*war to end all wars*." They prophesied that the airplane would transform war—and it did. However, the development of combat arms in a three-dimensional medium was not as straightforward as some had envisioned—including Orville and Wilbur.

The four forces of flight coupled with the three axes of control became the essential foundations that channeled the development of the warplane. However, with the advent of hostilities in August 1914, much of the knowledge of aerodynamics was still largely unknown. While the Wrights had established their work based on scientific principles, many of those who followed often failed to exercise such discipline.

World War I pioneered the introduction of the primary fighter attributes. The use of a single control "stick" for the pilot to control both pitch (elevator) and roll (aileron), defined by several pioneers including Glen Curtiss, become a standard feature. Louis Blériot, best remembered as the first to fly the English Channel from France to England in 1909, was one of the first to introduce rudders moved by the feet.

Airplanes were actually used in combat for the first time before WWI in skirmishes between the Italians and the Turks in 1911, when Italian Captain Carlo Piazza flew a Blériot to reconnoiter the Turkish positions. A lieutenant Gavotti achieved the distinction of being the first to drop small bombs, carried in a bag in the cockpit, on the Turks. A few airplanes also saw service in French Morocco in 1912. However, none of these encounters produced any proof of the airplane's value as an armed combatant. There were many in the general staff who doubted the usefulness of airplanes in producing "*death from the skies*" as prophesied.

In the United States, the airplane was initially incorporated into the combat arms for its ability to reconnoiter, as it had been in other countries. The concept of actual battle in the air was typically seen as illogical by those in high command—perhaps because they

Figure 01-01. Lieutenant Myron Crissy and Phillip Parmalee are credited with dropping the first bombs from a Wright Type B in January 1911, in a demonstration conducted near San Francisco. PD.

lacked personal understanding of the air environment (*battlespace*, as it is often referred to today) and the fragile nature of these early creations. Speed was not a factor, because the idea was to survey the battlefield carefully. The term "scout" was often applied to the role, as adapted from the Cavalry.

Initially airdropped notes, to speed the dissemination of information, augmented the returning pilot's personal descriptions of the battlefield. Cameras and air-to-ground radio communications via Morse code followed. To the reconnaissance role artillery spotting was added.

There were other more visionary members of the aviation fraternity, such as the Frenchman August Adolphe Pégoud. He demonstrated the first elementary aerobatics and made the first exhibition parachute jump from an aircraft. Pégoud is sometimes credited with performing the first loop on 21 September 1913—a most basic and essential combat maneuver. However, history records the Russian Pyotr Nesterov as being

Figure 01-02.
August Adolphe Pégoud demonstrated the first aerial combat maneuvers in 1913. He was shot down and killed early in 1915 by Unteroffizier Kandulski, one of his pre-war students. PD.

Figure 01-03. Lieutenant Jacob Fickel demonstrates how he fired his rifle while airborne. Glenn Curtiss is the pilot of this 1910 flight. PD.

the first on 9 September 1913. He was flying a French Nieuport IV monoplane.

Almost immediately, as aircraft began appearing over the troops on the front lines, rifle and machine gun fire from the ground was used to repel the "spies." However, the variety and newness of aircraft made positive national identification almost impossible. When a contingent of Royal Navy aircraft, which were setting up to land at a nearby field, came under fire by Royal Marines, the problem demanded an answer. Immediately, shield-shaped Union Jacks were painted on the underside of the wings of all British aircraft. Within months, the "*colors*" of each of the warring participants were displayed as colored "roundels" to establish the nationality of the combatants. The Germans were an exception, opting to use the "*Iron Cross*" as their emblem.

Airplanes of opposing armies occasionally saw each other while going about their reconnaissance duties, and it was not long before the obvious occurred. Each side recognized that it was important to deny the other the freedom to observe the battlefield. There is a famous legend that at least a few pilots carried bricks in the cockpit, which they allegedly threw at the opposition.

United States Army Lieutenant Jacob Fickel had demonstrated the firing of a rifle from a moving plane in 1910. Fickel wrote about his experience:

"*Mr. Glenn H. Curtiss conceived the idea of firing a service-rifle from an aeroplane, and suggested ... that an army marksman be detailed to make the experiment.* [I was] *sent to Sheepshead Bay* [Long Island, New York] *and Mr. Curtiss took me on two short flights.*" Fickel then goes on to describe '*three*' flights.

"*On the first flight, we were in the air for about a minute and a half. We fired one shot from a height of seventy-five feet, and missed. The breaking of the feed-pipe* [a problem with the airplane] *forced us to come down. After repairs, we went up for another flight of about seven minutes. This time we fired five shots. Only the last, from a height of about two hundred and fifty feet, hit the target.*

"*The next flight lasted about eight minutes and included a short cross-country run. This time four shots were fired, of which two hit the target and the other two were close misses.*" It is interesting that he described a flight of just eight minutes as a 'cross-country.'

"*The result of the experiments seems to indicate: (a) that the speed and the bobbing of the machine do not prevent accurate aiming; (b) that it is easy to load while in flight; (c) that the recoil does not affect the balance* [stability of the aircraft]; *(d) that practice and experience in estimating speed, wind, height, and distance are as necessary as when firing from the ground.*

"*The experiments seem to call for a light machine-gun to fire a tracer bullet of about thirty caliber. The sight should be very simple and admit of rapid adjustment for speed, wind, and distance.*

"*It is, of course, absurd to think that aeroplanes can be used in the near future as gun platforms for operations against an enemy on the ground. It is also highly improbable that they can be greatly damaged by gun-fire from the ground, provided they stay up for, say, three thousand feet.*

"*In the wars of the immediate future, however, aeroplanes will be used on each side, and must be prepared for both offense and defense. And that is where the machine-gun on the aeroplane will find its place.*"

Captain Charles Chandler fired the first machine gun while airborne in 1912. However, the ability of the pilot to both fly the airplane and fire a weapon at another was considered a difficult proposition.

Thus, with respect to aerial combat, conventional wisdom dictated two crewmembers—one to fly the plane and the other to do battle with a flexible machine gun mounted on a swivel. The first recorded downing of one plane by gunfire from another occurred on 5 October 1914. Joseph Frantz, flying a French Voisin pusher, and his gunner, Louis Quénault, destroyed a German Aviatik B.1.

Figure 01-04. Captain Charles Chandler and Lieutenant Roy Kirtland in a Wright Flyer Model B demonstrated the first firing of a Lewis machine gun from an airplane in 1912. The cooling shroud over the barrel was subsequently determined to be unnecessary for airborne applications. PD.

Figure 01-05. The French Voisin pusher is the type in which Joseph Frantz and his gunner Louis Quénault destroyed a German Aviatik B.I. Note that the gunner, with his "Hotchkiss," sat in front of the pilot in a fuselage that was called "The Chicken Coop." PD.

However, the weight of the second man (the gunner) became an issue in these underpowered wood and fabric creations. In addition, the ability of the gunner to communicate with the pilot to help position the aircraft—either for attack or for defense—was awkward at best. In the case of the Voisin, the gunner sat in front of the pilot so the communication was somewhat intuitive. Nevertheless, by April 1915 the first aerial combat units in the Royal Flying Corps became operational using the Vickers F.B.5 with a forward gunner.

The idea of mounting a fixed forward-firing machine gun to the fuselage and having the pilot aim the aircraft at his antagonist was an obvious alternative. However, many felt it was impractical, as it required firing through the propeller arc. Raymond Saulnier, an aircraft designer of that era, devised an interrupter mechanism to do just that. Working on a cam, the device momentarily stopped the firing of the Hotchkiss machinegun to allow for the passage of the propeller in front of the gun barrel.

Mounting the device on a Morane Saulnier Type I monoplane in November 1914, the development process included attaching some metal wedge shaped plates to the propeller. These would deflect any errant bullets that hit the propeller, as the mechanical linkage of the Hotchkiss 8mm machine gun to the synchronizer was imprecise.

Working with Saulnier was French pilot Roland Garros. Garros had achieved some recognition before the war for being the first to fly across the Mediterranean Sea (from France to Tunisia). Garros was impatient, and had determined that even

Figure 01-06.
To counter German aerial supremacy in mid-1915 and to sidestep the lack of a suitable interrupter gear, Geoffrey DeHavilland designed the DH.2, which was a pusher. PD.

without the interrupter, only one in ten bullets hit the prop—and a more robust deflector could handle that problem. Bringing the yet-to-be perfected invention into combat, he claimed his first victory on 1 April 1915 with the Morane Bullet (as the plane was often called). He had two more victories over the next two weeks before a mechanical failure (reportedly induced by antiaircraft fire) forced him down behind German lines on 18 April 1915. Garros attempted to destroy the plane but was unsuccessful, and on examining it, the Germans were quick to recognize the significance of the idea. However, because they tended to favor steel-jacketed bullets rather than the softer copper jackets of the French, the wedges were not an acceptable solution—a more efficient synchronizing gear was. The Germans approached one of their key designers to effect a solution.

The Dutchman Anthony Fokker, who would become renowned for his line of superior fighters, devised a simple interrupter mechanism based on a technique patented a few years earlier by Franz Schneider. While the legend states this work was accomplished in just three days, it more than likely took about two weeks and involved three of Fokker's engineers. Within two months, with this capability installed on the Fokker M.5K (a copy of the Morane Saulnier renamed the *Eindecker E.I.*), Germany's first

Figure 01-07. Roland Garros collaborated with Raymond Saulnier in equipping the Morane Saulnier Type L with a machine gun to fire through the propeller arc. PD.

fighter became a legendary component of the German Air Force (*Luftstreitkräfte*). The machinegun of choice was a modified air-cooled Maxim built by Spandau, firing the 9mm Parabellum cartridges—thus it was sometimes referred to as the "*Parabellum.*"

History records that two pilots are given credit for downing the first plane with the interrupter device on the Fokker M.5K/MG "E.5/15" *Eindecker*: famed German Ace Max Immelmann and Kurt Wintgens. Wintgens' claim was not recognized by the Germans because it fell in French-held territory and could not be confirmed. But the new capability caused German pilots like Immelmann and Oswald Boelcke to take a more innovative view of their role in the air war—and a new "hunting echelon," or *Jadgestafel*, was formed. For almost six months, the *Eindecker* reigned supreme and was the origin of the *Fokker Scourge* legend that grew from the innovation. So secretive were the Germans about their synchronizing mechanism that the *Eindecker* was restricted from overflying Allied positions for fear it might be shot down and the mechanism revealed.

It was at this time that the performance of the fighter came into question. A larger engine to provide more speed was an obvious part of the equation. Likewise, the ability of the pilot to maneuver quickly required more responsive controls and better training. Ailerons replaced the *Eindecker's* wing-warping, and the drag-producing open framework of the fuselage gave way to more complete fabric covering.

The Lewis .303 light machinegun (weighing 13 kg—28 pounds) was quickly adopted by the allies (principally France and Great Britain) as the primary armament for their fighters. Its 97-round circular cartridge magazine could be replaced in-flight. It had a firing rate of 500 rounds per minute and an effective range of 500 yards, making it a useful airborne weapon. The *"ring-and-bead"* gunsight was adopted to provide a reference for the pilot, who had to judge the turn rate against range to determine the appropriate lead on the target.

Because many pilots were skeptical of the imperfect Saulnier synchronizing mechanism, the allies began mounting the Lewis machine gun on top of the upper wing to fire over the arc of the propeller. By the summer of 1915 this was done with a new French fighter, the Nieuport 11, and it worked well. This arrangement, however, required the pilot to stand up in the cockpit to clear a jam or replace the ammunition drum. A Sergeant Foster of the Royal Flying Corp fashioned a mounting structure that allowed the pilot to slide the gun back to him while he remained safely belted to the seat. This also permitted repositioning the gun to fire almost vertically while flying under an enemy aircraft. This arrangement was adopted on several aircraft of the day.

Oswald Boelcke and Max Immelmann flew the *Eindecker* through the summer of 1915. Both quickly became Aces—a term originating with the French newspapers of the day that referred to sports stars as *Aces*. When Adolphe Pégoud, the famous French flyer, racked up his fifth kill, the newspapers used the expression to describe his feat and "five kills" became the coveted number for being considered an *Ace*. The German

Figure 01-09. A Lewis gun (less the cooling shroud) mounted on the top wing of an AVRO 504. The Foster mounting mechanism allowed servicing the gun in-flight and permitted the pilot to fire vertically at aircraft above him. PD.

Figure 01-08. The actual Fokker Eindecker flown by Kurt Wintgens when he scored the first aerial victory using the interrupter firing mechanism. PD

government did not recognize the term, instead awarding the *Pour le Mérite*, for gallantry, to aviators who destroyed eight aircraft (the number of "kills" to achieve the award was constantly raised during the course of the war). The common name for this award resulted from the color of the medallion and the fact that its first recipient for air combat was Max Immelmann—thus "*The Blue Max*." The British at first refused to track "kills," but soon recognized the value to morale—and propaganda. For America, Eddie Rickenbacker with 26 victories would be the leading *Ace*, although his squadron mate, Lieutenant Douglas Campbell, was the first American to achieve *Ace* status.

Garros eventually escaped from his German captors in February 1918 and returned to fly again. He was killed on 5 October 1918, just a day short of his 30th birthday. He is officially credited with two more victories (although reliable sources say only one of those was confirmed). History therefore remembers Roland Garros as an *Ace*.

With the advent of the fixed forward-firing machine gun, the ability of one aircraft to position itself (hopefully undetected) behind its adversary, and pointed at its target, determined the ideal stalking spot—the *six-o-clock* position. This tail-chasing method of pitting one plane against another—initially thought to be extremely difficult—was soon recognized as the most advantageous. The term *dogfight* became an established term to describe an engagement between two aircraft, and it quickly became obvious that maneuverability was the key to aerial combat.

Based on Boelcke and Immelmann's experiences with the *Eindecker*, the tactics and maneuvers they developed remain today a fundamental part of the fighter pilot's repertoire. They include the loop, roll, split-S and Immelmann. Boelcke described the six primary reasons for his success in a brief document called *Dicta Boelcke*. Among the factors of survival was the need to keep one's head turning, constantly scanning the skies—especially to the rear. This movement of the head and neck in the tight flying clothing of the day is what brought forth the use of the silk scarf—to avoid the chafing of the skin by the rough cloth of the collar. The white scarf, leather helmet and goggles would epitomize the dress of the aviator for posterity.

Aerial combat early in the war was often an individual effort, with a pilot flying out at dawn to catch the two-seater reconnaissance planes taking their first pictures of the day. Small groups of two or three might work together, but it was not until 1917 that larger formations were employed to secure the air space over the battlefield. The squadron (or *Jagdstaffeln* in German parlance) was the basic organizational structure.

The British and French, to provide for an orderly assembly of multiple aircraft, adopted the V-formation. This was a surprise to many of the newly trained pilots, who arrived at their operational squadrons without any knowledge of formation flying. It also served as an inherent defense for the lead plane, whose pilot could use hand signals to his flight, as each member had a clear view of his cockpit. The Germans apparently did not initially use any recognizable formation, as several accounts from the era observed, "*It was a constant source of surprise that Germans never flew in any recognized formation but just exactly like a cluster of flies,*" wrote RAF Captain Donald Hardman.

The Fokker *Eindecker* saw increasingly more powerful engines, as the E.II went from 80 to 100-hp and finally to the E.IV of 160-hp with two Spandau 7.92mm MG08 guns firing at 400 rounds per minute. The *Eindecker,* with its high-torque rotary engine, was a difficult aircraft to fly. It was surpassed by other designs on both sides by mid-1916. For the allies, the advent of the Hispano-Suiza aluminum block V-8 rendered the rotary radial obsolete, and successive versions provided 140 to 235-hp. On the German side, the in-line six-cylinder liquid-cooled Mercedes D.III was a primary power plant, growing to 180-hp by the end of the war.

As the essentials that governed aircraft performance became better understood, such as the significance of the *aspect ratio* (wing length to its chord, or breadth) and *wing loading* (aircraft weight per square foot of wing area), the airplane by 1918 had become a respectable fighting machine.

With the specialized fighting plane came the need to provide more effective training in basic airmanship, as well as fighting tactics. Early in the war pilot training was almost criminally negligent, with some receiving as little as five hours of solo flight time before being sent to operational units to finish the job. The advent of the dual-control airplane, actually another pioneering innovation of the Wrights, coupled with their mechanical flight simulator, was a key to the significant numbers of truly qualified aviators (approximately 75,000 from all participating nations) who took to the skies by the end of 1918. The American Army had only 26 trained pilots when it entered the war in April 1917; by Armistice Day in November 1918, more than 17,000 had completed basic flight training.

Aircraft designs went from the drafting board to the front line in as little as two months, and could be withdrawn within a year. The Fokker D.VII and D.VIII, along with the French SPAD XVII and British S.E.5, emerged from the Great War as the premier fighters. The Fokker's tubular steel frame and semi-cantilevered wings represented a significant step forward in construction techniques. The influence of the French in aircraft nomenclature was

Figure 01-10. The performance and structure of the German Fokker D.VII of WWI was so significant that Article IV of the Treaty of Versailles required all to be turned over to the Allies. It featured the "N" strut wing bracing without any drag-producing wires. PD.

forever established during this period, with such words as *fuselage*, *aileron*, and *empennage*. By the end of that conflict, the single-seat fighter was the dominant and romantic weapon for waging war in the air.

From 1914 through 1918, the advances in aeronautics were nothing short of amazing. Structures, controls, armament and power plants made major gains in the space of months rather than years. The Germans advanced aeronautical science with their laboratory at Gottingen University under the direction of Ludwig Prandtl. The thick airfoil employed on the Fokker D.VII generated significantly more lift and less drag than previous designs. With the availability of more interior space in the wing, fully cantilevered wings were possible—eliminating the biplane's truss-like and drag-producing external bracing of struts and wires.

The Fokker Dr.I, D.VII and D.VIII were perfect examples of these advances. Speeds of 140 mph were achieved with engines of up to 200 horsepower. With a gross weight approaching 2,000 pounds, these fighters were able to operate up to 18,000 feet. That altitude for the pilot was another problem.

Depending on the pilot's fitness and experience, the combined effects of decreasing oxygen (hypoxia) and increasing cold (hypothermia) could impair both his functions and judgment to a dangerous

degree, with effects combining fatigue, wooziness, euphoria, tunnel vision or "grey-out," decreased coordination, and even loss of consciousness; moreover, hypoxic and cold-induced numbness could render him more vulnerable to enemy attack. It was not until 1917 that German Ru.C.IV and Fokker D.VII pilots began to use a rudimentary oxygen supply system, whereby the pilot could squeeze a bladder to force oxygen through a pipe-stem held in his mouth.

As for the parachute, observers in balloons began using them when it became apparent that the balloon was a prime target—and hydrogen (the buoyant gas) burned rapidly! At first, it was felt that the balloon could be hauled down quickly when attacked, but that was not to prove an effective response. Therefore, the Observer wore a harness and the parachute was in a container outside the basket. With respect to the airplane, the Germans recognized the value of saving the pilot and were the first to provide a workable system. Germany's second-ranking air ace, Ernst Udet, was one of the first to use the parachute to bail out of a disabled airplane in combat. The British were slower to see the value, as the high command felt that if the parachute were available, the more timid pilot might opt for it rather than face the enemy. By the end of the war virtually all combatants had parachutes available, although many seasoned pilots refused to wear them, trusting more to their combat skills than a few yards of silk.

The parachutes of this era were simply stowed in a bag and connected to the harness worn by the pilot. It was believed that a person would lose consciousness if they fell at a high speed through the air. Thus, there was no "*free fall*" involved. It was not until after the war that the now famous "*D-ring*" (so named because of its shape) became a part of a parachute that the pilot wore. Army Lieutenant Harold R. Harris became the first recorded flyer to save his life using a backpack parachute in free fall on 22 October 1922, when the plane he was testing broke up over McCook Field in Ohio.

Aviation in the United States Army was initially included as the *Aeronautical Division* of the U.S. Signal Corps in August 1907, where it remained until 1914, when it became the *Aviation Section*. Aircraft development in the United States during this period was hindered by the legal action of the Wright Brothers in an attempt to protect their patents to the invention. As a result, the Europeans quickly developed more advanced aircraft. Thus, following its entry into World War I in April 1917, America was tasked by the allies to produce selected combat-proven French and English designs. An exception was the Curtiss JN-4 *Jenny*, which became the *de facto* American trainer.

Six months before the war ended, the Army General Staff recognized the increasingly important role that aviation was playing in combat and the *Aviation Section* of the Signal Corps became the *Army Air Service* in May 1918. Following the French vocabulary, which referred to the fighter as "*Avions de Passe*," the Americans adopted the word *pursuit* to define the genre.

Between the Wars

During the two decades between the world wars, pursuit ships continued to undergo refinement as more powerful engines and improved structures allowed mounting heavier guns. Although late to enter the fighter realm, American aircraft manufacturers of the 1920s, principally Curtiss and Boeing, soon provided competitive products despite the postwar frugal economic era endured by the military.

Prior to 1919, the Army Air Services used the manufacturers' designations to identify airplanes. However, in September of that year fifteen classifications were established to categorize military aircraft—with the prefix "P" assigned to pursuit ships. The Curtiss P-1 was the first in the new numbering scheme adopted by the U.S. Army in 1924.

In 1926, the Army *Air Service* was again elevated in the organizational hierarchy to the status of *Air Corps*. This was a result of several factors, perhaps most prominently the court martial of General William "Billy" Mitchell. The courtroom dramatics brought to light many of the problems hindering technological development and combat planning activities of the general staff.

By the end of the "*Roaring Twenties*," the typical fighter now weighed in at 3,300 pounds with a 700-hp engine. It could achieve 200 mph and reach 26,000 feet. While two .30 caliber machine guns were the standard, the .50 caliber was beginning to make its appearance.

The structural transition highlighted the recognition that engine power could produce only as much speed as the generated drag allowed. Drag increases as the square of the speed (twice the speed generates four times the drag), so it was important to streamline the form.

While Prandtl's aeronautical work in Germany was revolutionary, aviation research had not been completely

Figure 01-11. The Curtiss P-1 was the production version of the XPW-8B (the letter W defined the engine as water-cooled). U.S. Army Photo.

neglected in other countries. In America, the National Advisory Committee for Aeronautics (NACA) was created in 1915, but with less emphasis and funding than Prandtl's *Aerodynamical Laboratory of the University of Göttingen*. Orville Wright was a member of the first NACA board, and its initial fiscal allocation was $5,000. (Note that the organization was referred to by its letters N-A-C-A, rather than by a pronounceable word as was done with its successor—NASA.)

Following the war, one of Prandtl's disciples, Max Munk, immigrated to the United States at the urging of several influential American aerodynamicists. He brought with him many new ideas that included wind tunnel designs. NACA conceived many vital innovations between 1920 and 1940, especially those resulting from the development of, and research with, large wind tunnels. These included the NACA cowling for radial engine planes that significantly reduced their drag. The constant-speed propeller was another advance that dramatically increased the performance of both military and commercial aviation.

Likewise, tubular steel framework (truss structures), which had long since taken over from wood, and its fabric covering yielded to an all-metal semi-monocoque structure—where the aircraft skin carries much of the stress. Fokker had illustrated this concept during the war with his Dr.I, in which the wing was covered with a thin plywood rather than fabric and did not require external wire bracing. The German Albatross D.III had a cigar-shaped fuselage made of plywood. With these construction techniques, and the use of aluminum instead of plywood, only the control surfaces remained fabric-covered by the end of the 1930s.

Biplanes, thought to be more desirable than monoplanes because of their nimbleness and strength, soon gave way to the speed of the cantilevered (strut-less) monoplane by the early 1930s. Of course, the high wing loading of the monoplane fighters required higher landing speeds. The development of the trailing-edge flap and leading-edge slat that could be extended during take-off and landing provided more lift at low speeds, allowing 300-mph fighters to land at 80 mph. Retractable landing gear followed.

Figure 01-12. Jack Knight (right) demonstrated airborne voice radio communication. The cold environment of the open cockpit in winter is evidenced by Knight's heavy flying suit. U.S. Army Photo.

The open cockpit was given up reluctantly, as many pilots received useful information from "*the wind in their face*." Anyone who has flown in an open cockpit recognizes that there are important cues that the pilot can receive by feeling the slipstream and listening to the sounds of the airframe. Nevertheless, the drag and noise (as well as the cold of high altitudes) assured that the enclosed cockpit would prevail.

Even before turbo-charged and super-charged piston engines were permitting operations into the stratosphere (above 35,000 feet), it was apparent that, for the human body to survive let alone fight at altitudes above even 12,000 feet, provisions were required to sustain the pilot's primary physiological need—oxygen. Although oxygen had been discovered in the 1770s and increasingly used by balloonists during the 19th century, its use aboard pursuit ships of the Great War was scant. Post-war experiments were made as early as 1919, but it was not until the late 1920s that some fighters routinely carried a small tank of compressed oxygen from which a tube delivered the precious gas to the mouth of the pilot. The more formal oxygen mask followed quickly, in which the oxygen was delivered under pressure because the prevailing atmospheric pressure above 24,000 feet was not sufficient to allow the oxygen to be absorbed into the hemoglobin of the blood at those high altitudes. The oxygen was subsequently stored in a liquid state.

The fully cantilevered wing (all internal bracing with no struts) became strong and deep enough during the 1930s for some of the armament to be mounted within to fire outside the propeller arc. This allowed for more rounds per minute, because guns firing through the propeller were typically 15 percent slower due to the synchronizing requirement. However, wing-mounted guns required "*alignment to convergence*" at a point usually 100 to 250 yards ahead to focus their destructive power for maximum effectiveness.

The ability to communicate with the ground and other pilots that would become a critical factor for the effective application of fighters was pioneered by the U.S. Air Mail in 1922. Jack Knight first used the five-tube transmitter and seven-tube receiver equipment in a specially modified de Havilland DH-4.

Figure 01-13.
The Boeing P-26 was the first all-metal low-wing monoplane accepted by the Army. It retained the open cockpit, fixed-pitch propeller and non-retracting gear. Note the high headrest to protect the pilot should the plane end up inverted following a bad landing. U.S. Army Photo.

Another critical factor that allowed much more utility of the airplane was the development of electronic navigation and "*fog flying*" instrumentation. Unless the aircraft could safely take off and land with low ceilings and visibilities, their usefulness was severely limited in marginal weather conditions. Through grants from the *Guggenheim Fund for the Promotion of Aeronautics*, both of these capabilities were conquered by the mid-1930s (Daniel Guggenheim was a millionaire philanthropist of the time who had an interest in aviation). Gyroscopic heading and attitude indicators, coupled with advances in radio beacons, brought a high level of capability and reliability to "*instrument flying*"—as it is called today.

The "*Great Depression*," which essentially began in 1929, drove the military into a tight corner, with little money for new designs or training. It was fortunate that men like Guggenheim were able to step into the breach and fund critical ideas that otherwise might have taken many more years to develop.

During the 1930s, the ascendancy of strategic bombing put forth the idea that the bomber "*will always get through*" and that, when flown in formation, its defensive guns could effectively repel the fighter. This belief carried into WWII with devastating results.

While the single-seat single-engine configuration was most prevalent during this period, there were other fighter designs, such as the Bell FM-1 *Airacuda*. This twin-engine pusher aircraft employed a multi-place crew of five with flexible 37mm cannon in forward compartments of the engine nacelles. These types of designs, while they appeared good on paper, did not work in the real world, as the British discovered with the Boulton-Paul *Defiant* "turret fighter" during the Battle of Britain in 1940: its rear-mounted four-gun turret added drag that rendered it vulnerable to more agile German fighters, while its lack of forward-firing guns left it defenseless against frontal attacks; it fared better as a night-fighter and jamming aircraft until supplanted by newer and more capable fighters.

The Curtiss P-40 *Warhawk* typified the U.S. fighter at the close of the 1930s, with a 1,150-hp engine propelling a 7,200-pound airplane. Its early variant had both wing- and nose-mounted guns and was capable of fighting at altitudes of 25,000 feet and speeds of 320 mph. Although noticeably inferior to the best of both Japanese and German fighters at higher altitudes, this was not discovered until it entered combat. On the other hand, it did well at medium and lower altitudes, where its maneuverability and ruggedness were strong points; it could out-dive most of its opponents and was quite effective in a ground attack role. Despite its limitations, it was flown by 28 nations throughout World War II and, with its *Tomahawk* and *Kittyhawk* variants, was

Figure 01-14. The Bell FM-1 Airacuda first flew in 1937 and was defined as a "Fighter Multi-place." There were so many problems with the concept that it was never placed into production. U.S. Army Photo.

Figure 01-15. The Curtiss P-40 was America's "first line" fighter at the start of WWII. Although inferior in performance to the fighters of Germany, Japan, and Britain, it was effective when its advantages and weaknesses were understood and accommodated for by tactics. U.S. Army Photo.

the third most produced U.S. fighter ever, after the P-51 and P-47.

The P-40's most noted success was in the hands of General Clair Chennault's "*Flying Tigers*" (more formally the 1st American Volunteer Group, or AVG) in the China-Burma-India (CBI) Theater in 1941-1942. Here, the development of tactics to take advantage of its strong points and pilots' skill against more maneuverable Japanese fighters made all the difference. Chennault had been an Army Captain in the mid-1930s who advocated fighter development and tactics that opposed the policies of the "*bomber generals.*" He stressed speed, rate-of-climb, and maneuverability as the critical performance characteristics of the single-seat fighter.

In June 1941 the Army Air Corps became the *Army Air Forces*, and would do combat in the Second World War with its existing stable of fighters (P-38, P-39, P-40, P-47, and the P-51, which made its first flight on 26 October 1940). The single-seat configuration maintained its dominance. No other new single-seat fighter designs would see combat.

WWII - Adaptations of the Fighter
WWII saw the development of variations of the fighter to suit different requirements. The first was the basic point

defense obligation—the interceptor. The traditional role of the fighter is to gain air superiority over a specific location. That manifested itself in the Battle of Britain, where the *Spitfires* and *Hurricanes*, of rather short range, engaged the German Me-109s (a more correct designation is Bf-109) and Me-110s to secure the air over England.

However, the ability of the defending fighters to be in the right place at the right time was aided by an "*early warning system*" that included listening devices that could pick up the sound of approaching planes and visual spotters on the ground—but more importantly, there was the development of radar. The location and tracking of incoming bombers was fundamental. It was the ability to vector the defending fighters to the most appropriate location for interception based on radar plots that directed "*the few*" who saved England (per Churchill's phrase that "*never was so much owed by so many to so few*").

By comparison, in the CBI theater, where there were no warning radars, the sound of approaching Japanese aircraft was noted by a network of ground observers who relayed their current position and general course to the AVG by radio, thus enabling the AVG to plot the Japanese attack and scramble their shark-mouth P-40s in time for the intercept.

In the European theater, when the U.S. 8th Air Force's bombers started deep-penetration raids into Germany and Eastern Europe in 1943, they experienced heavy losses—in part because their P-38 and P-47 escort fighters were both in short supply and unable to accompany their bombers all the way to their targets and back. By 1944, longer-range P-51 *Mustangs* became available that could make the round-trip. As they progressively replaced the earlier escort fighters, they both ensured a significant reduction in bomber losses and advanced the fighters' ability to wage aerial warfare over the entire *theater* of operations. After the war, this escort capability became known as the *"penetration fighter."*

The importance of close air support for the ground troops was a hard-learned lesson for U.S. forces early in the war. The Tactical Air Force (later to become the Tactical Air Command) was the result. The outcome was the development of the fighter-bomber in preference to the more specialized dive-bomber, such as the Douglas A-24 and Vultee A-35, though not as accurate in their placement of bombs. The Republic P-47 in particular, using external *"hardpoints"* under the wings and fuselage, could both carry a large bomb load and was more than capable of engaging enemy fighter aircraft on equal terms of speed and maneuverability to fight its way back to friendly territory. Thus, virtually all fighters were eventually equipped with underwing racks for bombs, rockets

Figure 01-16. Many pilots who flew it considered the North American P-51 the best piston-engine fighter ever developed. U.S. Army Photo.

and fuel. This capability was also used for what is now termed *"interdiction"*—the bombing of critical points (bridges and railheads) to deny the resupply of the frontline enemy soldier.

A fourth iteration of the fighter was the removal of armament and the installation of cameras for air-to-ground reconnaissance—or *"recce,"* as those in the business called it. This was evident in the use of the P-51 being designated as the F-5—the "F"

Figure 01-17. The Lockheed P-38N was equipped with radar for night interception. A second crewmember to operate the radar squeezed in behind the pilot. U.S. Army Photo.

being phonetically used to denote "*photo,*" and the Lockheed P-38 (F-6). Because of their lighter weight (the cameras being lighter than the displaced machine guns and ammunition), these aircraft could often out-fly pursuing enemy fighters—theoretically that is.

The final fighter variant was the night interceptor. Initially, defending forces would try to illuminate incoming bombers with searchlights and the defending fighters would then be able to see the aggressor. Ground-based radar quickly supplemented searchlights, and ground controllers vectored the interceptors for the kill. However, the pilot still had to make visual contact with the intruder to bring his guns to bear.

Airborne radar was the next obvious step, but early versions of these were large and required a second crewmember to operate and interpret the scope, and thus provide the onboard guidance to the point of kill. These essential functions resulted in the development of the bulbous nose on the multi-engine, multi-crewed Douglas P 70 (an adaptation of the Douglas A-20 *Havoc*) and on the Northrop P-61 *Black Widow*, which served in the European, Pacific, CBI and Mediterranean Theaters. Late in the war, advances in centimetric radar wavelengths (or X-band range of frequencies) made antennas and supporting equipment much smaller and lighter, allowing for wing- and nose-mounted units to be installed on traditional fighter airframes, such as the P-38.

By 1944, the bomber was also employing radar to find targets; thus, overcast skies were no longer able to conceal an objective and the defending interceptors had to be able to operate "*in the clouds.*" Consequently, the development of the "night fighter" essentially enabled the *all-weather fighter-interceptor* capability.

At the end of WWII in 1945, the P-51H epitomized the fighter with a speed of 487 mph and its ability to climb to 40,000 feet. Powered by a 2218-hp engine, this fighter had grown in weight from 8,400 pounds to over 10,000 pounds.

Turbojet Engine Development

Royal Air Force Flight Officer Frank Whittle and the German physicist Hans Von Ohain developed the jet engine independently. Whittle received a patent in 1930, while Ohain's patent dates to 1935. However, the German Heinkel 178 was the first jet to fly (in August 1939), as it took Whittle longer to convince the British War Office of the merits of the new power plant. The British Gloster E.28/39 did not take to the skies until 15 May 1941. The Italians flew the Caproni Campini N.1 a "*ducted fan*" design, in August 1940, but it is not considered a true jet for several reasons, one being that it used a piston engine to drive the compressor.

The development of the turbojet engine came at a very opportune time in the evolution of fighter aircraft. The piston engine, by the early 1940s, was coming to the end of its ability to deliver the needed power. As aircraft came ever nearer to the fabled "sound barrier," the propeller-driven plane encountered many new and mysterious aerodynamic phenomena. Despite their ability to generate upwards of 4,000-hp, using either mechanical or turbo-supercharging, the piston-driven propeller was not the power source for the future. First, the complexity and maintenance of these engines was a major cause of aircraft downtime. Second, the ability to transfer the power from the crankshaft to the air brought diminishing returns, as the number of propeller blades increased from two, to three and

Figure 01-18. The German Heinkel 178 of 1939 was the first turbojet-powered aircraft to fly. U.S. Army Photo.

then four. Third, the aerodynamics of the propeller became increasingly difficult to master as their tips approached the speed of sound.

The jet derives its power by burning petroleum-based kerosene-like fuel with oxygen from the atmosphere in a parallel grouping of combustion chambers—typically eight. High-speed rotating compressor blades provide the volume of air needed and force it into the circular arrangement of combustion chambers originally called *burner cans*. The combustion process creates a high pressure that is relieved out the back of the chamber, resulting in a pressure differential. This creates the imbalance of force that propels the craft forward in accordance with Newton's Third Law of *"action/reaction."* The exhaust gas then passes through a turbine mounted to a shaft that drives the compressor, thus creating a self-sustaining reaction—so long as there is fuel and oxygen.

While the turbojet engine is much simpler than a reciprocating (piston) engine, its few moving parts must operate in an extremely hot and high-pressure environment while rotating at 10,000 rpm. Thus, during the first years of its introduction, jet engines had very poor reliability. It was not uncommon for an engine to fail after only 10 to 20 hours of operation. Advances in materials capable of standing up under the high temperatures for long periods were the key to the successful turbojet.

Jet engine technology, which was woefully lacking in America when the war began, was introduced when

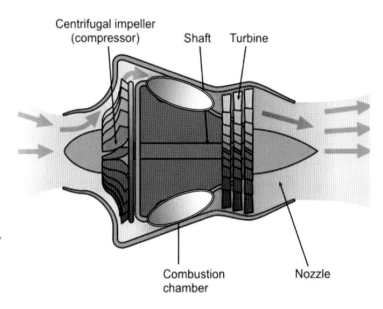

Figure 01-19. A diagram of the centrifugal flow jet engine. PD.

a copy of the Whittle W2B was imported from England in 1942. The General Electric Company, which had experience with turbo-superchargers, was tasked to build the engine, which became the 1,200-pound thrust model I-A that powered the Bell P-59—America's first jet-powered aircraft. That engine subsequently was developed into the I-16, which became the J31 when a standard naming convention was adopted.

Figure 01-20. The Bell P-59 was America's first jet-powered aircraft. It flew in October 1942. U.S. Army Photo.

By 1950, the jet engine had seen significant gains in performance, economy, and reliability since its development early in World War II. Thrust increased from the 1,200-pound I-A to GE's 4,000-pound thrust J33 that powered the F-80 of 1948. However, the technology began to shift from the British centrifugal flow compressor design to the German axial flow design embodied in the GE J35 that powered the first F-86. The centrifugal design compressed the air in a manner similar to most vacuum cleaners, providing only about a 4:1 compression ratio. Axial flow compressors can accommodate multiple compressor stages for higher compression ratios (up to 10:1).

The advent of the afterburner (AB) provided more options for fighter design. Afterburning is the process of injecting additional fuel into an extension of the jet engine's exhaust. Because a significant percentage of the compressed air is routed around the combustion chamber for cooling, there is still sufficient oxygen available in the exhaust stream for combustion. The added fuel burn increases the exhaust velocity and pressure, and can provide up to 50% more power. The down side is that it uses a relatively large quantity of fuel (doubling the specific fuel consumption) for the power it produces. Thus, the AB is typically used sparingly for take-off, climb, and limited combat operations. The Europeans usually referred to this process as "*reheat.*" Engine specifications refer to the engine power in the non-afterburning mode as "*dry thrust.*"

The AB was first used operationally on the early U.S. interceptors (F-86D, F-89, and F-94) to allow the fighter to catch the bomber before it could release its nuclear payload. This also meant that these fighters had to have a greater fuel supply. With the added weight of radar and fuel (and a second crewmember for the F-89 and F-94), the interceptor was heavier than point defense fighters like the F-86A.

By 1950, both major piston aircraft engine manufacturers in the United States (Pratt & Whitney and Wright) were competing in the development of turbojet technology. Because of General Electric's involvement in turbochargers, the War Department had assigned it the task of taking the British DeHavilland *Halford* H-1B engine and developing it into America's I-40. For large-scale production, the project was then turned over to the Allison Engine Company (a division of General Motors), which produced more than ten thousand of the resultant J33s that powered the F-80, F-94, and the T-33. (Westinghouse was another player attempting to enter the turbojet market, but the failure of its J40 engine for Navy jets led to its leaving the aircraft engine business in the 1950s.)

With the availability of reaction engines (jets and rockets), the U.S. military expanded their engine nomenclature to include the prefix J for turbojet and R for rocket. The J series began at "30," while the rocket naming started with the number "1."

With advent of the jet engine came some major changes to the basic configuration and handling of fighter aircraft, most notably their landing gear. Conventional landing gear, where the center of gravity is aft of the main gear, results in the tail resting on the ground, supported by a small tail wheel. This had been the dominant configuration since the fighter's inception in WWI. In that era, the tailskid was just that—a piece of wood that was used to keep the tail out of the mud and as a brake when back pressure was applied to the stick during the landing/taxi phase.

Through the early part of WWII the fighter, more often than not, operated from grass or dirt airstrips and used wide low-pressure tires to spread the weight over a large footprint to keep the wheels from being bogged down in the soil. The tail wheel was still preferred for these types of operations. However, the arrival of the jet engine brought a new set of problems that the Germans realized with the very first flight of their Messerschmitt Me-262. It too had a tail wheel, and the exhaust of its twin jet engines blew billows of dirt into the air during ground operations. Even when operated from hard surface runways the jet blast eroded the concrete. Thus, the jet engine dictated the use of tricycle landing gear and the hard surface runway— which also allowed for the use of narrower, high-pressure tires. The Me-262 quickly was converted to tricycle gear . . . and other nations' jet aircraft followed suit.

Like reciprocating engines before them, the new jet engines had their own characteristics and idiosyncrasies. First, the pilot needed to avoid rapid

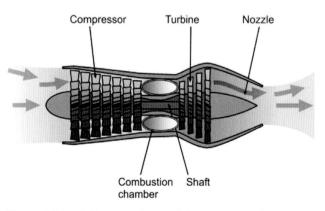

Figure 01-21. A Diagram of an axial flow jet engine. PD.

throttle movements at low power settings to avoid delayed engine acceleration or over-temperatures; improved engine controls alleviated that problem. A longer-lasting problem for some engines was an abnormal in-flight phenomenon called the "*compressor stall.*" The hundreds of small blades of the axial-flow compressor are airfoils that are subject to the same laws of physics as their larger cousin—the wing. The lift generated by the airfoil (which results in compression) can be impaired if the airflow is disturbed by a variety of factors, many related to the maneuver the pilot is attempting to perform or by outside influence, such as a bird strike or heavy rain. Most compressor stalls will return to equilibrium quickly after the incoming air returns to a normal state—but some may result in engine stoppage, and damage can result from very high engine temperatures.

When a compressor stall occurs, the loss of compressor efficiency impairs the thrust for periods of a fraction of a second to extended periods. The air/fuel mixture ratio is disrupted and a variety of visible, audible, and physical reactions can occur. These can range from a very loud explosive noise, accompanied by flame shooting out of the intake, to small pulses felt only slightly by the pilot.

There are two types of compressor stalls. The first is the "*rotational stall,*" which is the least intrusive, as only some of the compressor blades are stalled. However, these can progress to a more serious, completely stalled condition.

The second form is the axi-symmetric stall (sometimes referred to as a "*compressor surge*") and is more dramatic. In this instance, a complete failure of the compressor results and the high-pressure gasses within the engine's combustion chamber advance forward and out of the air intake. Loud noises and flame get the pilot's attention very quickly! While compressor stalls are infrequent in modern jet engines, for the affected *Century Series* aircraft (such as the F-100), it was a notable and nagging problem requiring careful throttle movements to avoid such events and quick reaction to mitigate their effects.

Other causes of early jet engine mechanical failures ranged from foreign object damage (FOD, while on the ground) to ingestion of birds or debris (while airborne)—both still a risk today—to turbine blade failures from imbalances or metal fatigue. This last susceptibility of primarily first-generation jets was not alleviated until c. 1960, when stronger nickel-cadmium turbine blades replaced the earlier metals.

A New Kind of War Strategy

The uneasy peace that followed WWII was brought about by the distrust between two of its victors—the United States and the Soviet Union. Uncomfortable allies during the war against Nazi Germany, the two quickly became antagonists after the defeat of Adolf Hitler. Soviet Premier Joseph Stalin made it clear to his Politburo and to the Soviet citizenry that their former ally, the United States, was now a mortal enemy.

It was behind this façade that Stalin made his own aggressive moves. His grip on eight countries in Eastern Europe (overrun by Soviet forces at the end of WWII) and the isolation his military forces imposed on them was brutal. Stalin's power rested, in part, on his ability to use the United States as an ever-present adversary.

Winston Churchill deftly defined the political situation in a speech in 1946: "*From Stettin in the Baltic to Trieste in the Adriatic an 'Iron Curtain' has descended across the Continent.*" The line running north and south through the divided country of defeated Germany established east and west partitions. From this emerged the terms Western and Eastern bloc countries—the latter dominated by the Soviets. (The term "*Iron Curtain*" had actually been used by the Nazis during the war in reference to the Soviets.)

Before WWII the Soviets were considered a backward nation, which threatened democracy only tangentially with a fanatical doctrine of communism and totalitarianism as evidenced by its own brutal terrorist regime. As it lacked a significant global military presence it was often dismissed as a menace.

However, following the war, the Soviets reverse-engineered the American B-29 (several of which had landed in the USSR during the war) and put that copy into production as the Tupolev TU-4 in the late 1940s. With the revelation of the USSR's development of the atomic bomb in 1949, coupled with the TU-4, the Russians now possessed an intercontinental threat. These factors, together with Stalin's blockade of Berlin in 1948 and his involvement in encouraging the North Koreans to invade the South in 1950, heightened the tension between East and West—a *Cold War*.

Accordingly, the policy and military mission of the United States and her WWII allies vis-à-vis West Germany and Japan changed from post-war occupation to collective active defense of Western Europe and the Far East against Communist aggression. The North Atlantic Treaty Organization (NATO), established on 4 April 1949 by 12 Western nations (the United States, Great Britain, France, Belgium, the Netherlands, Denmark, Italy, Luxembourg, Norway, Iceland, Canada, and Portugal) provided a political and military alliance for a collective self-defense against Soviet aggression. (Greece, Turkey and West Germany joined later, but in 1966 France withdrew from the military side.) In 1955 the Warsaw Pact, a Soviet-led Eastern European alliance, was established to counter NATO. This opposing alignment lasted until the dissolution of the Soviet Union in 1991.

Following the Korean and French-Indochina Wars, the Southeast Asia Treaty Organization (SEATO) was formally established on 19 February 1955, primarily to block further Communist gains in Southeast Asia. Its 8 signatory nations were Australia, France, New Zealand, Pakistan (including East Pakistan, now Bangladesh), the Philippines, Thailand, the United Kingdom, and the United States. It was militarily ineffective, in part because (unlike NATO) it had no standing joint military commands, and in part because France and Britain rejected military action on behalf of Laos when it was threatened by infiltration and insurgency, and again when the Republic of Vietnam was similarly afflicted. Instead, the U.S. (joined by Australia, New Zealand, South Korea and a few others) used the SEATO protocol as a rationale for direct intervention in what became a second Indochina (or Southeast Asia) War (1955-75). SEATO was formally dissolved on 30 June 1977.

Reorganizing the War Department

The *U.S. Air Force* (USAF) became an independent arm of the U.S. military in 1947, now on a par with the Army and the Navy as one of the three Military Departments under the renamed Department of Defense (DoD). With the restructuring of the Air Force, the fighter was redesignated with the prefix "F" and all aircraft in the inventory were switched after 12 June 1948—thus, the P-51 became the F-51 and the P-80 became the F-80, etc.

Evolution of the United States Air Forces

Identity	Year
Aeronautical Division, Signal Corps	1907
Aviation Section, Signal Corps	1914
Army Air Service, U.S. Army	1918
U.S. Army Air Corps	1926
U.S. Army Air Forces	1941
United States Air Force	1947

To counter the Soviet threat, the USAF structured itself for its strategic bombing (B-50, B-47 and B-36) and penetration/escort fighter roles within the Strategic Air Command (SAC). The Air Defense Command (ADC) provided initially for point-defense fighters

(F-86) and then all-weather interceptors (F-86D, F-89, F-94) for homeland air defense against the USSR's long-range bombers. The General Purpose forces (e.g., F-51, F-84, F-86) were the province of the Tactical Air Command (TAC). Both SAC and TAC required reconnaissance aircraft as well.

A nuclear strike force, as defined in the early 1950s, saw each bomber proceeding at high altitude and maximum airspeed towards its target. Unlike the dense formations of the one-thousand plane raids of WWII, SAC bombers would penetrate the Soviet Union individually at literally hundreds of points around its massive periphery. Strategic nuclear bombing would be the central theme of the United States' nuclear deterrence policy for the next 30 years, and SAC dominated the Defense budget during much of the period.

As soon as nuclear weapons could be made small enough for carriage aboard fighter-bombers, TAC deployed theater nuclear forces (TNF) to NATO bases in Western Europe and to bases in the Far East to augment SAC's long-range bombers with additional nuclear weapons to neutralize potential attacks by massive Communist armies. Following F-84Gs and Fs on Quick-Reaction Alert (QRA, per NATO's "forward strategy" of the early 1950s), *Century Series* fighters (F-100, F-101A/C, F-105) took on the U.S. share of what became "Victor Alert" as the 1950s rolled into the 1960s. In parallel, U.S. F-102As joined other NATO fighter-interceptor aircraft in European

Figure 02-02. The McDonnell F-85 was to be carried under the Convair B-36 bomber to provide fighter protection. It is shown here in tests with the Boeing B-29 in 1948. USAF Photo.

air defense, while U.S. composite strike forces responded to other crises as needed. In both standing and contingency operations, naval airpower also provided key support.

History had shown that the bomber was very much at the mercy of defending fighters unless provided some form of fighter escort. However, it was somewhat impractical to provide each bomber with its own escort (although several efforts were made to address the requirement). One concept recognized that the primary intercontinental bomber of the late 1940s and early 1950s (the B-36) was an immense aircraft. It not only could fly 10,000-mile missions without refueling, but also could carry several nuclear weapons of the period.

Figure 02-01. The relative size of the U.S. Navy airship Macon contrasts with the two small Curtiss F9C parasite fighters flying directly beneath the 780-foot dirigible. U.S. Navy Photo.

The B-36 was so large, in fact, that it was envisioned that perhaps it could carry its own fighter escort within its fuselage. The concept was a throw-back to the 1930s, when the giant airships *Macon* and *Akron* each carried a contingent of small biplane fighters to ward off attacks. They were lowered into the airstream by a trapeze-like mechanism from a hangar deck inside the dirigible.

McDonnell Aircraft received a contract in 1945 to design just such a fighter for the B-36. Without the need for a large fuel capacity or landing gear, it was extremely light with a gross weight of only 4500 pounds. The XF-85 "*Goblin*" fighter made six test flights in 1948 using a Boeing B-29 as the mother ship. The problems with flying into the wake of the B-29 for recovery operations gave McDonnell test pilot Ed Schock a difficult time and the project was cancelled. As one former Air Force pilot observed, "*This aircraft had all the aerodynamic stability of a knuckleball.*"

The concept re-emerged several years later, again using the giant B-36 as a standoff delivery ship. The small parasite, this time the F-84F, would carry a nuclear payload and be capable of making the final run into the target at a much higher speed than the B-36. This scenario was later revised to provide for reconnaissance with the RF-84F. Several modified B-36s and RF-84Fs became operational to perform this mission.

Revelation Over Korea

During the Korean War (1950-1953), the Soviet MiG-15 fighter made its surprise appearance in the conflict in November 1950. It was a better performing aircraft than TAC's jet fighter-bombers, such as the straight-winged F-80 and F-84, which were progressively replacing the still-operational F-51.

The MiGs were initially flown by North Koreans and Chinese—who were typically not well matched against the highly skilled U.S. pilots. The first jet-versus-jet dogfight occurred between an F-80 and a Russian-built MiG-15—Major Evans G. Stephens in the F-80 was the victor. The Soviets countered by having their own top pilots in the MiG cockpits, and this required the U.S. to send the F-86 into combat. Thus, subsequent encounters were primarily between the F-86 and the MiG-15.

While the new American jet aircraft (F-80, F-84 and F-86) typically performed well in Korea, there was a schism over the fighter strategy that would follow. Most pilots who fought the air war in Korea had been trained, and seen action, in WWII. They brought to the conflict their existing fighter doctrine, as did the Russian and Chinese pilots flying the MiG-15. Speed and altitude were the key attributes of a fighter. The MiG had a superior rate of climb and, having a lower

Figure 02-04. The Soviet MiG-15, although inferior by western standards, could be a match for the F-86 when flown by experienced pilots. USAF Photo.

wing loading, could turn tighter, and it quickly gained a formidable reputation as a very maneuverable fighter.

After the war, a brash Air Force fighter pilot named John Boyd, who had fought against the MiG-15 (albeit too junior to be an element leader, and as such, a "shooter"), made an exhaustive study of why the F-86 was able to achieve a very favorable kill ratio. Besides the very important aspect of pilot training, the MiG lacked the hydraulic-boosted controls that allowed the F-86 pilot to quickly and almost effortlessly input roll maneuvers. Although not known at the time it was being engaged in the skies over Korea, at high speeds the MiG-15 was incapable of effectively maneuvering and it lacked pilot protection, an unobstructed view towards the rear, and a radar compensating gunsight. It was not until a defecting North Korean delivered a MiG to the Air Force in 1953 that its limitations were truly appreciated.

In early 1952, little more than a year after the introduction of the MiG-15 into combat, design representatives from several U.S. aircraft manufacturers journeyed to the front-line airfields of Korea. Their objective was to talk directly to combat fighter pilots to acquire a better understanding of this new jet-age environment.

Under the tour direction of Lieutenant General Benjamin Chidlaw, the civilian group included Lee Atwood of North American Aviation. While no fighter pilot wanted to give up any specific attribute of the vaunted F-86, the agility and altitude capability of the MiG dictated more power while keeping the weight under control. The F-86 had performed well in its first encounters against the MiG-15, although heavier and slightly less nimble than its Korean War adversary. Nevertheless, the F-86 pilots wanted more speed and altitude capability to be able to have an overwhelming advantage.

Following the Korean War, the inability of the U.S. military to assess effectively the Soviets' capabilities often led to pushing the state-of-the art to ensure that there were no more MiG-15-like surprises. Just as the names "Fokker" and "Messerschmitt" during the World Wars symbolized excellence of the adversaries, the word "MiG" would likewise become the generic enemy fighter for half a century—representing a performance factor (real or imagined) (guesstimated or exaggerated) against which American aircraft would be compared.

By the end of the Korean conflict there were two primary thoughts about the role of the fighter. Those who had flown against the MiG continued to see the traditional gun-slinging dogfight scenario—they wanted lightweight agility. Those who foresaw the possibility of a Soviet nuclear strike envisioned the next conflict in terms of long-range interception with futuristic air-to-air missiles. In an atomic war, the scenario did not include mass formations. The Soviet intruders would fly individually to their targets—each bomber would carry one nuclear bomb—and one city, industrial complex, or military objective would be destroyed with it. The doctrine of strategic nuclear bombing clouded other possible war scenarios, and would closely confine the development of the fighter of the 1950s—as had happened in the 1930s.

To defend against the nuclear attack picture, the fighter would streak out from its base along the perimeter of the U.S., guided by ground radar, pick up the intruder on its own radar, and fire a guided missile (or cluster of unguided rockets) to kill the target. It was conceivable that the interceptor might not even gain visual contact with the enemy during the encounter—especially at night or in bad weather. There was no need to evade anti-aircraft fire or surface-to-air missiles. These fighters would be large and long-ranged and need not be very maneuverable, nor would they carry a gun. In fact, the pilot himself was being moved out of the picture. In some battlefield forecasts, the *Nike* and BOMARC surface–to–air missile programs would protect the United States with a ring of emplacements. It was conceivable to some military planners by the mid-1950s that "the fighter pilot" was becoming obsolete.

This strategy became dominant towards the end of the 1950s—especially with the surprise appearance of the Soviets' Sputnik earth satellite and their rapid development of atomic and then thermonuclear bombs. The "conventional" war was discounted in the U.S.'

Figure 02-05. Nike Ajax Surface-to-Air Missiles were installed around vital targets in the United States beginning in March 1954. U.S. Army Photo.

planning and training preparations, as well as in the types of combat aircraft and weapons to be carried. The emphasis was on nuclear warheads and missiles, not "iron bombs" and cannon. While this may appear forward-thinking, it did not reflect the actual reality of the world situation, nor the true capability of the technology of the times.

Command and Control

With the advent of the Cold War and the possibility of Soviet bombers attacking over the North Pole (the shortest distance from the Soviet Union to the heart of America), for the first time in history America had to maintain a *peacetime* alert within its own continental borders. With the establishment of the bi-national North American Air Defense Command (NORAD), Canada joined the U.S. in the rapid build-up of air defense elements throughout North America.

Area air defense across the U.S. (and Canada) required networked radar sites to control fighter-interceptors (and unmanned BOMARC interceptor missiles) as the major mission of the USAF's Air Defense Command (ADC). In parallel, point defense of high-value U.S. targets was the assigned mission of the Army Air Defense Command (ARADCOM), whose succession of surface-to-air missiles (SAMs) included *Nike-Ajax*, *Nike-Hercules* and *HAWK*

batteries during the *Century Series* interceptors' operations from the mid-1950s to the mid-1980s.

The basic doctrine of air defense was "D-I-I-D," for Detect, Identify, Intercept, and (if necessary) Destroy. Simplistically, the first two objectives were functions of the then-ground-based radar surveillance and control environment; the latter two were functions of the airborne interceptor forces. At the same time, these functional responsibilities could be shared, as when an interceptor needed to confirm the identity of an Unknown aircraft or "*Bogey*," or might (from its mobile high-altitude flight) detect targets below the ground radars' coverage or in mountainous terrain that blocked the ground radar's view. At the same time, the command and control (C2) facilities needed to "deconflict" the flight paths of the manned interceptors from those of the interceptor missiles or SAM areas of coverage.

Ground Observer Corps

In early 1950, the former WWII Ground Observer Corps was reestablished to supplement NORAD's planned network of ground-based radars and control centers for continental air defense. By 1952, this "*Operation Skywatch*" had expanded to more than 750.000 volunteers who were taking shifts at over

Figure 02-06. Atlantic Barrier WVII (Navy version of the EC-121) and a Destroyer Escort that served as radar picket lines off the coast of the United States. U.S. Navy Photo.

16,000 posts around the country to maintain continuous watch for suspicious aircraft, reporting through 75 relay centers to the ground control interception (GCI) centers of the Air Force's Air Defense Command (ADC).

By the late 1950s a major aircraft detection, warning and intercept control system, including both GCI sites and new Semi-Automatic Ground Environment (SAGE) facilities, was in the process of installation. In view of the dramatic technological and operational improvements provided by these networked military facilities, the Air Force canceled the Ground Observer Corps program in 1959.

Early Warning Radar
Although the Soviets were lagging in the development of a jet bomber, if the MiG-15 was any indicator, America could be facing a more formidable opponent in the decade of the 1950s. While the F-86 *Sabre* was effective in countering the MiG-15 over the skies of Korea, the prospect of intercepting Soviet bombers coming over the Arctic region and down into the United States posed yet another problem—the ability to effectively detect and identify them.

The MIT *Summer Study Group* of 1952 identified the critical nature of this need, and ultimately three separate lines of radar stations stretched from the Pacific to the Atlantic across North America (Canada being an active partner). The *Pinetree Line* was actually begun in 1951, and by 1954 there were 30 stations that extended across the northern U.S. and southern Canada on both sides of the 49th parallel. The *Mid-Canada Line* added to these in the late 1950s and provided eight manned stations and 90 unmanned Doppler stations along roughly the 55th parallel.

The *Distant Early Warning* (DEW) *Line* was built north of the Arctic Circle, along the 69th parallel from western Alaska across Canada to Greenland. It was begun in 1954, and within three years 58 stations were completed across these frozen wastelands. Each line provided progressively better radars, which extended the overall system's detection ranges—and thereby warning times for defense responses.

Supplementing these facilities was a series of structures set into the Atlantic Ocean about 100 miles offshore called "Texas Towers" for detecting possible intruders from the northeast. One final layer was the two *Barrier Forces* providing Early Warning radar coverage off the northeast and west coasts of North America from the mid-1950s into 1965. They comprised five destroyer escorts in the North Atlantic (BarLant) and Pacific (BarPac), teaming with long-range Navy Lockheed WV-2 maritime surveillance aircraft (later redesignated the EC-121). The innermost perimeter of radar stations were within the limits of the United States, usually located near the larger cities. Linking the input from these far-flung outposts and coordinating their detection, command and control capabilities was a daunting task that would become an essential basis for both coastal air defense operations and support for U.S. air operations over North Vietnam.

Defense Conditions—DEFCON
The level of America's military alert status depended, in part, on the relative threat posed by the Soviet Union (now Russia) based on political unrest, or overt military action in various parts of the world. A formal "*alert status*" was defined in November 1959 to provide a uniform level of understanding among the military and political leaders of the United States and Canada as to the significance of a perceived threat. A formal series of "*Defense Conditions*," or DEFCONs in military parlance, progressively elevate the alert status for American (and Canadian) armed forces. These levels range from DEFCON 5, which is defined as "*Normal peacetime readiness*" to DEFCON 1—"*Maximum force readiness*." The DEFCON level is controlled by the President with advice from the Joint Chiefs of Staff. The different branches of the U.S. military as well as specific bases can be operated at different DEFCON levels. (These DEFCONs remain in effect today.)

Exactly what actions are taken by the military services for each of these are classified. However, ICBM sites typically operated at DEFCON 4 level, as was much of the military until the end of the Cold War in 1990. The highest level ever declared was DEFCON 2— "*Further increase in force readiness but less than maximum*." This occurred for the Strategic Air Command during the Cuban Missile Crisis on 22 October 1962, with a return to DEFCON 3 on 15 November 1962. The remainder of the U.S. military went to DEFCON 3 for this period. Only two other periods saw elevation to DEFCON 3: the Yom Kippur War in 1973 and the 9-11 attacks in 2001.

Ground Control Intercept (GCI) Radars
By 1953, a then-modern radar system had been completed and additional radar units were programmed to blanket the country with medium and high-altitude radar coverage. At the same time, the Pinetree, Mid-Canada and DEW Lines, augmented by gap-filler radars, off-shore "Texas Towers" and Navy WV-2 radar-equipped (long-range over-water surveillance) aircraft, extended coverage as far from the American borders as possible.

After the powerful low-frequency early warning (EW) radars detected likely targets, their location and course data were passed to medium-frequency "acquisition" radars, which usually combined a circular sweep radar (that gave 360-degree azimuth coverage) with a height-finder radar (whose up-and-down beam sweep at the target's bearing provided refined elevation or altitude information). As these ground-based radars were essentially "horizon-limited," "gap-filler" radar sites were located where most needed to improve lower-level coverage of likely intrusion routes.

GCI Weapons Controllers at the designated acquisition radar sites then maintained assigned target and interceptor tracks and directed the interceptors into optimum position to acquire the targets on their own Fire Control System (FCS) radars to either identify them (if Unknown) or (if Hostile) shoot them down. The DEFCON level and prevailing Rules of Engagement (ROE) determined the normal course of action for such intercepts. The interceptor's armament and target's flight path, altitude and speed would determine which tactic would be pursued and in what order. For example, an interceptor armed with rockets or radar-guided missiles would normally attempt a lead-collision attack first, followed by a pursuit attack as necessary, while an interceptor with guns and/or heat-seeking missiles would normally fly a pursuit-type attack. If the target was flying significantly higher than the interceptor, then the interceptor would accelerate to a maximum practical speed while locking onto the target and then "snap up" to center the FCS steering dot in elevation when the attack display indicated about 20 seconds to intercept ("B-time"). (More on this later).

When *Century Series* interceptors replaced their subsonic predecessors the same tactical principles held, but the precise tactical parameters (intercept "geometry," speeds and altitudes) varied with the interceptors' enhanced performance and more advanced armament and fire controls. For example, the F-86D and L (with unguided rockets) would often attack in flights of two or more on a 90-degree crossing angle to provide a larger target surface than a frontal or tail-chase attack (with wingmen echeloned on the leader's opposite side from the approaching target). When lead fired and broke hard into the direction from which the target came, his wingmen would be in good position for follow-up shots as necessary. By comparison, the *Century Series* interceptor (with unguided nuclear rockets) would normally fly single-ship intercepts on a frontal lead-collision ("cut-off") attack, lock-on and fire at longer ranges, then break away as hard as possible while the nuclear warhead's timed detonation and large lethal envelope would destroy the target—and then start a re-attack for a pursuit launch of another weapon (if needed).

Whirlwind Computer

As the threat of the Soviet Union continued to manifest itself by aggressive moves and displays of power in the late 1940s, the specialization of the interceptor became

more pronounced. As with the Battle of Britain in 1940, directing fighters to the track of incoming bombers was a difficult problem—especially when the land mass of the United States is compared to the relatively small island nation of Great Britain. The coordination of radar data, command and control communications links, the launch of aircraft, and the final intercept and confirmation comprised a formidable undertaking.

Less than a decade earlier, Britain handled the intercept predicament with large horizontal plot boards 15 feet across with "fish boats" (locations of aircraft being plotted) pushed by pool cues, and the telephone and teletype. However aircraft speed, the large geographic area of the United States, and advent of the nuclear weapons threat demanded a system that operated with much greater responsiveness—in "real time," as it would be called. To assist in keeping control over the airborne battlefield, a few farsighted individuals looked to the power of a new device called an electronic computer. Some preliminary work had recently been done that would help establish the technology.

The U.S. Navy had initiated a project to create a flight simulator that would allow many problem variables to be calculated—some in real time—to produce a more realistic training environment than the Link Instrument Trainer. Working with the Massachusetts Institute of Technology (MIT), it was determined that an electronic simulator was possible—but not with the current analogue computing devices then available.

One member of the MIT team had an opportunity to observe the ENIAC digital computer originally built to calculate ballistic trajectories of artillery rounds (and which would eventually be a critical tool in the development of the thermonuclear bomb). Using the principle of a stored-program machine and incorporating a number of advances along the way, such as "core" memory, a prototype computer called *Whirlwind* was completed in 1951. This architecture formed the basis of a system that would profoundly change computing for the next half-century. For the Air Force and its *Semi-Automatic Ground Environment (SAGE)* project, it arrived at just the right time.

Semi-Automatic Ground Environment (SAGE)

The post-WWII air defense environment for North America changed rapidly from the late 1940s through the 1970s. The Soviet bomber threat increased exponentially, with first atomic and then thermonuclear bombs deliverable by faster aircraft (later augmented by air-to-surface missiles, or ASMs, that could launch nuclear warheads from

stand-off ranges). Meanwhile, the U.S.' expanding air defense ground radar network increased its areas of coverage and ADC's interceptors modernized first to subsonic and then to supersonic jets with increasingly capable FCS and armament options. However, these defense performance gains were being offset by the increases in information to be collected, shared and acted upon by the proliferating numbers of GCI sites and their upper levels of command and control (C2). The evolving air defense system was thus faced from the start with increasing risks of saturation, local breakdowns or ineffectiveness, and ultimately inability to neutralize a major attack. The defense's increasing challenge was: the attacker could engage at will and (given warning) the interceptors could be scrambled as needed, but the overall "battle management" system had to be operating at or near peak effectiveness *all the time* to avert a projected nuclear holocaust.

The solution was to automate as much of the air defense process as practical. All the GCI radar sites in given sectors were to be connected to high-power computers, which would then manage the in-and-out flow of information between all affected recipients. Thus, Weapons Controllers' workloads would be reduced, as *the computer* would process everything received and retransmit it to all affected recipients in "real time," albeit under human control.

The Air Force-funded *Project Charles* study in 1951 recognized that only a digital computer based on the MIT's "*Whirlwind*" project might be capable of handling such an enormous challenge. As *Whirlwind* was designed as a limited-area "demonstration" system, its successor needed to possess the power and speed to handle the millions of calculations that would be required for a full-scale national system. The incoming radar data had to be presented in a manner that allowed command and control from a network of *Direction Centers* to select specific targets and assign the most appropriate asset (aircraft or missile) to a spot in the sky for intercept—perhaps 200 miles or more from their bases.

Figure 02-07. The entire SAGE computer system, with its racks of vacuum tubes, weighed 275 tons and required a significant amount of air conditioning to keep its operating temperatures within bounds. USAF Photo.

Figure 02-08. The SAGE plot board for the northeast region operated out of McGuire AFB in NJ. The rooms were dimly lit with an eerie blue light. USAF Photo.

Figure 02-09. The SAGE console was one of the first uses of a CRT with a computer. Note the Light Pen (covered by the plastic box to protect this museum piece). USAF Photo.

These concepts were hammered out by the MIT *Summer Study Group* that convened in 1952. MIT's "air defense lab" would ultimately become the Lincoln Laboratories. The most advanced concepts in computing were then being explored at MIT by an engineer named Jay Forrester. He was involved in the *Whirlwind* computer and recognized that elements of that machine were compatible with the projected needs of the next-generation interceptors.

The companies that were competing for the resulting *Direction Center* contract included RCA, Raytheon, Remington Rand, Sylvania, and IBM. The system would be known as the *Semi-Automatic Ground Environment*—SAGE. IBM was selected to engineer the prototype, but was unsure if they would get the contract to build the production models. IBM president Thomas Watson decided that the challenge and reward were more than worth a maximum effort. He convinced Forrester that IBM would accept the risk to commit to full-scale production of a system that had yet to be proven, and that would require several advances in the state-of-the-art to achieve the objective.

Following almost a decade of definition, design, development and testing, the SAGE system emerged as a series of four-storey windowless "block-houses" that contained all the mission and support equipment that would make each "*Direction Center*" work. As of 1958, IBM was producing the requisite new computer, the AN/FSQ-7. Other contractors constructed the large reinforced concrete buildings to house them, along with power, cooling and communications to sustain them—plus system integration and test equipment to ensure that all the "parts" worked together. Phone lines were needed to connect the surrounding radar sites to their sector's SAGE facility for voice and data communication. System Development Corporation (SDC, a spin-off from RAND) developed the software—500,000 lines of assembly language code—and the new MITRE Corporation provided oversight and management during the program's deployment and operational phases.

The first *Direction Center* (DC) became operational at McGuire AFB (Air Force Base) in New Jersey in 1957. Ultimately, IBM built 48 FSQ-7 computers, as two systems were installed at each SAGE site to provide for 24-hour availability. The FSQ-7 was physically the biggest computer ever built: it used nearly 60,000 vacuum tubes, took a half-acre of floor space, weighed 275 tons, and consumed up to 3 megawatts of power. Not only was quality control necessarily rigorous, but each SAGE site had *two* FSQ-7s for redundancy (one on "hot standby"), with the result that, despite the relatively poor reliability of vacuum tubes of that era, overall system availability was as high as 99 percent.

The operational concept for the mature SAGE system was that target data from the radar facilities of the region's manual GCI sites would be fed, in digital format and via dedicated telecommunication links, to their *Direction Center*. The *Direction Centers* contained the (dual) FSQ-7 computers, and a large screen or "plot board" in their Control Rooms displayed regional air activity and status information overlaid on synthetic maps.

Each Control Room also contained multiple consoles with large cathode ray tubes (CRTs) and their controls. From one, the *Senior Director* would monitor his (and adjoining) sectors' air situation and oversee his site's operations, observing all the aircraft in his sector: friendly, unknown (or "*bogeys*"), and foe (or "*bandits*"). Computer-generated data-tags (in place of WWII "*shrimp boats*") would be electronically displayed to provide alphanumeric information about each "target" and about his Air Defense assets. To assign tasks to his *Weapons Directors* ("WDs" and their "Techs"), he would select a specific target for interception by spotlighting it with a "*light gun*" (later "*light pen*") and assigning its track electronically to a WD for action.

When fully deployed in the early 1960s, the 24 SAGE "*Direction Centers*" (23 in the U.S., one in Canada; the numbers varied over time) were managing the operations of more than 100 ground radar sites and about 60 interceptor squadrons, and reporting to three Region "*Control Centers*" (CCs, later "*Combat Centers*") in the U.S., plus the one underground at North Bay, Ontario, for Canada. The CCs used AN/FSQ-8 computers to monitor and control operations over North America, and to coordinate them with other military commands and civilian authorities in both countries.

Although developed as a part of WS-201A (the F-102), portions of the SAGE system were also used with the F-86D/L and F-89 and F-94 interceptors that, early on, shared the air defense mission concurrently with the F-102. The Air Force BOMARC interceptor missile (IM-99) was also directed by the SAGE system.

Operations of the SAGE system coincided roughly with the operational dates of the primary *Century Series* interceptors, the F-102, F-101, and F-106. SAGE data-linked target information and interceptor commands (backed up by SAGE

Weapons Directors on voice radio) controlled an increasing share of intercept missions, while manual control by the GCI controllers was still used as back-up or as delegated by SAGE. The effect on the interceptors was to replace the series of GCI voice transmissions by mostly data-linked displays in the interceptor's cockpit.

The act of committing an interceptor (aircraft, BOMARC or SAM) to a target became known as "*pairing*" them, analogous to a traditional GCI controller's "manual" actions to associate interceptor and target "blips," then following them with each sweep of his radar and giving voice corrections as needed. The difference was that, with *computers* now handling both tracks, intercept solutions (and corrections) were generated automatically—analogous to the situation aboard an interceptor aircraft once its pilot or radar operator had "*locked onto*" his radar target *blip* with his hand control, after which his FCS computer would continuously update his intercept solution to weapon launch and detonation (or break-lock, whichever came first).

For the interceptor, target position was indicated by a target marker circle that moved on the FCS radar scope according to the SAGE computer's projection; the target should eventually be detectable somewhere inside that circle. Meanwhile, target speed and altitude, command heading, speed and altitude, and the interceptor tactic—all comprised six signals that were shown on special interceptor displays: three via one SAGE update cycle, and the other three on the next cycle. Thus, ideally, the mission could be conducted in radio silence and, if the pilot coupled his autopilot to the FCS steering dot—and held the armament firing trigger down after lock-on—the SAGE-interceptor combination could complete an intercept practically automatically.

For pre-*Century Series* interceptors, or those whose data-links were not working, back-up voice transmissions by the SAGE WD were still needed— which were essentially the same as those of their traditional (and still operational) GCI control sites.

SAGE, however, did have early drawbacks—most of which were addressed by successive improvements to both SAGE programs and interceptor FCSs. For example, as SAGE computer storage space was limited, interceptor speeds were allocated only in indicated Mach numbers ending in '3s or '8s and altitudes only at 5,000-ft intervals. Speeds were also later designated for four conditions, each of which might also vary depending on whether the interceptor was "clean" or "tanked." These speeds (for each 5,000-ft altitude) were defined as: minimum

(Vmin, for endurance); maneuverable cruise (Vmc, for best range); maximum practical (Vmaxp, for highest sustainable during intercept maneuvers); and maximum attainable (Vmax). The speeds for each interceptor's performance envelope, however, were initially selected by engineers rather than experienced aviators, which, when combined with the '.x3 and '.x8 Mach number limitation, meant that the speeds transmitted were only approximations of the "ideal" interceptor speeds—and thus SAGE-directed speeds were often sub-optimal for the first several years.

Also, interceptor flight changes (of speed, altitude, or course) were initially computed as if made instantly, but as the interceptor needed time and space for such maneuvers, the WD had to reinitiate his interceptor track to update its computed track with the interceptor's real (lagging) position, thereby to compute an updated intercept solution.

Another limitation derived from the SAGE system's cycle time. Optimally, SAGE-computed updates were transmitted in roughly 16- to 20-second cycles (analogous to a GCI radar's sweep time)—but at longer intervals if the system was overloaded. While a GCI controller could often anticipate changes (based on target and interceptor track history), the SAGE computer could use only what it "saw" (or what was manually updated by the WD). This meant that unplanned changes between transmissions could result in "jumps" of target position and jerky updates of the intercept solution. If the cycle exceeded 60 seconds SAGE information was designated "unreliable," as the computer was projecting from stored (vice updated) track information; while presumably accurate at the time of transmission, the lengthened cycle would enable increasing errors of positioning and timing. The "old information" display was a short vertical bar on the interceptor's FCS scope.

Finally, "Tactics packages" (stored for each interceptor, based on its performance and current employment doctrine) were progressively improved from "T-1" (initially) through "T-4" (tested in late 1968). One early tactic that proved impractical was the "double-offset stern," where the interceptor was directed to an initial offset point, then turned onto a 60-second straight "J-leg" perpendicular to the target course to a second offset point, from which it made a 90-degree standard-rate turn to roll out two-to-four miles off the target's stern. This was based on the interceptor having a 1.2-to-1 speed advantage and the target maintaining a steady course and speed—neither of which would be likely under actual combat conditions.

Ultimately, and as a result of extensive testing of the T-4 tactics package (designed to overlay the preceding

T-3 program), tactics were simplified to more like the original GCI-directed lead-collision cutoff and pursuit options, but with more flexibility allowed to the interceptor crews, whose improved FCSs included more target acquisition options, as well as more responsive aircraft maneuvers. In addition, more realistic performance "numbers" were entered into the SAGE computer for both dedicated interceptors and back-up fighter aircraft, as agreed with the respective aircrews for each type. Thus, the automated system-to-interceptor relationship was rebalanced in favor of the interceptor's ultimate role in "making the kill"—though it took another few years to get the many T-4 test and follow-on recommendations into ADCOM's automated systems. (Effective 15 January 1968, ADC, the Air Defense Command, was renamed the Aerospace Defense Command, or ADCOM, in view of its increasing space mission.)

Despite SAGE's years of "growing pains" (not unlike the experiences of the aircraft it served and controlled), one fact became clear in retrospect— if not always appreciated by the interceptor pilots and RIOs at the other end of its directions. Much of the initiative, capability and responsibility for the conduct of the homeland air defense battle— had it come—had passed from the aviators "at the pointy end of the spear" to the relatively junior officers wielding their "electron guns" from swivel chairs in front of TV-like animations of their battle area...populated by clusters of "symbology." These were the people who, like their manual GCI controllers before (and alongside) them, effectively managed the battle. Moreover, they could train for its contingencies and "surprises" in ways usually denied those who "merely" complied with their computer-aided guidance—i.e., *"follow Dolly"*. (*Multiservice Tactical Brevity Codes* such as "Judy" and "Dolly" were used by American military (and NATO) to convey complex information with a few words.)

For example, routine *Direction Center* shifts could involve not only "live" missions (for manned interceptor or other aircraft), but also simulation program routines (for test or special training, especially for BOMARC or ARADCOM SAM "intercepts"), or combined "sim-over-live" activities (for combined operations, such as major exercises or multiple overlaid events or programs designed to stress the system in extreme ways).

In the face of such operational complexity an irony of the SAGE program is that the system, which consumed 3 *mega*watts of power (enough to service a community of 15,000 people), *had significantly less computing power, memory, and communication speed than the average cell phone of today.*

While the system itself was on the cutting edge of technology at the time, the hardware and software developed enabled several follow-on systems of the future that ultimately included the civilian air traffic control system now used across the world. The technology immediately found its way into IBM's first scientific computer (the 701) and its first business computer (the 702). The work done on the communication links provided a foundation for the ARPANET of the 1960s and the Internet of today.

Nevertheless, there were those who doubted all along whether SAGE (or any other defenses) could survive a massive nuclear attack, let alone prevail against it. IBM's President, T.J. Watson, Jr., characterized the $12 billion dollar project (in 1964 dollars) in his 1990 biography *Father, Son & Co.* as "...*a costly fantasy, the SDI* [Strategic Defense Initiative, a ballistic missile defense program] *of its day.*" This opinion may have been generated, in part, by the estimate that only 70% of the incoming Soviet bombers would be successfully destroyed. Assuming a force of a thousand or more, this meant that possibly 300 nuclear weapons would be detonated on targets within the continental U.S. However, based on the advances the SAGE system generated in computing and, as it remained in use until 1983, one might question Watson's perception, although he was not alone in his judgment.

In actual fact (though not well-known outside the defense community of its day), the risks of system destruction or failure were addressed to some degree all along. Three examples follow: two here and a third in a later chapter.

First, air defense sectors occasionally scheduled, or "sprang" mission days in which one or another SAGE or GCI site was "down" or failed, and adjacent sites had to expand their coverage to take over the downed site's area. Depending on the radar coverage by remaining sites, most missions continued as well as if full control capability had been available throughout.

Secondly, the next section below describes the Back-Up Interceptor Control (BUIC) series of "mini-SAGE" sites that were deployed in the mid-1960s (with simpler programs using newer technologies) to fill in for many of ADCOM's SAGE sites if they failed. In this way, the U.S. both added control sites and gave an enemy more targets he'd have to attack.

The third example, while not presumed to be unique to that airplane, may be found in chapter 7 for the F-101s.

Back-Up Interceptor Control (BUIC)

The first BUIC system (BUIC I) was a manual backup interceptor control system implemented in 1962 to provide limited command and control capability at selected GCI radar sites in the event a local SAGE center (or the entire system) was disabled. In 1964, the semi-automated BUIC II (416M) system, based on Burroughs Corporation's AN/GSA-51system's D825 modular data-processing computer, provided a semi-automatic back-up network to conduct more of the air battle in case one or more SAGE sites was inoperative. Starting in 1968, the AN/GSA-51 was modified into the AN/GYK-19, as BUIC III. The number of BUIC computer systems peaked at 22, each located at a long-range radar site. They performed most of the same Air Surveillance and Weapon Control functions as SAGE, but with more modern equipment, simpler processes, and at less cost.

From the interceptors' viewpoint, BUIC control looked the same as that from SAGE DCs. Moreover, T-4 test results and further recommendations were also applied to the BUIC system to keep it current with continuing SAGE updates.

Evolution of Automated Control Systems

As for the existential questions, such as how SAGE (BUIC) would fare under electronic countermeasures (ECM) or physical attack—the answers remain problematic. However (and as stated above), at intervals, sector-, region-, or system-wide exercises were conducted, both via internal computer simulations and with live interceptors against live "threat" targets, to test the survivability and effectiveness of SAGE (and other) sites under varying attack conditions. If one SAGE site was "down," adjacent sector sites expanded their coverage and control to sustain air defense functions. If SAGE as a whole was deemed unavailable, direct local control was assumed by BUIC and/or GCI sites. And, if they too were degraded, the interceptors still had opportunities to vector themselves towards target approach routes based on bare information command-relayed from the Early Warning radar networks and their owtn "dead-reckoning" courses to intercept.

In summary, despite the extra challenges to both Weapons Controllers and interceptor crews alike with the increasing complexities of automated systems and computer-driven battle management, both SAGE and BUIC were magnificent achievements for their time—especially in retrospect, as vacuum-tube technology was all that was available when SAGE was conceived, planned, constructed, and deployed. Moreover, as newer interceptors of all kinds were developed and deployed, they proved both worthy successors to their subsonic predecessors and increasingly able to capitalize on the expanded capabilities of their "supporting" ground environment system. From a "top-down" perspective, therefore, it was largely the SAGE/BUIC system's semi-automated control capabilities of the 1960s and '70s (backed up by traditional GCI control) that helped make their *Century Series* interceptors the integrated continental Air Defense force they were.

Ironically, even as SAGE and BUIC systems reached maturity, the evolving threat change from manned bombers with nuclear payloads to Intercontinental and Submarine Launched Ballistic Missiles (ICBMs and SLBMs) rendered the active air defense mission largely "irrelevant" to policy-makers, especially in light of continuing budget priorities. Interceptor assets were progressively transferred to the Air National Guard or deactivated, the active Air Defense mission was reduced to Air Sovereignty, and ADCOM itself was deactivated in 1980, with its remaining assets assigned to the Tactical and Strategic Air Commands (TAC and SAC). The last BUIC III sites in the U.S. and Canada were deactivated in the early 1980s, as the dual military-civil Regional Operations Control Centers (ROCCs) with digital computers became operational. The SAGE system itself was decommissioned in 1983, although Canadian forces continued to provide air defenses in their NORAD sectors. Meanwhile, U.S. command and control of atmospheric weapon systems had migrated to mobile airborne systems with longer-range detection (especially at low altitudes), and better and more ECM-resistant radar systems and communication links, most notably found in the E-3 Airborne Warning and Control System (AWACS) of the last 35 years.

The Development Process

The years that followed WWII were a period of prolific aircraft design, as the Cold War fighter doctrine by 1950 reflected a more diverse set of needs. With the move from piston to jet engines in the late 1940s, the unknown characteristics of the sound barrier opened up a new and challenging effort to explore the high-speed realm of aerodynamics.

The development process of military aircraft by 1950 had traditionally taken one of three paths. The most prevalent was a published Request for Proposal (RFP), in which aircraft manufacturers were asked by the military to respond to a set of specifications. Typically, a specific mission dictated a desired performance, such as speed, altitude, and range. In some instances, one or more technologies were suggested or required.

A second approach was for manufacturers who believed they might have a critical innovation or approach to a problem to spend corporate funds to develop their idea. In the early days of aviation (1920-1940), when the technology was less costly, the manufacturer might actually finance the building of a prototype. They then approached the military in hopes of convincing key individuals to create a requirement to which they would then respond. A third method was to propose changes to an existing aircraft in an attempt to elicit a response.

Regardless of the proposal's path, the actual design of an aircraft had taken on increasingly more complex aspects by the early 1950s. The designers themselves required progressively more academic knowledge of the environment. This new generation of aeronautical engineers discovered the need for better "*tools*" to cope with the unknown and more dynamic jet age.

The slide rule, or "*slipstick*" as it was more often called, was a simple mechanical analog computer that looked much like a simple ruler with a sliding inset (hence the moniker *slipstick*). Some were more than 20 inches long. They allowed for working a single constant against a variable—arriving at an answer interpolated from the many graduations on the face of the instrument. As the speed and complexity of aircraft increased, so did the number of variables and data points. With few exceptions, most of the *Century Series* fighter designs were implemented with the *slipstick*.

This method of calculation was augmented by a room full of electromechanical calculators that became available at that time. However, the need for much higher speed computing was obvious. By the end of the 1950s, although the *slipstick* could still be found on the desk of most engineers, a big room with a digital mainframe computer was available to most of the large aircraft companies.

Many new military aircraft designations began life with the prefix "X"—such as XF-86. This recognizes that the initial product is part of an experimental development. One or more of the model was produced, often by hand tooling rather than by production tooling. The simpler early jet aircraft, such as the P-80, were brought to life in a matter of a few months—with a skilled design team and a well-disciplined prototyping facility, such as Lockheed's "*Skunk Works.*" Of course, they were using the same type of aircraft structure used for propeller-driven aircraft. Thus, these were termed the "*first generation*" jet aircraft. The next step was to introduce some of the high-speed technology, such as the swept-wing and the all-moving horizontal tail (stabilator), as found in the later versions of the F-86. Most aviation historians consider these as part of the first generation; thus, the *Century Series* is the "*second generation.*"

At some point, the military would be enthused and confident enough in the product that they would authorize an initial batch for service testing. Here, production tooling may be used and the prefix "Y" (for "prototype") assigned to the military designation, as in "YF-100." About 10-20 aircraft were typically produced in this series, and the military then used them to test the functions and maneuvers required of the plane in a combat environment. The organizational structure necessary to support the aircraft, to include training, spare parts, maintenance and supply, was also set up during this period.

When the military is satisfied that they have a sound product, there is a formal acceptance of the aircraft and full-scale production takes place. (Nowadays, it is more often preceded by a low-rate initial production (LRIP) phase to allow problems to be addressed in a timely manner.) The ensuing production rate varies with the critical nature of the aircraft relative to the world's political situation and military priority, and to the funding available.

The jigs and fixtures for a production environment are very costly and time consuming to produce. Because a design may not meet the performance specifications—and might never be put into production—most of the pre-production models of post-WWII first-generation jet aircraft were "*hand built.*" This process would change with the *Century Series*.

It was also recognized that the time required for design, fabrication, test and production of higher-technology aircraft was constantly being extended. Because one of the significant time factors in the production chain was the fabrication of the required tools and fixtures to produce the plane, a plan was conceived to shorten this aspect.

Following WWII, General Orval R. Cook (Deputy Chief of Staff for Material) and Laurence C. Craigie (Deputy Chief of Staff for Development) proposed building prototypes with the production tooling so that quantity manufacture could proceed rapidly. (Craigie, in 1942, gained fame for being the first American military aviator to fly a jet-powered aircraft—the Bell P-59.) This plan was based on the assumption that when the technology was well understood, the plane would not require any significant structural changes following its test period. However, the Cook-Craigie Plan, while still widely used today and often referred to as *concurrent engineering*, resulted in some very costly decisions with several of the *Century Series.*

Performance Factors

Each of the four forces of flight (Lift, Thrust, Gravity, and Drag) represents primary factors that affect the performance of an aircraft. The principal attributes of the fighter are speed (a function of thrust and drag) and maneuverability—the management of lift and weight about the various axes of the aircraft.

The role of the aeronautical engineer is to determine the optimum aerodynamic configuration that manages these forces for the role of the aircraft. In the discussion that follows the F-86 is contrasted with the MiG-15, as these were the two primary contenders of the era that set the relative performance aspects considered by the designers of the *Century Series* fighters.

There are three weight definitions of an aircraft. The first is the *Empty Weight*, which is determined without any fuel, lubricants, armament or crew aboard. The *Combat Weight* (sometimes referred to as Loaded Weight) is with full (or most) internal fuel, armament and the pilot (or crew)—but no external stores. This is the nominal configuration of the fighter when typically engaging the opponent. Finally, there is the *Maximum Gross Weight* (or Maximum Take-Off Weight) that will include external stores (drop tanks and ordnance).

The *thrust-to-weight* ratio determines acceleration and climb performance. It is calculated by dividing the thrust of the engine by the weight of the aircraft. Climb rate is directly related to power available and the

weight of the aircraft. Thus, during encounters between the MiG-15 (13,460 pounds weight, 5,950 pounds max thrust) and the *Sabre* (16,220 pounds weight, 4,850 pounds thrust) the MiG had the climb advantage—a *thrust-to-weight ratio* of 0.44 compared to the *Sabre's* 0.30 *and* an acceleration advantage. Note that the empty weight of the MiG is 75% that of the *Sabre* while the thrust is about 10% more. In dogfighting, it is all about maneuvering and power. As will be revealed, however, the paradigm of the fighter's role began to change, and for some of the *Century Series*, dogfighting became less of a consideration.

Wing loading is a significant factor in the maneuverability of a fighter. It is the weight of the aircraft divided by the wing area (lb/ft²). For a given weight, an aircraft with a larger wing area will have greater maneuverability (as well as lower take-off and landing speeds). A part of the heavier weight of the *Sabre* was more fuel (20%), allowing for a longer range, engagement, and loiter time. The wing loading shows a slight advantage to the *Sabre*. These numbers are nominal, as the actual weight during combat determines the real values.

Roll-rate reflects the responsiveness of the plane to the pilot's aileron control input. The ability to roll quickly to a desired bank angle allows an aircraft the advantage of repositioning rapidly relative to its opponent. When a combat engagement (dogfight) has begun, the *turn radius* is critical to gaining the advantage behind the adversary to achieve the proper lead factor when guns are used. This turn radius is a function of the aircraft's weight, G-loading, bank angle, density altitude and, most importantly, true airspeed. An aircraft traveling at 800 knots requires a three-mile diameter to complete a 180-degree turn using a 60-degree bank angle, and will generate two Gs from centrifugal force. Level turns greater than 60 degrees of bank angle produce greater G-forces that can quickly approach six Gs and are common in close-in air combat engagements. The *Century Series* were typically designed for 7.33 Gs. Consider that the wings of a fighter that weighs 30,000 pounds will be supporting 180,000 pounds in a 6-G turn! The 180-pound pilot will be experiencing a body weight of over 1,000 pounds.

Table 03-01

Comparison of the F-86 vs. MiG-15 performance factors						
Aircraft	Empty Weight (lbs)	Combat Weight (lbs)	Engine Thrust (lbs)	Power / Wt Ratio	Wing Area (sq ft)	Wing Loading (cw/wa)	Internal Fuel (gal)
F-86A	10,535	16,220	4,850	0.30	288	56.32	435
MiG-15	7,900	13,460	5,950	0.44	222	60.63	364

Some specifications show the wing loading as 49 (F-86) and 58 (MiG-15) and Power-to-Weight as .38 and .54, depending on weight variables.

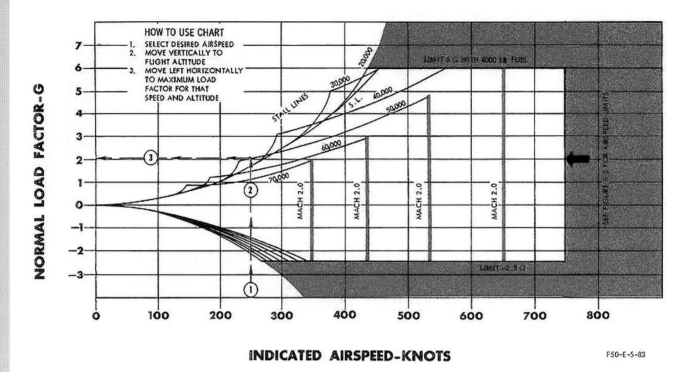

Figure 03-01. The V-G Diagram of the F-104. USAF Illustration.

The Velocity and G-loading are graphed in a chart called the V-G diagram. It defines the flight envelope within which that airplane can fly. Outside those conditions, the airplane will either stall or deform—to destruction in the extreme.

The MiG was a formidable adversary when in the horizontal plane at less than Mach .8, or in a climb. As the MiG had very slow roll response at high speeds and was unable to exceed Mach 1 in a dive, the *Sabre* was in its element in these conditions, retaining excellent roll and dive rates throughout its performance envelope. The maneuvering limitations of the MiG, however, were not truly quantified until after the Korean War.

While the MiG's numbers illustrate its built-in performance superiority in some areas of its flight envelope, the *Sabre* accounted for 792 MiGs with a kill ratio of 10:1 (though these numbers have been contested by the Soviets over the years). This attests to the significance of pilot training and experience in the equation—and some knowledge of the MiG's shortcomings.

It is important to note that *Century Series* aircraft spent little time at their top speed for several reasons. The most obvious is very high fuel consumption at high power settings (in AB). In addition, some of the *Century Series,* such as the F-104, had a maximum value on the skin temperature, which limited the time (measured in a few minutes) they could spend at high Mach numbers.

The optimum "*cruise*" for most was about Mach .9 at 35,000 feet—though if carrying external ordnance or drop tanks it may have been lower.

The performance of the fighter determines the offensive and defensive maneuvers that each pilot has available to him. In WWI the aircraft were relatively underpowered, and it was the pilot who was "fortunate" if they had the available energy to perform *tight turns, loops, rolls,* or *Immelmann*—the latter named for its originator. These are the basic stock-in-trade for the fighter pilot.

Even when begun at high speeds, a protracted dogfight will typically see the speed diminish to the realm of 4-500 knots as the pilots trade kinetic energy for potential energy—airspeed for altitude— and then altitude for airspeed. Wide varieties of combat maneuvers are derivations of the basic maneuvers and include such descriptors as the *high* and *low yo-yo,* and the *flat* and *rolling scissors.* These are executed in what is called the "*tactical egg*" of pursuit—the "*egg*" being the dynamic shape of the maneuver as defined by the effects of gravity and available power.

The key to a successful engagement, besides the obvious factor of remaining undetected until you fire on the enemy, is to manage the energy of the aircraft. Obviously, no two aircraft have the same performance characteristics. Thus, it is vital for the pilot to understand his aircraft and that of the opponent.

Supersonic Aerodynamics

Because the speed of sound through the atmosphere (763 mph at standard sea level conditions) decreases with altitude (air density) and temperature, the term *Mach* defines that speed regardless of the flight condition. The Mach number is the relationship of the plane's current speed relative to the actual speed of sound in its existing operating environment. Assume the speed of sound at 35,000 feet altitude is 660 mph. If the plane is flying at 594 mph, it is flying at about .9 (point-nine) Mach. High-speed aircraft have both an Airspeed indicator (for low speed operations) and a Mach meter. By using the Mach number as a reference, the pilot does not need to interpolate the relationship between airspeed and altitude to assure flying within the performance limitations.

The term "*Mach*" was derived from the name of the Austrian physicist Ernst Mach, who first measured the speed of sound and had theorized the aerodynamic effects of high speed on an object almost 100 years earlier. As an object approaches the speed of sound, its movement through the atmosphere creates pressure waves that radiate from its structure. Because these waves propagate outward at the speed of sound, they begin to accumulate along its direction of flight. These pressure waves are being compressed to form a shock wave. The actual penetration of Mach 1 by a streamlined object is, in itself, not a major achievement (a rifle bullet accomplishes the feat without much challenge to technology by simple brute force). However, when the object is being supported by airfoils, the problem quickly becomes more complex.

Shock waves form not only on the nose, but also on the leading edges and surfaces of the airfoils. Because the air is flowing faster across the top of an airfoil (from the Bernoulli Effect that generates lift), this portion of an aircraft will experience supersonic flow (at the critical Mach number) before other parts of the airframe. The shock wave may be observed by passengers sitting over the wing of a commercial airliner, which typically travels at .78 Mach. Looking closely about one-third of the way back from the leading edge, a ripple of air extending from the fuselage to the wing tip, perhaps a few inches wide, will undulate slowly back and forth across the top of the wing.

The pressure wave created by a supersonic object extends for several miles in all directions; its intensity is typically a function of the size of the object and prevailing atmospheric conditions. A supersonic bullet whistling a few feet from the ear will produce a "*crack*" sound similar to a whip. (The tip of the whip makes the crack sound because it is exceeding Mach 1.) As created by an aircraft, the shock wave's sound is heard on the ground as a loud sharp thunderclap. Thunder itself is created by the compression of air by a lightning strike, thus producing a sonic boom.

One key to achieving high-speed flight is the use of the swept-wing. It was first conceived and revealed publicly by Adolf Busemann at the Fifth Volta Conference in Rome in 1935. Eastman Jacobs of the National Advisory Committee for Aeronautics (NACA) also presented a paper on the work done in the United States, which pointed to a significant increase in drag as an aircraft approached the speed of sound. Busemann's research strongly suggested that a swept-wing would produce less drag at speeds between Mach .8 and 1.2—the transonic region. Within a year of the Volta Conference, whose theme was *High Velocities in Aviation*, the Germans classified Busemann's work.

Aircraft of the early 1940s, such as the Lockheed P-38, began to exhibit controllability problems in high-speed dives at Mach numbers in the transonic region. Unknown forces were at work that caused aircraft to become unmanageable at those speeds. The center of lift appeared to move aft along the camber of the wing, causing the nose to pitch down. What was known about these strange effects was that a shock wave was apparently building up on portions of the airfoil and upsetting its aerodynamic qualities—the phenomenon was known as *compressibility*. Control stick forces rose dramatically under these conditions, making it almost impossible for the pilot to pull out of the dive. Lockheed eventually fitted a dive flap on the P-38 that could be extended at high speed to slow the plane so that the pilot could regain control.

Figure 03-02. An FA-18 exceeding Mach 1 shows the effect of moisture condensation in the air caused by the rapid change in pressure in the shock cone. Note the small secondary pressure wave just behind the cockpit. U.S. Navy Photo.

It was not until the effects of *compressibility* began showing up in these power dives of piston-powered aircraft that a serious effort was begun in the United States to investigate this unknown region that had already killed several pilots. The U.S. Army and Navy, in collaboration with NACA, began a program to explore high-speed flight using the rocket engine as the power source for a series of experimental aircraft that would probe the mysterious region known as the *sound barrier*.

Former NASA Administrator Robert Gilruth worked on compressibility as an aerodynamicist in the 1940s at NACA. In a 1986 interview, he describes the phenomena encountered with WWII fighters in a dive. *"The wing-flow tests showed conclusively that a thick wing like you had on the P-47 lost its lift curve slope when you got above a Mach number of about .7 or .8, which caused it to have this so-called stick freezing characteristic. The stick didn't actually freeze; you could still move it the usual amount, but when the wing lost its lift curve slope, it wouldn't do anything for the airplane. It [the plane] kept going straight down, till it got to the lower altitudes where the drag was great enough to slow it down to a Mach number where the lift effectiveness was restored. Then you could pull it out — if you could wait that long. It was tough on the pilots the first time it came. They didn't know it was going to stop. To this day I still meet people who flew the P-47 who say, 'My God, I never knew why that was.'"*

Efforts to explore high-speed aerodynamics in wind tunnels were thwarted by the creation of shockwaves within the tunnel that *"choked"* the airflow. Thus, by 1944 research in the United States moved towards producing manned rocket-powered research aircraft, such as the Bell X-1 and Douglas D-558-2.

Gilruth continued: *"At Wallops Island we flew a whole model [in free flight] of the X-1, flew it right through the speed of sound... about four or five feet long, like a wind tunnel model, only it had to be designed and built to fly over the speed range you were testing. The center of gravity had to be in the correct place and you would control the elevators to go up and down the proper amount to produce the lift responses of the flight range. You would boost the model up to a Mach number of maybe 2, and then it would gradually slow down, and as it slowed down the elevators would move up and down to make pull ups and push downs and you'd record the response as it went back through the speed range... Without the rocket and without the telemetry you couldn't do this. But it all grew out of starting with simple models and finally we'd get to these pulse models. We did this with the X-1, the X-2 and with many of the new fighter designs of the Air Force and Navy."*

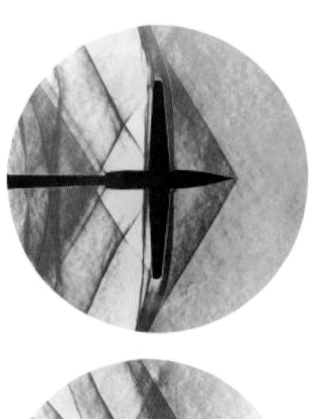

Figure 03-03. A Schlieren photograph shows the compression in front of an unswept wing at Mach 1.2. NASA Photo.

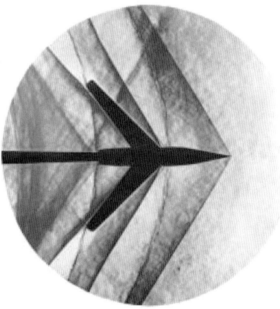

Figure 03-04 A Schlieren photograph shows the compression in front of a swept wing at Mach 1.2. NASA Photo.

These results fed back into supersonic flight research with reports that went to the industry. Gilruth: *"Then we got into all kinds of fights with the wind tunnel people, because they wanted to put a thick wing [10 percent ratio of wing chord to its thickness] on it because then you'd get lots of transonic flow. This was about the time that I was getting my wing-flow data, which showed that a thick wing would not permit flight through the speed of sound! I showed my boss, Tommy Thompson. It was awkward because Dr. Lewis, who was the head man in Washington, had made the wing flow data top secret."*

The thickness of the wing relates to the lift generated at a given airspeed by the Bernoulli Effect—a wing designed for subsonic flight might have a thickness of 10 percent of its chord (the width of the wing), while a supersonic wing might be 6 percent. The very thin wing (4 percent), while advantageous for extreme high-speed flight, requires much higher landing speeds and has less room for structure for hardpoints to accommodate external fuel and ordnance.

Gilruth: *"Anyway, I had showed Tommy my data and I had convinced him that we should not put that thick wing on because you'd never... get supersonic... We really wanted a 5 percent wing, that was the neatest wing, but 7 percent wasn't all that bad. It didn't lose its lift, it just had a certain amount of buffeting and so on but it still would respond. It still generated lift if you would increase the angle of attack, so that was the compromise, I think it was around a 7 percent wing, and so that was the reason, really, we were able to go above the speed of sound. If we had put the wing that the boys, Russ Robinson and Harvey Allen and those people wanted to put on, we would have waited a while before we got the first airplane to go supersonic. That was really a good effort, that research effort."*

NACA researcher Robert T. Jones produced a paper in February 1945 that strongly suggested that the swept-wing was also a factor in the supersonic equation. His work, however, was not widely accepted until the classified data from Germany began flowing into the United States following the end of the war. Jones had many notable innovative contributions to aviation despite his never having earned a college degree.

A sweptback wing reduces the effective velocity of the oncoming relative wind at the leading edge. The key point is that a component of the oncoming air is parallel to the leading edge, and is therefore not a part of that which is flowing over the wing. This effectively reduces the induced drag at critical transonic Mach numbers— the greater the sweep of the wing, the larger the parallel component. Of course, the effect of a swept-wing also has its drawbacks at low speeds (as during the landing phase), when it exhibits high drag and loss of lift.

The first-generation American jet fighters (F-80 and F-84), conceived before Jones' work became available and accepted, were of conventional design (straight wing). The second phase of these first generation jets (F-86 and F84F) took advantage of the swept-wing, which delayed the effect of compressibility resulting from supersonic airflow. Other countries were also hard at work addressing the problems of high-speed flight. The swept-wing Soviet MiG-15 flew just three months after the F-86.

Both Busemann and another German engineer, Waldemar Voigt, immigrated to the United States after the war to continue their research on supersonic aerodynamics. Theodore von Karman of Cal Tech's GALCIT laboratory recruited Busemann.

In 1945, in an effort to understand the low speed aerodynamics of the swept-wing, a Bell P-63

Figure 03-05. A modified Bell P-63, redesignated the L-39, examined the low speed flight characteristics of the swept wing. Note the wing fences and extended leading edge slat U.S. Army Photo.

Kingcobra was modified with a sweep of 35 degrees and redesignated the L-39. (What makes the L-39 designation a bit confusing is that the predecessor of the P-63 was the P-39.) Only the nose gear retracted because the wings were handmade with no provision for a complex retraction mechanism of the main gear. As it was primarily designed to explore the low speed regions, the added drag of the fixed gear was not a problem.

Various configurations of leading-edge slats were bolted on to explore the handling qualities during landing and take-off. One undesirable aspect of the swept-wing was its tendency to pitch up uncontrollably (beyond 45 degrees) at high G-forces and high angles-of-attack. If the pilot was not quick enough the plane would typically roll off into a spin that was recoverable—but used lots of altitude.

The ability to make aggressive pitch changes while maintaining control of the aircraft and allowing unrestricted airflow into the engine were major issues in several *Century Series* designs. A specific control problem called '*pitch up*" became apparent when swept-wing fighters exceeded their "*critical angle-of-attack*," resulting in a separation of the airflow over the wing—a condition referred to as a "*stall*." The swept-wing configuration exacerbates the stalled condition because it abruptly changes the location of the center of lift. This occurs when the outer portion of the wing stalls and moves the center of lift forward, upsetting the lateral stability of the plane by causing the nose to pitch upward.

Wing and tail placement (high, mid, or low) reflects the consideration for airflow interference, or drag. Typically a mid-wing has the least drag, but the low wing provides more convenient storage and shorter (lighter weight) landing gear. The T-tail normally keeps the horizontal stabilizer above the turbulence created by the wing at high angles-of-attack, as does one that is set below the wing position. A greater overall fineness ratio (the relationship of the aircraft's length to its width) was desired because it provides more inherent stability and typically presents less frontal area (drag).

Drag produced by the airplane determines how much available power can be turned into speed. Three forms of drag (*parasitic*, *induced*, and *wave*) produce a complex formula referred to as the "*drag coefficient*."

Parasitic drag is produced by the movement of an object (the aircraft) through a fluid (the air), and is composed of three elements: skin friction, interference, and form drag. Every effort is made in the design stage to create a sleek form (minimum cross-section), reduce or "*clean up*" all the perturbations, and provide a smooth surface (skin). Parasitic drag increases with the square of the speed. Thus, to fly twice as fast requires four times the power.

Induced drag is generated by the lift produced by the wing and is greatest at slow speeds. This is because a higher angle-of-attack must be maintained to produce the needed lift. Thus, this member of the drag family is reduced with increasing speed.

Wave drag is generated about the mid-section of the fuselage as the plane moves through the transonic region (Mach .8 to 1.2). This is one of the unknown factors that caused so much grief for the *Century Series* designers trying to attain supersonic flight, and which ultimately resulted in the "*area rule*."

The designs of the *Century Series* would exhibit considerable variation with respect to the layout of each aircraft and would include swept-wing, straight wing, and delta wing, as well as high tail and low tail.

The wing is primarily designed to perform at the normal cruise speed of the airplane and to permit excursions to its highest speed when necessary. However, the wing must provide enough lift at low airspeeds to allow the aircraft to take-off and land at a reasonable speed (speed typically equates to runway length required). A variety of auxiliary lifting devices can be designed into the wing to help lower the stall speed and provide maneuverability in the low speed range. *Trailing edge flaps* increase the camber and may increase the available wing area. Leading edge flaps (also called Krueger flaps) are hinged near the leading edge and typically deploy

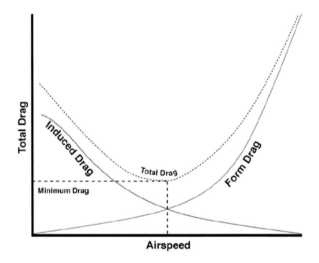

Figure 03-06. The "Drag Curve" illustrates the relationship of the various forms of drag graphed against airspeed. Minimum drag occurs at an airspeed that typically represents best economy/best rate of climb.

from beneath it, also increasing the camber. In some instances the entire leading edge is hinged to deflect downward.

Wing slats come in three types, and are a feature on the leading edge that again increases the camber and allows some of the relative wind to flow through from the bottom of the wing to the top. *Automatic slats* lie flush with the leading edge until reduced aerodynamic forces allow them to extend (by use of springs when needed). The slats on some aircraft were deployed based on airflow and angle-of-attack-only—there were no springs. *Powered slats* may be extended at the discretion of the pilot. *Fixed slats* are permanently extended and may also be referred to as a *slotted wing*.

Flutter is another undesirable aerodynamic issue. It is the rapid and increasing divergence of an airfoil (bending-torsion oscillations) from its static position, resulting from exciting the natural structural vibration frequency. It typically occurs at high speeds, which aggravate the imbalance. Most airplanes have a "never exceed speed" which is determined so as to avoid the critical flutter speed. The onset of flutter is so fast and the effect so damaging that few incidences result in recovery of the aircraft. The remedy is typically to provide improved torsional rigidity—stiffening— effectively changing the structural resonant frequency.

Airborne Radar

Prior to WWII there was little if any electronics in the cockpit of the fighter—the two-way radio being one of the first. This was a critical item in the Battle of Britain, as it allowed the point defense fighter to be vectored to the intercept position indicated by ground-based radar. Then the IFF (Identification Friend or Foe) transponder was developed. These "*parrots*" (as they were often called) provided a discrete code to be transmitted back to the ground radar facility to identify friendly fighters from those that were not "*squawking*" a code.

For the tactical, often multi-mission, fighters in the *Century Series*, airborne radars and supporting avionics were improved, but normally just enough to provide ranging and limited angle acquisition for their cannon, rocket and missile armaments. Air-to-air missions and equipage tended to be secondary to strike missions and their tactics, with the avionics focused on weapons delivery, both conventional and nuclear.

Meanwhile, as the Cold War grew colder in the late 1940s, the growing threat of Soviet long-range bombers—first carrying gravity bombs and then stand-off air-to-surface missiles (ASMs), all with nuclear warheads—gave a new urgency to the development of night and all-weather interceptors for in-depth air defense of North America.

The next step was dictated not only by the speed of the aircraft, but also the need to position the interceptor optimally with respect to its targets through the integration of ground and airborne radar information. This resulted in the progressive development of the fire control system (FCS), which would become a fundamental part of the *Century Series'* three dedicated interceptors: the Convair F-102, McDonnell F-101B, and Convair F-106. In 1948, aviation entrepreneur Howard Hughes created a new division of his diverse Hughes Aircraft Company, with two new Hughes engineers, Simon Ramo and Dean Wooldridge, as its nucleus. With the arrival of the transistor, many elements of an aircraft's electronics could be repackaged to make an integrated fire control system that would fit within a fighter aircraft. Thenceforth, "*aviation electronics*" were generally referred to by the contraction "*avionics.*"

Because of the requirement to operate in all-weather situations, the interceptor typically had to have a "*target acquisition*" radar. Radars of the immediate post-World War II era were large and heavy, and typically required a dedicated crewmember to operate them. For fighter-interceptors, they needed to be miniaturized, able to detect and track targets beyond visual range, and guide the interceptor into a firing position appropriate for its armament (guns, missiles, or rockets). Electronics were becoming a greater part of the fighter's complexity— and cost.

Starting with a contract to equip the early F-94s and F-89s (ADC's first interceptors) with its E-1 FCS, Hughes Aircraft Company went on to equip almost all the Generation 1 and 2 interceptors of the 1950s and '60s. From the E-1's pursuit guidance for gun-firing attacks to its E-3 through E-9 lead-collision positioning, first for the single-seat F-86D (and later L) and then for the F-94C, F-89D and F-89H—all firing volleys of 2.75-inch "Mighty Mouse" folding fin aerial rockets (FFARs)—Hughes FCSs grew more sophisticated. The F-89H's E-9 FCS, e.g., also retained the pursuit option so that it could fire its heat-seeking Falcon missiles as well as its radar-guided version.

As the *Century Series* interceptors began to replace their subsonic forebears in the later 1950s, Hughes's FCSs advanced to its "MG" series: the MG-3, then MG-10, equipped the transonic F-102A. The two-seat F-101B and F were equipped with the MG-13 to support supersonic launches. Finally, Ramo and Wooldridge completed development of the Hughes MA-1 system for the Mach 2-capable single-seat F-106A and two-seat F-106B to support their rockets and improved radar- and infrared-guided missiles.

From E-1 to MA-1, all the interceptor FCSs incorporated pulsed-signal radars (which could be susceptible to chaff and/or blinded at low level by ground clutter), plus relatively slow analog computers that used the radar location, speed, course and altitude of the aggressor to provide a real-time solution to position their interceptor for the kill. Concurrently, the required heading, speed, and altitude of the interceptor were transmitted to its crew, either by voice radio or data-link, so that the pilot or RIO could lock onto the target and let his FCS compute the firing solution. If the target and command information was transmitted by data-link (with voice backup, if necessary), the pilot could either follow his steering dot (and other commands) or couple the aircraft autopilot to the data-linked steering signal to let the command site "fly" his aircraft to the desired firing point. However, the aircrew still had to acquire and lock onto the target, and the pilot had to operate his engine throttle(s), select the armament, and hold down the trigger after lock-on to complete the firing sequence. Thus, although "the pilot was becoming a redundant part of the equation"—according to the technology visionaries—the facts of such dynamic air defense intercept operations continued to prove otherwise.

Infrared Search and Track (IRST)

In the mid-1960s, ADC interceptors added a basic infrared search and track (IRST) subsystem to augment their FCS's radar functions. Radars transmitted active pulses to acquire a target, and these could be detected and possibly countered by signal jamming and dispensing chaff (small strips of metal foil, cut to cover their object radar's wavelength band). The IRST passively received and exploited its target's emanations—its infrared "heat signature"—without necessarily giving away the interceptor's own position and intentions. It was also impervious to chaff, could detect "afterburning" targets beyond normal radar ranges, and low-level targets otherwise masked by then-pulse radars' ground clutter returns, and of course provided backup capabilities in case of radar failure or saturation by noise-jamming ECM. On the other hand, the radar was an all-weather system, while IRST operations were largely constrained to clear-weather conditions.

Moreover, as the IRST was added to an already mature radar-based FCS, the two sensors' search patterns were not always compatible, and their operating modes were complementary but not identical. In short, radar remained the primary sensor for direct collision-type intercepts, with IR

Figure 03-07. Captain Lowell H. Smith and Lieutenant John P. Richter perform the first aerial refueling between a DeHavilland DH-4B (tanker) and a DH-4 on 27 June 1923. The DH-4 biplane remained aloft for 37 hours. U.S. Army Photo.

Figure 03-08. A Boeing KB-50 tanker deploys three drogues to permit as many aircraft to "receive" fuel simultaneously. USAF Photo.

modes most useful for long-range high-altitude target detection and during pursuit attacks—especially if IR missiles became the preferred weapon choice. Even then, at the slower overtake rates and closer weapon launch ranges of a stern attack, an IR angle lock-on (and manual missile launch) could be upgraded to a radar angle-and-range lock-on (and auto-fire) if the radar could finally "burn through" jamming or ground clutter soon enough for weapon preparations to complete before minimum lock-on range was reached.

The benefits of this second FCS sensor were partially offset by the complexities of its added options—and the extra challenges thus presented to the pilot (and/or RIO)—but the overall net value-added was necessary to keep pace with the evolving bomber threat during the Cold War.

In-Flight Refueling

Perhaps no other single innovation has enabled the mission of the fighter to be expanded as has in-flight refueling. Extending the range or loiter time, increasing its load-carrying capacity, and allowing rapid deployment are just a few of the possibilities. Experiments carried out in the

1920s proved the concept. However, it was not until after WWII that the Cold War generated a need to perfect the technique. The two methods used were "probe and drogue" (where the "thirsty" client flies his aircraft's probe into the dispensing aircraft's drogue, or "basket"), or via "boom" (where the dispensing aircraft's boom operator "steers" his moveable boom into the receiving aircraft's refueling receptacle). Ultimately, most of the *Century Series* aircraft would have one or both methods available.

In the "*probe and drogue*" method, a flexible hose is extended from the tanker and trails behind. The receiver is responsible for flying up to and inserting his "*probe*" into the drogue—which employs "shuttlecock-like" aerodynamic stability.

The "*boom*" system, as developed by the Boeing Company for its KC-97 (and subsequent KC-135), uses a hard pipe-like appendage that hangs from beneath the tail of the tanker. The "*receiver*" flies into position astern and the "boom" operator uses small airfoils on the boom to "*fly*" the refueling nozzle into the receptacle on the receiver. The "boom" method allows four times the rate of transfer and is typically used for refueling larger aircraft, such as bombers.

Figure 03-09.
The Boeing "Boom" method
is employed from a KC-135
to refuel a General Dynamics
F-16. USAF Photo.

Tactical Nuclear Weapons

As noted, the fighter was adapted for delivery of conventional weapons in tactical support of ground forces. The fighter-bomber replaced the traditional dive-bomber before the end of WWII—although the Navy persisted and created a new series of "*attack*" aircraft as exemplified by the Douglas AD *Skyraider*, later redesignated as the A-1.

The Soviets were poised to roll over Western Europe following their conquest of the Eastern Bloc countries at the end of WWII. The threat of men and armor they had accumulated was brought to bear on the West with the Berlin Blockade of 1948. At the time, the U.S. possessed only a few nuclear weapons. These were physically quite large and heavy, and could only be delivered by America's *strategic* bombers (B-29, B-50, and B-36). Thus, there was not a significant nuclear deterrent. The yield of the bombs of that time, such as the MK (Mark) 5, ranged from 30 to 60 kilotons (KT). (The Atomic Energy Commission (AEC) originally designated atomic weapons with a Mark/Mod/Alt system.)

However, much of the weight and bulk of these weapons was a result of the conservative design philosophy in the rush to build the bomb during WWII. After the war, scientists from the Los Alamos Scientific Laboratory (LASL—where the bombs were designed) met with representatives of the various services to determine a wider variety of possible sizes and delivery options. Creating smaller weapons that could be carried by fighters brought a new dimension to the concept of "*tactical air support.*"

The question may be asked as to what type of tactical targets might warrant the kiloton power of a nuclear weapon? Obviously, targets involving massed infantry or armor and supply depots, as well as critical infrastructure, such as bridges. History recalls that there were several bridges during WWII that required hundreds of sorties over many days before critical hits finally dropped the structure. A delay of even hours in a modern war could prove disastrous. In a European war of the 1950s, the tactical "*nuke*" was an indispensable part of the deterrent plan.

One of the first nuclear weapons capable of being carried by a fighter was the 1700-pound MK 7. Specifically configured for the Republic F-84 *Thunderjet*, it became available in 1952 and served until 1967. Initially limited to subsonic delivery speeds, later versions allowed speeds well in excess of Mach 1. Its 15-foot length and 30-inch diameter made for a

Figure 03-10. The 30-inch diameter MK 7 bomb was an early effort to provide tactical fighter-bombers with nuclear capability. National Nuclear Museum Photo.

Table 03-02

Tactical Nuclear Bombs available for the Century Series fighter-bombers						
Designation	Width (in.)	Length (in.)	Weight (lbs.)	Yield (KT)	Fuzing	Service (yrs.)
MK 7	30.5	183″	1645 - 1700	8 - 61	Air, Contact	1952 - 67
MK 28	20; 22	96 - 170	1700 - 2320	17 - 1450	(Multiple)	1958 - 91
MK 43	18	150 - 164	2060 - 2265	70 - 1000	(Multiple)	1961 - 91
MK 57	14.75	118	490 - 510	5 - 20	(Multiple)	1963 - 93

tight squeeze under many fighters of that day; hence, it was fitted with retractable stabilizer fins. The MK 7 was a "dial-a-yield" bomb with field-selectable yields from 8 to 61 KT.

Tactical nuclear bombs available for *Century Series* fighter-bombers are shown in the Table 03-02.

Life Support

Improved oxygen masks developed on the eve of World War II provided for altitudes up to 40,000 feet. These "diluter-demand" oxygen systems sufficed for first-generation jet flyers. They would provide oxygen only when the aviator breathed in, with an increasing proportion of oxygen to ambient air as the aircraft flew higher, to include a 100 percent oxygen setting for upper altitudes. However, with the ability of *Century Series* aircraft to climb higher and faster—to 50,000 feet or more—the partial pressure of oxygen in the ever-thinner air (even at the 100 percent setting) became insufficient to sustain consciousness and even life. Accordingly, c. 1960 the *Century Series* aircraft were retrofitted with continuous-flow systems that delivered oxygen under pressure to the jet crews from the ground up. One of the first complaints was that, after the flight, it was hard to clear their ears quickly, and if the crews had been night-flying they would wake up with an ear ache in the morning. The dual remedy was to lower the aircraft's oxygen pressure to a more comfortable level and for the aviator to wait a couple of hours before sleeping and use the valsalva method (of holding the nose and "blowing out" the ears) to help release the residual oxygen inside the ear drums.

Moreover, as ambient temperatures above 18,000 feet are well below freezing, keeping the pilot warm was another concern. Electrically heated flight suits and gloves helped but were very confining. This problem was best solved by pressurizing the cockpit so it could sustain the warmth of heated air. However, the power to achieve that pressurization was not readily available until the advent of the jet engine. By simply tapping off the engine's later stages of compression, the air (heated by the compression) was available and the power loss insignificant.

With the ability of aircraft to zoom to altitudes above 60,000 feet, where the air pressure was a fraction of that at sea level, it became necessary by the mid-1950s to protect the pilot or crew should the cockpit pressurization system fail or a bailout become necessary. Under these extreme conditions of temperature and pressure the blood is near its boiling point, and rapid decompression can have a catastrophic effect on the human body.

Following WWII, the Army Air Force worked with the David Clark Company to produce the T-1, the first standardized mechanical pressure suit. The term *"mechanical"* comes from the fact that the fabric of the suit is drawn tightly over the pilot's frame by an inflatable tube-like structure called a "capstan" to maintain pressure on the body. Although uncomfortable when not inflated, it became almost unbearable when it was inflated, and work continued to find better pressure suits. Although some of the *Century Series* could fly to altitudes that required the pressure suit, they were typically not worn operationally unless a flight was planned above some specific altitude, such as 50,000 feet.

Performance increases and improvements in the structural integrity of the fighter during WWII led to yet another challenge. The pilot could be subjected to high acceleration forces (Gs) during combat maneuvers, such as rapid pitch changes or tight turns. The bank angle is directly related to the centrifugal force being placed on the aircraft and the pilot. Assuming coordinated turns in level flight, these forces increase dramatically at higher bank angles—2-Gs at 60 degrees and 3-Gs at 70 degrees of bank, and much higher during the more violent maneuvers of airborne combat.

Under these circumstances, the G-force drains the blood from the head (and brain) and pools it in the lower extremities. Although the pilot's natural defense is to tighten leg and abdominal muscles against the downward force, it is not uncommon for flyers to lose consciousness—from gray-out to black-out when exposed to 6-Gs or more for but a few seconds. The problem is also referred to as *G-induced Loss of Consciousness* (abbreviated G-LOC).

To extend the pilot's tolerance under these circumstances, a G-suit (as it is called) was developed that sensed the rising G-force and inflated tight cuffs around the legs and abdomen with air—further limiting the ability of the blood to drain from the upper body. Several of these "*Berger Suits*" and "*Frank's Flying Suits*" (named for their inventors) were in use before the end of World War II.

With the advent of the jet, the air pressure for the G-suit again came from the engine compressor. The suit had a tube that literally plugged into a port in the cockpit. The G-suit was subsequently incorporated into some versions of the pressure suit starting with the T-1. However, it was generally a garment, like a pair of "cowboy chaps," that the pilot slipped over the flight suit.

Another area of pilot protection is the helmet. Progressing from the leather (and sometimes cloth), the hard head covering evolved after WWII, as the cockpits of many fighters were quite small and the opportunity for the head to make contact with the canopy during violent maneuvers was a factor. Pictures of the post-WWII era often show some pilots with a modified football helmet. Helmet quality improved over the years, as those of the 1950s (which had pads glued to the inside, but which still left "hot spots" that caused discomfort) gave way to specially fitted lighter-weight versions that cushioned the head more evenly, as they were tailored to the aviator's own head. In addition, the original single sun visor was replaced by a double visor, where the sun visor could be used in bright conditions and the clear visor at night, so that the eyes were protected at all times.

Jonathan Myer: "*One more life-support item of note was the rubberized anti-exposure garment worn (by mostly interceptor crews) when making extended flights over water under winter conditions. Known as 'poopy suits,' they were both uncomfortable and (like pressure suits) tiring; it was wise not to challenge one's bladder by drinking anything before flight. Unfortunately, if flying beyond gliding distance to land and with ocean temperature below 50 degrees Fahrenheit, these rubber bags were mandatory for aviators flying from the coastal bases in winter. One could wear a metal ring inside the rubber neck to avoid chafing and allow a little air to circulate inside the suit, but if one forgot to remove it on ejection, the poopy suit would likely fill with water and sink—with the hapless human trapped inside; mere water wings would not suffice for flotation if the suit outweighed their buoyancy. A few escaped the discomfort by wearing a wet suit under their flight suit, but most just waddled to and from their aircraft in resignation.*"

The well-dressed pilot of the time wore a flight suit, gloves, helmet with oxygen mask and visor, parachute/torso harness, boots, G-Suit, and flotation gear. (OK, some still wore a silk scarf!)

The ability of the pilot to escape from the plane (when it was obvious that battle damage or system failure had rendered it incapable of controlled flight) became a major issue with the arrival of the jet. Even with some of the higher-performance piston fighters of WWII, there were situations where simply opening the canopy and jumping out was unsafe due to the force of the relative wind and proximity of the horizontal and vertical stabilizer. A study of more than 2500 combat bailout scenarios revealed that the pilot was injured or killed in 58 percent.

The ejection seat was the answer—the use of a small explosive charge that literally shot the seat (with the pilot strapped aboard) out into the slipstream at a velocity that assured clearance from the tail assembly. However, the early ejection seat was powered by a single impulse 37- or 40-mm cannon charge that resulted in high vertical G-forces and often caused injury to the pilot's spine.

Later improvements saw the use of a small rocket motor, with many of the escape sequences performed automatically. These included the release of a small drogue chute to stabilize the seat, a "butt-snapper" to ensure separation of the pilot from the seat, and an altimeter that opened the main chute when the flyer had descended into the lower reaches of the atmosphere. Life support, to include

Figure 03-11. Test Pilot Joe Walker models the T-1 pressure suit worn while piloting the Bell X-1E. There is no G-suit incorporated. Note the inflatable capstan (tube-like) segment running the length of the torso, arms and legs. USAF Photo.

the pressure for the suit and oxygen supply as well as survival gear, was included.

A small cadre of the dedicated researchers headed by Dr. John P. Stapp (USAF) pioneered the efforts to improve pilot survival during high-speed, high-altitude bailouts. Working at what was called the Aeromedical Laboratory at Wright Field, Dayton, Ohio, Stapp, along with Joseph Kittinger and David Simons, labored to understand the environment and develop equipment to address the problems of high G-forces, hypoxia, and depressurization.

The Flight Test Environment

With the more sophisticated designs of the *Century Series*, the interaction of the designer and the test pilot became more critical—yet the span of understanding between the two was often incongruent. Just fifty years earlier, Orville and Wilbur Wright were able to experience firsthand the effect of a design change, as they then went out and flew the aircraft. Their success, as opposed to those who designed without such a connection, was obvious.

When military aircraft undergoing development reach the flight test phase, the program is a joint undertaking by the designing contractor, the service development and testing agency, and the operational command destined to receive this new aircraft. The flight-testing program is divided into three parts or categories.

Category I requires the contractor to verify that the aircraft meets contract design specifications using the contractor's pilots and maintenance facilities. The basic flight envelope is explored and systems compatibility verified. Various stability and control issues are examined.

The contractor test pilots have the initial responsibility of feeding back to the company engineers the data derived from a series of flight assessment scenarios. By the early 1950s, automated recording of pressures, temperatures, and strain gauges was accomplished with film cameras and on-board strip chart recorders. These augmented the pilot's personal observations of the flight instruments and his subjective interpretations.

The pilot is responsible for getting the airplane into a specific configuration (attitude, bank angle, and G-force) at a given speed and altitude, and allowing the recording devices to do the measurements. Of course, there is the small detail of the airplane performing unexpected maneuvers because of unknown flight handling qualities. This is where the test pilot is worth his weight in gold, despite the fact that he is rarely paid the equivalent. Once the manufacturer believes

Figure 03-12. The Lockheed T-33 was used for several tests to evaluate the new ejection seats that were declared operational in 1949. USAF Photo.

they have worked most of the surprises out of the airframe, it is time for the next step.

In Category II, a military test pilot confirms the performance data and continues to investigate the flight envelope of airspeed, altitude, and G-force limitations. The test pilot verifies all emergency procedures and take-off and landing data, and documents cruise specifics with various external configurations and loadings, ferry ranges, and all other performance and maintenance data provided by the contractor.

Critical aspects, such as aerodynamic flutter and the interaction of armament and flight characteristics are explored. The maintainability of the aircraft is established by validating or revising the contractor-supplied manuals.

The plane is put through its combat maneuvers while evaluating and documenting individual aircraft systems' performance and relationships. While the company pilot had a close connection with the design team, the military pilot is typically one step removed—they were the experts in the application of the airplane to the intended role. Thus, the firing of its weapons or the dropping of ordnance under tactical conditions is the military test pilot's domain.

Category III is the final stage of testing—where the aircraft is delivered to the first operational squadrons to confirm that the aircraft can be flown and maintained to Air Force standards with Air Force resources using the documentation provided by the manufacturer.

Because the *Century Series* was driving the application of new technologies, it was typical for one of the first planes of each type to be turned over to NACA (the predecessor of NASA) for further testing.

These civilian pilots sought to fly profiles that would add to the sum total of knowledge about the mysteries of high-speed flight.

Virtually all test pilots, with few exceptions, came from the ranks of the military, for where else could a man learn to fly high-performance machines? Many of the pilots from the early years of aviation did not have college degrees, but as the complexity of the aircraft and the interaction of the pilot with the designers became increasingly sophisticated, by the mid-1950s an advanced engineering sheepskin became a prerequisite for any pilot who wanted to enter the test realm. James H. Doolittle, of WWII fame, was the first recipient of a PhD in Aeronautics from Massachusetts Institute of Technology in 1928. Chuck Yeager is a notable exception, having not completed a four-year degree.

The concept of providing a cadre of skilled pilots to perform the test function actually began in 1914, when the Army established a facility for advanced research and development at North Island, in San Diego. In 1918, it was transferred to McCook Field in Dayton, Ohio, but within a few years the operation, then known as the Material Division, was transferred across town to Wright Field.

The scandal created within the U.S. Army in 1934 because of the disastrous attempt to fly the U.S. Mail routes by regular Army pilots resulted in several recommendations from the investigating boards. Among these was that the Army, which had provided much of the engineering talent to design its own aircraft in concert with the various manufacturers, should end that practice. The Materiel Division was also to restrict its flight-testing role to verifying the performance of planes from private manufacturers and to a limited amount of research flying. During the Depression of the 1930s, the Army Air Corps selected its test personnel from a variety of sources. Some were flight instructors simply assigned to the job, such as one Lt. Donald Putt, who noted that *"... out of the blue, I got orders to report to Dayton...I had not shown any interest of wanting to be a test pilot."*

Colonel Ernest K. Warburton, chief of the Flight Section at Wright Field, formalized the selection process in the late 1930s along the lines of the Royal Air Force, which had established its *Empire Test Pilots' School* at Boscombe Down, UK. The need to standardize not only the selection of test pilots, but also their subjective understanding of the test environment, led to the establishment of the *Flight Test Training Unit* in September 1944. Positioned under the Air Technical Service Command, its first

commandant was Major Ralph C. Hoewing, who created a formal three-month-long curriculum that emphasized performance flight test theory and piloting techniques. Within months its name was changed to the *Flight Performance School* and was moved to the Vandalia Municipal Airport (now the Dayton International Airport) in Ohio.

Colonel Albert Boyd, a very experienced test pilot, became Chief of the Flight Test Division in 1947. Recognized for his high professional standards and discipline, he was the right man at the right time, as the Air Force entered the jet age with the P-59 and P-80; he has been referred to as the *"father of modern Air Force flight test."* Donald S. Lopez (Colonel USAF) described the program for the school in his book *Fighter Pilot's Heaven*: *"About half of the curriculum for the flight performance phase of the school consisted of classroom lectures; the other half was dedicated to planning and flying various tests. Then reducing the data and writing reports."*

The obvious need for not only a vast expanse of special use airspace but also good flying weather saw the *"test section"* move to Muroc Air Base, California, in 1949. (The name Muroc was the reverse spelling of the last name of two brothers who had been early settlers in the area, Ralph and Clifford Corum.) The base was renamed in December 1949 for Captain Glen Edwards, who had been killed test flying the Northrop B-49 flying wing.

The school was renamed the *Air Materiel Command Experimental Test Pilot School* and moved to Edwards Air Force Base in February 1951. Just months later the Air Force created the Air Research and Development Command (ARDC), and it assumed control over the base; the school's official designation was changed yet again, to the *ARDC Experimental Test Pilot School*. A few years later it became the *U.S. Air Force Experimental Flight Test Pilot School*. Selection to attend the school is very competitive, and candidates are carefully screened not only for their flying ability, but also for their academic qualifications.

Operational Feedback

John Boyd, a Korean War veteran with but limited combat experience as an F-86 wingman, went on to update fighter tactics and pilot thinking as an F-100 instructor at TAC's Fighter Weapons School (FWS) at Nellis Air Force Base, Nevada, and then revolutionize fighter aircraft design while at Eglin AFB, Florida. A masterly and forceful briefer throughout his career, Boyd was a reluctant writer. Nevertheless, before leaving Nellis in 1960 for an engineering degree at Georgia Tech, he dictated a 150-page tactics manual, his Aerial Attack Study, which codified air-to-air jet fighter maneuvers and was adopted TAC-wide. Once at Eglin and with mathematical, computer and writing support from Tom Christie (an Air Force civilian with a graduate degree in math and statistics, and who became a life-long friend), he developed the equations that both defined the essential requirements for the ideal dog-fighter and compared the combat performance of U.S. jet fighters with their Soviet counterparts.

Boyd's two-volume, initially secret report entitled Energy-Maneuverability Theory, was first published in May 1964. It showed that virtually every USAF jet fighter developed to that time (the *Century Series* and beyond) had been created or modified to perform multiple missions—and not optimized for any. Moreover, to the chagrin of the Air Force's leadership, the USAF fighters were inferior to Soviet designs in significant areas of performance, much as the MiG-15 had been more maneuverable aerodynamically than the F-86. His study and philosophy chronologically came after the *Century Series* fighters' development.

While John Boyd's influence on the designs of first the F-15 and then the F-16—and ultimately on the conduct of tactical war itself—are beyond the scope of this book's *Century Series* fighters, an additional contemporary factor must be mentioned: In the Air Force of the 1950s and '60s, the risk of nuclear war was the predominant national security concern, and its systems acquisition and budget priorities were driven by the "bomber generals". With the increasing demands of the Southeast Asia War, a resurgent interest in (and study of) fighter tactics in TAC and other fighter forces led to an expansion of General Purpose forces...and a new focus on the fighter pilot himself, with all his professional skills and ebullient personality. As a Mark Twain parallel, "Reports of [his obsolescence had] been greatly exaggerated."

Guns and Cannons

With the move to the jet engine, the propeller arc no longer represented an impediment to gun positioning in the nose. This not only allowed the gun to be centrally aligned for maximum fire power, but also permitted a thinner wing for better performance at high speed.

The F-86's six .50 caliber machine guns had long been the basic armament of the American fighter. The standard AN/M3 .50 caliber machine gun weighed 84 pounds and was an improvement on the AN/M2 of WWII, with an increase in rate of fire to 1200 rounds/min and a muzzle velocity of 2910 ft/sec.

However, even higher muzzle velocity and greater stopping power were needed with the increased speeds and shortened periods of firing opportunity in jet aircraft combat. Here, the Navy had taken the lead by equipping its aircraft with the 20mm (.79 inch) cannon at the close of WWII. (A "*gun*" is generally said to be a "*cannon*" when its bullet diameter exceeds 1/2 inch, or .50 caliber.)

The gyro-driven MK II gunsight was a manually adjusted optical device that was a product of British and American collaboration during WWII. It provided the aiming solution to determine the "target lead"—compensating for the aircraft movement and the bullet "*drop*." It was used on the P-51 and P-47 by the summer of 1944, but in combat it could be awkward to set. Following the war an improved version, the K-14, became the Air Force standard for the F-80 and F-84.

The radar gunsight made its appearance by the time of Korea and provided a significant advantage over the MiG. The later F-86As employed the A-1CM GBR gunsight with the AN/APG-30 ranging radar in the upper lip over the nose air intake. It had a sweep range of up to 3000 yards and was designed to calculate the required "*lead*" on the target to ensure that the path of the bullet would intercept the target's projected track. When the gunsight was activated, the radar automatically locked on the target and projected the sight image onto a glass plate behind the windscreen. The radar target indicator light illuminated one second before the optimum firing point. This allowed the pilot time to squeeze the trigger at the most favorable time.

Further advances in gun development following WWII responded to the requirement for increased firing rates. This involved the problem of *chambering*, *firing*, and *ejecting* the round in minimum time. The answer was to have multiple chambers so the various mechanical stages could be accomplished without interfering with each other. The German Mauser

.50 BMG   20x102 Vulcan   30x173

Figure 04-01. Relative size of .50 caliber (left), 20mm (center), and 30mm (right) rounds. The MiG-15 had two 23mm and one 37mm cannon while the Sabre had six .50 caliber guns. PD.

Figure 04-02. The General Electric M61 Vulcan 20mm cannon. USAF Photo.

213 was used as a basis by the U.S. for developing the single-barrel T-160, which incorporated a five-chamber rotating load mechanism—akin to the 6-chamber revolver handgun. Designated the M39, it had a long and distinguished career. Weighing in at 178.5 pounds, it had the ability to deliver 1500 rounds per minute with a muzzle velocity of 3300 ft/sec. The projectile weighed 3.56 oz. With the introduction of the F-89, the Air Force followed the lead of the Navy in making the 20mm the standard armament by the late 1940s.

Of course, in speeding up the firing rate the single barrel was prone to overheating. The obvious answer was to extend the multi-chamber concept to the multi-barrel gun. The "Gatling gun" got its generic name from the first machine gun developed during the American Civil War by Dr. Richard J. Gatling. The 1862 model had ten barrels that rotated with a hand crank. A drum of cartridges fed the process of loading at one station, firing at a second, and casing ejection at another.

The M61 20mm "*Gatling Gun*" began as '*Project Vulcan*' by the General Electric Company in 1946. It had six barrels, with each new round inserted at the two o'clock position of the counterclockwise rotation (as viewed from behind the gun). The round was fired electrically at the nine o'clock point and the casing ejected at the four o'clock point. Not only did this scheme provide for firing rates of up to 6,000 rounds per minute—100 bullets per second—but the rotation period allowed for cooling the barrel, which led to longer barrel life.

Despite these advances in gun design, bringing down a large bomber could require even more destructive firepower.

Unguided Rockets—FFAR

During World War I, solid-fuel Le Prieur rockets were launched from French Nieuport 17 biplanes as early as 1916. Used exclusively against hydrogen gas-filled observation balloons, the stick-guided missile required a very close launch to its target (125 yards) to assure success. Although attacks were also made against German Zeppelins, none was successful, and rockets faded from favor with the introduction of incendiary bullets.

The Germans had used some fin-stabilized unguided air-to-air rockets in the closing months of WWII against formations of B-17s, but their success was not definitive. One adaptation was the use of a vertically launched rocket-powered interceptor, the Bachem BA 349 *Natter*. This aircraft, essentially a manned missile, carried 33 solid-fuel R4M unguided

Figure 04-03. French Nieuport 17 with Le Prieur solid-fuel rockets affixed to the outer struts. PD.

Figure 04-04. The German Bachem Ba 349 Natter. A group of 33 R4M air-to-air rockets can be seen in the nose. U.S. Army Photo.

rockets. The design had not progressed far enough for combat use before the war ended; however, several aspects of the concept were soon resurrected.

Following the Second World War, the Naval Ordnance Test Center at China Lake, California, developed the German solid-fuel R4M into a four-foot long, 2.75-inch diameter, Folding Fin Aerial Rocket (FFAR). Weighing about 20 pounds and carrying a six-pound warhead, these rockets had an effective range of just over two miles.

However, the fact that they were unguided meant that they were fired in a volley of several dozen to assure a dispersion that would encompass the target

Figure 04-05. The North American F-86D with its 24 FFAR pod extended and a single rocket en route to its target. The unguided rockets were typically fired in volleys to ensure a hit. USAF Photo.

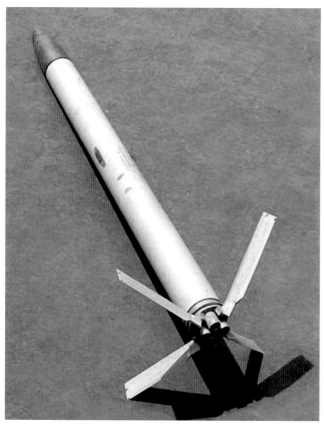

Figure 04-06. The 2.75-inch (diameter) Folding Fin Aerial Rocket. (FFAR). USAF Photo.

with their contact fuses. The all-weather interceptors (F-89 and F-94), originally armed with 20mm and .50 caliber, were switched to the FFAR by the early 1950s—some carrying up to 104 *"Mighty Mouse"* rockets, as they were also called. The F-86D's final design included a tray of 24 that extended from beneath the fuselage for firing; volleys of 6, 12, or all 24 could be selected.

However, as electronics began to shrink in size and increase in capability, the late 1940s saw several initiatives towards perfecting a Guided Airborne Rocket (GAR). Some predicted that the age of the manned fighter was reaching its limit. With closing speeds of over 1000 feet per second, it was thought that human reactions could not keep pace in a dogfight. So profound was the idea that the guided missile would eventually replace the manned fighter, the first air-to-air missile program (GAR-1 *Falcon*) was originally given the fighter designation F-98.

Guided Missile GAR-1/AIM-4 *Falcon*

The *Falcon* was the first guided air-to-air missile to see operational use by the Air Force. It employed a *"semi-active" radar homing* (SARH) guidance system via which the interceptor transmitted the high-powered radar beam to *"illuminate"* the target. The missile contained only the receiver that identified the electronic "echo" returns. This two-part system was dictated by the large size, weight and power consumption of the electronics in the 1950s.

Development was actually begun right after the close of WWII in 1946 as project MX-798. It was first conceived as a defensive missile for bombers against fighters, but that concept never advanced. Instead, as MX-904, its mission was changed to a bomber destroyer launched by a fighter. The first test firings occurred in 1949, when it was called the AAM-A-2. Its new F-98 designation in 1951 was in deference to the belief that missiles were simply an extension of the fighter. Just prior to its deployment on the F-89 in 1956, it was again redefined as the GAR-1.

The *Falcon*, developed by Hughes Aircraft Company, was initially 78 inches in length and 6.4 inches in diameter, with a "fin-span" of 20 inches; its weight varied from 119 to 135 pounds, depending on seeker and warhead. Propelled by a solid-fuel rocket, it could reach Mach 3+ in four seconds when its fuel was exhausted, giving the missile a range of about 6 miles. It initially carried a small 7.5-pound explosive warhead that had only a contact fuse along the leading edges of its fins.

The missile entered service in 1956 and was carried by the F-89, F-101, and F-102. It was later redesignated the AIM-4, and it progressed through a wide variety of models. The *Super Falcon* (GAR-3/AIM-4F), produced after 1958, had a 26-pound warhead and a larger, longer-burning engine for higher speeds and increased range.

A later variant (GAR-2/AIM-4B) employed the infrared heat signature of the exhaust of the enemy's jet engine to "*home-in*" on the target. Unlike the SARH version that required the host fighter to remain "*locked on*" to the target until the missile hit its target, the IR version was a "*fire-and-forget*" missile that allowed the launching aircraft to turn its attention immediately to other possible targets or evasive action. However, because its sensitive target acquisition electronics required a rather narrow launch angle, the attacker had to position himself almost directly behind his prey. Interference from the sun as well as ground heat sources could also cause the IR *Falcon* to lose its "*lock*." In contrast, the SARH *Falcon* could be fired at virtually any angle of encounter. An aural "*target acquired*" signal from the missile's sensor IR head was input to the pilot's headset. When the missile achieved a "*lock*" on a target—its IR sensor was picking up a strong signal—the pilot would hear a tone in the headset and could then fire at will.

The technology used liquid nitrogen as a coolant for the seeker head. The reservoir held only enough for about a two-minute period and required at least 6 seconds to cool down the sensors before firing. This proved to be the Achilles Heel of the missile in a tactical fighter environment: if the pilot activated the coolant too soon, he risked a dead missile by the time he was positioned to fire; and too late, and his quarry might evade him before the missile was ready to launch. While the launch/coolant timing appeared acceptable for intercepting a bomber, when the missile was used in Vietnam against fighters, where the rules of engagement prohibited "*beyond visual range*" firing and the dynamic engagements typically involved hard maneuvering throughout, it proved ineffective and frustrating for the pilots.

The Air Force's initial F-4Cs carried AIM-9B *Sidewinders*, but the newer F-4Ds came equipped with AIM-4D *Falcons* (which had been operational on Air Defense interceptors for several years). Robin Olds, in his book *Fighter Pilot: The Memoirs of Legendary Ace Robin Olds*, said of the IR *Falcon*s used on the F-4D in Vietnam: "*... we all hated the new AIM-4 Falcon missiles. I loathed the damned useless things. I wanted my Sidewinders back. In two missions, I had fired seven or eight of the bloody things and not one guided. They were worse than I had anticipated. Sometimes they refused to launch; sometimes they just cruised off into the blue without guiding. In the thick of an engagement with my head twisting and turning, trying to keep track of friend and foe, I'd forget which of the four I had (already) selected and couldn't tell which of the remaining was perking* [in reference to the coolant] *and which head was already expiring on its launch rail. Twice upon returning to base, I had the tech rep go over the switchology and firing sequences. We never discovered I was doing anything wrong.*"

Within days, Colonel Olds had banned all AIM-4Ds from his Ubon Air Base, ordered the F-4Ds reconfigured for *Sidewinders*, flight-tested their operation, and had all his Wing's F-4s using AIM-9s again—remarking to his Maintenance Officer: "*Oh, by the way, I don't think it's necessary to bother higher headquarters with our little change. They have far more important things on their mind.*"

Thereafter, the *Falcon* family—including improved variants—remained with Air Defense interceptors, where engagements would be at longer ranges against less-maneuverable (and hence more "cooperative") targets, until the last F-106s were retired in 1988.

In 1959, a previously cancelled program to develop a larger and more powerful *Falcon* missile with a nuclear warhead was resurrected as the

GAR-11 with a yield of 0.25 kilotons; a variant with a conventional (expanding-rod) warhead was designated the GAR-11A. Both used SARH guidance, plus a proximity fuse to detonate their warheads, thereby making them an all-aspect missile. In 1962 they were renamed AIM-26A (nuclear) and AIM-26B (conventional), respectively.

More than 40,000 *Falcon*s of all variants were built, some under license by other countries—but there were just five confirmed "*kills*" in Southeast Asia attributed to it.

GAR-8/AIM-9 *Sidewinder*

Development of *Sidewinder* began in 1950 at the Naval Ordnance Test Station at China Lake, California. The concept involved the creation of a simple heat-seeking "*fire-and-forget*" 9 foot 4 inch air-to-air missile propelled by a 5-inch diameter 4000-pound thrust solid-fuel rocket that burned for 2.2 seconds. This accelerated the missile to Mach 1.7 above the speed of the launching aircraft. The un-cooled lead-sulfide photocell that could detect IR radiation was enclosed in a hemispherical glass nose. The early missiles had a 4-degree angle-of-view and a tracking rate of 11 degrees per second. Because of these limitations, the *Sidewinder* could only be used for tail-on engagements at ranges from one-half to two-and-one-half miles. The missile was also very susceptible to other heat sources such as the sun.

Initial tests were conducted in 1951, with the first successful target intercept occurring in September 1953; the missile then received the designation XAAM-N-7 (later AIM-9A). General Electric initially produced the missile that became operational in 1956 with the Navy as the AAM-N-7 (AIM-9B), and which was subsequently also adopted by the Air Force. Starting from the AIM-9B's "*lead-pursuit*" or "*proportional homing*" guidance and "*blast-frag*" warhead, both services developed follow-on versions that improved seeker sensitivity and cooling, propulsion, warhead lethality and fuzing, and maneuver control. The Air Force variants of the era included the AIM-9E, J/N and P, while the Navy variants progressed through the AIM-9D, G, and H. In 1978 both services acquired the AIM-9L, the first all-aspect *Sidewinder*, and further developments have continued to this day—to include Russian IR missile equivalents, plus IR countermeasures (IRCM) to challenge U.S. capabilities. The latest *Sidewinder* is the AIM-9X, designed for the F-22 and F-35 and retrofitted to current fighters. More than 110,000 have been produced over its 50-plus year life span.

Nuclear Rocket MB-1/AIR-2A *Genie*

Development of the nuclear warhead *Genie* began with studies in 1951. The initial idea at that time was to ensure that the Soviets never contemplated saturating the skies with large formations that might overwhelm U.S. defenses. Following tests in Nevada, which confirmed that a nuclear weapon could be built of very small size and yield, the actual engineering began in 1955. However, by this time, the main objective was to provide an "*almost foolproof*" method of bringing down a single bomber. It was initially considered as a back-up to the *Falcon* (which was then ready to be declared operational, but which had serious reliability problems that would plague it for its entire life).

In operational use, the MB-1 would be launched towards an aim point in front of its target (i.e., on a lead-collision flight path, regardless of the intercept aspect angle—rather than attempting to hit the target). Its relatively large lethal envelope at its time-of-flight detonation would either enfold the target or the target would fly into it. With a yield of 1.5 kilotons, the maximum lethal radius for an airframe was calculated as 1000 feet (but this was never actually proven and might well have been two or three times that distance).

Jonathan Myer: "*Once operational, the Genie became the primary weapon for the three interceptors that carried it (two for each F-89J and F-101B/F; one for each F-106A/B), should the Cold War turn 'hot.' For one thing, the MB-1/AIR-2A's nuclear explosion offered a much better chance of 'weapon kill,' rather than simple destruction of the target: by actually destroying the bomber's presumed nuclear bomb load, there would be no risk of their detonation via 'salvage fuzing' (should they be so armed). For another, years of testing by squadrons deploying annually to Tyndall AFB, Florida, for live-firing practice showed that the Genie had a relatively high probability of kill (P_k), based on actual launches against drone targets, but with a spotting charge in lieu of a nuclear warhead; this weapon was designated the ATR-2A, and the real weapon's lethal envelope was calculated from the spotting charge's position relative to the drone target.*"

As for escape by the interceptor, that depended on the profile it presented to the blast at the time of detonation. Overpressure could more easily destroy the delivery aircraft if it presented a plan-view profile rather than a front or rear exposure. Escape maneuvers ranged from a tight level turn at low altitude, to a tight descending turn at medium

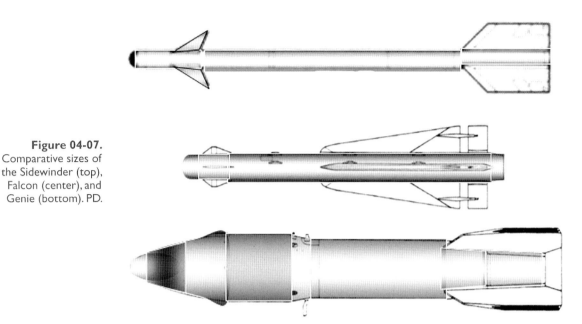

Figure 04-07.
Comparative sizes of the Sidewinder (top), Falcon (center), and Genie (bottom). PD.

altitude, to an inverted dive after a snap-up attack—all maneuvers to be continued until the shock wave passed.

The Douglas MB-1/AIR-2A *Genie* nuclear air-to-air rocket was 9 feet 8 inches long, had a diameter of 17.5 inches and "fin-span" of 3 feet 4 inches (when extended after launch), and weighed about 838 pounds. For live-fire training the ATR-2A was used, the nuclear warhead being replaced by a spotting charge. The *Genie's* speed reached 3.3 Mach after rocket motor burnout; its range varied with altitude- and tactic-based time-of-flight, at the end of which the warhead was detonated by its timer-fuze.

The only live nuclear test (shot *John* of "*Operation Plumbbob*," July 1957) was undertaken by a Northrop F-89J Scorpion at 20,000 feet (with the weapon detonated by a signal from the ground, for safety) that essentially proved the basic escape maneuver, with the weapon detonating 4.5 seconds after launch and the Scorpion 14,000 feet away (almost three miles). The explosion during this test actually had a yield of 2 kilotons. With the aircraft essentially turning away from the blast, the pilot would not have been in a position to observe visually the detonation and thus be blinded by its infamous brilliant fire ball.

There were two operational problems with using the combat-ready *Genies* (i.e., with their nuclear warheads installed). The first was that the live weapons had to be securely stored before use, guarded there and during transport to and from their aircraft, and also when they were loaded aboard their nuclear-alert aircraft in their alert hangars. The second was an edict that no one person should have control over a nuclear weapon—the so-called "*two-man rule*"—which mostly affected the aircrews, who would have sole control of their *Genies* in flight. For the F-89J, F-101B and two-seat F-106B, the presence of the radar intercept officer or second pilot met that requirement. The single-seat F-106A required the rule to be "bent." In all cases, certain cockpit switches were wired Off, with the wires to be broken only as part of the weapon selection process when cleared to fire by the appropriate control facility under appropriate DEFCON conditions.

A total of 3,150 MB-1s were built beginning in 1956 at a cost of about $1 million each. Many were later upgraded with improved, longer-range motors (and unofficially referred to as *AIR-2Bs*). All *Genies* were retired with the last F-106s by 1988—with none having been "expended" in anger.

Of all the factors considered in evaluating the capability of a fighter, none is as critical as the man who flies the machine—the fighter pilot. History has demonstrated repeatedly that a second-rate plane in the hands of a first-rate pilot can succeed in combat. The reverse is also true—a first-rate plane with a second-rate pilot can be a one-way flight.

The fighter pilot has often been elevated to the level of a super-human species, especially with writers such as Tom Wolfe. Expressing the notion of *"The Right Stuff,"* author Wolfe created a stereotype that has its own cult following. Certainly, the fighter pilot must possess all of the physical qualities of reflexes, eyesight, and stamina. To this must be added the emotions that allow a man to remain *"in control"* when his senses are telling him otherwise. The ability to exercise judgment and a high degree of situational awareness is perhaps what separates those who survive their first combat encounter from those who do not. For the *Century Series*, not only courage and skill were required, but an increasing level of intellectual ability to cope with the high-tech nature of the beast. The hunter's instinct coupled with a measure of natural aggression and self-confidence round out the qualities that make the successful fighter pilot. While such pilots have been characterized as "individualistic," their ability to work as a team has been demonstrated repeatedly, both in the air and while captive in POW camps in Vietnam.

All the military services comb their applicants to determine who has *"the Right Stuff"*—if the attributes listed can be assayed to that level. From the Great War through WWII and Korea, the majority of enemy aircraft were shot down by only a small percentage of the total of those in combat. Moreover, less than one percent of all fighter pilots ever score a single aerial victory. Furthermore, although most pilots would share some of their secrets of success with their compatriots, the dogfight was considered more as an "art" than a science. Most pilots who felt they could successfully and repeatedly execute the ritual, more often than not, could not explain the nuances to their brethren either in a combat report or over a beer, despite characteristic hand gestures maneuvering skillfully above the bar.

During WWII, the demand for fighter pilots far exceeded the supply, and many were accepted for training who might not have otherwise qualified. As the number of pilot "slots" in the Air Force steadily declined over the years (there are far fewer operational fighters in the inventory in the new millennium than when the *Century Series* was introduced in the mid-1950s), the competition for achieving the anointed status has become intense.

For those who initially flew the *Century Series*, the level of training involved many aspects that the WWII fighter pilot might find familiar and a few that were incomprehensible. The brief biographies that follow show the variety of paths that young men pursued to achieve the status of a *"Century Series* fighter pilot".

George Andre was a 20-year-old who was eager to become a fighter pilot in the mid-1950s. As there was no Air Force Academy, West Point and Annapolis graduates could request a transfer on graduation. The Reserve Officer Training Program (ROTC) offered another path for those who completed a four-year degree with the Air Force curriculum embedded along the way. However, the quickest route was the Aviation Cadet Program, which required only two years of college. Andre notes, *"As soon as I got the two years I was on my way!"* He was accepted into that program in January 1955, to begin his journey to earning his "wings."

First stop was Lackland Air Force Base (AFB), Texas, where eight weeks of "Pre-flight" provided the basics of Military Discipline and Courtesy, along with classroom academics in topics such as aerodynamics. Then it was on to Primary Training conducted by a civilian contract school at Malden AB in Missouri. This phase consisted of 20 hours in a Piper PA-18 Super Cub, a 108-hp fabric-covered "tail-dragger" that was little different from that flown 30 years earlier and provided the first milestone in an aviator's career—the solo. Andre now moved on to an airplane that was no mere "toy"—the North American T-6. Its 550-hp radial engine provided enough power that the fledgling student began to feel the excitement of the challenge, with the opportunity to experience basic aerobatics and instrument flying in the clouds. Andre recalls, *"We made instrument takeoffs and radio range approaches from the back seat under the hood... a real challenge and great training."* Andre's class was the last to use the T-6, as the Air Force was about to change its Undergraduate Pilot Training Program.

With 120 hours in type and 140 hours total time, Andre was transferred to Bryan Air Base in Texas for training in an even larger radial-engine airplane with tricycle gear—the North American T-28A. The 800-hp aircraft sat much higher and was more complex than the T-6. All of the basic fighter pilot maneuvers were experienced, as was the first introduction to formation flying. Forty more hours went by before the last step in the preparation process—transition to the jet—the Lockheed T-33 ("T-bird"). Perhaps the biggest impression was the sound—the T-33 transmitted very little sound and almost no vibration to the cockpit, and with a speed of 450 knots, here was a different environment. At the end of fourteen months and 300 hours of flight time, Andre received his Silver Wings as an Air Force pilot and the gold bars of a second lieutenant.

Along the way, Andre's class experienced its first loss when one of the students failed to return from a night cross-country flight. *"The first classmate to die leaves a BIG first impression. Later on, it happens so much that you get hardened to the losses. We must have heard the phrase 'There are old pilots and bold pilots, but no old bold pilots,' a thousand times."*

The flight training cadre apparently wanted to impress these young "tigers" that they needed to exercise caution if they were to live to become a competent combat pilot. Richard Greenlee (Colonel USAF retired) notes in his autobiography *Proud to Have Served*, regarding that cliché, *"One can't possibly fly fighter aircraft in the way they were meant to be flown and not be bold. Being bold is a way of life for most fighter pilots. It is the only way to do justice to superb aeronautical engineering. One can be bold and still fly safely. I suspect there are many Pollyannas writing about flying that haven't a clue as to the motivation and gut level courage of most fighter pilots."*

Andre then made the transition to the F-86D, which he found not too challenging. *"The first flight was solo, but we had probably 10 hours in a simulator prior to flight* [this was long before the fidelity of full motion simulators]. *The performance was not that big a change from the T-33. The biggest thing to watch for was now it was a swept-wing with different stall and handling features. Any of the other transitions that Air Force pilots made would have been in a 2-seat trainer—we did not have that luxury in the F-86."*

With the F-86D being an interceptor, there was virtually no air-to-air combat maneuvers (ACM) training included. Andre accumulated 1200 hours in the *Sabre-Dog* before moving up to his first *Century Series*, the F-101B.

For Craig Colter, the Air Force was his goal as a graduating member of the West Point class of 1960 (the Air Force Academy was then in the process of

Figure 05-01. The North American T-6 was the principal Air Force trainer during WWII and the Korean War. It was replaced by the North American T-28A *Trojan* in the late 1950s but continued to serve in a variety of roles especially overseas. USAF Museum Photo.

ramping up). The top two cadets from each third of his class would receive that coveted slot. For Colter, this meant having to "dumb down" a bit, as he was in the mid-point of the top tier. He made the cut and began Primary Flight Training at Moore Air Base in Mission, Texas, soloing the T-34 and then moving to the T-37. He went to Basic training at Laredo AFB, Texas, where he flew the T-33.

Colter was introduced to the *Century Series* fighters starting with the F-100 at Luke AFB, Arizona, where he logged about 150 hours of training, but only rudimentary Basic Combat Flight Maneuvers (BCM). It was here that he encountered a very high rate of fatal accidents among the fledgling fighter pilots, "... *typically one every two weeks or so. The accident investigations were not very thorough and the cause was most always attributed to the pilot.*"

Jonathan Myer was born in England, and had dual British-American citizenship for most of his boyhood. During WWII, his RAF father received liaison postings to Maxwell Field, Alabama, and then North Bay in Ontario, Canada. After seven postwar years back in London, he returned to the U.S., joined his college's AFROTC, became a naturalized U.S. citizen, and graduated in 1956, followed by his commission. Reporting to Lackland AFB in January 1957, he was sent to Stallings Air Base in Kinston, North Carolina, as a member of Class 58-J, arriving the day after his 21st birthday. After he completed T-34 training and T-28 ground school, Stallings became one of the three (of ten) Primary bases the Air Force closed in May 1957. He completed Primary in the T-28A at Bartow Air Base, Florida, one of few ROTC Lieutenants in his class to commit to the Air Force's sudden four-year obligation for new pilots ("*I needed the flight pay,*" he says).

For Basic flight school, he chose single-engine jets and went to Laredo AFB, Texas, and T-33s,

surviving "formation" to receive his wings in March 1958. Then on to Moody AFB, Georgia, for a month of Instructor Pilot Instrument School in T-33s (to include a couple of landings "under the hood") in preparation for all-weather interceptor training in the F-86L. He then went to the 13th Fighter-Interceptor Squadron (FIS) at Sioux City Air Base, Iowa, in the fall of 1958 to continue flying the '86L for a total of 160 hours, about which he quotes the old aviator's dictum: "*Six munts ago, I coulden even spell 'pylotte'—now I are one!*"

Jonathan got his driver's license in Sioux City after about 100 hours in the '86L. As for casualties, his first loss (during his senior year in college) was the former Commandant of his AFROTC unit, who had gone on to flight school and bailed out too low from his T-6 during a spin. The second was a former roommate, whose T-33 flamed out turning final at Laredo, and the third was at Moody, where a classmate's F-86L collided with his T-33 target aircraft during a night mission over Georgia's Okefenokee Swamp; thus, two of the eight who had committed to an extended tour to fly were dead in little more than a year. "*In fact,*" he later said, "*I lost more fellow-flyers to peacetime accidents during my 26-1/2-year Cold War career than to combat tours in Southeast Asia.*"

After the 13th FIS moved to the new Glasgow AFB, Montana, in mid-1959, its pilots and new Radar Intercept Officers (RIOs) brought back the squadron's new F-101Bs and Fs from the McDonnell factory and learned the fine arts of crew coordination and following GCI and SAGE control for practice intercepts on the Pinetree Line. In mid-1963, Myer joined the 98th FIS at Suffolk County Air Base on Long Island, New York, for 2-1/2 more years in the "*Mighty Voodoo,*" now flying intercepts over the Atlantic Ocean. His final

Figure 05-02. The Lockheed T-33 *Shooting Star* (more popularly known as the *T-Bird*) was typically a pilot's first encounter with a jet powered aircraft. While relatively easy to fly, it provided most of the critical cues and skills needed to make the transition to higher-performance fighters. USAF Photo.

Century aircraft assignment (following a Vietnam vacation in the O-1E "*Bird Dog*") was an F-101B/F Instructor Pilot slot at the USAF Interceptor Weapons School (IWS) at Tyndall AFB, Florida (1967 through '70). This gave him ten years and 1900+ hours in the *Voodoo* out of his 11 years flying active U.S. air defense before going on to staff tours, first at ADCOM Hq and then the Pentagon (5+ years at Hq USAF, where he also got his Master's in Public Administration; then, after the Industrial College of the Armed Forces/ICAF and promotion to Colonel, to 4+ years at OSD), where he retired in 1983 with a Defense Superior Services Medal (DSSM—which he still needs to have added to his DD 214...some day, he says). About flying, he claims, "*I always considered myself an interceptor pilot, rather than a fighter pilot.*"

Daniel R. "Doc" Zoerb enlisted in the Air Force in January 1969, served as an aircraft mechanic/flight engineer, "bootstrapped" to complete college, and was commissioned via Officer Training School (OTS) in December 1973. He completed pilot training at Webb AFB, Big Spring, Texas, in January 1975. He then went to Tyndall AFB, Panama City, Florida, where he spent 18 months flying/instructing in T-33s before moving to the F-106 Combat Crew Training Squadron (CCTS, or RTU) for about 6 months, also at Tyndall.

"Doc" Zoerb summarizes the melding of the attributes of pilot and plane: "*Dogfights require an ability to maneuver into a position to successfully employ weapons more quickly than an opponent. A variety of factors influence the outcome including altitude advantage, pilot proficiency, the ability to acquire and maintain visual contact, airspeed/energy, maneuverability, the ability to sustain maneuvers,* [and] *weapons capabilities....*"

Mark Foxwell entered pilot training at Webb AFB, Big Spring, Texas (July 1964), flew the T-37 and T-38, graduated #2 in his Class 66-A, and chose the F-106 as his first flying assignment. First he flew the T-33 and F-102 at Perrin AFB, Texas (ADC's interceptor

training school), to develop all-weather flying and combat skills, then went to Langley AFB, Virginia's 48th FIS (January 1966), to begin flying the F-106 and T-33 operationally. Flying virtually every day, he deployed with the 48th to Elmendorf AFB, Alaska, and flew active air defense alert out of Galena AFB on the Yukon and King Salmon AFB on the Aleutian peninsula.

Transferred to Nellis AFB, Nevada (July 1967), Foxwell checked out in the F-105D and then joined the 357th Tactical Fighter Squadron (TFS) at Takhli Royal Thai AFB, Thailand, where he flew 139 combat missions—100 over North Vietnam in Operation *Rolling Thunder*.

Next assigned to the 27th FIS at Loring AFB, Maine (October 1968), Foxwell resumed flying the F-106 and, as a USAF IWS graduate, became his squadron Weapons Officer. He returned to Tyndall AFB (September 1970) as an F-106 Weapons Instructor at IWS, earning ADCOM's highest skill rating of Master of Air Defense. He also conducted air-to-air fighter exercises with Navy and USMC fighter units, including the Navy's *Top Gun* School.

Foxwell's second IWS F-106 instructor tour (July 1976) included Operational and Testing supervisor for installation of USAF's first Air Combat Maneuvering Instrumentation (ACMI) system over the Gulf of Mexico test ranges, during which he conducted numerous mock air combat exercises employing other USAF, USN and USMC fighter units. His next assignment (June 1978) was to Hq TAC/Requirements as a member of the F-16 Multinational OT&E team to conduct the Air Force operational acceptance testing of the new F-16 aircraft.

In his introduction to the book *Wings* (Mark Meyer and Chuck Yeager, 1984, 20), Yeager writes, "*There is no such thing as a 'natural born pilot,'... a pilot's capabilities are commensurate with his experience. The more experience he has the better he is. It's that simple.*"

Figure 05-03
USAF Pilot wings (without star and wreath) are authorized for persons completing military pilot training. Senior Pilot Wings (with star but without the wreath) are awarded for 2000 hours of flight time and seven years as a rated pilot. Command Pilot Wings (with star and wreath) require logging at least 3000 hours and 15 years as a rated pilot.

Origin of North American Aviation

At the dawn of the 1950s, North American Aviation (NAA) was well established as the leader in the development of fighters, with the P-51 of WWII fame and then the F-86 as obvious indicators of that standing. No one could have foretold that their next offering, the F-100, would be the last operational fighter they would build for the Air Force.

Clement Melville Keys founded North American in 1928 as a holding company—as were several famous aviation-related companies of that era so defined. With interests in various start-up airlines and aviation activities, NAA was forced to divest itself of much of its holdings by the Air Mail Act of 1934. At that time, James H. "Dutch" Kindelberger was enticed from Douglas Aircraft to take the helm of the manufacturing entity that retained the North American name.

Then headquartered in Downy, California, NAA made its mark in history by designing and producing what many consider the finest piston-powered fighter of the Second World War—the P-51 *Mustang*. As the availability of the jet engine became a part of the design requirements of new aircraft, NAA responded to a Navy proposal for a jet-powered fighter to operate off an aircraft carrier. In January 1945, NAA produced a design that had the wings of the P-51 and a short fat fuselage for the minimal space aboard a carrier.

The Army Air Force evaluated the design, and it too ordered several prototypes. However, before the design could move to metal, the Air Force asked NAA to consider incorporating the swept-wing configuration. Information from German technology acquired after WWII appeared to support the assertions of NACA aerodynamicist Robert Jones with respect to its advantages at high speeds. Because of the suspected controllability problems of the swept-wing at low airspeeds, the Navy stayed with the straight wing configuration to address the carrier landing requirements. The airplane that took shape for the Army Air Force was to be the first American swept-wing fighter—the F-86 *Sabre Jet*.

From 1944 until his untimely death in 1954, George S. "Wheaties" Welch was a test pilot for NAA. He had first achieved fame on 7 December 1941, being one of a handful of pilots who managed to get airborne

Figure 06-01. North American Aviation's first jet, the FJ-1 Fury, was not an aesthetically pleasing aircraft. US Navy Photo.

Figure 06-02.
The classic lines of the North American Aviation F-86 Sabrejet epitomized the early swept wing fighters. USAF Photo.

in his P-40B during the Japanese raid on Pearl Harbor; he shot down at least four of the attacking planes that day. He had received the nickname "Wheaties" for his "quick energy" after joining the Army Air Forces in 1939; later he was featured on that famous cereal box with the notation, "*Famous test pilot starts the day with Wheaties, Breakfast of Champions!*"

Welch flew the XF-86 on its maiden flight on 1 October 1947. Less than five months later, he slipped it through the sound barrier in a modest dive—becoming the first production aircraft to break the sound barrier in April 1948. He claimed to have actually exceeded Mach 1 several days before Yeager's October 14th flight in the X-1, but it was never officially verified or recorded as such.

Figure 06-03. The NAA YF-93 was an attempt to upgrade the F-86 with a more powerful engine and expanded fuel capacity to compete as a penetration fighter. USAF Photo.

The prototype was powered by the GE (Allison) J35 of 4,000 pounds of thrust. However, early production versions used the GE J47, which produced 5,200 pounds of thrust. Using the information acquired by the X-1 research plane, later variants had an "all-flying" horizontal tail (stabilator) to assist in flight control in the transonic region. Many pilots consider the F-86 the finest handling jet to take to the skies.

The F-86 was still in its early testing stages when North American began to look at expanding its role to include the longer-range penetration capability. Initially designated the F-86C, the new design used the same wing, but with the Pratt & Whitney J48 engine, rated at 6,250 pounds of thrust, housed in a larger fuselage. The air intakes were placed on either side, rather than in the nose, to allow for radar. Designed to compete with the McDonnell F-88 and Lockheed F-90, two prototypes redesignated as the YF-93 were completed and test flown before the Air Force cancelled the project in 1950.

The basic *Sabre* design was refined yet again to produce the F-86D all-weather interceptor—the *Sabre-Dog*. Using the higher-thrust J47-GE-17B with 7,000 pounds of thrust in afterburner, the designation YF-95 was initially assigned. However, political implications dictated that its development be pursued as a model of the F-86—the Air Force was requesting too many new fighters and Congress was pushing back. Deliveries began in March 1951 and it set two speed records. In November 1952 it achieved 698 mph, and the following July it recorded 715 mph.

The F-86 airframe underwent several significant alterations, culminating in the H series powered by the J73-GE-3 with 9,070 pounds of thrust, and with a larger fuselage and wings. With a combat weight of 18,683 pounds, it was more than 2,000 pounds heavier than the A series. Produced between 1953 and 1955, the primary role of the F-86H was as a nuclear delivery fighter-bomber.

The F-86 demonstrated that a fundamentally sound design could be adapted for many roles and upgrades—provided the compromises involved were operationally acceptable. After some deliberation, NAA decided to create an entirely new airframe for a supersonic fighter, rather than attempt to squeeze more from the F-86.

Conventional Configuration

While some manufacturers toyed with less conventional configurations, such as Convair with its XF-92 delta wing, NAA decided simply to improve on a good thing. Within a year after the first flight of the XF-86, and before it became operational, in 1949 NAA began evaluating a new design labeled *Sabre 45* because it had a 45-degree sweep—ten degrees more than the F-86 wing and about half its thickness.

The NAA design team, headed by Ray Rice, NAA's Vice President of Engineering, embarked on a project that would take almost five years to its first flight. The objective was to design a fighter that was supersonic in level flight. However, wind tunnel research revealed a significant rise in aerodynamic drag in the transonic region of flight that required a considerable increase in thrust to overcome.

By 1950, the General Electric J47-GE-1 was the principal power plant for both the jet fighter (F-86A) and the bomber (Boeing B-47). More than 33,000 of these engines, which initially had 4,850-pounds of thrust, were produced. Although centrifugal flow compressors would continue to find application, the axial flow, as found in the J47, offered less cross-section, allowing a higher fineness ratio. The axial flow design also offered the promise of higher thrust with multiple stages of compression—NAA estimated it would need about twice the thrust of the J47 for its *Sabre* 45.

Westinghouse was developing the J40 for the Navy and it held much promise. However, engineering problems would ultimately cause significant delays in several Navy aircraft that had planned to use it. The failure of the J40 program ultimately put Westinghouse out of the jet engine business.

The GE XJ53, with 17,500-pounds of thrust, was also considered, but its large dimensions disqualified it. On the horizon, Pratt & Whitney was developing the Air Force-funded J57, which promised 9,700-pounds of thrust with an afterburner (AB) that boosted that figure by almost 50%. (The designation of the engines during this era reveals that odd numbers were primarily Air Force projects while even numbers were destined for the Navy.)

Several unsolicited NAA funded proposals for a supersonic fighter were rejected by the Air Force during the summer of 1950. Finally, in January 1951 NAA delivered its proposal for NAA-192 to the Air Force and was directed to proceed with a mock-up, which was completed in July of that year and accepted following more than 100 changes. The Air Force authorized construction of two prototypes known as the YF-100 in November 1951.

Among the changes to the design was the relocation of the horizontal stabilator to the lower portion of the aft fuselage to avoid airflow over it from being blanked by the wing during high angle-of-attack maneuvers, which could cause loss of pitch control. A speed brake was also configured on the underside fuselage between the wheels, effectively prohibiting centerline external stores from being carried.

The selection of the P&W J57 was somewhat of a gamble, as its two-shaft, dual-rotor, 16-stage split-compressor was a noticeable advance in engine technology. With this design, the low-pressure turbine (through which the exhaust from the eight-unit combustion chamber initially flowed) powered the 9-stage low-pressure compressor. The high-pressure turbine that followed drove the 7-stage high-pressure compressor. The low-pressure drive shaft was located within the high-pressure shaft and obviously rotated at a different velocity. The afterburner had about 10 percent variability in thrust from min to max with a throttle movement of about 1.5 inches. AB was selected by moving throttle outboard, then further forward to obtain maximum thrust.

The use of the two-stage (also called two-spool) turbine/compressor arrangement allowed for higher compression ratios while hopefully reducing the possibility of compressor stalls and surging, and reduced the stress on the turbine blades themselves. The downside was that the engine had grown to a length of 20 feet and weighed over 5,000 pounds.

The cockpit pressurization used air diverted from the compressor stage of the engine. Working as a part of the cockpit environmental control, this air was temperature-controlled by a heat exchanger and refrigeration unit.

Leonard S. Hobbs of United Aircraft (P&W's parent company) was awarded the Collier Trophy in 1952 for the development of the J57. Perry W. Pratt (no relation to Francis Pratt, the co-founder of P&W) initiated the design, which relied significantly on their experience with the T34 turboprop and the two-shaft T45.

Wind tunnel tests of models determined that the initial configuration would not achieve the desired goal of Mach 1.3. Back to the drawing board, the engineers redesigned the engine air intake to achieve a thinner taper of the inlet lip. They also increased the length of the nose by 9 inches—improving the fineness ratio. A variable inlet ramp to slow the incoming air to subsonic values was proposed, but was rejected in favor of the more conventional fixed ramp ram-air intake similar to the F-86. The long intake duct allowed for appropriate deceleration of air to a subsonic value before entering the compressor. The inlet design changes reportedly added 50 knots to the F-100's top speed. (The use of knots instead of miles-per-hour by the Air Force occurred during this period.)

The final significant change to the F-100 design was to reduce the thickness of both the horizontal and vertical stabilizers by half—to 3.5 percent of their chord. As the elevator control function is incorporated into the all-moving horizontal tail, the surface is defined as a *stabilator*.

To move the control surfaces, it was no longer practical for the pilot to exert direct pressure from the control stick. Two completely independent 3,000-psi hydraulic power systems were now employed for redundancy, with a manual back-up of direct linkage. To ensure that the pilot did not overstress the plane, spring bungees provided an artificial feel. To further eliminate drag and complexity, the aircraft control surfaces were positioned by the *trim actuators*, rather than *trim tabs*.

The F-100 wing was for its time very thin—only 6 percent of the chord (the F-86 was 10 percent). This required a heavier internal structure for the F-100 to avoid the aero-elastic twist of the wing when the ailerons generated differential lift. These two-section movable control surfaces were placed mid-span to reduce the torsional twisting motion. While allowing up to 200 degrees of roll per second at Mach 1, this also meant that traditional flaps were not employed on the F-100A, as there was insufficient trailing edge space.

Another aerodynamic addition, to assist in low-speed/high angle-of-attack and high-speed high-G maneuvering, was the use of leading-edge *slats* that would deploy automatically, based on air pressure, to delay the onset of wing buffet and stall. These would allow for a tighter turning radius while maintaining a constant altitude for a given airspeed.

Manufacture of the traditional semi-monocoque (stressed skin) construction presented several challenges because of the large performance envelope.

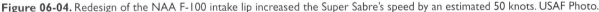

Figure 06-04. Redesign of the NAA F-100 intake lip increased the Super Sabre's speed by an estimated 50 knots. USAF Photo.

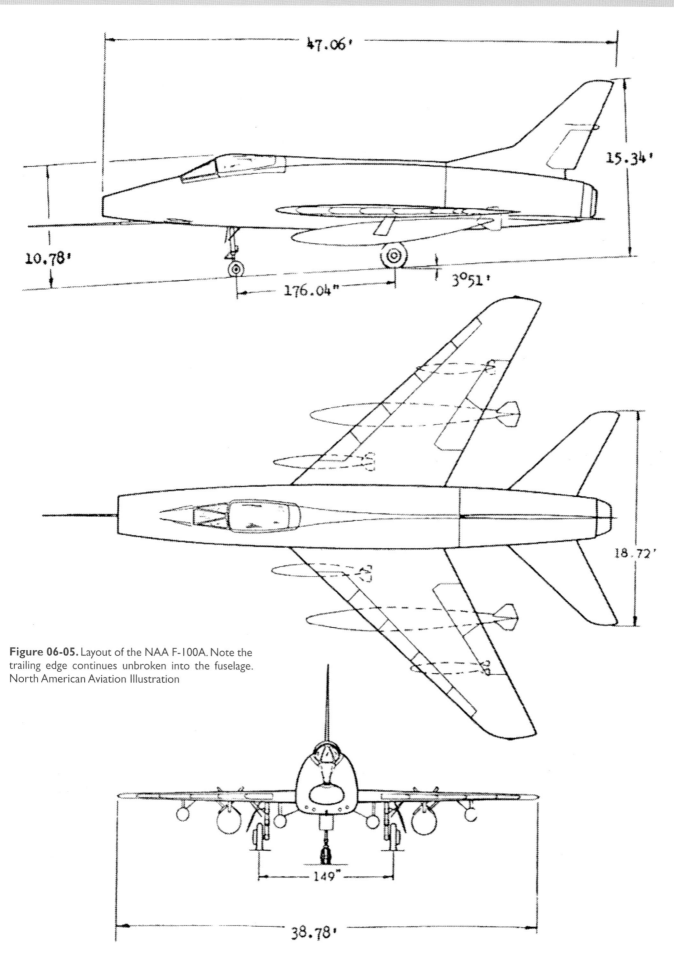

Figure 06-05. Layout of the NAA F-100A. Note the trailing edge continues unbroken into the fuselage. North American Aviation Illustration

As the structure was not only subject to high Gs but also to more severe temperature extremes generated by the J57 engine and its afterburner, the rear third of the fuselage was built from titanium (a heat-resistant metal). This required much closer tolerances of the components than with previous aircraft. NAA had to develop new processes and procedures for working with titanium, as more of it was used in the F-100 than any other aircraft to that point. Even the manufacturing facilities had to control closely the environmental temperature and humidity to ensure the tolerances of the parts.

With the Korean War and the MiG-15 threat as a major issue, the need to bring a more capable fighter into operation as soon as possible dictated not only a conservative approach to the design, but a more high-risk approach to production. The Air Force contract provided for the fabrication of production tooling and the procurement of long-lead items early in the production cycle (the Cook-Craigie Plan). Should the aircraft experience problems in the flight test program that required noticeable design changes, this approach could cause millions of dollars of equipment and fixtures to be scrapped. The F-100A would be built using this tooling philosophy.

Fabrication of the first YF-100 began in January 1952. A production order for 23 F-100As was issued in February 1952 and an additional 250 were authorized the following August—even before the first flight. The Cook-Craigie procurement strategy would prove a costly decision that was repeated during the same period with the F-102.

Figure 06-07. The titanium aft third of the fuselage is conspicuous by its off-color in many photos of the NAA F-100. USAF Photo.

Employing the new Air Force standard armament of four M-39 20mm cannon with 200 rounds per gun, the F-100 was also a candidate for the first Air Force air-to-air guided missiles then under development. The new fighter promised a significant improvement in performance over the F-86 and was given the moniker *Super Sabre*. However, the design did not significantly benefit from the insight gained from the interviews with veteran pilots of the Korean War. These pilots were looking for lighter weight and high maneuverability. Instead, incorporation of the afterburner required greater quantities of fuel and the weight of the *Super Sabre* kept increasing. The first aircraft (52-7554) rolled out on 24 April 1953 with an empty weight of 18,135 pounds—almost twice that of the first F-86.

Figure 06-06. The leading-edge slats are just visible on the leading edge of the wing in this view of the Super Sabre as its landing gear is in the retract cycle. USAF Photo.

Test Flights

The first flight of the YF-100 occurred on 25 May 1953 with a de-rated XJ57-P-7 engine—seven months ahead of the schedule projected two years earlier. George Welch was again selected as the primary test pilot. Climbing to 35,000 feet, he had been told that if all the systems were functioning properly and the aircraft felt solid, supersonic flight could be attempted—and this he did. With the afterburner lit, the plane accelerated to Mach 1.05 on its very first flight.

Despite the initial enthusiasm, several problems were apparent. Rudder flutter observed on subsequent flights was resolved by adding hydraulic rudder dampeners. (Flutter is the vibration of an aerodynamic surface and most often results in catastrophic failure.) Because it lacked flaps, the high pitch angle during takeoff and landing resulted in poor visibility over the nose. Additionally, it exhibited poor low-speed handling characteristics (instability about the pitch axis) and landings required a much higher approach speed. The Pilot Handbook (known simply as the *Dash-1* in military slang) called for flying the downwind leg at 230 KIAS (knots indicated air speed) with the base leg at about 175 KIAS. Recommended touchdown was 155 KIAS (with 2,000 pounds of fuel remaining). The speed brake proved very effective, producing little buffet and requiring only small pitch changes when extended.

Pilots also noted neutral (or even negative) static lateral stability at speeds greater than Mach 1. Another factor now entered into the complex equation of the F-100 performance envelope—the decision to reduce the size of the vertical stabilizer—saving weight and reducing drag.

The first plane was turned over to the Air Force for their Category II test series on 30 June 1953. Initial reports from Lieutenant Colonel Pete Everest, who was chief of the Air Force Flight Test Operations at the time, indicated that stability problems at low and high speeds were troubling.

Speed records in those days were a common occurrence, as the Soviet Union, the United Kingdom, and the U.S. were constantly vying for the honors. Of course, not to be overshadowed by the junior service, the Navy was also "in the hunt" during this period. Its Douglas XF4D-1 *Skyray* was the first carrier aircraft to exceed the speed of sound and took the record on 3 October 1953 with 655 knots (753.4 mph).

Little more than three weeks later, on 29 October 1953 Everest flew the F-100, at an altitude of less than 100 feet AGL (above ground level), to a new world's speed record for a turbojet aircraft, reaching 656 knots

Figure 06-08. First NAA YF-100 as it appeared during initial flight tests. USAF Photo.

(755.149 mph). This was one of the last low-level record flights, as subsequent attempts were made at higher altitudes because of the inherent dangers of high-speed low-altitude operations and the problem of tracking.

Kindelberger, NAA chairman and chief executive officer during this period, was awarded the Collier Trophy for 1953 for the development of the F-100. Sharing the trophy for that year was Douglas Aircraft Chief Engineer Ed Heinemann for the *Skyray*. No doubt, the performance of the F-100 during its initial flight tests was instrumental in the selection. However, the euphoria of the Collier Trophy was about to be subdued.

Everest, despite setting a new speed record with the F-100, had also discovered an unsettling aspect about the new fighter. At both high and low speeds, he encountered a form of *inertia coupling*—a complex relationship of interactions between the aircraft center of gravity and the three axes of control (roll, pitch and yaw moments). Because of the distribution of mass along the longitudinal axis (centerline) of the F-100, a rapid roll could cause movement about the pitch and yaw axes and—in the extreme—the aircraft could tumble.

Along with this was an adverse yaw problem—a movement about the vertical axis generated by drag from the downward deflection of an aileron in an attempt to raise the wing by creating more lift. It moves the nose opposite to the direction of the intended roll. A roll, initiated at high speed, caused the aircraft to yaw to the outside of the turn. At low speeds, the effect of adverse yaw was much more pronounced than with other aircraft.

The minimum controllable speed (Vmc) at max gross weight, (power off, gear extended) was 137 KIAS. The power-off stall speed (Vso) was 131 KIAS. Both NAA and Air Force pilots reported that

Figure 06-09. The shortened tail of the NAA F-100A is evident in this photo. USAF Photo.

the aircraft response to control inputs was sluggish at slow speeds—a not unexpected factor.

Both roll and yaw anomalies, which occurred only in very specific flight conditions, caused Everest to report that these properties needed further evaluation and resolution. NAA, however, felt the problem was not significant, and by September 1954 seventy F-100As were declared operational with the 479th Fighter Wing at George AFB. George was chosen because, being a few miles from Victorville, California, it was within easy driving distances from both the NAA factory (at Los Angeles International Airport) and Edwards AFB, so factory support was readily available. (The base was named for Brig. Gen. Harold Huston George, a WWI ace and director of air operations at Clark Air Base in the Philippines at the start of WWII.)

October 1954 found Welch putting an F-100 through its paces to examine further characteristics of the plane at high Mach speeds in a shallow dive by applying maximum G during a symmetrical pitch-up. It was an effort to either prove or dispel the critics. As the Mach meter reached 1.5 (the highest approved speed), the airplane was observed to yaw and roll inverted. It broke up in-flight (observers said it appeared to explode in an orange ball of flame). Nevertheless, Welch was able to eject and descended under chute. However, the severe lacerations from the sharp fragments of the plane disintegrating around him

caused Welch to succumb to his injuries before he could be transported to the hospital.

An intense investigation revealed that the instabilities Everest previously identified were responsible for the loss of control and subsequent disintegration. Surviving motion picture film from cameras located in the aircraft revealed tail flutter had induced a rapid yawing movement that led to the breakup.

Additional data showed that more area was required for the vertical stabilizer to address the yawing moment, so 13 inches (27%) were added to its height. An additional 12 inches were added to each wing, increasing the span to 39 feet. That change moved the ailerons further out—creating a higher aspect ratio to provide greater aileron control over the rolling moment. Even with these changes, the Dash-1 cautioned about making rapid aileron input at low airspeeds. All A and C series that had been built were returned to NAA for the modifications.

Because of the flight instability, hydraulic system failures, and in-flight structural failures, all F-100As were grounded for two months on 11 November 1954, by which time six fatal accidents had occurred. Another incident on 26 February 1955, a few months after Welch's ill-fated flight, caused the F-100 to find its way again into the darker corners of history on a routine production test flight. NAA test pilot George Smith had taken one of the new fighters for a series of standard maneuvers prior to delivery. While in straight-and-level flight, a hydraulic failure occurred at 35,000 feet that caused the plane to pitch down suddenly and uncontrollably.

By the time Smith determined that he was not going to be able to save the plane he was traveling at just over the speed of sound. At 6,000 feet Smith elected to eject. The seat functioned as designed, and Smith was shot clear of the plane into the high-speed slipstream. For an instant, his body was subjected to tremendous deceleration estimated at greater than 30 Gs. The force of the air tore the helmet and oxygen mask from his head and face and knocked him unconscious. The automatic ejection sequence separated Smith from the seat and the parachute deployed. As he was just off the coast of California, near Palos Verdes, a small fishing boat saw the descending chute and pulled him unconscious from the water.

Smith survived this first supersonic bailout, but it was obvious that improved protection for the pilot was mandatory. The accident resulted in an increased emphasis on enhancing the flight suit, helmet, and arm and foot restraints.

Brakes were never a strong point on the F-100 and an anti-skid system was installed that, according to several pilots, "*worked most of the time.*" The tail-mounted drag chute was often used to help decelerate the plane. Using more than 6,000 feet of runway was a common occurrence, and the standard NATO runway was subsequently lengthened to 8,000 feet.

While the plane reached operational squadrons in record time for its size and complexity, the hundreds of changes that were now required—some major—were taking a toll on the price tag. The per-unit cost of the F-100A was nearly one million dollars, compared to the F-86's $200,000. These problems, as revealed during operational suitability tests in August 1955, labeled *Project Hot Rod*, kept the plane from being widely deployed. Centered at North Field (an auxiliary of Pope AFB in South Carolina), *Hot Rod* put the aircraft through a concentrated variety of missions.

It was not until the following month (September 1955) that an intense effort cleared all the deficiencies, and the F-100A was then flown without restriction, but the Air Force realized the basic design did not have the superior performance they desired. The A series continued to have problems, and the Air Force began phasing them out by 1958 in favor of later variants. The 188th FIS of the Air National Guard at Kirtland AFB in New Mexico was the first unit to receive the F-100A in February 1958.

Unfortunately, when the last F-100A was removed from operational status in 1961, 47 (of the 203 built) had been lost to accidents. However, they were recalled to operational status from Davis-Monthan AFB in February 1962, due to escalation of the Cold War.

Fighter-Bomber Development

As the Air Force had done with virtually all its fighters, the F-100 airframe was evaluated for its ability to provide tactical delivery of conventional as well as nuclear weapons (initially, the Mk 7). In an effort to compete with the Republic F-105 as a nuclear delivery aircraft, the design was radically modified by NAA with the air intake placed over the cockpit, and this version was labeled the F-100B. However, a new designation, F-107, was quickly applied to that proposal, so there were no F-100B series built. The Republic F-105 was selected to fill the supersonic nuclear strike role, but the time lag in its development program resulted in the development of the F-100C to fill in on a temporary basis.

The F-100C series fighter-bomber (with modifications to overcome some of the inherent design problems of the F-100A) first flew in January 1955. The up-rated J57-P-21 engine had almost 2,000 pounds more thrust, but compressor stalls were a constant problem. Its extended wing now had 385 square feet of area as opposed to the 376 of the A series, but adverse yaw at low airspeeds was still considered troublesome. A yaw dampener, installed beginning with aircraft 146

Figure 06-10. Note the relative size of the vertical stabilizer following the modification to solve the inertia-coupling problem. USAF Photo.

of the C series, addressed the inertia-coupling issue and was retrofitted to previous aircraft. A pitch dampener was added beginning with aircraft 301.

Despite all the modifications, the adverse yaw problem gave the F-100 (especially the A series) a very bad reputation. It was called the "lieutenant killer" because so many new pilots failed to learn its idiosyncrasies fast enough to stay alive.

Craig Colter, a former F-100 pilot, notes: "*Because of the adverse yaw problem, we learned very quickly that the Hun* [the unofficial but widely used moniker derived from a foreshortening of "hundred"] *was a 'rudder' airplane. You led every turn with rudder, and held rudder in every turn—especially in slow speed, high angle of attack situations and in the traffic pattern. You did not throw ailerons around without rudder. I had no problems transitioning back to high power piston airplanes because I used more rudder in the Hun than any airplane I ever flew afterwards, including ones with big props and radial engines.*"

The increased thrust of the J57-P-21 enabled the F-100C to take 6,000 lb of external load on eight underwing pylons (four on each wing)—a confirmation that the F-100 would not be the air superiority fighter for the next decade, but would live out its years as a fighter-bomber. As a part of the underwing ordnance, twelve 5-inch High Velocity Aircraft Rockets (HVARs) could be carried for close air support.

The F-100C could deliver the Mk-7 nuclear bomb and employed the Low-Altitude Bombing System (LABS)—sometimes called "toss bombing." With LABS, the aircraft approached the target at a low altitude and then initiated a pull-up. Just before the vertical, the LABS, having calculated the optimum release point, would "loose" the bomb so that its trajectory would follow a parabola along the initial line of flight while the F-100 completed what was essentially an Immelmann vertical course reversal, departing at high speed in the direction it had come from so the fighter could avoid the effects of the blast.

Despite engineering features, such as the ability of the high- and low-stage compressors to run at different speeds, compressor stalls and surges continued to be a significant problem. Even after incorporating both yaw and pitch dampeners (among other improvements), 85 F-100Cs of the 476 built (18%) would be lost to accidents.

On 20 August 1955, an F-100C flown by Horace A. Hanes set the first supersonic world speed record of 714 knots (822 mph) for turbojet-powered aircraft. Hanes was awarded the Air Force Mackay Trophy "for the most meritorious flight of the year." The *Super Sabre* appeared on its way towards a firm footing in the Air Force combat-ready inventory. Several other notable flights demonstrated the versatility of the plane. An F-100C won the Bendix Trophy Race for 1955 and again in September 1956. But despite these remarkable events, one former Air Force F-100 pilot noted, "*None of these had 'Jack Spratt' to do with operational suitability.*"

A particularly notable occurrence happened while a motion picture crew was filming at Edwards AFB in January 1956. As the pilot of an F-100C was entering the round out (flare) for landing, he inadvertently allowed the plane to get too slow and a sudden pitch-up occurred before touchdown. The film dramatically shows the pilot fighting the airplane and bringing in the afterburner in an attempt to fly out of the condition. The pilot was unsuccessful and the crash that followed took his life. The dramatic segment of film was subsequently used in the movie "*X-15.*" This type occurrence (referred to by *Hun* pilots as the *Sabre Dance*) victimized several less experienced pilots.

Air-to-Air Refueling

Recognizing the need for long-range missions and the ability to take off with maximum ordnance, the C series also featured in-flight refueling capability. A long pipe-like extension with a probe at the end was affixed under the right wing, allowing for use of the "probe and drogue" method. This significantly improved the versatility of the F-100C, along with an increased internal fuel capacity in the form of a "wet wing." The external racks could carry up to four fuel tanks (200, 335, or 450-gallons) commensurate with gross weight limitations.

On 17 May 1957, three F-100Cs set a new distance record for single-engine aircraft by flying 6,710 miles from London to Los Angeles in 14 hours and 4 minutes using in-flight refueling. This flight provided ample proof to the Soviets that this capability allowed rapid deployment of assets to virtually anywhere in the world. However, meticulous advanced planning for a record flight and the rapid deployment of an entire combat-ready Composite Air Strike Force on short notice are worlds apart.

This situation was made apparent just one year later when trouble in the Middle East in July 1958 prompted the deployment of two squadrons of F-100s to Incirlik, Turkey—along with RF-101s, B-66s, B-57s and KB-50s—to provide a "show-of-force" to bolster American political interests in the region.

The two F-100 squadrons (the 352nd and the 355th) deployed from Myrtle Beach AFB, and while in Incirlik were under the command of Lt Colonel Frank Fisher, who was the senior commander of the two squadrons. Fisher recalls that they deployed on very short notice and did not have the right frequencies for the tankers on the second refueling off the Azores. As a result,

Figure 06-11. The addition of in-flight "probe and drogue" refueling from the Boeing KB-50 provided a wider range of combat and deployment versatility for the F-100. USAF Photo.

many of the fighters that were unable to contact the tankers had to divert into Lajes, in the Azores. Fisher comments, "*With respect to communication, it points up how uncoordinated we were with some of these early crossings. We became a lot better as we learned from each deployment.*

"*The F-100s normally flew at 31,000 feet, but the KC-97 and KB-50 tankers could only make it to about 10,000 feet with the fuel load they carried, so we would have to come down to refuel. If you fell off the tanker [became disconnected from its drogue] before you got a full load it was difficult to get back on again because you were too heavy to join up at the slow speed of about 210 knots. Tankers were typically asked by the F-100 pilots to descend gradually to increase their speed—it was called 'tobogganing.'*

"*The tankers provided the navigation bearings for rendezvous by using radio direction finders. You would key the mike and say 'ahhh' to provide a signal to locate your relative bearing to them. You never wanted a head-on rendezvous. They should always be flying away from you when joining up. Occasionally*

you would get a reciprocal bearing. That meant they were behind you! If they gave a heading you thought was wrong (such as a reciprocal) you would always ask for another steer or request a back-up steer from another tanker [there were several]. There was no onboard radar. Some of the equipment we have today (like GPS) would have made that whole process a lot easier."

Of the two squadrons, only four F-100s actually made it non-stop to Incirlik. These F-100 pilots flew more than 12 hours while refueling four times in-flight and overcoming turbulence, weather and the blackness of night to accomplish the mission. The others diverted to safe havens along the way, except for one pilot who had to eject over Greenland when he was unable to take on fuel. Weather prevented him from reaching his abort base, but he was rescued the next morning. All fighters were in place and "mission ready" in Incirlik by the end of the day following takeoff.

"*We flew 'show of force' missions over Lebanon—once with all aircraft of every type in a very long string formation led by the fighters. Both the SecState and the SecDef communicated through channels their appreciation for a 'job well done.' I made four more transatlantic crossings in the F-100 during my tenure with the 352nd, including the first high altitude passage [using the Boeing KC-135]."*

Fisher continues: *"I remember one crossing when I flew in the KC-135 tanker. We had an experience on that mission that was really gut wrenching. The forecast winds aloft were wrong. Instead of a cross wind—we had a strong tailwind. When we discovered this we were obviously a lot further along the route than planned and further from our departure base which was our abort base [where you went if you couldn't take on fuel]. One of our fighters was unable to refuel at the first refueling point. Tanker crews had been briefed that should an abort occur, one of the tankers would accompany the fighter to the abort base to aid in navigation and to determine his position if he had to eject.*

"The question was should this F-100 pilot return to the planned abort base or land at a non-military airport that was closer. The Tanker Wing Commander, who was mission commander, made the decision for him to return to the departure base. I had authority to counter his decisions if I thought it affected the safety of the fighter. I was sitting in the tail of his tanker monitoring the conversation. I got on the radio and asked what the fighter's fuel status was. Using my old E6B (an analogue circular slide rule used by pilots for cockpit computations) I determined that he didn't have enough fuel to make his abort base. I countermanded the mission commander and directed him [the F-100] to a civilian airfield. In a subsequent transmission a few minutes later I heard his tanker pilot say 'Good luck little buddy we will see you later.' To me this meant the tanker was not going with the fighter... as briefed. I communicated with the mission commander and told him that one of the tankers had to accompany this guy. He called the tanker and directed him to follow the fighter, which by then was miles away. The tanker asked the fighter 'How about slowing up so we can catch you.' Well, if the F-100 pilot did that he would not be at a fuel-efficient speed that was needed if he was going to make it. Once again, I had to intervene and tell the fighter he was to maintain proper cruise speed.

"Still later, the fighter pilot called that he was getting really low on fuel and said he had a ship in sight and asked should he bail out over the ship? Well, in thinking about the bailout situation I had to consider the water temperature, how does he contact

Figure 06-12. "Refueling off a KB-50 was sporty in the Hun. Very nose high mushy attitude at 200 Knots, the KB going its top speed with four turning and two burning. The KB would be in nose down 'race' mode, while Hun is wallowing nose high." Craig Colter Photo.

the ship, will they see him eject, can they launch a boat to pick him up. I directed him to press on. He did and made the landing OK... but he flamed out taxing off the runway. You know, it's things like that that age you.

"On those deployments where we knew in advance that we were going, the pilots would be put in 'crew rest' in the afternoon in dormitories on-base and given a sleeping pill and monitored by a flight surgeon. Air Police would be stationed to keep the area quiet. We were awakened at about 1 AM, got a steak for breakfast [low residue food] *and bused to the flight line to brief. Takeoff was normally around 2 AM. Our objective was to arrive at the destination during daylight hours—so we would fly through the night and land in the afternoon (about a six hour time change). Maintenance was then done on the aircraft and pilots were briefed on the missions to be flown the next day."*

Craig Colter recalled: *"Learning to perform aerial refueling at night from the KB-50 using the 'probe and drogue' in the F-100 was an interesting experience. You had to get the right 'sight picture' of the tanker to know where your probe was. You couldn't look at your probe* [that extended from the right wing] *because it was out of your normal line-of-sight so you had to know where it would be when the tanker was in a certain position on your windscreen. Any turbulence and the KB-50s hose would start whipping around. There were several occasions where the drogue broke the F-100 canopy or ripped the slats off the wing.*

"Rendezvous with the KBs at night in weather were really sporty—all done with DF steers from the tanker down at low altitudes around 10K, because that was his ceiling limit with a full load, which was the worst altitude for weather and turbulence— really made those long hoses whip. Very nose high mushy attitude at 200 Knots [IAS], *the KB going its top speed with four turning and two burning* [some KB-50s had two underwing J47s to augment their speed]. *The KB would be in nose down 'race' mode, while Hun is wallowing nose high.*

"The Hun had terrible exterior lighting, and usually had a wing tip and/or at least one fuselage light out. Horrible being a wingman at night trying to fly wing on one light that was constantly moving in bad weather. Had many severe cases of vertigo out there and just hung on sweating and terrified. When we got luminescent strip lights on the sides of the F-4, all the old F-100 wingmen thought they had died and gone to heaven."

Perfecting the "Hun"—the F-100D

The F-100D, with the larger vertical fin, was the last major production variant, entering the inventory in September 1956 with 1274 built. The changes addressed some inherent deficiencies in the design by revising the wing to incorporate trailing edge flaps—moving the ailerons outboard. This improved the slow-speed characteristics and the view over the nose during the landing phase of flight. Enhancements to the airframe increased its structural service life from 3,000 hours to

Figure 06-13. The F-100C in formation. USAF Photo.

7,000 hours. This would prove to be a very cost-effective change when the D series became an important ground support asset in Vietnam.

The new series provided increased ordnance (1,500 pounds more external stores) and expanded nuclear delivery (Mk 7, B28, B43, B57 and B61). It also had the ability to carry four GAR-8 (AIM-9B) *Sidewinder* air-to-air missiles and the AGM-12G *Bullpup* air-to-surface missile. Upgraded electronics and an autopilot completed the list of major changes. Because of the rapid introduction of the F-100D, most of the C series were transferred to Air National Guard units by 1960.

The D series also provided for "Buddy System" refueling, where one F-100 could provide fuel to another via a special external pod. In November 1956, two F-100Ds performed the first demonstration of "Buddy" refueling.

A USAFE air demonstration team called the *Skyblazers* (36th TFW in Germany) flew shows in Europe with the F-100C from 1957 to 1962. The U.S. Air Force "Thunderbird Flight Demonstration Team" operated the F-100C from 1956 until 1964, when they made the transition to the F-105. However, problems with the F-105 caused them to change back to the F-100 (D variant) before they completed the 1964 demonstration season.

One in-flight airframe failure of a Thunderbird F-100D occurred during a performance over Laughlin Air Force Base near Del Rio, Texas, on 20 October 1967. The pilot was future Air Force Chief of Staff Merrill A. "Tony" McPeak, flying #6, a solo position. In his own words (from "Tony McPeak Story"):

"...*We approach the climax, the signature Bomb Burst. My job is to put 'pigtails' through the separating formation, doing unloaded, Max-rate vertical rolls.... I start the aggressive [6.5-G] pull into the vertical—and the aircraft explodes.... Any F-100 pilot who hears a loud 'BANG!' automatically thinks, 'compressor stall,' and unloads the jet to get air traveling down the intake in the right direction.... SO, INSTINCTIVELY, the explosion causes me to relax stick-pressure to unload the airplane...[but—] That's no compressor stall!!...*

"*In retrospect, the airplane had already unloaded itself, making my remedy superfluous, but there was some pilot lore at work here. No matter what else happens...fly the airplane. Forget all that stuff about lift and drag and thrust and gravity, just fly the damn airplane until the last piece stops moving. Good old 55-3520 has quit flying. But I have not.*

"*Now there's fire, and I don't mean just a little smoke. Flames fill the cockpit. I have to eject. I grab the seat handles and tug them up, firing the canopy and exposing ejection triggers on each side of the handles. I yank the*

Figure 06-14. Cockpit of the F-100D. USAF Photo.

triggers and immediately feel the seat catapult into the slipstream...."

He lost his helmet in the high-speed bailout, but landed safely—despite a damaged parachute. He talked to Mike Miller, Thunderbirds narrator, who said "*maybe we should leave 'that thing, whatever it is,' out of the show sequence.*"

McPeak: "*That's when i learn i'd pulled the wings off the airplane.*"

Meanwhile, over in war-torn Southeast Asia, pilots making high-G pull-ups from their bomb runs in F-100s had also been losing airplanes. These were simply considered "combat losses," as it was impractical for recovery teams to visit crash sites or search for wreckage for Accident Boards to examine. But now here was a "Hun"—fallen into their laps, as it were.

McPeak: "*After I jumped out, my aircraft continued on a ballistic trajectory, scattering parts and equipment along the extended flight path. Most of the engine and the main fuselage section impacted about 2 miles downrange from my initial pull-up spot. All the bits and pieces landed on government soil, and there was no injury or property damage. My aircraft was destroyed—I signed a hand-receipt for $696,989—but if there is a good kind of accident, this was it. Nobody was hurt, and all the scrap metal was collected for post-game analysis.*

"*The F-100's wings mate into a box at the center of the fuselage, the strongest part of the airplane. When my aircraft's wing center box was inspected, it was found to have failed. North American Rockwell, the manufacturer, tested the box on a bend-and-stretch machine, and it broke again at an equivalent load of 6.5 G for the flight condition I was at when the wings departed.*

"*Later, specialists discovered considerable fatigue damage in the wing center boxes of other Thunderbird aircraft. USAF immediately put a 4 G limit on the F-100 and initiated a program to run all the aircraft through*

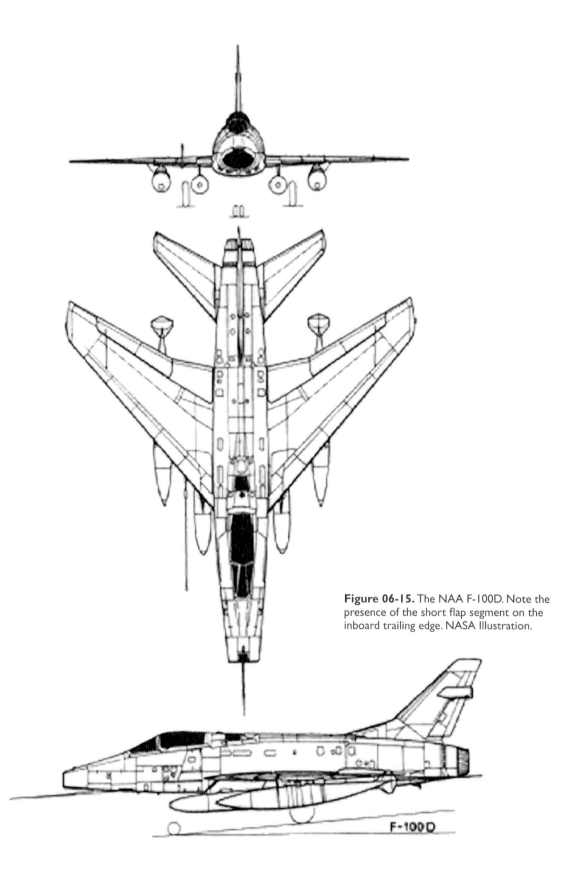

Figure 06-15. The NAA F-100D. Note the presence of the short flap segment on the inboard trailing edge. NASA Illustration.

F-100D

Figure 06-16. The Air Force Flight Demonstration Team known as the Thunderbirds flew both the F-100C and D series from 1956 to 1968. USAF Photo.

depot modification to beef up the wing center box. My accident almost certainly saved lives by revealing a serious problem in the F-100 fleet."

The Thunderbirds performed with the D series from July 1964 until November 1968, when they upgraded to the F-4E Phantom II.

Zero Length Launch Capability

To provide more flexibility, several tactical fighters of the era, including the F-100D, had the capability of launching from a flatbed trailer using a Zero Length Launch (ZEL)

facility. This entailed attaching a 130,000-pound thrust solid fuel rocket booster of the type used with the B-61 *Matador* (an early cruise missile) that accelerated the aircraft to flying speed (300 mph) within four seconds and then was jettisoned. The pilot experienced 4-Gs of acceleration.

This capability would negate a first strike by the Soviets of U.S. airbases on the European continent. These aircraft could be trucked to virtually anywhere in Europe or the Far East and launched without the need for a long concrete runway. The initial test to prove the concept took place at Edwards Air Force Base on 26 March 1958. While the first test went as expected, the booster failed to drop-off on the second attempt and test pilot Al Blackburn had to eject. The failure occurred because one of the attachment bolts had failed to shear. The appropriate items were redesigned and a total 20 flights were conducted, although none of the unique ZEL fighters were actually deployed.

The F-100F Two-Seater

The two-seat F-100F appeared in March 1957. It was an attempt to reduce the training accidents by allowing instructors to fly with trainees in a tandem seating arrangement. Prior to the F series, new pilots flew the F-100 for the first time without the benefit of any dual instruction in type. Design studies had actually begun as early as 1954, but the first flight did not take place until

Figure 06-17. An F-100D launched from a Zero Length Launcher (ZEL). USAF Photo.

August 1956. The addition of a second seat required a lengthening of the fuselage by three feet. To allow the aircraft to maintain its performance, only two 20mm cannons were carried and the external load was limited to the 6,000 lb. There was no noticeable change in accident rates with the introduction of the F series. However, its availability would prove providential in two unique applications in Vietnam.

Transitioning to the F-100

Many pilots, like Craig Colter, made the transition to the F-100 as their first duty assignment: *"I went into the Hun right out of pilot training in May of '62, after waiting at Laredo for 6 months for my training slot at Luke (I flew the T-34, T-37 and T-33 in pilot training—and acquired about 265 hours there). After 9 months of gunnery school at Luke, I went to Cannon AFB [New Mexico] for 2.5 years, and deployed all over world in the Hun, including a seven-month combat tour in SEA [Southeast Asia—Vietnam]."*

The F-100 was a challenging aircraft as Colter recalls:

"The J57 engine was slow to spool up. This meant that you had to be way out in front of the airplane in your head and get the throttle up before things got dicey. It was a real pleasure later to fly planes like the F-4 and F-16 that had instant acceleration out of the engines—they were much more forgiving of mistakes than was the Hun. I firmly believe that if you could fly the Hun, you could fly anything. Everything else was a breeze to check out in after flying it.

"It was ironic that when I was least experienced and prepared, I got to fly the airplane that demanded the most and was the most unforgiving. I lost many friends in the Hun from accidents. But, those that survived and learned her ways grew to love the airplane."

Vietnam

While the conduct of the Vietnam War is beyond the scope of this book, it is appropriate to relate the political objectives. Vietnam had been divided along the 17th parallel by the 1954 Geneva Accord following the French defeat at Dien Bien Phu. The North, under Marxist revolutionary Ho Chi Minh viewed that peace cease-fire agreement as simply another staging point to reunification of Vietnam under his control. As he represented Communist ideology, this insurgent movement, which was going on in all of Southeast Asia, had been opposed by the preceding Eisenhower and Kennedy administrations. In 1964, with Lyndon Johnson as president and with the "Gulf of Tonkin Resolution," the United States sought to use military means to inflict economic damage to achieve a political settlement.

Although similar in some respects to the Korean War, major ground operations were restricted to South Vietnam. The air war was used initially to interdict supplies flowing to the South over the roads and railways of the North, particularly through the *Ho Chi Minh Trail* that led through Laos and Cambodia. The Secretary of Defense, Robert McNamara, a former Ford Motor Company "whiz kid," envisioned progress in a conflict of this type as being measurable in number of sorties flown, tons of bombs dropped, and number of enemies killed—"body counts." The targets and weapons used were tightly controlled by McNamara to ensure that the U.S. did not aggravate our relations with China or the Soviet Union, who were backing the insurgency. These limitations and others were referred to as the "Rules of Engagement," or ROE. These rules, which were changed, often capriciously, were not popular, as they required the pilots to operate in an environment for which few of them had been trained or their aircraft adequately equipped. Most believed that the ROE resulted in higher losses and a protracted war. McNamara admitted in his book *In Retrospect: The*

Tragedy and Lessons of Vietnam, that the philosophy and strategy were dreadfully flawed.

The F-100D was one of the first combat aircraft deployed to Southeast Asia when six arrived at Don Muang Royal Thai Air Force Base (RTAFB) in Thailand on 16 April 1961, to be used for close air support and ground attacks within South Vietnam. Three years later, following the Gulf of Tonkin incident in August 1964, Craig Colter's entire wing flew across the Pacific within days of the Congressional Resolution. He then spent four months flying Combat Air Patrol (MIGCAP) missions out of DaNang. He notes: "*There was not much knowledge transfer from guys who had flown combat in WWII and Korea, very little intelligence regarding the capability of the MiG-17 or MiG-19, and virtually zero information on tactics. Early on there were no maps of the country and perhaps three or four TACAN stations (DaNang, Takhli, Laos, and Udorn) in the whole of SEA at the time, making navigation a real bear, especially when flying at low altitudes.*"

With the escalation of the war into the North in August 1964, the F-100s initially escorted the bomb-laden F-105s, providing MIGCAP to ensure any MiGs sent to intercept would be effectively countered. The first loss of an F-100 was recorded just a few weeks later on 18 August 1964, when First Lieutenant Colin Clark was shot down by ground fire, ejected, and was rescued. F-100s also performed anti-aircraft suppression using the 2.75-inch FFAR or the 5-inch HVAR.

However, the MiGs stayed out of the fighting until operation "*Rolling Thunder*," in the spring of 1965, began to hurt the North. On 4 April, a large *strike package* of 79 aircraft went North to provide follow-up strikes on several roads and bridges hit the previous day. Four F-100s, positioned to assault AAA positions, were attacked by two Mig-17s. In the ensuing brief dogfight one F-100 pilot, Capt Donald W. Kilgus, claimed hits with 20mm cannon on a MiG but could not confirm that it went down. This was the first aerial combat of the war, and the loss was confirmed years later when the pilot of the downed MiG actually stated that three NVA (North Vietnamese Army) aircraft were lost at that time.

Another four F-100Cs flying MIGCAP, alerted by the pilots under attack, had just turned toward the action when they observed two other MiG-17s hit the F-105 formation. Because of their heavy bomb load, the F-105s (flying at about 350 knots) were easy targets. Two F-105s were hit and one went down immediately. The F-100s (carrying *Sidewinder*s) immediately engaged the MiGs but had to

Figure 06-19. One of the obvious changes to the F-100 brought about by the Vietnam War was the return to camouflage paint in 1965. Even Korea had not required that. USAF Photo.

hold their fire until they cleared the F-105 formation. A *Sidewinder* fired by one of the F-100s passed within 15 feet of one of the MiGs but failed to detonate. However, the F-100's high wing loading (75 lbs/sq ft as opposed to the MiG-17's 48 lbs/sq ft) caused the F-100 to have problems combating the nimble Soviet fighter. The MiGs went vertical, using their superior maneuverability to disengage. This first encounter between a *Century Series* fighter and a MiG was not encouraging.

Initially limited to daylight visual combat conditions, installation of the Motorola SST-181 X-band radar for ground-directed bombing (Operation *Skyspot*) turned the F-100 into a marginal all-weather/day-night aircraft. By late 1966 they were restricted to targets in the South, as more capable F-4 Phantoms became available. Two-hundred forty-two F-100Ds were lost in Vietnam before the last *Super Sabre* departed SEA in 1971—the longest serving of any first line combat aircraft in Southeast Asia.

Wild Weasels

On 24 July 1965, an Air Force F-4C *Phantom* was shot down over North Vietnam by a Soviet-supplied SA-2 *Guideline* surface-to-air missile (SAM). What is ironic about the incident is that the pilot, Capt. Richard Keirn, who successfully ejected and became a POW, was shot down during WWII and had been a POW twenty years earlier.

With the NVA employment of sophisticated missiles and radar-directed anti-aircraft guns (AAA) the war entered a new phase. Technology began to play a more important role in a concerted effort to suppress these radar stations. However, the tactic to do so was fraught with risk—some felt that the days of the manned strike force were numbered. The concept of defeating defensive radar actually goes back to WWII, when specially equipped bombers were employed to jam the radar frequencies and drop "chaff."

The political strategists in President Lyndon Johnson's administration, primarily his Secretary of Defense, Robert McNamara, insisted that the SAM sites, whose construction was monitored almost daily by the U.S., should not be attacked for fear of killing Soviet technicians who were supporting the installation—and exacerbating an already precarious political position. Thus, it was not until these sites became operational (as evidenced by the downing of the *Phantom)* that the threat required a response; the SAM sites now became "politically acceptable" targets.

Although the Soviet SAM threat had been known for more than a decade, little had been done in the Tactical Air Command to address that danger; however, SAC and the Navy had made significant progress. Colonel Edward Rock's commentary in the book *First In, Last Out* notes: "*This was a clear failure in tactical thinking. In general, it was thought that the SAM could be defeated or degraded to an extent simply by flying at low altitude* [using ground

clutter to mask the radar return]... *or so it was thought. Low altitude penetration and weapons delivery* [such as LABS] *were taught in all Air Force... training courses, practiced religiously... and prescribed in every major war plan....*" However, flying down low exposed the aircraft to the low-tech AAA fire that would claim far more U.S. aircraft in SEA than the SAM.

Rock notes that with the SAM threat now a reality, the Air Force formed "*a special anti-SAM task force... headed by Brigadier General K.C. Dempster to study this 'new' threat and recommend ways to counteract it.*" This resulted in several proposals. First, that a small number of fighters should be equipped with electronics to enable locating and marking the SAM sites in real-time for attack by strike aircraft, as traditional methods of photo and electronic reconnaissance were neither timely nor effective, since many of the sites were reasonably mobile. "*Various concepts were tried including putting fighters on alert and launching them as soon as an occupied SAM site was identified by photo-reconnaissance. In every case, the occupied site was empty by the time fighters arrived. It was necessary to find the sites while they were still occupied, hence the need for 'real-time' location capability. The EB-66 electronic reconnaissance aircraft could provide information on the general SAM site position but not accurate enough for identification of a camouflaged SAM site.*"

Thus, a "*Radar Homing and Warning*" (RHAW) device was needed immediately so that the fighters would at least know when they were being tracked (targeted). Second, missiles were needed that could be fired from a fighter to "home in" on the radar antenna to destroy it. The Navy had taken the lead on this with their *Shrike* anti-radiation missile that was just being deployed with the fleet. Third, more effective jamming equipment was needed that could be carried by the fighters.

In defining a system to counter the threat, the most obvious answer was to use the radar's own signal to find its location. Destroying the antenna would disable the most vulnerable part of the site. At that time (1965) most of the electronic equipment aboard aircraft employed large and relatively fragile vacuum tubes and their supporting power supplies. These were heavy and bulky and required a lot of cooling air. Thus, the first anti-radar counter-measures (used in the bombers) were too cumbersome for fighter aircraft. With the first use by the NVA of the SAM-2, the U.S. was driven, in what some say was a "panic" mode, to make something available in the shortest possible time.

The two-seat F-100F was chosen as the "pathfinder aircraft" for its obvious availability and relatively high-speed performance. Flown by highly experienced pilots and with well-qualified Electronics Warfare Officers (EWOs) in the back, these aircraft would be equipped to locate and mark the SAM sites.

Applied Technologies Inc. (ATI) developed a lightweight "transistorized" Vector Homing and Warning system in less than 30 days that was the answer to the "size" problem. The IR-133 Panoramic Scan Receiver represented the heart of the RHAW system. It provided for a 360-degree scan on a 3-inch Cathode Ray Tube (CRT) cockpit display to provide the bearing to the signal. It differentiated the various frequency bands (S as a solid line, C a dotted line, and X a dashed line) and pulse rates to identify the presence and type of radar signals being received— surveillance, missile tracking, or AAA radar.

The project was so intense and the lead-times so compressed that Dr. John Grigsby (then a member of the ATI engineering staff) notes that the production contract with ATI was defined on a blackboard during a meeting. A Polaroid picture was taken of the board and the appropriate representatives of the military and ATI signed the picture. Grigsby believes it was at this meeting that one of the attendees asked the famous question "*You want me to ride in the back of a two-seat fighter with a teenage killer in the front seat? You Gotta Be Shi...ing Me!*"—the start of the *Wild Weasel* slogan "YGBSM." Other memories recall the YGBSM slogan from a top-secret briefing of the *Weasel* mission presented at Clark Field, in the Philippines. As the phrase was widely used in the military, multiple origins may have equal validity.

The concept required the IR-133-equipped F-100F to fly within 20-30 miles of a suspected SAM site—allowing itself to be tracked by the *Fan Song*—NATO code name for the Soviet radar. The presence of the missile guidance signal, as indicated by the Pulse Repetition Frequency (PRF), would indicate that launch was imminent. On the early units, although the length of the strobe on the screen gave some indication of range and threat level, there was no specific indication of the radar's distance. Rock comments: "*A long strobe indicated a near threat along with a high probability that you were the target.*"

Thus, the pilot had to make a visual identification of the target, using the bearing indicator to fly directly towards it. This often proved very difficult, as the NVA were masters of camouflage. Because anti-aircraft guns heavily protected the SAM sites, this was also a very hazardous mission. Only after making visual contact would the *Pathfinder* dive on the radar location, marking it with 2.75-inch air-to-ground rockets from LAU-3 canisters.

The second part of the team was the attack aircraft—four F-105s that carried more substantial ordnance to complete the job. Of course, the time between the presence of the missile

Figure 06-20. The Wild Weasel patch features the abbreviation YGBSM—an expression of incredulity among aviators of the period when told of the tactics and mission. Air Force Museum Photo.

guidance signals and the firing of the missile was quite short, and the *Pathfinder* often had to dodge the incoming SA-2 before completing its attack on the radar site. The Launch Warning Receiver (LWR-300) provided a simple yellow light in the cockpit to warn when the launch was imminent, and a red light when missile launch occurred (detecting that guidance commands were being transmitted to the SAM after launch).

Rock notes: "*If a SAM was launched, then the azimuth strobe associated with the threat was supposed to blink at 3 cycles per second. I can say that I probably had more than 100 missiles launched at my aircraft and never, not even once, saw the strobe blinking. Probably busy with more important things like saving my life.*"

Four two-place F-100Fs, modified with the RHAW gear and code-named *Wild Weasel*, arrived at Korat RTAFB in November 1965. Their objective was to evaluate the effectiveness of the equipment and training. Lieutenant Colonel Allen Lamb conducted the first successful *Wild Weasel* attack on 22 December 1965. He writes: "*...we didn't just mark the target...we went in first with rockets and came back around with cannon even before some of the Thuds* [the popular name for the F-105 *Thunderchief*] *had started on a first run. The F-100F was an excellent hunter-killer in that it was very agile. I was very fond of it, and of my ability to fly it.*"

Rock: "*Due to the limited number of Wild Weasel aircraft we were considered a high value limited asset... we normally flew only the most dangerous missions and in an area where the threat was the very highest.*"

More than 180 SAM sites were destroyed by an estimated 19,000 Iron Hand sorties (attacks on SAM sites were called "Iron Hand" whether flown by Wild Weasel or other USAF or Navy strike missions). The use of the *Wild Weasel*, while successful, generated another round of electronic counter-warfare "one-upsmanship"—the NVA then using bogus radar sites in an attempt to confuse the *Wild Weasels*. Another NVA tactic was to spoof the incoming Americans by increasing the PRF, which normally indicated that a SAM had been launched. The hoped-for result was that the American planes would take evasive action, perhaps even jettisoning their ordnance, and abort the mission. This was more probable if the flight was "on top" of an overcast, where the ability to observe the SAM was severely restricted.

Beginning in 1967, the SA-2 was modified with an optical target acquisition and tracking system to help counter ECM jamming and the ability of the *Wild Weasel* to home on the enemy SAM radar in a timely manner. This optical system could be used only during daylight and when the weather was clear.

The courage and intensity of the flyers was exceptional, as they proved new tactics and equipment as the war progressed. Thirty-four Americans lost their lives, while 19 were taken prisoner in this era before the availability of effective "stand-off" weapons and laser-guided smart bombs.

The F-100F was withdrawn from the *Wild Weasel* program in July 1966 with the introduction of the F-105 Wild Weasel-III. (More on the *Wild Weasel*s in the F-105 Chapter.)

"Misty" Forward Air Controllers

The function of the Forward Air Controller (FAC) became a critical asset in that hard-fought war over the dense jungles and anonymous rice paddies of SEA. Low and slow, FACs were used to spot targets for intelligence gathering and close air support, not only for the U.S. and Vietnamese forces in South Vietnam, but also for then-secret operations in Laos and later Cambodia. Initially the standard Cessna O-1 *Bird Dog* was used, then the twin-engine Cessna O-2 *Super Skymaster* and twin-engine and armed OV-10 *Bronco* were added. However, the range and speeds of these aircraft were not enough to keep up with this fast-paced war and often left them vulnerable to ground fire.

Augmenting these aircraft would be yet another adaptation of the two-seat F-100F called *Commando Sabre*, in which "Fast FACs" performed under the call sign "*Misty*". (*Misty* was a popular jazz song of the era by Erroll Garner.) The plan to form a secret squadron of volunteer pilots was originally conceived by General William W. Momyer, then commander Seventh Air Force in Saigon, in 1967. Their ability to maneuver tightly at low altitude and to accelerate rapidly when called on provided a new dimension to the FAC mission. The F-100F performed well in the role assigned to Detachment 1 of the 416th TFS.

First stationed at Phu Cat Air Base in South Vietnam, the Fast FACs were tasked with identifying targets that ranged from SAM sites to trucks moving down hidden jungle highways. They had to fly low to spot the enemy in the tall grass and heavy foliage that was Vietnam. They would usually operate singly, scanning the jungle for enemy movements. They had the ability to use their own firepower to effect an immediate attack while calling in other fighter-bombers via the Airborne Battlefield Command and Control Center (ABCCC). The ABCCC was an "orbiting" C-130 that provided 24/7 response. Initially the backseater was from the O-1 crowd, but this gave way to both members of the crew being F-100 pilots—they would trade seats on alternate missions.

There would be only 157 *Misty* pilots in this close and endangered fraternity, each with a numbered call sign. Typically, there were no more than 14 "volunteers" in the group at a time, serving TDY tours of 90 to 120 days. Like the *Wild Weasels*, the *Mistys* were very vulnerable and 28 percent of the aircraft assigned were shot down. The first *Misty* commander, Colonel George E. "Bud" Day (call sign *Misty 1*), spent five years and seven months in the Hanoi Hilton following ejection from his disabled *Hun*.

Another famous member is *Misty 40*, Dick Rutan of the famed Rutan Brothers (Bert being the other sibling). Known for their innovative aircraft, Dick Rutan was the first to fly around the world non-stop without refueling with his co-pilot Jeana Yeager. Rutan flew 105 of his 325 combat missions as a *Misty*. Rutan's F-100F was shot down over Vietnam, but he was able to eject and was rescued. Another *Misty* of future note was "Tony" McPeak, whose Vietnam tour followed his Thunderbirds assignment. After flying the F-100 with the 612th TFS at Phu Cat AB, South Vietnam, from December 1968 to January 1969, he served as Operations Officer of the *Misty* Fast FACs at Phu Cat from February to April 1969, and then as their Commander, first at Phu Cat and then at Tuy Hoa Air Base, South Vietnam, from April to August 1969; his call sign was *Misty 94*.

The Fast FAC operation formally came to an end in June 1970.

Foreign Service

In 1958, the French were the first foreign country to receive the F-100. They operated both the F-100D and the F-100F. The Danish Air Force operated 48 F-100D series and 10 F-100Fs starting in 1961. The accident rate was abysmal, with a loss of almost one-third of the aircraft by 1968. They continued to operate the F-100 until 1982, when it was phased out for the F-16. The Turkish Air Force operated 87 beginning in the late 1950s and eventually acquired 206. They were reportedly the last country to use the F-100 operationally when it was retired there in 1985. The

Figure 06-21. The Cessna O-1 (L-19) Bird Dog used by Forward Air Controllers (FAC) preceded the Misty F-100Fs. USAF Photo.

Chinese Nationalist Air Force operated the largest number of F-100s outside the U.S., including the RF-100A *"Slick Chick"* reconnaissance version.

Variants

Numerous variations of, and modifications to, the F-100 over the course of its service allowed it to keep pace with advances in avionics, and in aerodynamic and maintenance improvements. Production ended in October 1959 with an average unit cost of about $800,000.

One interesting change was the replacement of the original afterburner of the J57 engine with the more advanced unit from retired Convair F-102s. Both units had two-position nozzles in "afterburner"; however, the original F-100 unit had a tendency to fail to close when the pilot moved the throttle out of the AB position. This resulted in less power, and in some flight operations required the pilot to go back into AB—increasing fuel consumption. This mod changed the facade of the aft end "petal-style" exhaust of the F-100. The afterburner modification started in the 1970s and reportedly solved maintenance issues as well as operational problems with the old type—including most compressor stalls.

Table 06-01

North American F-100 *Super Sabre* Versions

Type	Notes	No. Built
YF-100	Preproduction models.	2
F-100A	Single-seat day fighter.	203
RF-100A	"Slick Chick" F-100A mod for photo recce 1954. Retired USAF 1958.	(6)
	Four transferred to Republic of China Air Force, retired 1960.	
F-100B	Became North American F-107.	0
F-100C	Added fuel wet wings, fighter-bomber capability, probe-&-drogue.	476
	Refueling, up-rated P-21 engine on late prod A/C	
TF-100C	F-100C converted to a two-seat trainer.	(1)
F-100D	Fighter-bomber, advanced avionics, larger wing, tail fin, flaps.	1,274
F-100F	Two-seat training version, two cannon.	339
QF-100	D & F models converted to unmanned drone and drone directors.	(209)
Total Build		**2,294**

Phase Out

What began as the first combat aircraft in United States Air Force inventory capable of exceeding the speed of sound in level flight found itself struggling towards the end of its career over the rice paddies of South Vietnam—delivering iron bombs. While its long-term association with the Thunderbird Aerial Demonstration Team fostered its positive image with the public as the quintessential jet fighter of the 1950s, the reality of its long series of mechanical and aerodynamic problems caused it to fall from favor in its combat role. More than 500 of the 2,286 F-100 types were lost to accidents during its operational lifetime. The Air Force completed the phase-out of the F-100 in TAC by June 1972, but it remained in some Air Guard units until November 1979.

The F-100 also represented the last fighter that NAA would contribute to the USAF inventory. Subsequent proposals, such as the F-107 and F-108, would fall to the budget axe and competitive efforts by the other aerospace manufacturers.

Nevertheless, those who have flown the *Hun* are attached to its soul and, in 2006, Les Frazier (Colonel, USAF Ret.) organized the *Super Sabre* Society. Complete with a quarterly magazine and other "accoutrements" of such an organization (hats, mugs, etc.), it provides its members with a nostalgic tie to a temperamental airplane that they skillfully guided through often hostile skies.

F-100 Specifications

	YF-100	F-100A	F-100C	F-100D	F-100F
Length	46'3"	47'1"			50'4"
Wing Span	36'7"	38'9"			
Height	14'5"	15'4"	16'2"		16'2"
Short tail		(13'4")			
Wing Area	376	385	385	400	
J57 version	P-7	P-7	P-39 P-21	P-21	P-21
Thrust Dry	8,700	10,000	10,200	10,200	
AB	13,200	14,700	16,000	16,000	
First Flight	May-53	Oct-53	Jan-55	Jan-56	Mar-57
Number Built	2	203	476	1,274	339
Empty Weight	18,135		19,270	20,638	21,712
Gross Weight	28,561	28,899	36,549	38,048	39,122
Combat Wt		24,789	28,700	30,061	31,413
Max Speed	634	742	715/805	795	798
Initial climb fpm	4,700	5,000	4,200	4,300	4,230
Svc Ceiling	41,000	45,100	43,500	43,200	42,700
Normal Range	400	402	541	564	555

Table 06-2. North American F-100 Super Sabre Specifications

Origin of McDonnell Aircraft

James Smith McDonnell (1899-1980) graduated from Princeton University with a Master's in Aeronautical Engineering, and then served as a pilot in the Army Air Corps reserve in 1923. He worked briefly for the Huff Daland Airplane Company before forming his own business in 1928, to produce a small personal aircraft in pursuit of the Guggenheim Foundation's *Safe Aircraft Contest*. Unfortunately, his entry crashed during the trials and the company folded with the Depression. He then joined the Glenn L. Martin Company as an engineer.

With signs of an economic recovery (on the eve of WWII), "Mac," as he was known to his employees, left Martin to reform his company in 1939 as the McDonnell Aircraft Company, in St. Louis, Missouri. Originally, the 15-person enterprise simply manufactured parts for other companies, but in 1940 McDonnell responded to a U.S. Army Air Corps RFP (R-40C) for a high-speed, long-range, high-altitude interceptor. This RFP (which also had spawned the unorthodox configurations of the P-54, P-55 and P-56) encouraged respondents to think creatively in terms of configuration and technology. Although his first submission placed 21st among the 23 respondents, the Army provided $3,000 for additional design work on an interesting *blended wing* concept, which was subsequently rejected. A third iteration finally netted a $1.5 million contract in April 1942 for two prototypes of the XP-67.

Following several flights of the XP-67 *Moonbat* in 1944, an engine fire resulted in an emergency landing and the aircraft was essentially destroyed. The then-U.S. Army Air Forces (USAAF) determined that the anticipated performance would not be significantly better than existing types and cancelled work on the second prototype.

However, McDonnell had been approached by the Navy in 1943 to develop what would become the first jet powered carrier fighter. Using two small 19-inch diameter 1600-pound thrust Westinghouse axial-flow engines, three prototypes were ordered. As with the XP-67, the XFD-1 *Phantom* would

Figure 07-01. The XP-67 Moonbat was ready to be turned over to the Army Air Force for their flight evaluation when it was destroyed by an engine fire. U.S. Army Photo.

Figure 07-02. Lt Cmdr. James Davidson conducted the first trials of the McDonnell XFD-1 Phantom fighter aboard the aircraft carrier USS Franklin D. Roosevelt (CVB-42) on 21 July 1946. USN Photo.

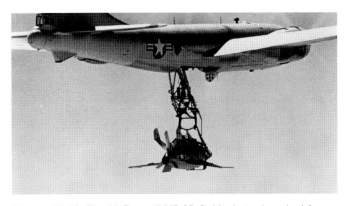

Figure 07-03. The McDonnell XF-85 Goblin being launched from a B-29. USAF Photo.

Figure 07-04. The McDonnell F2H Banshee had a long Navy career for a first generation fighter. An FH-1 is in the background showing the family resemblance. USN Photo.

blend the engines, their intake, and exhausts into an unswept-wing. The first flight in January 1945 showed promise and the plane went into limited production at the end of the war. The Navy also changed the designation from FD-1 to FH-1 at this time because Douglas Aircraft Company, which had been previously assigned the "D" manufacturing code, was about to put an aircraft into production for the Navy. McDonnell then received the "H" manufacturing code.

An interesting note to the first flight of the XFD-1 *Phantom* was that Westinghouse had only been able to deliver one engine. Thus, the initial test flight was accomplished with ballast in place of the second engine. Carrier qualification occurred in July 1946, and the airplane served with the Navy using the Westinghouse J30. This was the true precursor of McDonnell's more than sixty years of providing two-engine fighters to both services.

While the follow-on F2H *Banshee* was being designed with the Westinghouse J34 engine that was almost twice the thrust of the J30 (note the rearrangement of the Navy FH2 designation), the Army placed a contract with McDonnell for a parasite fighter FICON (Fighter-Conveyer) that became the XF-85 *Goblin* and was also powered by the J34. As with the XP-67, only a single prototype flew and the project was cancelled after several flights in 1948, but McDonnell had now grown to over 5,000 employees.

XF-88 Development

In early 1946, the USAAF issued an informal request for a "penetration fighter" with a speed of 600 mph,

McDonnell XF-88
USAF Museum Photo Archives

Figure 07-05. The clean lines of the XF-88 are apparent in this early photo of the plane, which does not have the afterburners. USAF Photo.

a combat radius of 900 miles, and an operating altitude of 40,000 feet. McDonnell responded with what was known in-house as the Model 36—initially powered by two 3000-pound thrust Westinghouse J34 engines. When work began in April 1946, the design called for the engines to be faired into the roots as had been done with the F2H. However, production engines were to be the Westinghouse J46 and its larger 34-inch diameter did not allow for this. Thus, both engines were placed together in the fuselage with the air intakes in the wing root and the exhaust exiting well forward of the empennage. This arrangement also facilitated the larger internal fuel supply needed for its mission. With completion of the mock-up, a contract for two prototypes was issued in June 1946. However, the J46 would never complete its development cycle.

The Chief Project Engineer Bud Flesh and his creative design team, lacking any hard data on wing sweep, followed the conventional wisdom of the day and employed a 35-degree angle as was done with the F-86. A V-tail arrangement was originally selected because of the desire to lessen the number of airfoils experiencing compressibility effects in the transonic region (about which little was known). It was thought that reducing the number of tail structures from three to two might help—but a more traditional tail was quickly adopted when wind tunnel tests revealed some possible problems with the V configuration. Armament was six 20-mm M-39 cannon and the name *Voodoo* was chosen—some have speculated that "Mac" was a student of the occult, thus the use of demonic names for McDonnell aircraft.

The XP-88 (46-525) that rolled down the runway for its first flight on 20 October 1948 was a clean looking single-seat fighter with Chief Test Pilot Bob Edholm in the cockpit. Several problems were apparent during the initial flight tests. Lack of full thrust early in the take-off roll occurred because of a poor design in the engine intake. This was ultimately resolved with spring-loaded "blow-in" (or "suck-in") doors in the wheel well, as had been used on other early jets, such as the Republic F-84.

Poor roll rate was resolved by increasing the aileron chord. However, this in turn resulted in an undesired wing twist at high speeds. Added torsional rigidity required yet more structural weight. With a specified gross of 15,000-pounds, the XF-88 was now nearing 18,500 pounds—so the two engines and large fuel requirement needed to meet the performance numbers doomed that objective. Despite its striking good looks, the aircraft's performance was lackluster, with a maximum level-flight speed of only 641 mph. Edholm was able to achieve Mach 1.175 only in a shallow dive.

In an effort to improve the performance, McDonnell wanted to have afterburners installed on the J34. However, Westinghouse did not think that they could configure the aft section of the J34 with an AB because the existing tail structure limited the available length to only 52 inches. However, the second prototype (46-526), designated XF-88A, did accommodate a short AB segment (constructed by McDonnell) as part of its Westinghouse XJ34-WE-15. It also had the "all flying" stabilator and bladder cells in the wings, which increased the internal fuel capacity to 834 gallons.

With its first flight on 26 April 1949, the effect of the AB in providing 34 percent more thrust was readily apparent. The take-off run was reduced by 20 percent and the top speed increased to 700 mph, while the time to climb to 30,000 feet was reduced by 4 minutes. Despite these improvements, or perhaps because of them, the plane was now encountering the effects of compressibility.

Fortunately (for McDonnell), the competition, Lockheed's XF-90 and North American's XF-93, were faring no better. The fly-off between these penetration fighters occurred just as the Korean War erupted in the summer of 1950. Although the XF-88A was scored highest by the Evaluation Board, all three designs failed to meet the required specifications. Thus, a production contract was not awarded pending a reappraisal of the role of the penetration fighter in light of the Korean situation.

The now-United States Air Force (USAF) issued another penetration fighter RFP in February 1951. Virtually all of the traditional fighter manufacturers responded, including Northrop with an escort iteration of its F-89 and Republic with a stable of aircraft based on its F-84F airframe. The XF-88A returned to flight status in February 1952 for additional tests.

An interesting footnote to the XF-88's development was the incorporation of an Allison T38 turboprop in the nose of 46-525 for evaluation by NACA. Flight tests began on 14 April 1953, and it was the first propeller-equipped aircraft to achieve supersonic flight. The thought was that the turboprop would provide for better economy during the long cruise into enemy territory. (Republic had likewise toyed with the supersonic turboprop with their XF-84F—covered in a later chapter.) Both XF-88 prototypes were scrapped by 1958.

Pushing for the Penetration Fighter

The Air Force continued to redefine the role of the penetration fighter in the early 1950s. Although most of the Air Force bomber fleet still consisted of B-29, B50 and B-36 bombers, the B-47 (and soon to be B-52) continued to make significant strides in performance and were as fast (in cruise) as any of the contemporary fighters of the day. It was assumed that this performance relationship would probably continue, and some planners felt that escort was not required.

However, events in Korea added another factor: B-29s bombing the North required escort. The F-86 did not have the range to accompany them all the way to some targets and to loiter. The Republic F-84 was called on, and it was

noticeably inferior to the MiG-15. A long-range fighter, by whatever name, was still needed.

It was also apparent that, in an all-out war, the penetration fighter could provide cover during the initial ingress into Soviet territory, but would not accompany the bomber all the way to the more distant targets. Nor would there be any effort to cover the egress portion of the bomber's flight. Most SAC pilots recognized that a nuclear war would effectively be a one-way mission, although the RTB (return to base) factor was always a part of the mission plan.

Nevertheless, the McDonnell design team leader Ed Flesh continued to persist in trying to advance the XF-88 concept. The company was in trouble with a single-engine variant of its Navy fighter, the F3H *Demon*, which was to have used the Westinghouse J40. (That engine proved disastrous for several Navy programs and ultimately forced Westinghouse out of the jet engine business.) The F3H was thereupon revised to use the Allison J71 engine, and McDonnell accordingly proposed the F-88C powered by a pair of J71 engines with afterburning.

As the team went back to reworking the design with the much larger engine, it became apparent that the airframe was no longer an extension of the XF-88 and a new designation was assigned in November 1951—the XF-101. The push by McDonnell resulted in a Letter of Intent from the Air Force in January 1952, but it specified

Figure 07-06. The XF-88B configured with the Allison T38 turboprop shown here with the prop feathered. The short AB segments are also apparent. USAF Photo.

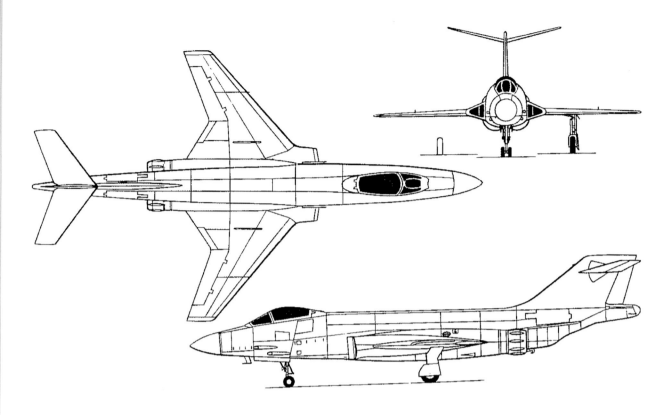

Figure 07-07. McDonnell F-101A Voodoo single-seat fighter three-view. NASA Illustration.

the use of the Pratt & Whitney J57. The basic layout continued, however, with the pair of J57s being fed by a much larger wing root intake. The fuel capacity was increased to 2,341 gallons to account for the larger engine's fuel consumption.

The all-moving horizontal "stabilator" was repositioned to almost the top of the vertical stabilizer. The wing area was enlarged from 350 sq ft to 368 sq ft by increasing the inboard chord. Split flaps were used, and the ailerons moved slightly inboard to avoid torsional twist. Air brakes were installed on either side of the massive rear fuselage. All F-101 versions were equipped with extendable probes for in-flight "probe and drogue" refueling. (The F-101B/Fs exchanged theirs for IR Search and Track seeker heads c. 1963-64. The later RF-101B was retrofitted during its conversion in the early 1970s to add the "boom-type" aerial refueling capability.) The armament was reduced to four 20mm M-39 cannons, and provisions were made to carry four *Falcon* air-to-air missiles (then in development) and 12 unguided folding fin aerial rockets (FFARs). The weight continued to grow.

F-101A Single-Seat Fighter
The mock-up inspection was completed in July 1952, and the Air Force issued a contract for 39 pre-production F-101A aircraft. This designation is unusual, in that these

would normally have been referred to as YF-101, since all of these aircraft were used for Category II suitability tests and none saw operational service.

With an uneasy peace finally restored to Korea in July 1953, some of the pressure was off the Air Force. By May 1954 they decided not to proceed with full-scale production, but to defer that decision until completion of the Category II testing in early 1955. Moreover, yet another change of operational direction saw the emphasis shift from SAC to TAC with a nuclear strike capability—Weapons System WS-105A. As with most of the *Century Series*, the F-101 would be adapted as a fighter-bomber with nuclear delivery as a primary objective. As the initial aircraft rolled off the production line, they were equipped for both the air-to-air (with the MA-7 Fire Control System) and tactical delivery of nuclear weapons (with the Low Altitude Bombing System—LABS).

Flight Test
The first F-101 was delivered to Edwards AFB in August 1954 for initial testing. McDonnell test pilot Robert C. Little made the first flight on 29 September 1954. Taking the new plane to 35,000 feet, he elected not to exceed the speed of sound, although some reports indicate he did so while in a shallow dive. There were several "small" problems noted, but the first flight is

Figure 07-08. The single-seat F-101A Voodoo was an impressive airplane. USAF Photo.

usually not the place to start expanding the performance envelope. A double flameout on the fourth flight was apparently the result of an incorrectly wired boost pump. Little was able to restart the engines and the flight ended successfully.

On the seventh flight, as he approached Mach 1.4 for the first time, both engines experienced "violent" compressor stalls. After decelerating to Mach .8, Little was able to get a relight and again completed the flight successfully. Several modifications were made to the engines and the airframe, which involved a redesign of the air intakes to include the addition of "turning vanes" to assist in channeling the air through the intake.

These early flights revealed an airplane that was relatively easy to fly with few vices—save for the notorious swept-wing pitch-up. The swept-wing stalled at the tip first and at high angles of attack or with adverse yaw, and the longitudinal center of lift moved forward—resulting in the pitch-up and the almost certain oscillating spin that would follow. Even with a spin-recovery tail-chute available, several airplanes were lost during the test phase. As with most of the *Century Series*, the pitch-up problem was a continuing liability.

Despite these problems, the Air Force released the plane for full-scale production on 28 October 1954. Phase II flight tests began in January 1955, and a high incidence of compressor stalls began to plague the program. Then, following the evaluation of a pitch-up accident that killed Korean War Ace Major Lonnie Moore in January 1956, the Air Force temporarily ceased production of the F-101A in May 1956.

Ultimately, the F-101 used an *Active Inhibitor* that generated an audio signal and a *stick pusher* as the critical angle-of-attack was approached, to warn the pilot. The conditions under which the pitch-up would occur were clearly defined in the *Dash-1* (Flight Operating Manual). This included a warning that a successful recovery was unlikely if the event occurred below 15,000 feet above terrain—requiring the pilot to abandon the aircraft.

Jonathan Myer: "*Pitch-up, or loss of control, could occur if too many Gs were pulled for the airspeed (or pulled too fast) and/or adverse yaw was induced, thereby allowing the wings to blank the airflow over the high T-tail section's control surfaces, which exerted a downward pressure that raised the nose. Our birds eventually had three warning devices (along with increasing buffet, if subsonic): a command signal limiter (CSL) in autopilot that limited the control stick pull to 4 Gs max, a horn warning, and finally a pusher that applied a 27.5-lb forward pressure on the stick. If a malfunction (or ham-handed pilot) still allowed a pitch-up, the recovery was to come out of afterburner (if in 'burner), push and hold the stick forward until zero or negative-G was felt—while pulling the drag-chute T-handle—then relax the stick while holding the rudders in a neutral position. That would restore flyable conditions by lowering the nose (perhaps with a snap roll). The drag-chute would fail at 250 knots (its job done) and speed should be allowed to increase to 350 knots before the pilot did anything else. If not recovered by 15,000 ft above ground (or pitch-up entered below that level)—eject.*"

Meanwhile, the *Active Inhibitor* "fix" allowed the production ban to be lifted, but rates were limited to eight aircraft per month for the rest of 1956, as McDonnell attempted to address the more than 300 other problems that had been identified by the Air Force in the test program. Mac's boys also tackled some 2000 additional issues identified "in-house" during this time.

As with virtually all the *Century Series*, the relatively small main landing gear provided poor braking action. In addition to an anti-skid device, a drag chute was installed—and its use was virtually mandatory as an additional safety feature to get the *Voodoo* stopped. What was also to plague the plane for its service life was the inability of the gear to take any significant side loads without structural failure. Tire wear was also considerable, with initially only 4 to 6 landings between tire changes; an improved tire addressed this issue. One simple problem that nagged pilots through the operational life of the F-101 was the ease with which the plane could exceed its gear retract airspeed of 250 knots on takeoff. George Andre comments on the F-101B: "*The nose gear was the problem as it retracted forward. The massive acceleration on a cold day would allow the airspeed to increase to a value that the airloads overpowered the hydraulic retract system. We made non-afterburner take-offs when below freezing temperatures existed.*"

Jonathan Myer: "*The dual nose gear also had another problem: increasing wobble above 75 knots on take-off roll if the tire pressures were uneven. On my first instrument check (in early 1960), I was in the back seat of our two-stick then-TF-101B as my check pilot in the front seat lit the 'burners on take-off roll. By 115 knots, the shaking was so strong he followed procedure by aborting the take-off. However, this is where real trouble began. Even with throttles in idle, drag chute deployed and braking hard enough to engage the anti-skid (so we wouldn't run out of runway), the residual momentum*

took us above 125 knots before slowing down — with the aircraft shuddering violently all the way as deceleration put more of its weight on the nose. The combining glass of its optical sight above the front seat instrument panel shattered and (we were told later) most of the black boxes in the nose were also broken. From then on, I determined that it would be better to lighten the weight on the nose gear and continue the takeoff, so that after the mission we'd be landing with a much lighter airplane and could then ease the nose down carefully and with less risk of damage during rollout. This technique worked fine over the years when I needed it."

The F-101 was the first production aircraft to exceed 1000 mph in level flight. Of course, this required the use of the ABs, which were limited to six minutes of continuous operation at the time. By this time, however, Air Force planners realized that the primary threat to U.S. bombers might not be the Soviet interceptor (which the long-range F-101 was being developed to combat), but the surface-to-air missile, or "SAM," as evidenced by the Army's progress with the *Nike Ajax*. Moreover, SAC had lost interest in the long-range fighter as a viable option; its relatively high wing loading (124 lbs/ft^2) implied that the F-101 would not be an agile dogfighter (it had the heaviest wing loading of any of the *Century Series*).

The first 77 single-seat F-101A aircraft, with two J57-P-13 turbojet engines with afterburners, became operational with four 20mm cannon and were assigned

Figure 07-09. The drag chute and drop tanks are evident in this early F-101A photo. USAF Photo.

Figure 07-10. The two-seat F-101B Voodoo was turned into a long-range interceptor to fill the gap until the F-106 achieved operational status. Here, a flight of 13th FIS "Black Bull" F-101Bs patrols the skies of northeastern Montana, circa 1960. Neal Mishler Photo.

to the 27th Strategic Fighter Wing at Bergstrom AFB, Texas, on 2 May 1957. However, as SAC was no longer interested in the F-101, the 27th was transferred to TAC in July—the A model having the ability to carry a single "special store" (Mk 7) nuclear weapon. The last units were delivered by November 1957. Despite the problems uncovered, the F-101A would achieve the lowest "first year" accident rate of any of the *Century Series*.

Major Adrian E. Drew set a new absolute world speed record of 1207.6 MPH on 12 December 1957. (The previous record was held by the British Fairey *Delta* FD-2.) On 25 September 1958, an F-101A flew nonstop and unrefueled from Carswell AFB in Texas to Bermuda, a distance of 1,896 miles.

F-101B Interceptor

The *Voodoo* had also been considered as a long-range interceptor at various times since its conception. However, it was not until the F-102 program ran into big problems in late 1953 that the Air Force again looked to the F-101. The urgency was ramping up with the disclosure that the Soviets had exploded a thermonuclear "device" in August 1953. With the flight testing of the area-ruled F-102A revealing a top speed of only 825 mph, its role as an effective interceptor was in serious question. The follow-on F-102B (which would become the F-106) had yet to fly, and was not expected to be operational until 1959. The Air Force needed a "back up."

Of the various options, the F-101 was selected to fill the interim role as a two-seat all-weather long-range interceptor. Initially the Wright J67 was chosen to power it—a derivation of the British Bristol *Olympus* 201 with 17,000 pounds of thrust in AB. McDonnell was authorized

to proceed in February 1955 with a Letter of Intent following in March. The official designation "F-101B" occurred in August.

Almost immediately the J67 program was in trouble and, in an effort to avoid any extensive delay, it was decided to go back to the J57, but to employ first the P-53 and then the P-55 version, which had a 24-inch longer AB section making it 900 lb heavier. Moreover, this increased the maximum thrust from 15,000 to 16,000, and then to 16,900 pounds per engine, making it competitive with the proposed J67—and the highest-thrust J57 installed in any aircraft.

While close in appearance to the F-101A, there were several significant structural changes in the F-101B. Among these was the provision for a second crewmember dictated by the workload of the all-weather radar intercept mission, and the installation of an extensive Fire Control System (FCS)—both of which increased the length of the fuselage. These changes required a reduction in the internal fuel capacity to 2,053 gallons and limited the G-force from 7.33 (the Air Force standard) to 6.0. This change also highlights the dynamic relationship of weight and configuration to G-loading: if the weapons bay's rotary armament door ("rotodoor") was in the "MB-1 launch" position then the limit was 5.33 Gs; on the other hand, with no more than 8,200 pounds of internal fuel, no tanks and rotodoor "normal," the limit increased to 6.8 Gs. With external fuel tanks the F-101B was limited to 4.0 Gs for all conditions. Negative Gs were proportionately less.

The F-101B was also heavier by some two tons, requiring the landing gear to be strengthened. The larger tires protruded slightly when retracted and made necessary a small bulge in the gear door covers. The first F-101B (56-232) took flight in March 1957.

Employing the Hughes MG-13 FCS, this version of the aircraft used only air-to-air armament—no guns. ADC's F-101Bs (and the two-seat Fs) were equipped with two MB-1 (later renamed AIR-2A) *Genie* unguided rockets with nuclear warheads as Primary weapons, mounted on the aircraft's rotodoor. In accord with the nuclear "two-man rule," the Radar Intercept Officer (i.e. backseater) enabled the *Genie* and the Pilot launched it.

Secondary weapons were a pair of Hughes *Falcon* missiles, initially the semi-active radar-guided GAR-1D (renamed AIM-4A) or the infrared-homing GAR-2A (renamed AIM-4C); both options were later replaced by the improved GAR-2B (AIM-4D). Thus, the fully loaded F-101B/F interceptor carried two *Genie* unguided rockets fired individually and two Hughes *Falcon* guided missiles ripple-fired as a salvo, enabling three weapon launches per combat sortie.

Sharing the production line with the F-101B was the two-seat trainer F-101F (originally designated the TF-101B). These maintained all of the interceptor capabilities of the B series but had dual flight controls. However, while the back-seater could essentially fly the aircraft throughout a mission, he did not have control of the landing gear, wing flaps, speed brakes, drag chute or afterburners; these were under sole control of the front-seat pilot.

Fifty aircraft underwent extensive testing that exposed several problems related primarily to the integration of the MG-13. The performance of the F-101 was much greater than the aircraft for which it had been designed. A recommendation to replace the MG-13 with the (then) F-102B's prospective MA-1 was rejected because of the anticipated costs. As a final "fix," a redesigned Central Air Data Computer (CADC)

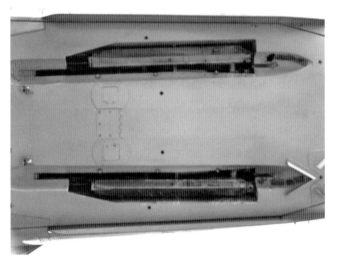

Figure 07-11 The underside of the F-101B/F interceptor showing the Falcon missile bay. USAF Photo.

in the MG-13 resolved most of its initial problems, and successive FCS upgrades added features both to improve basic intercept operation and to add electronic counter-countermeasure (ECCM) improvements to keep pace with the projected ECM threat. As noted with other *Century Series* fighters, the electronics were becoming a more significant aspect of the total "weapons system" environment.

For those *Century Series* interceptors based near the Pinetree Line (along the U.S.-Canadian border), the early years (1959 to the early '60s) involved flying intercepts mostly under Manual GCI control until their sector Semi-Automatic Ground Environment (SAGE) sites became operational. For the 13th FIS flying its new Voodoos around northeastern Montana, restrictions were few. Cruise-climbing was still permissible (which added noticeably to cross-country ranges), and sonic booms—the *original* "sounds of freedom"—were not yet restricted to altitudes above 30,000 feet. Moreover, some intercepts were flown with restricted or even no GCI control to prepare units for operation under degraded air defense conditions.

Jonathan Myer recalls one such mission: "*Back in the early 1960s, after my FIS had been flying its F-101Bs for a while, we were given a mission where our 'targets' would be making a high-altitude dash over Canada to our Montana area of responsibility—and no GCI control would be available; our sole target information would be occasional location plots from our early-warning networks across Canada ... in latitude and longitude. My RIO pulled out his local area map, entered target locations on it as they were reported, and then plotted a course to intercept and gave me a heading. I followed it as he updated our respective positions until within likely detection range of our now-confirmed Mach 1.25 target. He locked on and the target was clearly above our altitude. I'd already 'lit the pipes' in anticipation, so we were supersonic too. A few seconds later, my steering circle shrank at B-time (20 seconds to go), and I started 'up the hill' to center the dot. When I casually cleared us right and left (for safety), I saw another Voodoo a few hundred yards off to my left—converging on 'our' target. With one eye on our 'wingman' and the other on my steering dot, I held down the trigger to get our firing 'X,' then broke hard left over our fellow Voodoo as he broke hard right, under us. Two 'MAs' (for 'Mission(s) Accomplished') ... with next to no control at all!*"

The F-101B was integrated into the SAGE environment (see chapter 2), and interceptors focused more on trying to make SAGE's computerized "tactics" and aircraft performance assumptions work than was comfortable at the time. However, when the

RIO got a solid target lock-on and called "Judy," all was up to the interceptor's fire control and armament system capabilities.

The F-101B/F's MG-13 fire control system (FCS) was designed to launch both *Genie* and *Falcon*s at their optimal points, as determined by the intercept tactics, aircraft performance, and selected weapon range and timing factors. After the RIO locked onto the target, the pilot would depress the control-stick trigger while steering his attack display to "bury the (steering) dot" at weapon launch. If the weapon was a Primary MB-1/AIR-2A, the pilot would then immediately perform a tight escape maneuver to put maximum distance between his interceptor and the anticipated nuclear explosion. For roughly co-altitude intercepts, the breakaway was a max-rate level or (preferably) descending turn, while for snap-up attacks, the pilot would roll the 101 upside-down and pull...at least until the *Genie's* anticipated time-of-flight had elapsed, at which point it was prudent to relax the Gs somewhat to minimize the buffet of the nuclear detonation's shock wave.

If the intercept was being controlled via the SAGE data-link, the pilot could couple the autopilot to the steering dot directions transmitted by his Weapons Director until the RIO completed his lock-on—at which time the steering dot transferred to the MG-13's internal steering directions as before. Jonathan Myer: "*Using all the automated features could prove exciting, especially if the steering dot after lock-on (and now giving three-dimensional corrections) proved 'sensitive.' Although the autopilot kept the aircraft within safe G-limits and no more than 70 degrees of bank, most pilots preferred to 'average out' the steering error before deciding whether to couple to the dot during the last few seconds before weapon launch.*" Both weapons could also be launched manually if necessary, as would be the case if lock-on could not be maintained or the MG-13 was inoperative.

An early 1960s requirement to complete an intercept without being detected by the fighter's own electronic radar emissions led to the installation of an Infrared Search and Track (IRST) subsystem in the nose of all three *Century Series* interceptors (F-101B, F-102 and F-106). The F-101B/F update program, known as *Project Bold Journey* (1963-1966), installed a fixed IRST sensor in place of the retractable refueling probe, with a rear fairing to streamline it. A modification to the autopilot at this time again addressed the pitch-up problem.

Jonathan Myer: "*Besides being a passive 'stealth' system, the IRST operating modes could be used in conjunction with the interceptor radar's modes to optimize target detection and interception—especially at low altitudes, where our pulsed radars were blinded at short ranges by ground clutter. Moreover, it could often 'see'* higher-altitude afterburning aircraft at longer ranges than the radar, rendered defensive chaff 'invisible,' and provided a back-up FCS capability in cases of radar failure or degradation by advanced ECM. While as an optical system it was rarely useable in solid weather (where the radar remained primary), it could still 'see' farther into mist or fog than the human eye. Correlating radar 'blips' with IR 'pings' in Search modes could be a bit tricky, as the angular height of our IR sensor aperture was half the height of our radar's now-'pencil' beam, but the initial IRST's real limitation was its tendency to use up its liquid nitrogen coolant during a single mission. Upgrading to a closed-cycle cooling system (for the F-101B/F and F-106s) rectified the problem and the IRST became as reliable (if not as popular) as our radar from then on.*"

Note too, that the addition of the IRST for air defense intercept aircraft could mitigate the risk of early selection of IR *Falcons* and their subsequent possibility of premature coolant depletion. Even though the IRST operated in the medium-wavelength band (roughly 3 to 5 microns), while the AIM-4 IR missiles used the 1.7 to 2.8-micron short-wavelength band, there was no evidence of operational incompatibility. Thus (absent weather constraints), the aircrew was enabled to acquire their target in an IR (or radar) mode while delaying activation of the IR missiles until much closer to their launch point.

Jonathan Myer: "*Another interesting IRST feature was the ability to set up an "estimated ranging" function. It began by selecting an estimated overtake rate (for the particular intercept) while acquiring the angle-lock onto the target's tailpipe. When the IRST recognized a 13-db increase in IR signal strength, a "range blip" appeared on the scope—representing 'half' the original range; this was known as 'range coincidence.' (The FSC calculation was based on a 12-db or four-fold increase in IR signal strength equating to a halving of the (actual) range—with the '13th' db allowing for atmospheric attenuation of the signal strength. Each successive 'coincidence' represented a further halving of the range to target—with adjustments of the 'blip' range becoming less each time—so that, by weapon launch range, the target would almost certainly be within the weapon's lethal envelope for a manual launch—even if no radar range burn-through had been achieved. In fact, even if the initially estimated overtake rate proved wildly off (as in a maneuvering intercept), the successively smaller range errors with each 13-db 'coincidence' increased range accuracy—down to a zero error if the intercept were to be flown to actual collision with the target! ... Thus said the math; I never put it to the ultimate test.*"

Other features of the several MG-13 upgrades during its lifetime included the addition of more RIO scope

Figure 07-12. The rocket is extended under the belly of the F-101B while the IRST sensor is clearly defined on top of the nose. The complex air intake structure is also visible. USAF Photo.

ranges, a home-on-jam (HOJ) mode to select pursuit steering (in azimuth) to a continuous noise-jamming source, improvements in target discrimination at low levels and against chaff-droppers, and ever-faster tuning speed options for the radar's magnetron (the last of which made it practically foolproof against any known noise jammers of the era).

Jonathan Myer: *"During its life in the Active air defense force, the F-101B/F went through five FCS and armament upgrade 'cycles,' the last two of which (Cycles 4 and 5) were also known as Interceptor Improvement Program (IIP) I and II. For example, the initial installation of the* Century Series *interceptors' IRST subsystems occurred during IIP-I (the Voodoo's Cycle 4); that configuration used a 'Dewar flask' as container for its coolant. Only when 'closed-cycle cooling' replaced the (leaky) Dewar flask equipment during IIP-II (Cycle 5) did the IRST become reliable. It was also during IIP-II that the F-101B (and F-106) fleets got the highly variable-speed magnetron tuning options that could defeat all then-known noise-jamming ECM threats."*

Operationally, the F-101B/Fs were delivered to the 60th Fighter Interceptor Squadron (FIS) at Otis AFB in Massachusetts in January 1959. Eighteen ADC squadrons eventually flew the F101B and F. They were preceded (in the fall of 1958) by deliveries to existing ADC training and test units of the 4756th Air Defense Wing (later the Air Defense Weapons Center—ADWC) at Tyndall AFB, Florida. However, formal Category III operational testing was conducted at Otis AFB, Massachusetts, by the 60th FIS, whose initial pilot checkouts were assisted by *"a handful of guys"* (i.e., experienced single-seat F-101A/C pilots from the 27th TFW at Bergstrom AFB, Texas) *"to give the squadron some core F-101 experience when they received their F-101B's,"* as one of them, Frank Murray, put it.

F-101B Transition Training

George Andre's F-86D unit, the 322nd FCS, was based at Larson AFB in Moses Lake, Washington. They had done very well, received many awards, and were their Air Division's competitors in the 1958 ADC-wide *William Tell Weapons Meet*. Their sister unit at Larson was an F-104A operation that was often grounded.

Andre: *"We had expected to be deactivated, however in late 1958, we were suddenly advised we were moving to Kingsley Field in Klamath Falls Oregon, and would be getting the F-101B. We were among the first four units to get the One-O-Wonder. This was not altogether great news as most of the pilots would have preferred the F-102 since most true fighter pilots would rather fly alone, and in a single engine airplane. Nevertheless, we were happy to get out of 'Moses Hole'* [as it was sometimes un-lovingly called].

"We all had trepidations about this big heavy 2-seater. Our training was accomplished by a mobile ground school along with a cockpit procedures trainer in a trailer. Flight training was done in a dual controlled TF-101B and we had about 2 or 3 former F-101A pilots assigned who would act as our IPs

[Instructor Pilots]. *We soloed rather quickly and began the task of becoming operational. We brought out F-86Ls from Larson* [to remain proficient while the transition took place], *so for a while, we were operating two very different airplanes. Once a pilot started on the 101, he was grounded from further 86 flying.*

"*A MAC test pilot (Don Stuck) came and gave us a pep talk, but all he did was scare us with tales about the pitch-up dangers. I think our first several flights all were with one eye on the airspeed indicator. This is an airplane that could have used an angle-of-attack indicator, much like the 104 or the typical navy airplane.* [This feature was added a few years later.]

"*Another weird thing was to find we could only do one 360 degree roll and then we had to stop and let the plane settle down before rolling again. There was this thing called an inertia roll coupling problem in which continuous rolls would cause the plane to swap ends due to the mass being concentrated in the fuselage.*

"*Another adjustment we had to make was working with the back-seater. In the 86D, we acquired the target on radar, locked on and flew the attack by ourselves (as would be done in the 102 also). Now we had to rely on our radar observers in the back seat for the radar work. Most of them were right out of school and we usually knew more than they did about the job. It was frustrating to have a visual on the target and our RO could not find it on the radar screen. In the 101B, we were relegated to being the driver, although we had the job of skillfully flying the steering commands* [via GCI voice radio, or from the SAGE data-link] *to effect the missile or rocket launch.*

"*Upon solo, we would be given a patch and lapel pin from MAC. Pilots got a One-O-Wonder patch and our ROs got a Scope-Wizard patch.*

"*Nearly all of our tactical training was to employ the MB-1 [Genie] rocket of which we carried two. Our mission profile would usually have us attempt a head-on attack, simulated launch and then fly an escape maneuver to minimize the destructive overpressure to our plane from the nuclear detonation, which was programmed to occur about a mile in front of the target. The Falcons we carried were usually the radar version which steered itself along the reflected radar return from the target. The MB-1 was totally unguided and was simply a ballistic rocket relying on a hell of an explosion to kill the target.*

Figure 07-13 The "One-O-Wonder" patch and a lapel pin were awarded by McDonnell to pilots who soloed the F-101 (left) and the "Scope Wizard" patch to the radar officer (right). USAF Photo.

"*As we became combat ready, we started sitting alert with 2 planes on 5-minute and 2 on 15 or 30-minute status. We were armed with 2 hot MB-1s plus the Falcons.* [In today's] *era we make a giant affair when a nuclear bomb is airborne and some Air Force brass lost their jobs when a weapon was inadvertently transferred, yet in 1959, we were flying all over the Northwest with two nukes aboard. We were short of pilots and I was slated for alert duty all the way to my discharge date. On my last night in the Air Force, I was on 5 minute alert and had two actual scrambles. One was to intercept a lost Flying Tiger Line Constellation coming in from Hawaii. I thought it was a nice way to end my active duty. I would depart the base the next day, heading for the California ANG and a new job flying the F-86H at Van Nuys.*"

Myer adds: "*Unless we were actively preparing for war (as with the Cuban Missile Crisis), our 'hot-five' birds would be armed with the two Falcons only. Their basic mission was to scramble to identify 'bogeys' (unknowns, if/when detected by our GCI and then GCI-fed SAGE Direction Centers) and perform an ID pass to get the type and number of the 'offending' aircraft. No 'nucs' would be necessary or even appropriate for such a mission; moreover, there was always a remote risk of a mishap, or having to recover elsewhere in case of an emergency—per 'Murphy's Law.' Our MB-1s/AIR-2As, were always maintained under tight security, thus remained safely in their storage bunkers, or in our guarded Alert hangars, loaded aboard the alert aircraft in continuous readiness.*"

Andre: "*The 101 was really a hot plane and takeoff acceleration was unbelievable. It was possible to see 400 knots by the departure end of the runway. You had to confirm the nose wheel was straight before releasing brakes as it would head for the boonies immediately if not centered and steering engaged. On one occasion, I had the opportunity to ferry a new Voodoo from the factory in St Louis to a squadron at Oxnard AFB in CA. This was one of the few occasions I flew with two 450 gallon drop tanks and I made it non-stop which was the longest range flight of my career at that point.*"

While the maximum speed was redlined at Mach 1.73, Andre recalls that was "*...easily attainable. Once I was in a 'tail chase' intercept, and as I passed thru about Mach*

1.65, I pulled the throttles back to min burner. After the simulated missile launch (code word 'splash' [i.e., for an actual "kill"]), I noted I was going 1.78! Pretty good for min AB!"

In the summer of 1959, Jonathan Myer's F-86L unit, the 13th FIS, left Sioux City, Iowa, for the new Glasgow Air Force Base (GSG) in northeastern Montana, "...best described as 'miles and miles of horizon . . . unbroken by scenery,' where we teamed up with our RIOs, many of them there ahead of us and waiting. As GSG's runway was still under construction, we transitioned into our Voodoos off its 75-foot-wide taxiway. Our only restriction was 'No formation take-offs or landings'; fortunately, nobody blew a tire. We checked out in rough order of rank: our Commander and Ops Officers brought the first three aircraft back from MacAir's factory in St. Louis and then checked out our three flight commanders. They, in turn checked out their deputies, and so on; three rides apiece to 'solo' (with a senior RIO in the backseat), and then start flying with our RIOs to really learn how to use the '101B as a weapon system. The only 'tech orders' we had at the time were MacAir checklists; the rest we learned for ourselves and from each other.

"As I awaited my turn to check out, I heard how different the Voodoo was going to be from the '86L. We already knew its performance would astound us. We'd seen Don Stuck's movie about the extensive test program to understand 'pitch-up' and how to avoid or recover from it, followed by his flight demonstration of the Voodoo's maneuverability—and we'd been warned that its speed and altitude gauges had significant errors at high subsonic speeds—only becoming accurate above Mach 1. Our squadron's coolest flight commander, Charlie C., was giving a first ride to his flight RIO, Bob S., who relayed the following afterwards: 'Charlie was demonstrating an AB take-off and climb, holding a 20-degree pitch attitude as he was used to in the F-86, while explaining how smoothly the '101 performed.' Passing 15,000 feet, Bob asked him how to tell when they went supersonic. Charlie explained that the Mach needle would jump a tenth of a Mach number as it passed Mach 1 and the altimeter would suddenly wind up two or three thousand feet. 'Oh. Like it just did?' said Bob. 'I'll be damned!' said Charlie."

Myer: "I remember little of my own checkout, except that it was exciting and uneventful—probably due to my 160 hours flying the F-86L, where I'd smoothed out my formation flying and qualified in all aspects of our NORAD air defense mission: D-I-I-D, Detect, Identify, Intercept, and (if necessary) Destroy any invading aircraft.

"Another 'rite of passage' came when we went to Fairchild AFB, Washington, in early 1960 to get fitted for partial-pressure suits. They were specially tailored to fit over thin two-piece long-johns and had capstans that ran from wrists up to shoulders and down to ankles, with a hook-up to our '101's pressurization system so that, if cabin pressure were lost or we had to bail out at very high altitude, they would expand and draw the suit evenly tight, thereby keeping our blood from 'boiling' if above 63,000 feet. For demonstration in the altitude chamber, our small group watched a balloon expand as the chamber reduced pressure (and we got colder), simulating ever-higher altitudes as shown on a cabin altimeter. But, it wasn't until the water in a coke bottle began boiling furiously as we 'passed' 63,000 feet that we recognized the enormity of our situation. Suddenly I realized that my groin felt exceedingly cold, as the suit was looser in that area to enable movement.... Fortunately, all was normal after we 'returned to earth....'

"Back at the squadron we'd fly P-suit missions every three months or so, and I realized that: (1) a single P-suit flight in a day was as tiring as three regular flights; (2) their initial pressure all over the body from the ground up had the effect of reducing our normal 1-G sensation to 1/2-G as if we were nosing over, so we had to fly more by our instruments, especially at night; and (3) our over-size P-suit helmets restricted head movement to the sides while cockpit lights at night were reflected on the visor—all combining to give a sense of unreality while flying our intercept missions. A few short years later, when I was then in the 98th FIS at Suffolk County Air Base, New York, our suits were recalled for good. They had been costly to buy and fit, costly to maintain, tiring to wear, and with our training altitudes now restricted to 50,000 feet we'd never really need them.... They were not missed."

F-101C Fighter-Bomber

With unsurpassed speed and range for its time, the F-101 was an obvious candidate for tactical nuclear delivery from bases in Europe and England. To improve on this capability, McDonnell made a series of modifications to production numbers 51 through 98, which were designated as the F-101C. The internal structure was strengthened to accommodate the fighter-bomber role and it was thus 500 pounds heavier, and could again pull up to 7.33 Gs.

With its unrefueled range of 1,700 miles at a cruise speed of Mach .9 with external stores, the Soviets would have a new set of problems. Use of the AB was extended to 15 minutes. Its first flight was 21 August 1957, and it became operational with the 27th Fighter-Bomber Wing at Bergstrom AFB, Texas.

On 1 July 1958, the 27th FBW was redesignated the 27th Tactical Fighter Wing (TFW). Later that year the 27th TFW transferred its aircraft and personnel to bases in the UK—RAF Bentwaters and RAF Woodbridge, just a few miles apart in eastern England—to assume their nuclear strike mission in defense of Western Europe.

This operational deployment of the USAF's combined F-101A and C fighter-bomber force was to the 81st TFW of the United States Air Forces in Europe (USAFE), the U.S. air component of NATO. It lasted from the fall of 1958 to November 1965. The *Voodoos* replaced F-84F *Thunderstreaks*, and were in turn replaced by F-4 *Phantom IIs* some seven years later.

RAF Bentwaters hosted the 81st TFW's Hq and two of its three Tactical Fighter Squadrons, the 91st and 92nd TFSs; RAF Woodbridge, its sister base, was home to the 78th TFS. The Wing's primary mission was to have a number of aircraft on "Victor" Alert—"cocked and ready" for nuclear strike missions into Eastern Europe "24/7" (to use the modern term).

Dudley Potter transferred into the 81st TFW's 92nd TFS after 4-1/2 years flying the F-101B interceptor with the 13th FIS: *"I arrived at RAF Bentwaters, UK, on 25 May 1964. After a quick checkout in the single-seat version of the F-101, I was deployed to Wheelus Air Base, Libya, for bombing and gunnery qualification prior to becoming combat-ready. We were required to qualify in strafing and low- and high-drag bombing. This was accomplished by using a practice bomb dispenser on the centerline position of the aircraft. We had three 20-mm cannons in the nose of the '101.*

"Upon return to the UK, I passed a check ride and assumed combat-ready status. I then began to stand 'Victor' Alert. This entailed an alert status with a tactical nuclear weapon on the centerline position. The mission was low-level nuclear strike....

"This was my duty until October 1965, when the 81st TFW went off alert status to transition to the F-4C. We ferried the entire wing of F-101s to Air National Guard units in Kentucky, Arkansas, and Nevada. The aircraft were to be modified for service as RF-101s. My last flight in an F-101 was to ferry one of the Guard's aircraft to Little Rock AFB, Arkansas, thus ending my six years of combat-ready status in the F-101."

Although the LABS technique was still the primary method of nuclear delivery during the 1950s, the Low Angle Drogue Delivery (LADD) system, introduced in 1960, was soon favored by the F-101 nuclear strike pilots. It provided for a parachute-retarded method that, according to Bob Hanson, a five-year F-101A/C veteran, allowed the pilot *"to break away short of the target and escape the AAA [anti-aircraft artillery] and blast from his own weapon"* while the nuclear bomb was delayed in its arrival and subsequent detonation. *"We did away with the LABS delivery, and targeted solely with the LADD, or Lay Down deliveries. The LABS made you a beautiful target near the top of the maneuver (around 14,000 ft.), and limited the escape parameters —Not that it would matter."*

Although the F-101A/Cs, once launched, would fly to their assigned targets at high subsonic speed and at low level to avoid enemy defenses, this basic mission profile would leave most of the fighters without enough fuel to recover safely after ordnance release. All the pilots were thus prepared for a one-time one-way mission—after which they'd return as far as their remaining fuel would permit and then eject, hide for some days, and finally E&E (evade and escape) towards the European coast in the hope of pick-up by a friendly vessel.

Dudley went on to say, emphasizing the grim nature of this operation: *"These were one-way missions into East Germany and Poland, for the most part. Most would not have enough fuel to get to the Baltic, so ejection over the great Polish forest was planned, dig a hole, cover it with the parachute and dirt, crawl in and wait ten days for the fallout to subside, then hike to the Baltic, where a Sub (ours hopefully) would pick you up! Comforting.... By the way, our 81st Wing had 12 aircraft on 15-minute status and we sat 24-hour alert. With our ground mapping radar, we could fly our mission all 24 hours and deliver in all kinds of weather."*

RF-101A/C Reconnaissance

The speed and size of the F-101 made it obvious that the Air Force would consider it for reconnaissance, as was proposed in January 1953. The workhorse Republic RF-84F Thunderflash was high subsonic, but the promise of the F-101 would certainly increase that capability. Thus, the 16th and 17th F-101A airframes (54-149 and 54-150) were converted to photographic reconnaissance as the YRF-101A (note the emergence of the "Y" prefix). (Also, the Air Force's decision to field RF-101s also served to cancel parallel proposals for an RF-104 and RF-105.) The F-101A's nose was redesigned without any cannon to house four low-altitude cameras—both frame and strip film for vertical and oblique orientation. Two high-altitude cameras were situated behind the cockpit, reducing the internal fuel load to 2250 gallons.

The first flight occurred on 30 June 1955, and 35 were built as the RF-101A and delivered to the 17th Tactical Reconnaissance Squadron (TRS) at Shaw AFB in South Carolina by mid-1957. When production switched to the C series, 166 more were completed as RF-101Cs. At this time, the USAF decided to have the last 75 F-101C fighters built as RF-101Cs for tactical reconnaissance, although it retained the capability to carry a single Mk.7 nuke on the centerline store station "just in case."

To demonstrate the new high-speed capability, four RF-101As set new transcontinental speed records between California and New Jersey on 27 November 1957. Perhaps not coincidentally, this record was designed to take the edge off the recent launching of the Soviet's new Sputnik satellites that had the world in a spin. Refueled by KC-135s, two landed at McGuire AFB while the other two returned to March AFB.

First Lieutenant Gustav Klatt set the new eastbound record of 3 hours 7 minutes (average speed of 781.7 mph). Captain Robert Sweet set a westbound record of 3 hours 36 minutes, 33 seconds (average speed of 677.7 mph). He also set a new Los Angeles-New York round trip record of 6 hours 46 minutes 36 seconds (average speed of 721.85 mph). This was followed in December by an RF-101A that flew from Tachikawa AFB in Japan to Hickam AFB in Hawaii in 6 hours 3 minutes to set a new point-to-point record. With three drop-tanks configured, the total fuel was now at 3,467 gallons.

Many of the RF-101A/C TAC Recce Squadrons that were deployed to Europe under the 66th Tactical Reconnaissance Wing (TRW) flew out of bases in France and Germany until 1966 (when France withdrew from the military side of NATO), after which all USAFE RF-101 assets were consolidated at RAF Upper Heyford in Oxfordshire, UK, by September of that year.

Other TRSs had deployments to Taiwan, Japan and the Philippines before being stationed at Kadena Air Base, Okinawa (15th TRS), and Misawa Air Base, Japan (45th TRS), during the 1960s. From there and from Tan Son Nhut Air Base in the Republic of Vietnam (RVN; aka South Vietnam) and different air bases in Thailand, both units provided photo-recce support over South Vietnam and the rest of the Southeast Asia theater (SEA) from late-1960 through late-1970. (These operations are summarized in the later section on "Vietnam.")

An airborne reconnaissance unit consisted not only of the aircraft, but also their supporting infrastructure. The cameras needed to be loaded with film and maintained. After each flight, the film was transferred to a "photo laboratory" to be developed. It was then taken to "plotting," where each frame was related to its position on a map, after which the "photo interpreters" determined the information that was on the film. Finally, the photos were ready to be sent to the command and general staff for action to be taken. (This process, like so many others, would be improved and accelerated during the SEA War.)

During its active USAF service, the RF-101C received two major upgrades. First, following the Cuban Missile Crisis [see below] and in light of its major role in Europe, its inherent nuclear weapon option was refined and bomb delivery became part of its pilots' training at Wheelus Air Base in Libya.

Secondly, in late 1964, its initial manual camera operation was automated (and most original cameras replaced) via "Modification 1181." This upgrade gave it improved high-speed low-altitude and night capabilities, along with in-flight processing, cassette ejection, and an increase in sensor reliability due to

Figure 07-14. A flight of four RF-101s air refueling over the UK, and it's Neal Mishler's "turn at the tap" in No. 1475, while the others wait patiently. Neal Mishler Photo.

Figure 07-15
RF-101C clearly shows two of the four camera positions. Note the internal structure of the air intakes. USAF Photo.

automatic exposure control. The centerpiece of the modification was the Hycon KS-72A framing camera being developed for the RF-4C *Phantom* II. Once initial problems were resolved, this upgrade further enabled the RF-101C to perform with distinction in combat. As Doug Gordon wrote in *Voodoo Eyes*, "*There is no doubt that the European experience paid dividends for the pilots who went on to serve in SE Asia.*"

RF-101 pilot Don Karges: "*For most of us a European tour was where we really learned how to fly and navigate. The lack of airspace restrictions, bad weather, constantly being intercepted by our own friendly forces (UK, French, Canadian, German, U.S., etc.) and the soberness of sitting alert with a nuclear weapon only 30 minutes or so from enemy airspace made confident, proficient pilots of us all. The training and experience did, in fact, lead to a high level of proficiency in SE Asia. All of us who had tours in Europe were able to fly combat missions immediately on arrival in SEA. There was no time for checkout flights etc. You arrived in SEA as a combat qualified crew member and were expected to perform immediately.*"

Initial plans to transfer RF-101Cs to the Air National Guard in the mid-1960s had to be postponed to continue meeting tactical recce needs (and replenish losses) in the Southeast Asia theater (see below). However, as more RF-4Cs deployed to SEA, RF-101C units were progressively replaced starting in the late 1960s; the 45th TRS was the last to leave in November 1970. Once back in the U.S., RF-101Cs continued to serve in both Active and Guard units until the last one was retired in 1979.

RF-101G, H, and RF-101B

The increasing need for combat and contingency photo-reconnaissance support led to conversions of some other F-101 series to RFs, as they were successively replaced by newer aircraft. In 1965/66, the 81st TFW traded its F-101A/C series for the F-4C *Phantom*. First, 18 F-101A and 31 F-101C series were extensively modified to reconnaissance configuration and given the designations RF-101G and RF-101H, respectively. The G's modification was superior to the original RF-101A's capability, and a few RF-101As were upgraded to the RF-101G standard. The RF-101H differed from the RF-101G only by virtue of its parent F-101C's stronger airframe; the same USAF "*Dash-1*" Technical Order covered both series.

The first deliveries to ANG recce units occurred in 1966 and continued into 1967. They were federalized in response to the 1968 Pueblo Crisis (in which North Korea captured the intelligence gathering ship *Pueblo* and incarcerated its 83-man crew in late January 1968). Elements of the Arkansas 154th TRS, Kentucky 165th TRS, and Nevada 192nd TRS flew their RF-101G/H series from bases in Japan and Korea. They compiled impressive flying and photo records supporting the theater reconnaissance operations.

After returning home, both subtypes served with all three units until it was decided to station all the RF-101Gs with the Arkansas ANG and the H series with the Kentucky ANG, to supplement the RF-101A and C series returning from Southeast Asia. In addition to the RF-101A/C, Nevada eventually used the RF-101B, which was modified from returning Canadian F-101B/F interceptors in the early 1970s.

Bob Hanson: "*These machines were our remaining 101s from Bentwaters and Woodbridge when we went to the F-4Cs. We'd lost roughly a squadron's worth—18 101s in the 6+ years of operations. Quite a few accidents, but repairs were made. Some VERY extensive! I believe we only lost 7 pilots, 8 if you count Lonnie Moore, but he was* [in pre-operational] *Test. Sad day to see the beautiful nose on the A/C, turn into a camera lens!*"

Figure 07-16.
The detail revealed in these Cuban Missile Crises photos highlights the skill of the photo interpreters to define effectively what is contained in the picture. USAF Photo.

These RF-101 fleets were supplemented by RF-101Cs from the active force. They served only a relatively short time with the Guard and were retired in 1972, traded for RF-4Cs now augmenting the ANG recce force.

Meanwhile, when Canada returned its first CF-101s to the U.S. (under the 1970-71 Peace Wings exchange), 22 of those CF-101Bs, plus a former ADC F-101B, were converted to RF-101Bs. Their armament and fire control systems were replaced by a reconnaissance package that included three KS-87B cameras and two AXQ-2 television cameras, while a TV viewfinder control indicator was added to the pilot's cockpit.

The ex-Canadian 22 RF-101Bs were transferred to the 192nd TRS (Nevada ANG), which sent its RF-101Hs to the 165th TRS (Kentucky ANG), which in turn sent its RF-101Gs to the 154th TRS (Arkansas ANG)—thus "rationalizing" their units' RF-101 configurations. However, the RF-101Bs (like the Gs and Hs before them) proved costly to operate and were replaced by RF-4Cs in 1975.

The last RF-101A and RF-101C were both retired from military service in 1979.

Cuban Missile Crisis

While the traditional fighter was often modified to perform in the photo intelligence role, larger and sometimes more specialized aircraft were sometimes needed to accommodate the bulky cameras and other "listening" devices that became part of the trade. Throughout the 1950s, the United States sent a wide variety of aircraft deep into the Soviet Union to perform strategic reconnaissance. These included the Boeing RB-47 and the high-flying U-2. Several RB-47s (and a number of other clandestine aircraft) were shot down during the 1950s, but the obligatory U.S. cover story of "navigation error" always tended to defuse Soviet allegations.

Two realizations came together in the skies over the Soviet Union on 1 May 1960. The first was that reconnaissance was a critical asset—the United States continued to risk provoking the Soviets by repeatedly flying the U-2 spy plane deep into their territory. The second was that the surface-to-air missile had come of age with the successful downing of a U-2 on that date.

President Eisenhower, in owning up to the U-2 missions during the crises that ensued, emphasized the need for being able to assess the capabilities of our Cold War enemy. For many in America, and others around the world, this was the first open recognition of the importance the U.S. placed on this form of intelligence. However, reconnaissance flights 30 months later would bring the world to the brink of a nuclear holocaust.

Following the failed attempt to overthrow Cuban dictator Fidel Castro in the Bay of Pigs debacle of April 1961, the U.S. closely monitored the Soviet presence in Cuba. The U-2 first brought to light the deployment of offensive weapons in Cuba in August 1962 when Soviet IL-28 bombers were noted by U.S. photo interpreters. Then, an over-flight on 14 October revealed the presence of six Soviet R-12 (SS-4)medium range missiles sites being prepared. Surrounding these sites were SA-2 surface-to-air missiles and antiaircraft batteries—apparently to protect them.

There followed intensive reconnaissance at low level (to avoid the SA-2 threat) by RF-101A/C aircraft of the 363rd Tactical Reconnaissance Wing starting on 23 October 1962. High-flying U-2s and Navy RF-8A Crusaders were also a part of the intelligence-gathering effort.

U.S. President John F. Kennedy announced, during a nationally televised speech on the evening of 22 October 1962, that photos from American reconnaissance planes had determined that the Soviets were putting long-range offensive surface-to-surface missiles—with nuclear warheads—into Cuba. The Soviets vehemently denied the allegation, but the overwhelming evidence that was supplied by the recce flights left them no credibility. The U.S. placed a naval blockade around Cuba that was, for political reasons, called a "quarantine"—all ships bound for that island were subject to search.

While these forces concentrated on Cuba's new missile installations and Soviet naval activity, the rest of the U.S. combat forces went on heightened alert and prepared for war. Jonathan Myer describes his unit's homeland air defense preparations: "*In the Air Force, while our bombers reinforced their around-the-clock airborne alert flights, fighters deployed to and near Florida, in preparation for tactical strikes while our air defense units sent interceptors to emergency fields, for both survival and readiness should Soviet bombers attack. I remember our 13th FIS aircrews listening tensely to President Kennedy's October 22nd speech, as some of us prepared to deploy from Glasgow AFB, Montana, to the municipal airport at Billings. We flew there fully loaded, in pairs and with our AIR-2A nucs and IR missiles ready for war, while maintenance and supplies followed by truck. Landing on Billings' unprepared runway*

Figure 07-17. One of many photo-recon pictures taken during the Cuban Missile Crisis of October 1962. The shadow in the lower right corner leaves no doubt what aircraft took the picture or the low altitude. USAF Photo.

MRBM LAUNCH SITE 1
SAN CRISTOBAL, CUBA
23 OCTOBER 1962

Figure 07-18.
Dismantling of each
MRBM site was
carefully documented
by the RF-101s.
USAF Photo.

incurred a few cut tires, while our makeshift alert area was cordoned off and a 24-hour phone alert set up in a hangar. Our Ops Officer and flight commanders took turns by that phone while the rest of us shared patrols around our aircraft, sometimes chasing away (with drawn .38 revolvers) local citizens who crossed the wire 'to see the jets.' Fortunately, no Soviet escalation ensued and a couple of weeks later we returned to Glasgow to resume regular alert and training."

In parallel, Bob Hanson reports on his F-101C nuclear strike mission preparations across the Atlantic Ocean at RAF Bentwaters with the 81st TFW and its F-101 nuclear strike fighters: "*...I was on alert the day the Cuban Missile crisis balloon went up. It was around 0900, and we went to RED cockpit alert until nightfall, and then reverted to 15 min. But, initially we really thought we were going! And for the next week or more the whole wing was loaded and ready to launch! It was serious!*"

Jonathan Myer concludes: "*...It was ten years before I got a first look—from Robert Kennedy's 'Thirteen Days: A Memoir of the Cuban Missile Crisis'—at what had been going on, beyond our local horizons and above our pay grades, those tense 24-hour days.*"

Compounding the problem was the shooting down of Air Force Major Rudolf Anderson during a U-2 flight on 27 October. The showdown that followed over the next few weeks resulted in the withdrawal of the Soviet missiles—with the then-secret agreement that the U.S. would remove its Jupiter IRBM missiles from Turkey. This removal process from Cuba was confirmed by subsequent overflights. The point was again made that, both militarily and politically, aerial intelligence was of the highest national importance. One of the most significant military confrontations in modern history had been uncovered by airborne reconnaissance.

During the period from 26 October to 15 November, RF-101s flew 82 "combat" missions with no losses—Major Anderson's U-2 was the only casualty. However, the flights revealed several weaknesses in the overall reconnaissance capability of the US—which were even then being discovered halfway around the world.

Vietnam

Of all the roles that aircraft may play in combat, none is as understated as reconnaissance. Flying into enemy territory unarmed is a challenge, but to do it almost daily in an environment that not only presents surface–to–air missiles, but radar-guided anti-aircraft and small arms fire, requires great courage. This was the setting in Vietnam. The RF-101 had actually been employed in Southeast Asia (SEA) since late 1960, when Communist insurgency reached new and alarming levels of aggression.

Using the newly "liberated" country of North Vietnam as a base, the Soviets and Communist Chinese sought to destabilize no fewer than four countries: Laos, Thailand, Cambodia, and South Vietnam. With the defeat of the French in Vietnam in 1954 (followed that July by the Geneva Convention, which partitioned the country into North and South at the 17th parallel) and the ousting of British and Dutch influence in the region, newly independent nations (to include India) walked a fine line. They needed the major Western powers, particularly the United States, to help them remain "free" of Communist domination—yet they did not want to antagonize the Russians or the Red Chinese by getting "too close" to America.

However, while many of these new governments were "friendly" towards the United States, they were also quite corrupt and were little better for their people than the Europeans who had been driven out. Thus, the Communists often had strong local support within these countries. This prevailing situation created a difficult political environment in which the U.S. then attempted to use "measured" military power to keep the Communists at bay.

Initially augmenting a weary Lockheed RT-33, a few PACAF RF-101s deployed to the area and quickly became the mainstay for providing aerial intelligence to U.S. political and military planners with respect to infiltration of Communist forces into these countries. At first these missions did not meet much opposition, although the various political "no fly" zones, altitude restrictions, and weather created a challenge for the pilots and mission planners.

However, compounding this situation was inadequate navigation support. In the era before GPS, TACAN had become the primary U.S. military navigation system, and initially only two facilities were available in SEA—hence, dead-reckoning (the use of heading, time and ground speed) was the primary means of routing, with an occasional ADF (Automatic Direction Finder beacon) or radar fix available. A pilot who violated the airspace of one of the less friendly countries (to include Cambodia and Burma—and of course North Vietnam and China) could be subject to a court martial, as well as death from the antiaircraft weapons of that nation. Both low- and high-altitude missions were flown, from 200 feet above ground level (AGL) to 40,000 feet. Occasional damage to the RF-101s was inflicted by Communist ground forces as they began to bring in flak guns of up to 37mm.

These recce missions brought a new reality to the profession that had been lacking in the ten years prior. In an effort to maintain a high level of proficiency, many of the NATO and SEATO nations engaged in periodic "competitions" among their military. These were designed to evaluate the effectiveness of their respective air forces. Now, in SEA, real targets, hidden by jungles masked by seasonal weather and protected by real antagonists, were taxing the abilities of the photo-intelligence community. The various altitudes and speeds flown also challenged the camera technology and new developments were undertaken.

The RF-101 and the close-knit community of pilots that flew them were uniquely qualified to address this reality. The high speed and long range of the RF-101, coupled with the variety of cameras it carried, provided the optimum platform. Tactics to help the pilot survive the run into the target area were developed. These included a variety of "pop-up" techniques to permit ingress and egress patterns that would increase his chances of survival, as well as the occasional use of a second aircraft to provide another pair of eyes for the pilot making the run.

By early 1964, the *"One-O-Wonders"* (as they were sometimes called) were essentially flying full combat missions in an as-yet undeclared war. It was clear to the photo-interpreters that the North Vietnamese were stepping up military action against the South when the infamous and somewhat mysterious torpedo boat attacks against U.S. destroyers operating in the Gulf of Tonkin took place in August 1964. The congressionally approved retaliation (*Gulf of Tonkin Resolution*) opened the war into the North—yet with strict political limitations on military action.

RF-101 missions now flying into North Vietnam saw an immediate escalation on the part of the North with the appearance of MiG-15 and MiG-17 aircraft at the Phuc Yen air base that was "off limits" to U.S. air strikes. The NVA would flex this new muscle against the U.S. for the first time on 4 April 1965, when MiGs shot down two F-105s. While the *Voodoo* could easily out accelerate and outrun the older subsonic MiG-15 and MiG-17, the Mach-2 capable MiG-21 usually had the advantage—yet only one RF-101 was lost to a MiG-21 during the war. The unarmed RF-101s had only one option: to break off their photo run when attacked.

As the war continued to escalate, what made the situation frustrating from the U.S. military viewpoint was that virtually every target had to be approved by President Lyndon Johnson or his Secretary of Defense, Robert McNamara. Although President Truman had established the "limited war" precedent during the Korean campaign, his dictates were comparatively simple—no over flights of Manchuria—where the Chinese stockpiled the supplies for the war and sheltered the MiGs that attacked the United Nations forces. Now, 15 years later, not only were the targets themselves subject to presidential approval, but the

Figure 07-19. An RF-101 in camouflage colors, which highlighted the bitter combat that recce pilots encountered over Southeast Asia. USAF Photo.

types of weapons used required prior authorization. Thus, even after the U.S. military was given approval to attack targets in the North, there were many military objectives that were considered "politically out-of-bounds."

Virtually every target in the North had to be identified by photo-reconnaissance and, following bombing strikes, had to have bomb damage assessment (BDA) flights to determine the effectiveness of the attack. Thus, recce pilots saw extensive combat. The SAM threat was effective above 3,000 feet AGL, but to fly lower exposed the pilot to flak and small arms fire. From January 1965 to June of that year, the number of AAA (or "Triple-A") batteries more than doubled in North Vietnam. After recognizing that some areas of the North were extremely dangerous, the missions that RF-101 pilots (and other aircraft crews) flew into these areas were referred to as "counters." After flying 100 counters, the pilot was eligible for rotation back to the States.

For those who were shot down, the *Voodoo*'s ejection seat was designed to operate at a minimum 50-foot altitude with a low speed of 120 knots to a maximum velocity of 525 knots (zero-zero was not an option). A small rocket that fired for less than a second propelled the seat and allowed it to clear the tall tail. The pilot typically wore a backpack parachute, and the ejection mechanism

Figure 07-20. The cockpit of a well-used RF-101C at the Air Force Museum in Dayton, Ohio. AF Museum Photo.

separated him from the seat at a predetermined time interval (within a second or so) that anticipated the apogee of the ejection profile. The seat separation also deployed the chute unless a barometric device sensed that the pilot was above 15,000 feet—in which case it was delayed until that altitude.

The effectiveness of radar-tracking anti-aircraft guns and the anticipation that Soviet SAM missiles would soon be employed caused the U.S. to begin using active Electronic Countermeasures (ECM).

Under-wing QRC-160 pods carried by the RF-101s attempted to jam the radar frequencies and provide erroneous return signals to confuse the tracking computers. However, the effectiveness of these early ECM measures was not easy to determine, and their drag and G limitations caused the pods to quickly fall out of favor with the pilots. Compounding this was the secrecy of the electronics in the pods, which inhibited their "black boxes" from getting effective preventive and corrective maintenance.

At the time of the first SAM-inflicted casualty in July 1965, all NVN sites were located in politically "protected areas." The SAM itself was relatively easy to spot at launch, since it left a very visible smoke trail during its early solid-fuel boost phase and quickly acquired the moniker of "flying telephone poles," which they resembled. Also, the RF-101's RHAW (radar homing and warning) receiver alerted the pilot as to what type of radar was tracking him (Early Warning, SAM, Airborne, or AAA), and a special tone in his headset provided the differentiation. So, although the RF-101s could not out-run the SAMs (which approached at Mach 3), they could outmaneuver them—if seen. With their high speed and small control surface areas (which gave them a very high wing loading), the SAMs could not make rapid changes in direction.

Thus, if the pilot saw the incoming missile early enough (or was warned by a wingman or headset tone of its approach from the rear), he could wait until the last possible moment to execute an abrupt "SAM break" that he hoped could not be countered within the SAM's modest 3-G turning limit. In addition, once the missile had passed the plane, there was no possibility that it could turn for a second attempt. As George Andre noted, *"If you could see it you could evade it. The most dangerous place to be was right on top of an overcast layer of cloud where the SAM could pop out and hit you."*

Of course, this required nerves of steel and an understanding that the missile's tracking radar, when it determined that the missile was making its closest pass to the target, would send a signal to detonate its warhead. Even a near miss could bring down a plane, but with the robust construction of the RF-101 and the durability of its J57 engines, many pilots were able to bring their

Figure 07-21. An RF-101 casts a shadow over a missing span of the My Duc highway bridge in North Vietnam, April 22, 1965. USAF Photo.

battle-damaged aircraft back. It was estimated that the ECM and evasive maneuvers required the SAM sites to fire 60 missiles to down one aircraft. But this number fluctuated dramatically during the war, as various countermeasures were employed by each side.

Even as another McDonnell aircraft, the RF-4C *Phantom II*, began to replace the RF-101 in SEA, the *Voodoo* still had its advantages where photo-reconnaissance was concerned. In his *Tactical Reconnaissance in the Cold War: 1945 to Korea, Cuba, Vietnam and the Iron Curtain*, Doug Gordon notes, as one example: "*The KA-1 camera carried by the RF-101 was a significant factor in its remaining in SE Asia when the RF-4C Phantom squadrons had been fully operational for two years. The large format photographs produced much sharper images even at low level and the RF-101 was the preferred photo recce vehicle for certain targets. The Phantom, though a much more sophisticated aircraft in many respects simply could not provide satisfactory photography in certain circumstances. Commencing in August, 1967 the RF-101s were tasked with regular KA-1 photography of the 'electronic barrier' a system of sensors which had been set up along the Ho Chi Minh Trail and in Laos to detect the passage of vehicles or people.*"

The RF-101 was finally withdrawn from SEA in November 1970. During the preceding eight years, 35 aircraft had been lost along with 13 pilots.

Foreign Service—Nationalist China

The Republic of China (also known as Nationalist China since 1912) lost the Chinese mainland to the People's Republic of China (PRC) during the Chinese Civil War in 1949 and withdrew to the island of Taiwan (Formosa), off the mainland's east coast. The PRC (Communist China) has continued to claim Taiwan as its province, while the latter prepared to defend itself against periodic PRC aggression and the threat of invasion.

When the PRC again shelled the offshore Nationalist-controlled islands of Quemoy and Matsu in 1958, the USAF sent a composite strike force to Taipei Air Base on Taiwan to support the Chinese Nationalist Air Force (CNAF) if necessary. In October 1959, the USAF followed up with a then-secret Operation *Boom Town*, whereby eight RF-101As were "acquired" by Nationalist China and select CNAF pilots were secretly trained in their use by 15th TRS pilots at Kadena AB on Okinawa, then began flying their RF-101As both around Taiwan and over the mainland. This operation did not make any friends with the Red Chinese, who had long been the object of aerial reconnaissance by the Nationalists. The PRC claimed to have shot down two of these planes in the years that followed.

Meanwhile, for the next 20-odd years the "ChiNat" RF-101As conducted both routine photo-recce flights and covert low-level sorties over the Chinese mainland, their already-impressive range and endurance augmented by refuelings from USAF KB-50s. In 1962, the 45th TRS discreetly lent four of their RF-101Cs to the Nationalist Chinese to fill in while some of the RF-101As underwent needed maintenance. The RF-101s' reconnaissance products greatly improved the level of intelligence for both Nationalist China

Figure 07-22 Originally USAF F-101B s/n 59-0546 until its transfer to the then-Royal Canadian Air Force (RCAF) under the "*Queens Row*" program of 1961-62, this photograph shows it in its Canadian markings as CF-101B s/n 17546. Orv Malcomsom, RCAF Photo.

Figure 07-23. This four-ship formation of Canadian *Voodoos* flown on 18 June 1984 represented a farewell to their CF-101B/F aircraft by squadrons 409, 416, 425 and 414 (410 had lost its CF-101s in 1982), and a welcome to their CF-18A/B replacements. Orv Malcomson, RCAF Photo.

and the U.S. with respect to their major threat in the Far East. The last CNAF flight took place in the late-1970s, following which the surviving RF-101As were returned to the U.S.—except for one retained for display outside the Taipei airport museum.

Foreign Service—Canada

The year 1959 was also notable because the Canadians cancelled work on their Mach 2+ fighter—the Avro CF-105 Arrow. This was a very controversial decision which involved several issues. First, in 1957 Canada had joined the North American Air Defense Command (NORAD), which extended the defense-in-depth needed to meet a possible Soviet long-range bomber attack against the North American continent. Accordingly, the U.S. offered participation in its new SAGE computerized command and control system, plus acquisition of new BOMARC unmanned interceptor missiles, whose SAGE-controlled high-altitude Mach 2.5+ flight profile would enable quick response to the emerging Soviet jet bomber threat. Initially, the BOMARC-A (then IM-99A) with conventional warheads was ordered.

Meanwhile, the CF-105 had already experienced several engine and armament changes, followed by

cancellation of its advanced fire-control system—all of which incurred delays and increased program costs. Although the Arrow had already reached 1.98 Mach in an early test flight, the government concluded that it could afford either the SAGE plus BOMARC acquisitions or the CF-105 program, but not both. With no foreign sales in sight to share costs and risk, the CF-105 program was abruptly cancelled on 20 February 1959—a day that became known as "Black Friday" in the Canadian aviation industry.

To replace the CF-105, the Canadians bought 66 F-101B/F *Voodoo*s (then operational with the USAF) as their manned interceptor. They were delivered from July 1961 through May 1962 under Operation *Queens Row*. The 56 F-101Bs were designated "CF-101B," while the ten two-seat F series became "CF-101F"; all could carry two MB-1/AIR-2A *Genie*s and two AIM-4 IR-seeker missiles as their combat load. The Royal Canadian Air Force (RCAF) all-weather fighter squadrons (AW(F) Sqns) receiving these 66 CF-101s were, in order of delivery: the No. 425 Conversion Training Squadron (which became an AW(F) Sqn when its CF-101 aircrew training work was done), followed by AW(F) Sqns 410, 416, 409, 414, and 425 (redesignated). During the early

1960s, three of these units moved to locations further northeast for better defense against likely Soviet bomber attack routes, while one was deactivated. Thus, four AW(F) *Voodoo* units provided continuous defense in depth for the next 20 years.

Meanwhile, in 1963 Canada's new government changed to the BOMARC-B (now CIM-10B), thereby giving both its manned and unmanned interceptor forces nuclear capabilities, until its two BOMARC squadrons were deactivated in 1972.

In 1970-71, the now-Canadian Armed Forces (CAF)'s 46 surviving CF-101Bs and CF-101Fs were "traded" to the USAF for 56 modernized F-101Bs and 10 F-101Fs under Operation *Peace Wings*. These *Voodoo*s, while older airframes than those "traded back" to the U.S., had already been upgraded with IRST infrared sensors and the latest fire control system improvements during their active USAF service under ADC/ADCOM.

From the early 1960s through the next 20+ years, at least four Canadian all-weather fighter squadrons flew North American air defense missions, until their CF-101 interceptors were replaced by McDonnell Douglas CF-18A/Bs from 1982 through 1984.

The last two CF-101s flying were with the (reactivated) 414 Electronic Warfare (EW) Sqn at North Bay, Ontario, from 1982 to 1987. The last USAF F-101B (58-0300), flying with the 2nd Fighter Interceptor Training Squadron at Tyndall AFB, Florida, was actually the first (and only) *Voodoo* equipped with an electronic countermeasures (ECM) suite, the same as that carried by ADC/ADCOM's EB-57E ECM target fleet. It was retired on 21 September 1982, whereupon it was leased to Canada and flown to North Bay three days later, on September 24th. There it was assigned to 414 EW Sqn (101067), where it was outfitted with standard Canadian equipment, unofficially dubbed "EF-101B," painted black, and popularly known as the "*Electric Jet.*"

As it flew only ECM missions with an Electronic Warfare Officer (EWO) in the back seat, averaging 50 sorties a year, a 1971 *Peace Wings* F-101F was used to maintain the *Voodoo* pilots' flying proficiency.

During its 4-1/2 years as an EF-101B, the "*Electric Jet,*" supported by its CF-101F trainer companion, provided a challenging ECM aggressor-target—first to Canada's remaining CF-101 units and, as they retired in 1984, to their CF-18A/B replacements. On 7 April 1987 EF-101B 101067 was returned to the United States, where it was eventually displayed in an air museum near Minneapolis. On 19 April, with false antennas added to simulate the "Electric Jet," CF-101F 101006 flew the world's last *Voodoo* flight to Canadian Forces Base (CFB) Chatham, New Brunswick, for eventual display at CFB Cornwallis, Nova Scotia.

Figure 07-24. The USAF's last F-101B, equipped with an EB-57E jamming suite, was leased to Canada's 414 EW Squadron, where (as "EF-101B" s/n 101067) it provided ECM training to CF-101s and then CF-18s until returned to the U.S. on 7 April 1987. Orv Malcomson, RCAF Photo.

Variants

Table 07-01.

McDonnell F-101 *Voodoo* Variations			
Type	Configuration/ Role	Notes	No. Built
F-101A	1-seat Fighter	1957-65 w/USAF TFSs (27 to ANG; 18 as RF-101Gs 1966-72)	77
RF-101A	1-seat	Photo-Recce 1967-71 w/USAF TRSs (8 to CNAF)	35
		Oct-59 - 1979) (1 to ANG 1966)	
F-101C	1-seat Fighter Bomber	1957-66 w/USAF TFSs (To ANG 1965-75) (31	47
		as RF-101Hs (1966-72)	
RF-101C	1-seat Photo-Recce	1957-79 w/USAF TRSs (1969-75 w/ ANG)	166
F-101B	2-seat Interceptor	1959-71 w/USAF (1969-82 w/ANG) (1961-84 w/CAF)	479
		(22 CAF to ANG as RF-101Bs 1971-75)	
F-101F	2-Seat Trainer/ Interceptor	To Apr-71 w/USAF (ADC/ADCOM FISs)	79
		(1969-82 w/ANG) (1961-84 w/RCAF, CAF)††	
		Totals	883

Figure 07-25 As this F-101B, (from the Portland OR ANG's 123rd FIS) flies past Mt. Hood, it presents an imposing picture. Note the longer AB extensions and the IRST sensor on the top of the nose. Bill McDonald, USAF Photo.

Operation *Queens Row:* 56 F-101Bs and 10 F-101Fs delivered to then-RCAF (later CAF) July 1961 - May 1962; redesignated CF-101B and CF-101F, respectively. They shared NORAD's air defense mission with ADC/ADCOM for the next ten years.

Operation *Boom Town:* 8 RF-101As delivered to the Chinese Nationalist Air Force (CNAF; aka Republic of China Air Force / ROCAF), Oct 1959. Two were presumed shot down over the People's Republic of China (PRC). The last was retired in 1979.

Operation *Peace Wings:* 46 surviving CF-101Bs plus CF-101Fs were returned to USAF, and 56 fully upgraded F-101Bs and 10 F-101Fs were delivered to now-CAF 1970 - 71; again redesignated CF-101B & F, respectively, and operated into the 1980s.

Phase Out

While the F-101 never served in the role for which it had been designed—that of a long-range penetration fighter—it performed quite successfully as a nuclear strike fighter-bomber, a tactical photo-reconnaissance aircraft (in combat), and an air-to-air nuclear rocket- and missile-carrying interceptor.

The F-101A/C fighter-bombers met operational needs from 1957 into the mid-1960s. Most of them initially deployed to France and West Germany before being consolidated under the 81st Tactical Fighter Wing at RAF Bentwaters and Woodbridge in the UK during the height of the Cold War. Part of that force was on continuous nuclear alert, ready for quick-reaction sorties against targets in most of Eastern Europe.

Figure 07-26. Four F-101B *Voodoos* in close formation. Note the dark high temperature titanium structure protecting the tail. The weapon bay under the cockpit is also visible. USAF Photo.

RF-101A/C TRSs were deployed to both Europe and the Far East, beginning in 1958. The 67th Wing based its TRSs in Okinawa and Japan, from which increasing numbers of aircraft were sent during the 1960s to bases in Thailand and South Vietnam to fly photo-recce missions primarily over South Vietnam, Laos and (initially) North Vietnam. Increasingly lethal AAA, SAM and MiG threats limited their operations to south of the 17th parallel, while they too were progressively replaced by RF-4Cs. Nevertheless, as the only *Voodoo* type to fly continual combat missions during the Southeast Asia War, the RF-101 provided essential photo-intelligence throughout the 1960s.

Meanwhile, back in the U.S., *Century Series* interceptor coverage saw predominantly F-101 and F-106 FISs interleaved across its northern border and along its east and west coasts throughout the 1960s. Active F-102 FISs steadily transferred their aircraft to ANG units, which were themselves reequipped a few years later with F-101s and F-106s. These changes were driven by the twin pressures of a projected strategic threat change from long-range Soviet bombers to predominantly intercontinental ballistic missiles (ICBMs), plus increased budgetary constraints arising from growing SEA War demands.

The Air Force began phasing out its F-101B/F FISs in 1968, with many aircraft progressively transferred to Air National Guard FISs (from 1969 to 1971, where they flew air defense until the early 1980s), while others went to Canada during 1970 and '71, where they flew as CF-101s for another dozen years. The last ADCOM FISs, the 60th and 62nd, were deactivated in April 1971. A few F-101Bs continued with the 2nd Fighter Interceptor Training Squadron at Tyndall AFB in Florida until the last, a specially configured F-101B s/n 58-0300, was retired on 21 September 1982— and was immediately leased to Canada, where it provided ECM training for Canadian interceptors for another 4-1/2 years.

The net result was that, as ADCOM's F-101 interceptor units progressively transferred their aircraft to the Air Guard and Canada, the U.S. *Voodoo*s dedicated to North American air defense, which had numbered 16 to 18 squadrons from 1960 through 1967, declined to about a dozen from 1969 through 1975, and then to zero in the early 1980s. By that time both U.S. and Canadian interceptor forces had been modernized with new aircraft, while their NORAD mission evolved from active air defense in depth against a bomber threat to primarily peripheral air sovereignty sorties.

The ANG units started phasing down in 1976, with the 178th FIS being the first to get F-4s (in 1977) and the 111th FIS being the last to yield its F-101s (in 1983).

McDonnell F-101 Voodoo

Configurations, Characteristics, and Performance Data	GENERAL PURPOSE FORCES				AIR DEFENSE FORCES	
	F-101A 1-seat Fighter	RF-101A 1-seat Photo-Recce	F-101C 1-seat Fighter Bomber	RF-101C 1-seat Photo-Recce	F-101B 2-seat Interceptor	F-101F 2-Seat Trainer/Interceptor
Length (ft in)	67' 5"	69' 4"	67' 6"	69' 4"	71' 1"	
Wing Span (ft in)	39' 8"					
Height (ft in)	18' 0"					
Wing Area (sq ft)	368 sq ft					
Engine (2 x J57:)	J57-P-13		J57-P-13		J57-P-55#	J57-P-55
– Military Power (lb)	10,200		10,200		10,700	
– Max A/B Power (lb)	15,000		15,000		16,900	
Max G (combat weight)	6.33	6.33	7.33	7.33	6.8^	
First Flight	9/29/1954	6/30/1955	8/21/1957	7/12/1957	3/27/1957	8/21/1957
First Delivery (for op'ns)	5/2/1957	May-57	1957	Sep-58	1/5/1959	Jan-59
Last Delivery	11/21/1957	Oct-57	Jun-58	3/31/59	3/24/1961	Mar-61
Production Total	77	35	47	166	479	79
Service w/USAF units. (Most then sent to ANG. A few F-101As to CNAF; many 'B/Fs to RCAF/CAF)	1957-65 w/ USAF TFSs (27 to ANG; 18 as RF-101Gs 1966-72)	1967-71 w/ USAF TRSs (8 to CNAF Oct-59 - 1979) (1 to ANG 1966)	1957-66 w/ USAF TFSs (To ANG 1965-75) (31 as RF-101Hs 1966-72)	1957-79 w/USAF TRSs (1969-75 w/ANG)	1959-71 w/USAF (69-82 w/ANG) (61-84 w/CAF) (22 CAF to ANG as RF-101Bs 71-75)	To Apr-71 w/USAF (ADC/ADCOM FISs)(69-82 w/ ANG)(61-84 w/ RCAF, CAF)
Empty Weight (lb)	24,970	25,335	26,277	26,136	28,970ª	
Gross Weight (lb)	48,120	47,331	48,908	48,133	45,664∞	
Combat Weight (lb)	39,495	39,495	39,495	39,495	40,853	
Max TO Weight (lb)	50,000	50,000	51,000	51,000	52,400§	52,400
Internal Fuel (gal)	2341	2250	2250	2250	2053	
Max Fuel (gal)	3467	3150	3150	3150	2953	
(w/Drop Tanks) (gal)	3 DTs	2 or 3 DT	2 x 450 DT	2 x 450 DT	2 x 450 DT±	
Max Speed, 35Kft (mph)	1009	1012	1012	1012	1134	
(Mach no.)	M 1.539	M 1.544	M 1.544	M 1.544	M 1.73•	
Initial climb (ft/min)	44,100	46,600	45,000	45,500	49,200	
Service Ceiling (ft)	55,800	55,800	55,100	55,300	58,400	
Combat Ceiling (ft)	49,450	51,540	51,540	51,540	51,000	
Normal Range (stat mi)	1900	1100	1315	1715	1520	
Max Range/DT (stat mi)	2925	2195	2125	2145	1930	
Key Mission Avionics	APS-54 Rdr, MA-7 FCS & MA-2 LABS	(Manual camera operation)	MA-2 LABS/ LADD Bombing System	Mod 1181 for auto-cntrl of cams. Kept KA-1; added: KS-72&A, KA-56A (Nuc wpn option)	MG-13 FCS (IIP-2/Cycle 5): Int Radar w/ECCM + IRST subsys. Data Link (TDDL) for T-4 Tac pgm	
Latest Mission Payload and/or Armament	4 x 20mm M-39 Nuc options: Mk-28, 7, 43, 57	Cameras: 1 KA-1, 3 KA-2s, 1 KA-18	Nuc bomb options: MK-28 or Mk-43 ≤ 4 x 20mm M38		2 x AIR-2A "Genies" 2 x AIM-4D IR "Falcons"	
Converted RF-101s	RF-101G		RF-101H		RF-101B	
Key Mission Equipment	(Various cam suite options)		(Various camera suite options)		3 KS-87B cas & 2 AXQ-2 TV cam's. TV viewfinder cntl indic on pilot's panel	

Source: T.O. 1F-101B-1 FLIGHT MANUAL: USAF Series F-101B and F-101F A/C – Issued 1 Jun 66, update thru Chge 11, 15 Jun 70

Table 07-02. McDonnell F-101 Voodoo: Series.

Figure 08-01. The Consolidated Vultee XP-81 was the first attempt at creating a turboprop fighter. U.S. Army Photo.

Origin of Consolidated Vultee

Consolidated Vultee Aircraft, as the company was known toward the end of World War II, had taken a circuitous path to its corporate structure. Its origin was the Gallaudet Engineering Company of Connecticut—formed by Edson Gallaudet in 1908. Reuben Fleet, a former military pilot during the First War, who organized the first U.S. Air Mail flight in 1918, became Gallaudet's general manager in 1923. A disagreement among the board of directors of the ailing business prompted Fleet to purchase the Gallaudet contracts in 1923. He formed the Consolidated Aircraft Company with the amalgamation of other entities to include the Thomas-Morse Airplane Company. Its first real product was a design acquired from General Motors' Dayton-Wright subsidiary—the PT-1 primary trainer.

In 1928, Consolidated (being low bidder) manufactured the prototype of a "large" flying boat designed by Navy Captain Dick Richardson and Isaac Machlin "Mac" Laddon, who subsequently became Consolidated's general manager. Although Consolidated did not win the contract for subsequent production of the XPY-1, they did build fourteen of an improved version for civilian use, where it was known as the *Commodore*. The plane found a home with the fledgling NYRBA (New York Rio Buenos Aires) airline (a predecessor of Pan Am) that formed in 1929 to open service to South America.

Consolidated moved out of Buffalo, New York, to San Diego in 1935. Its success with the follow-on flying boat projects, the P2Y Ranger and then XP3Y-1 (better known as the PBY *Catalina*), gave it a more firm financial foundation.

While this was taking place, a young and very dynamic Gerard Frebairn Vultee was working his way through the mainstream of aviation companies that made Southern California the cradle of aeronautical innovation during this period. Moving from Douglas Aircraft to Lockheed, "Jerry" Vultee had made a name for himself and had acquired significant depth and breadth in aeronautical engineering principles. By the early 1930s Vultee had several designs he wanted to produce and, along with Vance Breese (a prominent test pilot of the time), formed the Airplane Development

Corporation. They acquired the backing of Errett Lobban Cord (of automobile fame) who had formed the Aviation Company (Avco)—and the Vultee Aircraft Division was created.

The relatively high-performance single-engine 8-place Vultee V-1 and the V-1A provided some financial security for the young company. Unfortunately, the 38-year-old Vultee and his wife died when he flew into a mountain near Flagstaff, Arizona, during a snowstorm in January 1938.

Despite Vultee's death the company continued, producing the YA-19 for the Army and a series of training planes that included the notable BT-13 and BT-15. It became a separate corporation in 1939. By 1943, Vultee had made an effort to expand by producing the XP-54 fighter. Unfortunately the design, which offered a pressurized cockpit and a downward "ejection seat," did not progress any further than two prototypes because of weight growth and the unavailability of its original power plant.

In 1941, Reuben Fleet decided to retire from Consolidated and the company merged with Vultee—although completion of the deal did not take place until March 1943. This union was logical, in that Consolidated was producing large multi-engine aircraft, such as the Army Air Force's B-24 and the Navy's PBY. However, their efforts to enter the fighter realm had never met with much success. During the 1930s they built a series of two-place fighters that were lackluster in performance. With the inclusion of Vultee, Consolidated Vultee now had more expertise in the fighter realm.

The earliest fighter to be developed following the merger was the XP-81—an attempt to create the first turbo-prop powered airplane. However, the XT31 engine, on which it trusted its fate, would never produce the promised horsepower. This was the status of Consolidated Vultee as the war drew to a close.

Figure 08-03. Lippisch's DM delta wing never took flight, but the prototype was shipped to the United States for analysis and wind tunnel testing. U.S. Army Photo.

Futuristic Designs

For aircraft manufacturers in the United States, the period following World War II was uncertain. The drawdown was difficult for the aircraft industry, as defense plants across the country closed and hundreds of thousands of workers were out of a job. On the engineering side significant cuts were also experienced.

Nevertheless, virtually all of these companies had some level of optimism. The advent of the jet engine, coupled with the revelation of the amazing array of advanced German designs that became known, stimulated the imagination. Many of the designers were a product of the exciting days of the 1930s, when futuristic artwork (that had little basis in aerodynamic reality) appeared in aviation magazines. Without any hard evidence, a variety of swept-wings, flying wings and triangular "delta" platforms began to appear on the drawing boards. The term "*delta*" was an obvious descriptor taken from the Greek letter Δ.

The flying wing, in its many permutations, had taken form between the World Wars. In Germany, with Alexander Lippisch and the Horton brothers, in America with Jack Northrop, and in Russia with Boris Cheranovsky, attempts to get the most from the only truly essential part of an airplane—its wing—caused a great deal of innovation. Even the NACA had done a cursory study in the 1930s. Because much of the experimentation was undertaken with very little funding, many of the early creations took the form of gliders.

The desperate designs that took shape in the death throes of the Third Reich were evaluated in America following the close of hostilities, and several of those who had participated in their engineering were interviewed. Some, such as Lippisch, came to the United States at

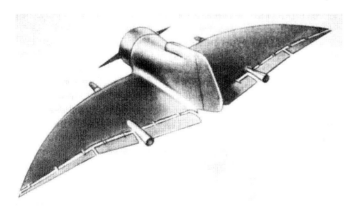

Figure 08-02. Boris Cheranovsky's BICh-17, designed in 1936, would have used a radial engine had it ever been built. PD.

Figure 08-04. Convair's first proposal for a "ducted rocket" interceptor looked very stylish, but hid a confused power plant package beneath its clean lines. Convair Photo.

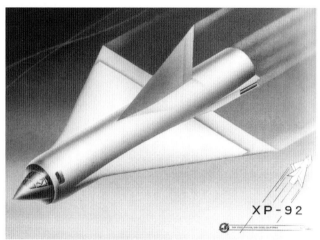

Figure 08-05. The XP-92 interceptor as it appeared in its second iteration using a delta wing configuration. Convair Photo.

the end of the war and could be "contracted" for their ideas. Lippisch's wartime designs included the P13a, DM-1, and the Messerschmitt Me-163. When Convair learned that Lippisch was available, they arranged for him to consult with their design staff. Work by Jones at NACA and preliminary wind tunnel testing gave strong indications of the possible benefits of the swept-wing and the promise of the delta planform.

American manufacturers were not alone in their desire to explore radically different shapes in hopes of achieving an aeronautical breakthrough. Several countries moved quickly to exploit the intellectual property of the German aeronautical industry. The British, French, Russians, and even the Swedes would all make efforts to determine if these new shapes held any promise.

Birth of the XF-92

The Army Air Forces (as it was then known) circulated many Requests for Proposals (RFPs) in an effort to upgrade both bombers and fighters into the realm of the jet age prior to the end of WWII. There was a lot of competition between the major aircraft companies, and the desire to stand out from the competition was (and is) a major marketing consideration—Consolidated was no exception.

Consolidated Vultee Aircraft, which was becoming known as *Convair*, submitted an initial point-defense interceptor proposal in October 1945. It used a 35-degree swept-wing and a V-tail. A novel "ducted rocket" power plant consisted of a set of 16 small (50 pounds of thrust) liquid-fuel rocket engines embedded within the combustion chamber of a ramjet. These would provide a "heated environment" into which fuel would be sprayed to create a ramjet-like "pressure wave" to produce thrust.

Four 1,200-pound thrust rocket engines were mounted at the tail around the periphery of the ramjet exhaust. These would provide the initial energy to get the fighter airborne and the necessary airflow through the ram-tube to allow the action-reaction process to begin. Finally, a 1,560-pound thrust Westinghouse XJ30 jet engine was to be used for the return to base. Having a very short range, it would have been deployed in the "point defense" role, much like the German Me 163.

The proposal was accepted by the Army in April 1946 as project MX-813 (MX being a War Department designation of the times for *material experimental*) and funding provided for a full-scale mockup, a structural test article, and two prototypes—termed XP-92. The chief engineer for the project was C.R.

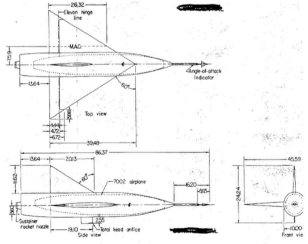

Figure 1.- Three-view drawing of the ⅛-scale MX-813 rocket-powered flight model; all dimen in inches. Consolidated Vultee 7002 airplane is sketched in for comparison.

Figure 08-06. This diagram is from an NACA report on the MX-813. The outlines of the Consolidated Vultee 7002 are shown as dotted lines. (Note the crossed-out classification at the time was CONFIDENTIAL.) NACA Illustration.

"Jack" Irvine, with Adolph Burstein as the assistant chief engineer of the San Diego Division. Ralph H. Shick was the chief of aerodynamic research and Thomas Hemphill was a project engineer of the design team. However, the configuration that made its way to the mockup stage was significantly different from the proposal. Displaying the influence of German design concepts, the delta wing appeared and the cockpit became mounted in a "shock cone" located in the center of the engine inlet.

Because the aircraft involved two very new and untried technologies, the Army agreed to allow Convair to separate the engine development from the airframe in September 1946. This proved fortunate, as the "ducted rocket" concept was abandoned in 1948 as being too expensive and development of the turbojet was progressing at a reasonable pace—thus an Allison J33 turbojet would be the only source of power.

The delta provided two important aspects: it presented a 60-degree sweep to delay the formation of the sonic shock wave—compressibility—and, because of its long chord at the wing root, it allowed the thickness of the wing to be reduced while still permitting good structural integrity.

Convair began design work that would culminate in what was termed a "flying mock-up"—a somewhat ambiguous term. The MX-813 project has been variously identified over the years as the Model 115 (Convair's internal designation) and as the Model 7002 (the latter was the internal model for the XF-92A), because much of the NACA test data referenced drawings with that number.

While the delta wing survived the mockup inspection by the Air Force, the cockpit was deemed unacceptable and was moved back to a more traditional position on top of the fuselage. It was also decided that the current design did not appear to be worth pursuing as an interceptor, but that the airframe should be completed for use as a "proof-of-concept" delta wing demonstrator. The objective was to determine the basic flight characteristics of the delta—both at low speeds and in the high-subsonic region. Thus, the XP-92 interceptor died but the one-of-a-kind "flying mockup" would continue as the XP-92A.

Many shortcuts and cost savings were achieved in building this unique aircraft by using existing parts from proven aircraft. These components included the main landing gear (North American FJ-1), nose gear (Bell P-63), canopy (YP-81), and hydraulics (P-80) as the "flying mockup" proceeded to completion in October 1947. It was immediately shipped to the new NACA "40 by 80" wind tunnel at Ames Aeronautical Laboratory in Sunnyvale, California, for a month of tests. (The term "40 by 80" referenced the wind tunnel's 40-foot by 80-foot test section, which allowed full-scale aircraft to be tested. These tests confirmed the validity of subscale tests and engineering analysis.)

The XP-92A was shipped back to San Diego in January 1948, where the J33-A-21 was installed and complete ground tests of all its systems were accomplished. It was then trucked to Muroc AFB, where the first taxi tests were performed in May. It was noted that the large vertical fin area made taxiing in crosswinds in excess of 30 mph difficult.

Without the traditional horizontal stabilizer on the empennage, the XF-92A employed a single set of control surfaces to provide for two of the three axes of control. Hinged to the trailing edge of the delta wing, the "elevons" (as they were named) provided the function of the elevator when used together for pitch control. When used differentially, they acted as ailerons to provide for roll control—thus the contraction of the two words into one—*elevon*.

Because it was unencumbered with operational requirements, such as guns or armor plating, the XF-92A weighed only 8,500-pounds empty and 14,600-pounds at gross weight.

Figure 08-07. The XF-92A as it appeared in natural aluminum finish for initial tests. USAF Photo.

Figure 08-08. Prior to supersonic wind tunnel capability, rocket boosted models were used. The Deacon rocket provided 6,000 pounds of thrust for 3.1 seconds and was 6-inches in diameter. NACA Photo.

Convair's premier test pilot, Ellis Dent "Sam" Shannon, learned to fly in 1929 as an Air Corps cadet. He had spent three years in China helping to train a viable Chinese Air Force long before Claire Chennault arrived. He had worked as a test pilot for Martin and had flown virtually all their big flying boat creations. He took over the flight test operations at Consolidated in 1943 and established a high level of professionalism. However, flight test of the XF-92A was Shannon's first experience with a jet fighter (although he had tested the hybrid XP-81).

It was while exploring the high-speed taxi characteristics on 9 June 1948 that Shannon made an "unofficial" flight of about 2 miles at an altitude of 15 feet above the runway at Muroc. He elected to continue the short flight as he cautiously explored the control responses. These he observed were unacceptable, as the plane exhibited "*rapid lateral and longitudinal oscillations.*"

A series of changes were made to the aircraft and the engine was replaced with a J33-A-23, which provided slightly more power using water-alcohol injection. Shannon was very cautious about this new wing design and elected to make two more low hops as the engineers tweaked the control system.

The first official flight of a true delta took place on 18 September 1948. After several flights, he determined that it was almost impossible to stall the plane. High angles of attack simply caused the plane to descend at extremely high rates while the airspeed remained at 80 mph indicated. Recognizing these drag characteristics, he elected to use high approach speeds to allow full control authority—and to avoid any unwelcome surprises.

Six months of cautious testing resulted in 47 flights of the XF-92A, with but 20.5 hours flown between Shannon and another of Convair's test pilots, William "Bill" Martin. This effectively completed the manufacturer's analysis and the plane was turned over to the Air Force in October 1949, with Major Charles "Chuck" Yeager and Major Frank "Pete" Everest assigned as test pilots.

In September and October 1948, NACA conducted a series of tests using scale models of the configuration with the cockpit located within the engine inlet and propelled by solid fuel Nike-Deacon rocket boosters. The stubby booster accelerated the model to Mach 1.4 and 40,000 feet, where a smaller rocket motor within the model held that speed constant for the few seconds during which the control surfaces were moved and their effectiveness noted. This was a common method of test before supersonic wind tunnels were available. It is interesting to note that these tests were made *after* the first XF-92A prototype had already flown.

Of his flights in the XF-92A, Yeager comments in his autobiography (Yeager/Janos, 1985, 159): "...*Colonel Boyd assigned me the testing of the XF-92. The old man* [Colonel Boyd] *raised hell with Convair because their own test work proceeded so slowly. Their chief test pilot* [Shannon] *had flown the plane for about a year, but was so spooked by the XF-92's supersensitive handling characteristics that he refused to take-off if the wind was blowing at more than ten miles an hour. He had only had it out to .85 Mach and landed it no slower than 170 mph. The Air Force yanked it away from Convair and gave it to me shortly after my supersonic flight.*"

Yeager's unabashed style of remembrance is a trademark that sets even his thought patterns apart from many of these early test pilots:

"*The controls were the first to be hydraulically operated* [the P-80 used hydraulics for ailerons only], *so light there was hardly any feel. My comment after flying in it for the first time was that it would be easy to handle if the stick were 18 feet long. It was a tricky airplane to fly, but on only the second flight I got it out to 1.05 Mach, and coming in, I decided to see how slow I could land it, and kept pulling up the nose until it was pointing at a forty-five degree angle of attack. I was amazed and landed at a speed of only 67 mph, more than 100 mph slower than Convair's pilot—a good example of how experience in high performance aircraft pays off. I had hundreds of hours more flying time in jet fighters than he did.*"

Yeager, not known for his modesty, doesn't mention that he used Shannon's 170-mph approach speed, but held off the touchdown by applying continued backpressure to the elevons a few feet above the runway.

Everest observed (Aviation History Magazine, 1998, Website): "*Unfortunately, the XF-92 was built for wind tunnel studies only. There was an argument among the engineers–some felt that it could never fly. So Convair, to make it fly, stuck an engine in it, and we started flying it. It wasn't a very stable airplane because they didn't attempt in those days to run stability tests on it, per se.*

"*Then Convair decided it wanted to get the XF-92 to go supersonic. Since it didn't have an afterburner on it, we dove it like you would an F-86 and other early jets to break the sound barrier. But, we just couldn't get it to go supersonic.*" Note Yeager's previous comment about getting it up to Mach 1.05. Memories are tricky.

Initial Air Force tests were completed on 28 December 1949, and the plane returned to Convair in San Diego for installation of the afterburner. It was during this 14-month hiatus that the XF-92A received its all-white paint scheme. Although Convair had predicted significant gains in performance, the plane was still subsonic in level flight when it returned to flight status in July 1951.

Everest continues: "*Convair then took it back to the factory and put an afterburner on it. We then were able to dive it supersonic. There was another argument that's still going on between the pilots and engineers. The engineers figured the XF-92 was going supersonic in level flight. But we pilots said it couldn't have, because we never saw any indication on the Mach meter or saw the airspeed indicator jump. Normally, you get a reading on your instruments when you go supersonic.*

"*One of the deficiencies of the XF-92 was that it had only one flight-control system–a single hydraulic*

Figure 08-09. Convair XF-92A following the change to all white finish and installation of the afterburner to the J33, which made the tail appear unusually long. USAF Photo.

flight-control system. One of the last flights made in that aircraft was by me. I took off from Rogers Dry Lake and shortly after the takeoff, the master caution warning light came on. I looked down and saw I was losing the flight control system's hydraulic pressure. I then turned around to land on the lake bed, and the controls froze just as I touched down. We stopped flying that bird. We had done everything with it we had really wanted to, and felt there wasn't any sense in taking a chance on losing both pilot and plane in further testing."

Nevertheless, the lone XF-92A was still useful for giving new test pilots (and some old hands as well) a "feel" for something different. Thus, it remained in the stable of test aircraft at Edwards until 14 October 1953. On that date, Scott Crossfield was flying a test of wing fences. During his landing the nose gear collapsed. The plane was not badly damaged until a recovery crane dropped it; as repair would now be uneconomical, it was decided to retire it. Crossfield recalled, *"Nobody wanted to fly the XF-92. There was no lineup of pilots for that airplane. It was a miserable flying beast."* During its five-year life the XF-92A flew 118 flights for a total of 62 hours. It now resides in the National Museum of the U.S. Air Force.

Some pictures of the XF-92A (before the addition of the AB) show it in a striking green/blue paint job. Hollywood had talked the Air Force into using some airborne footage of the plane to be portrayed as a Soviet MiG-23. That designation was in large print on the tail, lest any moviegoers not be able to identify the bad guys. Unfortunately the release of the picture, *Jet Pilot* (with John Wayne as the star), was delayed by several years, and by then the scenes with the "MiG-23" were cut.

1954 Interceptor and SAGE
As the first generation of all-weather, jet-powered interceptors was becoming operational in 1949 (the F-86D, F-94 and F-89), the Air Force looked to the next level of performance. It recognized that the complexity of the problem demanded a more managed approach—thus was born the concept of the "weapons system". In the case of the all-weather follow-on to the first-generation fighters it was labeled "*The 1954 Interceptor*"—the target year for its intended operational date. However, its official designation was WS-201A, and it included not only the aircraft and its engine, but the missile it would carry and the fire-control system. WS-201A would be the first U.S. fighter designed from the start without guns—it would use missiles.

With respect to the electronics, the Hughes Aircraft Company was selected in July 1950 to develop the Fire Control System—Project MX-1179. It was not coincidental that Hughes had recently been chosen to develop an air-to-air guided missile—Project MX-904 (the *Falcon*). Thus the two components, obviously tied together operationally, would be developed concurrently by the same company.

The WS-201A airframe was defined as project MX-1554, and an RFP in June 1950 saw all the major aircraft companies submitting their designs. By July 1951 the "final three" (Republic, Convair and Lockheed) were awarded contracts for mock-ups. Lockheed, however, had already set its eyes on a "light weight" fighter towards which their chief designer, Clarence "Kelly" Johnson, was moving. Johnson was unsure of the "weapons system" concept, as he recognized that many of the critical elements of WS-201A would be outside his direct area to influence. Moreover, the winner of the MX-1554 contract would have all the headaches of system integration. Lockheed elected to withdraw to concentrate its "Skunk Works" on what would become the first Mach 2 fighter—the F-104.

Republic, on the other hand, under the guidance of Alexander Kartveli, wanted to leapfrog the Mach 1.5 interceptor and move to a Mach 3 design that would become the XF-103. The Air Force recognized that the concept would be unable to compete for an operational date of 1954. However, they decided to encourage Republic by authorizing a contract for continued study to be known as WS-204A—the XF-103. Therefore, Convair became the sole contender and was awarded a contract in August 1951 for WS-201A—which would spawn the F-102.

As the various elements of WS-201A came into focus, the magnitude of the electronic monitoring and control problem became apparent. The F-102 was the first of the *Century Series* designed to use the SAGE system as described in chapter 2. While IBM was building a complete production facility for the SAGE computer, work proceeded on the F-102 fighter.

Developing the F-102
Convair determined that the XF-92's delta planform would be the basic configuration. However, to provide for the large onboard radar in the nose that would acquire the target for the final intercept, the air intakes were moved to the sides of the fuselage beneath the cockpit. Unlike its

Figure 08-10. The missile bay of the Convair F-102 with both forward and aft launchers extended. USAF Photo.

two-seat all-weather predecessors (F-89 and F-94), the F-102 would be flown by a single pilot/radar operator (as with the F-86D). It was believed that the plane would fly most of the mission as directed by the SAGE system and autopilot—relieving the pilot of many tasks and allowing him to oversee the radar intercept functions. It should also be noted that from the pilot's perspective, the idea of being a *"chauffeur for a missile platform"* was not in keeping with the mystique of the fighter jock's perception of himself.

Convair was awarded the contract in August 1951, but by December it was obvious that the engine selected, the 10,000-pound thrust Wright J67, was behind its own development schedule. The J67 was actually a British Bristol-Siddeley *Olympus* engine that Wright was to build under license. Thus, the first of many costly changes and delays began to plague the program.

The Westinghouse J40 of 7,500 pounds thrust was selected as an interim replacement for the J67, but this was a short-lived choice. The Pratt & Whitney J57 of 10,000-pounds thrust held much promise and a change was made to that engine. This proved a good alternative, since the J40 experienced its own set of engineering problems and never materialized. However, as a result, five months were lost on the F-102 development schedule—partly from slippage in the Hughes MG-3 Fire Control System.

The MG-3 aboard the F-102 weighed 1,700 pounds and occupied 28 cu ft. The electronics consisted of more than 100 pluggable units for quick

diagnostic replacement through a set of fast-opening access doors. Beneath the large radome in the nose was housed the powerful radar antenna.

Two different weapons were initially defined for the F-102. The first was an extendable "tray" of 24 2.75-inch FFAR unguided fin-stabilized air-to-air rockets similar to those used in the F-89, F-94, and F-86D. Although used as the primary armament on those aircraft, on the F-102 the FFARs were considered a backup to the high-tech but questionable "guided missiles." This set of missiles was a complement of six GAR-1 semi-active radar homing (SARH) *Falcon*s paired in a three-segment internal weapons bay. The bay doors opened rapidly and just long enough for the missiles to be moved out into the slipstream and fired before closing automatically. The FFAR "tray" arrangement was later changed to house the FFAR rockets in the doors of the *Falcon* bays.

Like the XF-92A, the F-102 had elevons to control both pitch and roll. There would be no provision for flaps to provide for slower take-off and landing speeds, but the big delta wing area of 695 square feet, coupled with the "cuffed" leading edge, allowed for reasonable low speed operations.

By the time the design was frozen, it was realized that the target date of 1954 was not going to be met for the original specification. The Air Force decided to proceed with a version of lesser capability designated as the F-102A, while the more advanced version would be the F-102B. Working within the Cook-Craigie plan of procurement, the initial build

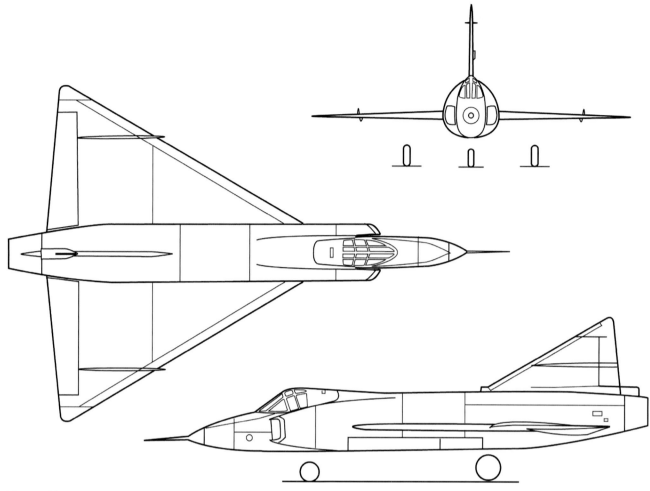

Figure 08-11. The YF-102 exhibited the clean lines of the classic delta, but a major defect in aerodynamic design was lurking. USAF Photo.

of ten YF-102 prototypes and the first 32 F-102A aircraft would use production tooling.

The full-scale mockup was completed and approved by the Air Force with relatively few changes. The most prominent of these was the requirement to carry external stores in the form of drop tanks and possible future ordnance that might not be accommodated in the planned internal weapons bay. However, all of the previous problems and requested changes would soon pale in comparison to the revelation that came from the wind tunnel in the first months of 1953.

Area Rule

Tests with scale models showed rather conclusively that the transonic drag generated by the current F-102 wing/fuselage configuration would be significant, and that the plane would not reach its expected Mach 1.3

Figure 08-12. The Sears-Haack body shape is the aerodynamic configuration with the least theoretical "wave drag." Two independent researchers, Wolfgang Haack (1941) and William Sears (1947), determined this configuration. PD

specification, and would not even exceed the speed of sound in level flight. Earlier indications from NACA that this issue would occur had been ignored by Convair.

A young engineer at NACA, Richard Whitcomb, had been probing the generation of transonic drag (Mach .75 to 1.2) for several years at their Langley facility. He discovered an important aspect of the Sears-Haack body shape. This contour (determined decades earlier) provided the optimum form for supersonic penetration to minimize wave drag.

Whitcomb realized that the entire structure, not just the fuselage, entered into the Sears-Haack equation. Thus, the cross-sectional area of wings, cockpit, and tail (and any other "perturbations" on the plane) had to be considered to achieve the least drag. With respect to the F-102, the almost unchanging barrel shape of the fuselage coupled

Figure 08-13. Consider the similarity of an early XF-92 wind tunnel model to the Sears-Haack body shape in the previous figure, but note the obvious absence of the intake and exhaust truncations. NACA Photo.

with the ever-increasing span of the delta wing created a virtual "worst-case scenario" as far as conforming to the Sears-Haack shape was concerned. Major changes would be needed in the contour of the F-102 fuselage—the new fuselage contour would be called the "area rule."

Only after several iterations between Langley and Convair did the message finally take root in August 1953. However, by then it was too late for the first batch of ten YF-102s that were starting to roll out the door. The "design error" would eventually cost more than $20 million in wasted tooling and about $35 million in additional R&D.

Convair test pilot Richard Johnson had the privilege of making the first flight on 24 October 1953. There was no denying the problem—even with the 10,000-pound thrust J57, the YF-102 (52-7994) would not achieve Mach 1 in level flight. Worse yet for Johnson, an engine failure on take-off for the seventh test flight a week later on 2 November resulted in major damage to the airframe and serious injuries for the pilot.

The second YF-102 began flight test in January 1954 as the performance envelope was explored—the maximum speed was Mach .98 in level flight and the highest altitude was 48,000 feet. Noticeable buffet was encountered at Mach .9 and Mach 1.06 was achieved in a shallow dive.

A modified wing with a cambered leading edge was then installed on the second plane, along with a fillet between the elevon and the fuselage to reduce the buffet. Testing resumed in April and the YF-102 reached Mach 1.29 in a 30-degree dive on 2 May 1954. To reach the goal of Mach 1.3 and 57,000 feet, another two years and significant effort and money would be required.

Figure 08-14. The Convair YF-102 displays the original fuselage configuration before the redesign with the area rule. USAF Photo.

Soviet Imperative

The Soviets were not as revealing to the world of their technology as was the United States. While espionage was not a major factor at this point, the yearly military displays in Moscow's Red Square provided the only real intelligence that the United States could rely upon. The Soviets' jet bomber force initially consisted of the Tu-16 *Badger*, which was smaller and lighter (at 168,000 pounds) than the American B-47 (230,000 pounds). Although it was almost five years behind its American counterpart, having first flown in 1952, it exhibited superior speed and altitude capability. However, its limited range essentially restricted it to being more of a European threat.

The Soviet Tu-95 *Bear* (the B-52 equivalent) made its first flight in 1952, and its estimated range made it a true intercontinental threat. It used turboprop engines and was about 50 knots slower than the B-52. Yet a third bomber, the Myasishchev M-4, NATO code name *Bison*, also made its appearance at this time.

In exercises against the B-47, America's first-line interceptors of 1952 could not keep pace. It was obvious that the year 1954 was not an arbitrary date for the deployment of the F-102, as that was the date the *Badger* was due to be operational—the *Bear* was delivered to operational squadrons in 1956.

Because of the inability of the interceptors then in service (F-89, F-86D and F-94) to counter effectively the B-47 and B-52 in exercises, their firepower had to be increased—the nuclear tipped MB-1 *Genie* air-to-air rocket was the answer: even if you "missed the target by a mile," you could still bring it down.

Just as the Americans probed the perimeter of the Soviet Union (and occasionally penetrated well into it), so did the Soviets survey America's intercept capability. On more than one occasion, a TU-16 entered U.S. airspace in Alaska and then departed before it could be intercepted. The presence of the *Badger* and the *Bear* were influencing decisions in the Pentagon.

"Coke Bottle" Fuselage

The expected delay in developing the *1954 Interceptor* that had been anticipated in 1952 was

Figure 08-15. The Soviet Tu-16 Badger was a most formidable opponent in the mid-1950s. USAF Photo.

much more protracted and expensive than anyone imagined. Instead of being able to move the interim configuration (F-102A) to operational readiness, the "area rule" delay would require more engineering and yet another major schedule slippage. This

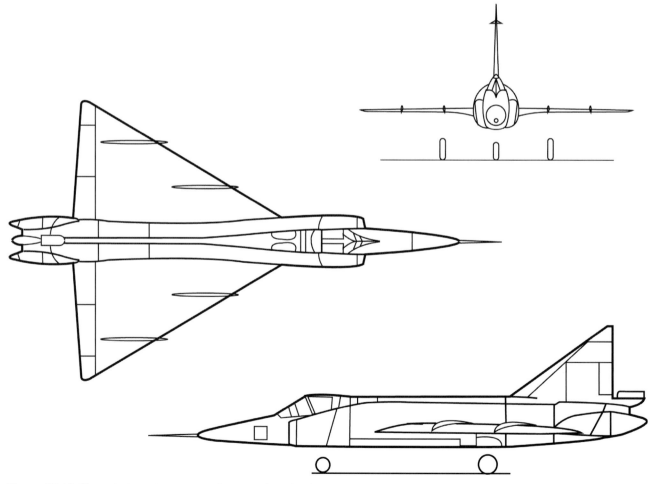

Figure 08-16. The redesign to incorporate the area rule is clearly apparent in this three-way view of the F-102A. NACA Illustration.

in turn would set back the timetable in bringing the ultimate variation, the F-102B, to flight.

It has sometimes been said that the best way to design something correctly is to do it a second time. That was the case with the F-102. With the extensive electronics of the fire control system, access to the various components for maintenance had not been well planned, nor was the basic assembly of the airframe as a whole. Thus, the opportunity to rework many of the structural details allowed the engineers to "make it right" the second time.

The most noticeable changes to the F-102, now defined with the suffix A, would be the "pinching" of the waist of the fuselage and the addition of two bulbous appendages to each side of the tail called "Whitcomb bodies." The modification was referred to as the "coke bottle fuselage" because it resembled the famous contours of the popular soft drink container (in the era before aluminum cans). It was also occasionally referred to as the "wasp-waist" for the same reason. The air intakes also were squared off to provide improved airflow. The cuffed leading edge of the wing was further refined to provide a "partial conical camber"—a progressive increase in the leading edge curvature from the wing root to its tip. This changed the effective angle of incidence and resulted in improved controllability at high angles-of-attack and a slight drag reduction at higher altitudes.

The wing was reduced in area from 695 sq ft to 661.5 sq ft., and an additional wing fence was installed (which had already been introduced on later versions of the YF-102) to improve the handling at high angles-of-attack. The fineness ratio of the fuselage was enhanced by adding eleven feet to its length, which reduced the form drag and, along with a redesign of the canopy, improved the pilot's vision. The cockpit was pressurized to 7.2 psi and an MC-1 partial pressure suit was required for planned flights above 50,000 feet.

The vertical tail was redesigned by decreasing the sweep to 52 degrees and increasing the height from 104 to 137 inches. This increased the total surface from 68 to 95 sq ft to address roll-coupling. The trailing edge, which had a slight forward lean on the earlier design, was made perpendicular to the longitudinal axis.

Extensive use of forgings was planned to deliver complete fuselage frames, wing spars, and longitudinal members. This manufacturing technique would reduce the weight of each aircraft by over 100 pounds and the individual component count by 273 items, as well as 3,200 rivets.

The ejection seat was built by Weber Aircraft Corporation and used what was the standard method of activation—lateral handgrips. The ejection process required two steps and took about two seconds. Step 1, raising the handgrip, resulted in several actions that began with depressurizing the cockpit, jettisoning the canopy, and elevating the forearm guards, which locked the inertia-reel shoulder harnesses. Step 2 was the squeezing of the trigger that fired the seat.

The design changes were completed in just 118 days following a sign-off on the engineering drawings— the first F-102A (painted a light grey) flew on 20 December 1954. The results were impressive—given the same J57 powerplant, test pilot Johnson (now fully recovered from the accident 13 months earlier) took the F-102A through the speed of sound in level flight on the second test run to Mach 1.22 and was able to reach 53,000 feet. (The F-102A reached Mach 1.535 on a flight in January 1956.) With these confirming assessments, the F-102A was released for production.

A two-seat trainer version (the TF-102), with the pilot and instructor sitting side-by-side, made its first flight on 31 October 1955. This required significant restructuring of the nose of the aircraft (to include the air intakes) and a disruption to the area rule. The

Figure 08-17. The Whitcomb Area Rule modifications are apparent in this photo of the F-102A. USAF Photo.

TF-102, although combat capable, was not able to exceed the speed of sound in level flight; 111 were built.

Operational Use

The F-102A was given the nickname *Delta Dagger* in 1957—only after it started its operational career. Like most combat aircraft, the aircrews almost never used the official name and the F-102 was universally called *The Deuce.*

The F-102's radar display mounted in the cockpit provided the pilot with a graphical representation of the target in relation to his aircraft. After lock-on (and with the pilot depressing his trigger), when the radar determined the optimum convergence of the missiles' projected flight path with that of the target it automatically opened the missile bay doors and fired a pre-selected salvo.

The F-102A began its operational service with the 327th Fighter Interceptor Squadron at George AFB, California, in April 1956—two years after the 1954 deadline that had been established in 1949. This was not as bad as it might have been, thanks to an exceptional effort on the part of all the contractors and the Air Force personnel to work exceedingly difficult schedules. The F-102A served continuously in 32 squadrons with 889 aircraft built (including the 14 prototypes). While the early squadrons were in the contiguous 48 states to "work out the bugs," the F-102A ultimately operated out of Alaska, Greenland, Iceland, and in other NATO-European and SEATO countries.

George Andre recalls the layout of a typical alert base: "*Most featured an alert hangar at the end of the longest runway with high speed taxiways leading on to the runway for immediate scramble. These buildings all had a common design with hangar bays 2 or 4 on each side of a central two story building with the pilots upstairs and the ground crew downstairs. A few of them featured the fire pole* [for rapid movement down to the first floor]. *Each story had its own food prep area and lounge and sleeping area.*

"*Generally, a pilot stood alert for an 8, 12 or sometimes 24 hour period. We slept with our boots on, and always could make a less than 5 minute airborne time from the sound of the scramble horn. By the time we got to the plane, the crew had started the doors opening and had the ground power running, and often, while we strapped in, they started the engine leaning into the cockpit.*"

By 1961 there were three squadrons of F102s in Japan, one in Okinawa, and one in the Philippines. As the F-102A had been designed as an interceptor, in-flight refueling was not included and these overseas transits required cocooning the aircraft and transporting them by

Figure 08-18. The TF-102 featured side-by-side seating and the full interceptor capability—except it would not exceed Mach 1.0 in level flight. USAF Photo.

ship.

As its pilots would soon learn, flying the world's then-fastest interceptor and working the radar was not as simple as it had been made to look by the engineers who designed the systems.

Jerry Bjerke, who flew the F-102 for four years and 1200 hours, recalls: "*I transitioned from the F-86D to the F-102. Since both were all-weather ADC aircraft using acquisition radar, the transition went well. The F-102 training was handled at the former Perrin AFB, Sherman, Texas. The most challenging part was getting used to the coordination of flying the aircraft and use of the radar controls. The hand control for the radar was on the same stick as used to fly the aircraft.*

"*The F-102 was very easy to fly and being delta wing, very stable. The aircraft was limited to subsonic speeds due to the drop tanks. Since we always flew with the tanks, supersonic was never attained. The aircraft was easy to fly in formation and, compared to current-day fighters, the cockpit was fairly simple and easy to learn and use. Due to the small, forward fuselage intakes, we had to be aware of the susceptibility of compressor stalls at high angle-of-attack and low speed maneuvers. This could happen during 'snap up' attacks.*"

Advances in electronics came rapidly during this period, and the Hughes MG-3 system was upgraded to the MG-10. Despite the early use of the transistor, there were still many of the relatively delicate vacuum tubes in the system and reliability was a major issue.

The Hughes GAR-1 *Falcon* missile was the F-102A's initial armament. followed closely by its heat-seeking cousin, the GAR-2. When an intercept was flown with the intent to use the GAR-2, a stern approach would be set up to give the IR heat-seeker head the optimum view of the heat source—the hot engine tailpipe. When flown together with the GAR-1, the GAR-2 was positioned on the rear launcher. If fired as a salvo the IR would be the first to launch—for two reasons. If the forward missile was launched first, debris from its exhaust impinged on the rear missile's nose cone. If both a radar-guided missile and heat-seeker were launched in that order, the heat-seeker would simply follow the greatest heat source—the missile ahead of it— rather than the target. In 1962, the *Falcon* missile family was again redesignated as the AIM-4.

Unfortunately, the *Falcon* had significant reliability problems. It was designed to explode "on contact," as the warhead fusing was contained in the fins. Thus, even a close approach would not down the target. As the Air Force would learn in Vietnam, the *Falcon* had too many problems to be an effective weapon against other than relatively stable targest. Moreover, its heat-seeker version employed an internally cooled seeker head. The pilot would activate its coolant when he selected the missile. However, if he delayed more than two minutes before launching, the coolant would be depleted and the missile would no longer track.

More advanced versions of the *Falcon* were successively employed during the F-102A's operational tenure. Although the nuclear MB-1 *Genie* was considered, and a single non-nuclear test conducted in 1956, this weapon was never carried operationally.

The intercept scenario used the SAGE system's ground-based radars to "position" the F-102 on a 135-degree (optimal) convergence point within 20 miles of the target (if the GAR-1 was to be employed) for a "forward-quarter" intercept. If an FFAR rocket attack was planned then a 110-degree beam angle was calculated. At that point, the pilot used his onboard radar to pick up the target, and after he locked on the F-102's fire control computer (FCS) continually updated the predicted "lead" should the target take evasive action. When inside "B-time" (indicated by steering circle shrinkage at about 20 seconds to intercept), the pilot could hold down his trigger for an autofire at launch time, or reselect a manual launch option if lock-on could not be sustained.

For intercepting very high-flying aircraft—those at 10-15,000 feet above the interceptor—head-on "snap-up" attacks could be employed. Several seconds before the expected launch point the pilot would pull up to center his steering dot in elevation, and thus position the nose to the point of convergence, in time to "bury the dot" and fire the armament.

One of the original SAGE objectives—that the system would fly the aircraft to its intercept point and fire the weapons—was never achieved. SAGE (or manual GCI) sent the aircrew command and target information (via SAGE data-link displays and/or voice), but the actual flying and weapon launch was the responsibility of the pilot.

Roger Pile: "*On-board radar searched for the target, but it was up to the pilot to locate it, select the appropriate armament, lock on to it and fly the plane to the release point computed by the MG-10 system. The pilot was also responsible to retain the attack in spite of radar jamming, dispensing of chaff, and to switch to alternative modes should it be necessary (i.e. switching to an infra-red [IRST] tracking mode to avoid those counter-measures).*"

It was realized that the search radar of the interceptor could be detectable by its prey, and that the enemy might employ a variety of electronic countermeasures (ECM, signal jamming and dispensing chaff being the most obvious) either to render the FCS ineffective, or to affect missile guidance after launch. (FFARs, once launched, would not be affected by ECM, but might be evaded by strong target maneuvers.)

Thus, in the early 1960s a program to provide additional capability to defeat these ECM measures was underway. A part of this was the installation of passive infrared search and track (IRST) equipment in the F/TF-102 for stern attacks, beginning in 1963, to augment its FCS radar functions.

Roger Pile recalls: "*It was a softball sized sensor-head located immediately in front of the center of the windshield. IR search tactics were part of the flight profile when I attended the Interceptor Weapons School (IWS) at Tyndall in 1963. The detection system was cooled by liquid nitrogen to -196 degrees Fahrenheit and it was used for low altitude stern attacks where the radar would be degraded due to ground clutter. The pilot could select IR dominant with the radar in standby, search or slaved to the IR tracker after lock-on to the target. If the radar was in standby, the target might never know you were locked on to him as the IRSTS was a passive receptor only and did not emit any signals. If in 'search mode,' he might think you were still searching for him.*

Figure 08-19. Two of the three Falcon bays of the F-102A can be seen here with the 2.75-inch rocket tubes visible on the front edge of the doors. Note that the middle bay contains an advanced GAR-11A (AIM-26) Falcon. USAF Photo.

If the radar was slaved to the IR head, you might get 'burn-through' (pick him up on the radar) to give you an accurate distance from him and lock on to him with the radar. This would also allow the radar-guided (AIM-4A) missiles to also lock on to him and be guided to the target as well as the heat seekers (AIM-4Ds)."

George Andre provides some detail for the intercept process: *"As one of the last squadrons to use the 102, we never ever got into the pure, pie in the sky, SAGE control. The controller used SAGE to filter out the enemy and assign the interceptor, but the plan to have it all handled automatically using data-link never bore fruit. In my last year as a 102 pilot (1974), I was earning the 'Master of Air Defense' rating (a crew qualification level, the highest) and had to qualify as a controller. I went to the SAGE blockhouse at Luke AFB Arizona and learned the controller tasks. All this business with pencil light guns was shaky at best and never fully replaced the manual control."*

The F-102As of the 509th FIS were sent to Tan Son Nhut Air Base, South Vietnam, from Okinawa in March 1962 for use in the air defense role as a deterrent against possible air attack by North Vietnam on the South. With the ramping up of the war in 1965, it was also used as bomber escort for later B-52 operations. Because the North Vietnamese tended to avoid the more advanced American fighters there were few encounters during the early stages of the war. Only one incident occurred where MiG-21s bounced a pair of F-102s—shooting down one with missiles.

To provide the F-102A with greater flexibility in meeting the obligations of overseas operations it was decided to equip them for in-flight "probe and drogue" refueling. As the internal structure had not been designed to accommodate this feature, the "probe" and associated piping was configured to run along the outside of the fuselage. Although it degraded the performance, it could be easily removed.

Jerry Bjerke recalls: *"The most exciting experience for me and the other 82nd FIS Pilots was the in-flight refueling deployment from Travis AFB to Naha, Okinawa [Feb 1966]. We were the first squadron to have the F-102 modified for a trip across the ocean. Since the Air Force wanted a quick deployment without cocooning the A/C for a long ship trip, this was the only solution. The aircraft were modified with a rigid [refueling] probe on the right side. The challenge included engine oil consumption vs. amount of oil available and [the pilot's] oxygen limitation for an extended trip (each of the three legs about 6-hrs). The oxygen issue was solved by adding another tank and the oil—by monitoring usage during practice flights with the tankers.*

"Training was a real challenge since none of us had ever had any in-flight refueling experience. We had six shorter trips with the KC-135s, to practice the techniques of hook up and back off. The final practice run simulated actual time of a leg of the trip, 6 hrs. This trip was certainly a measurement of our abilities. The drop tanks could not be refueled in air. We were to use that to insure safe return to departing base should

Figure 08-20. The "probe" in-flight refueling system was retrofitted to the F-102 to permit long-range ferry. Note the Boeing KC-135 has a drogue adapter attached to its boom. USAF photo via Jerry Bjerke.

CONVAIR F-102 *DELTA DAGGER*

Figure 08-21. The external "plumbing" for the aerial refueling probe is evident on the right side of the F-102. The small softball-size IRST sensor can also be seen just in front of the canopy. This photo was taken 14 February 1966 as the first 16 F-102s prepare to depart for the trans-Pacific crossing. USAF Photo Roger Pile collection.

we have to abort and return. Tanks were turned on once we were assured of making our destination."

George Andre provides the following regarding *Palace Alert*, a program in which combat-ready F102 pilots from the Air National Guard could fill a pilot slot in any of the many active duty squadrons around the world. It was often used to get a tour with a combat unit in the Vietnam war.

Andre: "*Orientation flying out of Clark* [AB in the Philippines] *included training on the particular weapons we would be carrying since the combat load did not match what we were using stateside. In particular, we would be equipped with the AIM-26B, a super model of the Falcon missile equipped with, what was then, the highly classified expanding rod warhead.*

"*Additionally, since our mission also included the possibility of air-to-ground strikes, we qualified in launching our 2.75-inch folding fin rockets (called 'Mighty Mouse') at ground targets.*

"*Our mission at Udorn* [Thailand] *was varied. Our primary purpose was to have 2 or 4 airplanes on five-minute alert status, ready to scramble airborne to repel any intruders from the north.. I was sitting alert at Udorn one lazy day, and the scramble horn went off. This was rare. As I buckled in and put on my helmet, I could immediately hear on guard channel—'two blue bandits coming through the fish's mouth.' There were red, white and blue bandits as code words for MiG fighters and a blue one was the MiG-21. The fish's*

mouth was a geographical landmark on the border of NVN and Laos that looked, on a map, like a fish's mouth. We were under radar control from an EC 121.

"*My partner beat me to the runway so he was leader, but shortly after takeoff, his radar failed and I took the lead. The two MiGs were going very fast, probably supersonic and came down over the Plaine des Jarres in central Laos, made about two 360s, and went back into their NVN sanctuary. We were never able to get a contact on them, and if so, we could not fire unless fired upon* [per the Rules of Engagement]. *The mere action of flying into another country, and acting aggressive was not enough to classify them as hostile. Anyway, for a little while, I thought this was the fight I imagined would maybe happen someday. Interestingly, I found out later that Ho Chi Minh had died the day before. This incursion was rare for the MiGs to come so far from their bases and always wondered if there was any connection.*

"*We also had a few other missions. It was a time of heavy carpet-bombing going on by B-52s interdicting supplies coming out of North Vietnam (NVN) supplying the Viet Cong (VC) in the south...(the famous 'Ho Chi Minh Trail'). Our job was to escort the bombers and be there to intercept any MiG attacks on them. Our 102s would generally fly high cover on the NVN side, while sometimes a flight of F-4 Phantoms would fly low cover on the other side.*

"*NVN anti-aircraft guns were often locked in on us, but we were too high for them. The shells would explode under us, and one could often feel a concussion from the blast. Rolling up on a wing and looking at them usually did a number on one's night vision."*

Because of the built-in FFAR rockets, the F-102 was used briefly in the close air support role in 1965 and the two-seat TF-102 saw some missions with forward air controllers. The type was withdrawn from the SEA Theater in 1969. A total of 15 F-102s were lost in Vietnam—of which four were combat-related.

While the F-102 avoided the pitch-up problem experienced by traditional swept-wing aircraft of the day, it did have an engine stall problem caused by excessive angle-of-attack—typically during departure—that caused a large percentage of the 259 which were lost throughout its service life. The F-102 had a lifetime accident rate of 13.69 per 100,000 flight hours, which is about three times worse than the F-16, which ran around 3.0 (though it has lately been closer to 4.0).

With a power-to-weight ratio of .56, acceleration was poor compared to the F-101B (.75) and the F-104 (.78). Its big 661 sq ft wing provided a wing loading of just 35-pounds per square foot. This compared very favorably with the other *Century Series* and allowed *The Deuce* to have an advantage in certain aspects of its flight envelope, although it was not designed as a traditional "dogfighter."

Ron Standerfer: *"I flew the Deuce for three years with the Florida Air National Guard after flying the Hun on active duty and can tell you that hassling with my squadron mates who had no air-to-air combat training was a piece of cake. With its delta wing it could turn on a dime, and using a few basic maneuvers like the 'low speed yo-yo' you could be on someone's [six] before they knew what was happening."*

Bill Jowett: *"I flew the F-102 transitioning into the F-106. I was very impressed with its turning ability. Many pilots claim their aircraft turns better than another. Of course, aerial combat will prove this, but short of that, I found another way to measure the turning capability of different aircraft and used that for comparison. That is to take the aircraft to 10,000' at initial approach airspeed and perform a split-S as tight as possible. The F-102 would do it under 2,500'. The T-33 about 3,300'. The F-106 at 3,100' and the F-4 at about 7,000'. I repeat the F-4-at 7,000."*

In the 1960s, as responsibility for stateside air defense shifted to the Air National Guard, so did most of the F-102As. Former president George W. Bush flew the F-102 during his tour with the Texas Air National Guard. Bush enlisted in 1968 following his graduation from Yale. He was selected for pilot training and, following basic training at Lackland AFB, Texas, he was sent to Moody AFB in Georgia for flight training in November 1968. He received his commission as a Second Lieutenant and trained in the T-41, T-37, and T-38. He completed his training in the F-102A in June 1970 and logged a total of 625 hours of flight time before finishing his service in October 1973. He is the only former President to have flown a jet fighter, while his father (George H. W. Bush) is the only one who has flown combat (TBM *Avengers* in WWII). President Dwight Eisenhower is the only other Chief Executive to have been a certified pilot.

Foreign Service

Fifty F-102A and TF-102s were exported to Turkey and about 25 to Greece, and they reportedly saw combat during the short-lived Turkish invasion of Cyprus in 1974. It is conceivable that they may have engaged each other, but neither side reported losses. The F-102 was finally retired from both of those air forces in 1979. Those were the only foreign sales of the type.

Variants

Table 08-01

Convair F-102 Variants

Variant	Notes	No. Built
YF-102	Prototype Non area ruled unable to exceed Mach 1 in level flight	10
YF-102A	Area-ruled 4 converted from prototypes	4
F-102A	Production model. 8 non area-ruled remainder redesigned with area rule	875
TF-102A	Two-seat mission capable— Unable to exceed Mach 1 in level flight	111
F-102C	Fighter-bomber—Two converted as YF-102C	(2)
QF-102	F-102A converted to target drones	(6)
PQM-102A	F-102A converted to target drones (unpiloted)	(65)
PQM-102B	F-102A converted to target drones (piloted or unpiloted)	(146)
	Total Built	**1,000**

CONVAIR F-102 *DELTA DAGGER*

Phase Out

In 1973 six of the older aircraft were converted to target drones, receiving the designation QF-102A (later defined as PQM-102). Eventually about 400 F-102As were converted to drones and fell as targets to the testing of advanced air-to-air and surface-to-air missiles. The last PQM-102 drone was expended in 1986.

The F-102 was developed on the cutting edge of both supersonic and computer technology. As such, it suffered from significant teething problems in each. The quick follow-on of the F-106 and solid-state electronics allowed both these new frontiers to mature, with the result being an effective air defense weapon. The F-102 left U.S. service in 1976, and there are no F-102s remaining on flight status.

Characteristics & Performance Data	YF-102 1-seat Prototype	F-102A 1-seat Interceptor	TF-102 2-seat Mission Capable/Trainer
Length (ft in)	61' 5"	68' 4"	68' 5"
Wing Span (ft in)	38' 1"		
Height (ft in)	18'1"	21'2"	21'2"
Wing Area (sq ft)	695sq/st	661 sq/st	661
Engine	J57-P-13	J57-P-25	J57-P-25
– Mil Pwr /AB (lbs)	10,000 / 15,200	11,700 / 17,000	10,200 / 17,000
Max G (combat weight)	7.33	7.33	7.33
First Flight	Oct-53	Dec-54	Nov-55
First Delivery (for op'ns)		Apr-56	
Empty Weight (lb)		19,350	19,050
Combat Weight (lb)		24,500	24,500
Max TO Weight (lb)		31,500	31,500
Internal Fuel (gal)		1,085	1,085
Max Fuel (gal)		1,900	1,900
(w/Drop Tanks) (gal)		(2) 215 gal	(2) 215 gal
Max Speed, 40Kft (mph)		825	646
Mach no.		1.25	0.9
Initial climb (ft/min)		13,000	12,500
Service Ceiling (ft)		53,400	54,000
Normal Range (sm)		1,350	1000
Wing Loading		35 lb/sqft	35 lb/sqft
Thrust/Weight		0.7	0.7

Table 08-02. Convair F-102 Specifications.

Alexander Kartveli

What is remarkable about most of the *Century Series* is that they were designed by aeronautical engineers who began their careers while aviation was still in its infancy—when fabric covering and open cockpits were still the standard. This is particularly true of Russian-born Alexander Kartveli, who graduated from the High School of Aviation in Paris in 1922. After working for Blériot-Aéronautique (a company founded by Louis Blériot—the first person to fly the English Channel in 1909), Kartveli emigrated to the United States in 1927. He worked for the Fokker Company until he was brought into the Seversky Aircraft Corporation in 1936 by Alexander de Seversky. A fellow Georgian, de Seversky came to the United States in 1918 to escape the Communist Revolution.

Figure 09-01. Alexander Kartveli was hired into the Seversky Aircraft Corporation by Alexander de Seversky. PD.

Although de Seversky left the company in 1939 amid company political pressure, Kartveli continued as the Chief Engineer at Republic Aviation (the corporate successor to Seversky). These pioneers pushed technology in an age before the digital computer, television or the internet (more on de Seversky and

the genealogy of Republic aircraft in the F-105 segment).

Design Concepts

The 1949 study by the Air Force for an advanced fighter known as the *"1954 Interceptor"* (the target year for it to be operational) resulted in the establishment of Weapon System program WS-201A. The RFP for the Mach 2 airframe (MX-1554) was issued in June 1950, and there were nine proposals submitted by six aviation companies by January 1951.

Republic Aviation's response was orchestrated by Kartveli's design team and had actually been born two years earlier in 1948. It resulted from a review of data distributed to the aviation industry from the X-1 program that had taken Chuck Yeager through the sound barrier for the first time. Inspired by the prospects of creating a Mach 2 airplane, Kartveli initially produced the plans for the Republic model AP-44A (Republic's "AP" designation originally stood for "Army Project," but was changed to "Advanced Project" when the Air Force became a

Figure 09-02. An artist's conception of the Republic F-103. USAF Museum Archives.

Figure 09-03. In this XF-103 mockup, the main landing gear appears too small for the massive plane. USAF Museum Archives.

Figure 09-04. The size of the XF-103 mock-up cannot be appreciated without a human form present. USAF Museum Archives.

Figure 09-05. The configuration of the MX-1787 reveals the XJ67 (on the right) feeding into the XRJ55 unit (on the left). USAF Museum Archives.

separate entity). By the time of the contract award in August 1951, the competition had narrowed to just three companies—Lockheed, Convair, and Republic.

Republic's proposal, which was now defined as AP-57, was so far advanced over the other entrants that it was obvious it would not meet the 1954 target date. Kartveli believed that rapidly advancing technology would push the performance envelope and the Mach 3 bomber threat would follow too closely to allow yet another procurement iteration before the need became critical. However, Convair was awarded WS-201A, which became the F-102.

Nevertheless, the Air Force recognized that Republic's entry was actually a generation beyond the *1954 Interceptor*, and that it would undoubtedly involve a protracted development cycle. WS-204A was the answer. Instead of a Mach 2 interceptor flying at 55,000 feet as specified for the *1954 Interceptor*, WS-204A would fly at Mach 3 and 70,000 feet. The Air Force encouraged Kartveli by awarding a letter contract to Republic in September 1951.

The key to the XF-103, as it was for all the *Century Series*, was power. Jet engine technology was experiencing significant advances in many areas. Yet "materials science," for all the progress that had been made, still presented a formidable obstacle in the "hot section" of the engine—the turbine wheel and blades. Sitting in the extreme temperatures of the exhaust, the blades were exposed to high levels of stress as they transmitted some of the engine's energy to spin the high-speed compressor stage. To some designers of the era, the answer lay in simply avoiding the turbine and replacing it with the ramjet. However, the ramjet required a high-pressure wave of intake air generated by accelerating the engine to near-sonic speeds before the shock front of the incoming air would provide usable thrust. Convair had addressed

this issue with its XP-92 "ducted rocket" engine—a concept that quickly died.

Kartveli proposed a dual-cycle powerplant. The first was a relatively conventional turbojet engine—the Wright XJ67 that would produce about 10,000-pounds of thrust (dry). The exhaust of the XJ67 fed into a hybrid ramjet/afterburner designated as the XRJ55. There were several operational aspects that made this arrangement, labeled MX-1787, unique. The XJ67 thrust would propel the F-103 on takeoff and accelerate the plane to Mach 2 using the afterburner properties of the XRJ55 to generate about 20,000 pounds of thrust. However, the temperature limitation at the turbine inlet would not allow that speed to be maintained for more than a few minutes. At this point, a "deflector plate" would bypass the XJ67, redirecting all the intake air through the XRJ55, which would begin operating as a ramjet. It was anticipated that the thrust would initially decay to about 14,000-pounds, but as the various environmental aspects of airflow, temperature, and fuel flow stabilized over a period of several seconds, the thrust would increase to 16,000 pounds and the aircraft would accelerate towards Mach 3. As it did, the increased airflow into the ramjet would raise the thrust to about 18,000 pounds until the thrust-drag equilibrium was established.

Because the F-103 was expected to fly out at high speed to a point of intercept and launch its missiles at the incoming bombers, there would be no need for a highly maneuverable planform. Nor would the ramjet be throttleable. After a successful intercept, the F-103 would slow to subsonic cruise using its XJ67 alone and return to its base. The XJ67 was actually the Bristol *Olympus*, to be built under license by the Curtiss-Wright Corporation.

Figure 09-07. The lack of a traditional canopy and the forward-raked shark-like intake set the XF-103 apart from its contemporaries. USAF Museum Archives.

Figure 09-08. The F-103 exhaust featured a slab-sided square-shaped variable nozzle. The outer sides of the exhaust nozzle had the ability to extend outward to 45 degrees to form speed brakes as demonstrated in the photo. USAF Museum Archives.

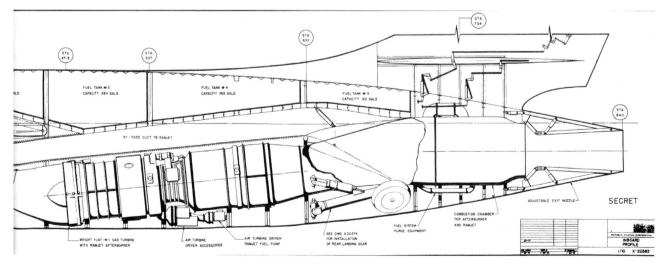

Figure 09-06. The AP-57 tail configuration had the horizontal stabilizer set in the vertical fin. The bypass air duct for the XRJ-55 is the area directly above the J67. USAF Museum Archives.

Figure 09-09. A forward-raked Ferri-type two-dimensional intake on the underside of the F-103 presented a menacing shark-like profile. USAF Museum Archives.

Figure 09-10. Two mockups of the F-103 cockpit area provided for evaluation of the embedded cockpit against the more traditional canopy. USAF Museum Archives.

Moving to the Mockup

The design that was displayed for the mockup in June 1953 represented a very sleek, high-fineness-ratio fuselage with short delta wings swept to 55 degrees. The conventional horizontal stabilizer had been attached to the vertical stabilizer in the AP-57 design, but was subsequently moved to the very bottom of the aft fuselage, which took on a square configuration. Both the vertical and horizontal stabilizers were of delta configuration but used a 60-degree sweep.

The XF-103's most notable feature was a cockpit buried within the fuselage. A forward-raked Ferri-type two-dimensional intake on the underside presented a menacing shark-like profile. (The configuration was named for the NACA investigator of supersonic intake flow—A. Ferri of the Oswatitsch, Ferri and Nucci trio.) The deflector plate divided the intake airflow internally.

Of particular note was that the wings were mounted on a pivot that allowed them to change their angle of incidence (the Navy's Vought F8U *Crusader* would have a similar feature). This not only allowed the plane to fly at the optimum pitch angle, but also avoided the need for other forms of aerodynamic trim surfaces. The outer third of the wing also pivoted to provide for roll control. These surfaces were referred to as "tiperons." This arrangement allowed the inboard trailing edge to employ traditional flaps. Also, a folding ventral fin extended in flight to provide added directional stability at high speed.

The original configuration of the plane provided for a cockpit that was embedded completely within the fuselage. Republic attempted to verify the adequacy of periscopic forward vision for this arrangement and modified an F-84G that had an unusual structure on

its nose through which the pilot viewed the world. It spent 50 flight hours roaming the airways over Long Island in 1955. A mockup of the cockpit was also placed on a truck to help understand the various ground handling factors. A second mockup of the cockpit area provided for a more traditional canopy arrangement, as Kartveli was concerned with the ability of the single pilot to have adequate vision for take-off and landing.

It was envisioned that the F-103 would use a fire control system compatible with the SAGE system then being developed for the F-102. The armament initially consisted of two trays of 18 FFARs and four *Falcon*s that were to be carried internally and extended from the sides for firing.

Figure 09-11. To verify the adequacy of periscopic forward vision, an F-84G was modified to incorporate the unusual structure through which the pilot would view the world. USAF Museum Archives.

Figure 09-12. The two portside Falcons, carried internally, are shown in their extended launch position. USAF Museum Archives.

Too Many Problems

As the design team moved deeper into the details, it was realized that aerodynamic heating of the structure would be a more critical Mach-limiting factor than the engine. Efforts to find and use a variety of materials (to include aluminum, steel, and titanium) slowed the project. Other high-tech aspects included an escape capsule for the pilot that ejected downward—a direction that the F-104 would eventually abandon.

Although Republic had been awarded a contract for three prototypes in July 1954, the lack of progress by 1955 caused some of the funding and priority to be removed. By October of that year, the Air Force issued a new RFP to the aviation industry for a Mach 3 interceptor, essentially acknowledging that the F-103 was a dead-end and the program was cut to a single prototype.

Republic was unable to deal with the necessary fabrication problems that titanium presented and, coupled with delays in the J67 by Bristol, the end came in August 1957. Both the F-103 and the XJ67 were cancelled by the Air Force after having spent over $100 million dollars on development. The engine and materials challenges for a Mach 3 interceptor would be resolved in the early 1960s in a project that was not initiated as an interceptor but as a photo-reconnaissance platform—the Lockheed A-12.

Figure 09-13. The 18 FFAR unguided rockets are shown in their firing position extended into the slipstream on a tray. USAF Museum Archives.

Characteristics & Performance Data	XF-103 1-seat Prototype
Length (ft in)	81' 11"
Wing Span (ft in)	35'10"
Height (ft in)	18'4"
Wing Area (sq ft)	401 sq/ft
Engine	XJ-67-W-3/XRJ55-W-1
– Mil Pwr /AB (lbs)	15,000/18,800
Max G (combat weight)	7.33
First Flight	Mock-up only
Empty Weight (lb)	24,950
Combat Weight (lb)	38,505
Max TO Weight (lb)	42,864
Internal Fuel (gal)	3,730
Max Speed, 50Kft (mph)	2,600
Mach no.	3.0+
Initial climb (ft/min)	20,000
Service Ceiling (ft)	75,000
Normal Range (sm)	431
Wing Loading	96
Thrust/Weight	.57/.95

Table 09-01. The Republic F-103 Specifications.

Figure 10-01. U.S. Air Corps Y1C-12 military version of the Lockheed Vega. U.S. Army Photo.

Origin of Lockheed Aircraft

The Alco Hydro-Aeroplane Company was originally formed in 1912 by brothers Allan and Malcolm Loughead, who built their first plane in San Francisco in 1913—the *Model G*. They chose the designation "G" so as not to alarm potential buyers that this was their first creation. The company was later renamed the Loughead Aircraft Manufacturing Company and located in Santa Barbara, California. Neither of these ventures proved financially successful, although Malcolm would go on to make a very good living with his Lockheed hydraulic brakes. In 1926, Allan Loughead formed the Lockheed Aircraft Company with the spelling changed to match the phonetic pronunciation. This company was sold to Detroit Aircraft in 1929, but the Great

Depression essentially forced many manufacturers out of the aircraft market, including Detroit Aircraft, which went bankrupt after delivering nine of the company's principal product—the high-wing *Vega*.

A group of investors headed by Robert and Courtland Gross bought the company out of receivership in 1932 and relocated it to Burbank, California. The new Lockheed continued to build more-capable versions of the *Vega*. With its high performance (range and speed), it was ideal for such luminaries as Amelia Earhart and Wiley Post to set aviation records in the early 1930s. Lockheed then developed a small twin-engine transport, the L-10 *Electra*. It was in this aircraft that Amelia Earhart and navigator, Fred Noonan, were lost in their attempt to fly around the world in 1937. It was

Figure 10-02. The Lockheed Electra L-10 was the type that Amelia Earhart took on her ill-fated Round-the-World attempt in 1937. Lockheed Photo.

Figure 10-03.
Lockheed's P-38 was a dramatic step up in high-performance fighter design in 1939. U.S. Army Photo.

Figure 10-04. Thirteen Lockheed YP-80As were built, receiving the nickname Gray Ghost because of their polished gray lacquer finish, as were the two XP-80As that preceded them. U.S. Army Photo.

also at this time that a young Aeronautical Engineering graduate from the University of Michigan, Clarence L. Johnson, joined the engineering department. He became a major driving influence in the design of most Lockheed aircraft for the next 50 years.

Known as "Kelly" to his friends and associates, Johnson was a key member of the design team for the radical P-38 *Lightning* fighter in 1937. Kelly was particularly effective as the protégé of Lockheed's Hall Hibbard—an executive who recognized the talents of the young Swede.

When the Army Air Forces went looking for a new design for the emerging jet engine technology in 1942, Johnson turned the Lockheed design team's talents to the XP-80 and the new plane was built in just 143 days.

Its first flight in January 1944 revealed an airplane that attained 490 mph. This was almost 100 mph faster than contemporary piston-engine fighters—despite being powered by an early version of the British-built Halford H-1B that produced only 2,240 pounds of thrust. This single XP-80 prototype, called *Lulu-Belle*, proved the basic design concept and was superseded by the XP-80A, a larger and much heavier version (13,700 pounds vs. 8,900 pounds) powered by the General Electric I-40 (J30). Later production versions used the J33 with 4,000 pounds of thrust.

Working out the problems with the new jet resulted in 15 accidents in a period of less than a year. These began with the death of Lockheed test pilot Milo Burcham in October 1944. There was no single primary cause for the loss of six pilots and eight aircraft. Top-scoring American Ace Major Richard Bong was among those killed. He had been transferred from the combat zone in the South Pacific to keep the hero "safe." The flurry of accidents brought about the realization that jet aircraft required higher levels of quality, redundancy, and more careful preflight preparation.

Tony Levier, one of Lockheed's best-known test pilots, narrowly escaped death when his XP-80 lost its tail. It was determined that the structural failure was the result of the engine's high-speed turbine disintegrating and severing the airplane in two. Levier parachuted from the jet but was injured during the landing. The engine's turbine wheel, to which the turbine blades were attached, had been made from the upper portion of a steel ingot.

Figure 10-05. The Lockheed XP-90 was a beautiful airplane that "looked right" but was too heavy and underpowered. USAF Photo.

Further investigation revealed that this part of the ingot contained some impurities. From then on, only the lower portion of the ingot was used in the manufacture of the turbine wheel. The investigation also resulted in the marking of the turbine's location with a red line around the fuselage to warn ground crew to remain clear of that area.

In early January 1945, four P-80 *Shooting Stars* (as they had been named) were sent to Europe to counter the threat of the German Messerschmitt Me-262, which had appeared in increasing numbers during the previous six months. The British Gloster *Meteor* jet was also in operational use against the V-1 *Buzz-Bomb*. None of the P-80s actually engaged in combat operations before the end of hostilities in Europe in May 1945. However, the P-80 had been given the same high production priority as the Boeing B-29. Had the Pacific war continued, the P-80 production would have reached 30 aircraft per day, with the objective of having 1,000 aircraft in operation by 1946 for combat against Japan.

Following the war, the Air Force looked forward to regaining the World Speed Record that was held by the *Meteor* Mk.4 of 606 mph set in November 1945. The last time the United States was in possession of that record was 24 years earlier when a Navy pilot, Lieutenant Al Williams, had flown his Curtiss R2C-1 to a speed of 266 mph. The new attempt was made as part of a project to determine the feasibility of using water-alcohol injection to increase the power of the P-80's jet engine at high thrust levels. However, despite the 5,400-pounds of thrust and fairing over the gun ports and polishing the craft smooth, the best that could be attained was 596 mph (Mach .78).

By September 1946 the British had increased their record to 615 mph, again with the *Meteor* Mk4. Just a day later, the J35-powered Republic XP-84 flew at 611 mph, but this was not enough to bring the record home.

Lockheed, working with the Air Force, modified a *Shooting Star* (redesignated the P-80R—"R" for its nickname of *Racy*) with a sharper leading edge, reconfigured air intakes, and a smaller canopy. Now re-engined with the Allison J33-23, developing 4,600-pounds of thrust, Colonel Albert Boyd attained a new world speed record of 623 mph in June 1947.

The P-80 (redesignated F-80 in June 1948) went on to achieve greatness as a fighter-bomber in Korea and as the basis for the venerable two-place T-33 trainer, more commonly known as the "T-bird." The T-33 in turn became the basis for the F-94 *Starfire* all-weather interceptor of the early 1950s. However, the basic engine and airframe combination of the F-80/T-33 had been pushed to its limit, and the next generation of Lockheed fighters would employ the swept-wing—starting with the F-90.

"Kelly" Johnson's design team began to formulate the F-90 in 1947. In addition to the swept-wing, the long-range escort or "penetration fighter" requirement was its basic premise. The size of the plane was dictated by the fact that the new F-90 required two of the fuel-thirsty Westinghouse J34-WE-11 engines, which produced only 3,100 pounds of thrust each. Much of the airframe was stainless steel to achieve the 12-G design load factor.

Developed in competition with the McDonnell F-88, the F-90 was a beautiful airplane that "looked right" when it first flew in June 1949. However, the lack of efficient and powerful engines, coupled with a gross weight of 27,200-pounds and the yet-unidentified transonic drag factor resulted in a speed of just 600 mph. The engines were augmented with afterburners on the second plane, which brought the thrust up to 4,000-pounds each. However, the fuel load of 1,665 gallons internally, coupled with the weight and drag of large tip tanks doomed the performance to a lackluster 665 mph.

A *penetration fighter* "fly-off" against the McDonnell F-88 was completed in June 1950, but the start of the Korean War caused a pause in the procurement cycle, as the Air Force wanted to assess how its current first-line aircraft, the F-80, F-84 and F-86, performed. As the war progressed and the Soviet Mig-15 was introduced into combat in November 1950, it was realized that a fighter with the power-to-weight ratio of the F-90 would not have much chance against such competition.

Design Considerations

The December 1951 meeting of contractor representatives with combat fighter pilots at front-line air fields in Korea included Lockheed's "Kelly" Johnson. During the interviews, pilots asked for a simple Day Air Superiority Fighter with exceptional climb rate, high speed, and high altitude capability. The Air Force concurred and encouraged Johnson to design for these attributes. "Kelly" felt that weight and complexity should be held

to the absolute minimum to ensure that high performance was achieved.

Although there was no formal requirement for such an aircraft, Johnson returned to the States with a new focus. With the backing of Lockheed management (Hibbard in particular), he began to explore a series of configurations. This independent approach was occasionally promoted by the military services because it offered an opportunity for unrestricted innovation.

Swept-wing, straight wing and delta wing layouts were all considered—each having its strengths and liabilities. The delta wing imposed too much drag and the weight penalty was too high for the flight envelope being considered. The swept-wing, while reducing drag in the transonic region, lost out to the relatively straight wing beyond Mach 1.2—where this new fighter was to operate. It was decided that the aerodynamics of an exceptionally thin and straight wing (18-degree sweep) could provide the ability to fly at speeds up to Mach 2.2.

The weight of the various proposed designs fluctuated greatly from a low of 8,000 pounds to more than 30,000 pounds. By early 1953, the Lockheed L-246 design emerged as the most likely contender with an empty weight of 12,000 pounds and a gross weight of under 16,000 pounds—less than half that of most of the *Century Series*. It was to carry two 30mm cannon.

The most striking visual aspect of the proposed fighter as it was laid out on the drawing board was the short wing span of just under 22 feet and a total wing area of 196 square feet that was mounted far aft. This was incredibly short when compared with the 47-foot span and 385-square foot wing of the F-100 then being readied for flight test. However, the Lockheed plane was built for speed that would come at low angles of attack. It would give up some maneuverability because of high wing loading, and greater induced drag at high angles-of-attack and G-forces. The wing would literally "slice" through the air with a leading edge radius that was only 0.016-inches—sharp enough that it would be covered by a felt protector during ground maintenance.

Another notable oddity was the negative 10-degree dihedral (slant of the wing). More correctly called "anhedral," this feature was necessary to provide better roll control because of the large vertical fin.

With a wing of such small area, special attention was directed to the landing configuration to provide a reasonable approach speed. Of course trailing edge flaps were employed, but to increase their effectiveness a technique called "boundary layer control" (BLC) was used. High-pressure air from the 17th stage of the engine's compressor was routed into the wing. This flow was directed through a series of small openings (holes) over the upper surface of the flaps when extended. This

Figure 10-06. The wooden mockup of the XF-104. USAF Photo.

Figure 10-07. The unmanned Lockheed X-7 explored speed ranges well beyond those available to contemporary wind tunnels. USAF photo.

Figure 10-08. The XF-104 was noticeably shorter than the production version and lacked the ventral fin and air intake "spikes." USAF Photo.

reduced the turbulence in the "boundary layer"—that layer of air that flows directly against the structure. This technique delayed the stall (boundary layer separation) to a noticeably lower airspeed.

Another feature, designed to increase the camber of the wing during low speed operations, was to include full-span leading edge flaps that lowered in concert with the trailing edge flaps. George Andre notes: *"For takeoff and combat maneuvering, both were extended to 15 degrees. For landing, leading goes to 30 and trailing goes to 45. As the trailing edge flaps further extend past the 15-degree point, a duct slowly opens and allows bleed air to wash over the flap for increased lift. Only after the flap gets to the full 45 degrees, is BLC air at full flow. BLC is dependent on power setting, so reducing power diminishes BLC effect. For this reason, we land with some power on and do not go to idle until the main gear touches. A problem would be a crushed or failed duct, which would result in full BLC on one wing and not the other—causing a violent roll. For this reason, you kept your hand on the flap handle and if you got a roll, you'd go immediately back to 15 degrees."*

Bleed air from the compressor was also used to pressurize the cockpit, the G-suit (on early models), and electronics, as well as to de-ice and defog the windscreen and to purge the gasses from the M-61 gun compartment.

The "area rule" was a known factor, but in analyzing the design, the short wings coupled with the air intake position and fineness ratio presented a minimal drag profile. The "area rule" would not be a major consideration! The symmetrical fuselage was adopted mainly because it looked right and the position of the mid-wing resulted in less drag. It also allowed for more easily extending the fuselage length in the future.

The "all-moving" horizontal stabilizer (stabilator) was positioned at the very top of the vertical stabilizer to minimize the possibility of *inertia coupling*—the tendency for an aircraft to lose stability while maneuvering with rapid or high-G rolls. With its low-aspect-ratio wing, the L-246 would be susceptible to this not fully understood phenomenon.

Several aspects were critical to achieving the hoped-for performance. One was the ability of the General Electric Company to produce an engine with more than 10,000 pounds of thrust—the J79. The second was the exceptionally small and thin wing, which would produce less drag. If the engine could generate the needed thrust, then the L-246 could power itself through the high-drag transonic region without a highly swept-wing or pronounced area rule.

Once it was decided to use the thin wing—just 3.36 percent of the chord—other design considerations began to fall into place. It was obvious that the gear had to be retracted into the fuselage and that the air intakes for the engines would best be positioned at the wing roots on each side of the fuselage. This left the nose available for the radar and armament.

After considering more than a dozen possible configurations, the design was completed and Lockheed management approved the project in October 1952. It was presented to the Air Force several weeks later. They liked the concept. Because no formal request had been made for the proposal, it was necessary for a General Operational Requirement to be issued for a "light-weight air superiority fighter." The only serious competition came from North American, who put forward a version of the F-100 originally designated the F-100B, but later redefined as the F-107. However, Lockheed obviously had the inside track and the L-246 (now called the Lockheed Model 083-92-01) became the XF-104 *Starfighter* in March 1953 with a contract for two prototypes. The mockup was assembled by April 1953, and the first two airframes began taking shape in the "Skunk Works" prototype shop in the summer of 1953.

To examine the aerodynamic properties of the proposed wing, versions of it were used on the ramjet powered X-7. This unmanned test vehicle was designed to fly at speeds up to Mach 2.5 and to altitudes of 80,000-feet. Using various wing shapes, data were collected about the wing as well as the ramjet itself.

The research craft was air-launched from under the wing of a B-29 (and later the B-50) during the years 1952 through 1960. After it was released, a 105,000-pound-thrust solid-fuel rocket motor accelerated the X-7 to the Mach 2 operating speed of the ramjet. It was then discarded and the ramjet continued powering the X-7. Sixty-one X-7s were flown during that period, reaching speeds of up to

Mach 4.3 and altitudes to 106,000 feet. Models of the F-104 wing design were validated for lift and drag, as well as structural integrity and susceptibility to flutter in the early flights.

The aero-elasticity of the thin wing (its tendency to bend) was countered, in part, by its short span and the "end plate" effect of long jettisonable tip tanks. Additional testing of both the wing and empennage (tail) was done with high-velocity aircraft rockets of the type that were used as air-to-ground weapons. Also, a similar wing had been employed on the Douglas X-3 several years earlier and Lockheed was able to review the data that resulted from that program.

The nose fairing was a challenge, in that it was to be an exceptionally sharp cone. At the most forward point, the pitot tube (for measuring the airspeed) was positioned out in front of any turbulence induced by the airframe itself. The nose cone fairing was made from a new plastic filament-wound material. The challenge was to allow the radar to "see through" the nose and around the pitot head. A Douglas DC-3 was configured with the "Pinocchio-like" F-104 nose and some of its avionics for airborne testing.

The XF-104 incorporated two completely independent hydraulic systems powered by engine-driven pumps that provided boost to the three-axis flight control surfaces and the speed brakes. These primary flight controls were activated by servos which received signals sent by the pilot's movement of the control stick, as well as inputs from the stability augmentation system and the auto-pilot.

There was also a third emergency hydraulic pump that could be extended into the air stream, where a small wind turbine provided the pressure source for the primary flight controls. The landing gear was designed to use a manual release when hydraulic power was lost. This allowed the gear to fall into place and lock using gravity and aerodynamic forces.

The first XF-104 required almost a year to fabricate, and the airplane was transported from Burbank to Edwards AFB in January 1954.

Flight Test

Because of the advanced nature of the F-104's systems, there was extensive ground testing before the Category I flight test program was begun by Lockheed. As the GE J79 engine was not going to be available for the initial flight tests, the first two XF-104s were completed with the Wright J65 *Sapphire* (built under license from the British company Armstrong Siddeley).

The first official flight occurred in March 1954 with Tony LeVier at the controls. The first plane (37786) did not have an afterburner and was unable to exceed the

Figure 10-09. The XF-104 is easy to recognize in photos because of its lack of intake cones, in addition to its AF serial number 37786. USAF Photo.

speed of sound in level flight (the lack of wing sweep and area rule prevailed against the relatively low thrust of 7,800 pounds). The afterburning version was installed in July 1954 and the plane, with 10,200-pounds of thrust, easily slipped through to Mach 1.49 at 41,000 feet, with an absolute ceiling of 55,000 feet.

Tony LeVier discovered an interesting flight anomaly early in the test program when he was performing high angles-of-attack (AOA) profiles. As the plane approached a positive 15-degree AOA, its nose suddenly and spontaneously pitched up to about 60 degrees. This was followed by a violent yawing roll and the aircraft descended at rates of up to 15,000 fpm. Further investigation revealed that this condition could result in a spin if the center of gravity was near its aft limits.

If the "un-commanded pitch-up" happened at relatively low altitudes (under 10,000 feet), the result would probably be the loss of the plane. To avoid this, an automated stall warning system was developed which received input from an external angle-of-attack vane that

Figure 10-10. Lockheed Test Pilot "Tony" LeVier poses in full pressure suit with the XF-104. USAF Photo.

activated a stick shaker to warn of an impending stall. If the pilot took no action, the system would pitch the plane forward if the stall became imminent. The pilot could override any of the automated responses. Despite these modifications, the pitch-up problem remained for the life of the plane—especially for the less experienced pilot.

Dudley Larson: "*We had a 'stick shaker' and 'stick kicker' that was based on angle-of-attack. For those who flew it aggressively in the air-to-air role, the shaker was where you wanted the airplane to be—because you knew you were flying it on the edge. If you pulled too hard and got a kicker the airplane would unload and you would lose many degrees of angle off that you were trying to gain. Watching from the ground at the Gunnery range, you could see the 'stick kicker' work if the pilot pulled too aggressively following the pass—you could see that nose pitch down and a little PIO [pilot induced oscillation] until he got it under control.*"

A second and potentially even more serious problem was revealed during a flight involving that same XF-104 flying chase for an XF-104A during a low-altitude flutter test at Mach 1.6 in July 1957. Apparently, the XF-104 encountered flutter of its horizontal stabilizer and the tail was torn off. The pilot, Bill Park, successfully ejected from the tumbling jet.

In the days before advanced computer analysis of structural models the engineering was occasionally imprecise. In the case of the F-104, there was no definitive mathematical determination of the added stiffness required for the stainless steel box structure that comprised the tail. As this flutter situation occurred after the production tooling had been built, it was determined that the greatest thickness of material that could be accommodated by the existing fixtures was one-fourth of an inch. This serendipitous dimension was subsequently used and it turned out to be sufficient. There were no more incidents of tail flutter.

Lockheed test pilot Ray Goudey achieved the highest speed of the XF-104 with the first prototype: Mach 1.79 (1,324 mph) at 60,000 feet in 1955. What resulted from the fertile minds of the small group of Lockheed engineers was exactly what the fighter pilots had asked for—an extremely high performance day-fighter. However, even higher performance was yet to come.

Integrating the J79

Despite the problems with the XF-104, the Air Force was impressed with the plane and ordered 17 Category II service test versions in July 1954 (which received the "Y" prefix). The YF-104 was 5 feet 6 inches longer than the X model to accommodate the new J79 with which it was equipped—for a total length of 54.77 feet. The vertical stabilizer was a foot taller as well.

The General Electric J79 was a marvel of engineering, but it would take some time for the inevitable problems to be ironed out. Weighing just 3,500-pounds, the engine employed a 17-stage compressor and a three-stage turbine, augmented by the afterburner, which used a variable-area exhaust nozzle. This latter feature was continuously variable to optimize the thrust available at different throttle settings and to maintain the tailpipe temperature within acceptable limits.

Figure 10-11. The production of F-104 added the ventral fin and the arresting gear seen in its retracted position adjacent to the fin. USAF Photo.

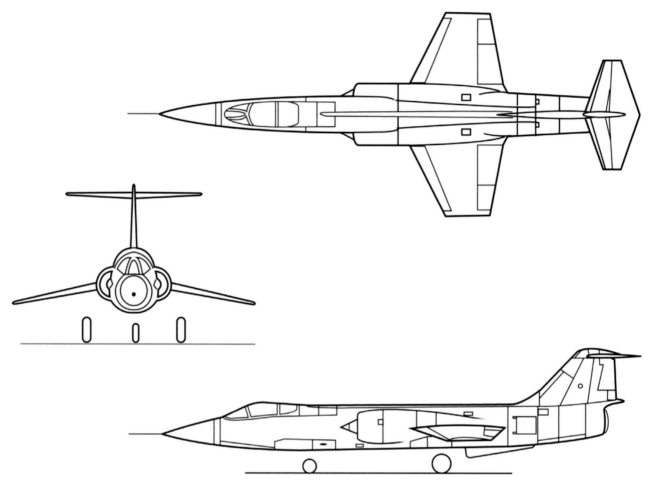

Figure 10-12. Three-view layout of the YF-104. NASA Illustration.

Larsen: "*When you pulled it out of AB you couldn't just yank it, you had to sneak it back to minimum AB and let the aircraft slow down, otherwise you could mess-up the nozzle closure mechanism. It took a while to get down below Mach 1. It wasn't real comfortable up at high altitudes unless you were going fast* [that high wing loading again]. *You'd fly at Mach .9 (about 540 KIAS) on a XC* [cross-country flight]."

However, the biggest technological addition that came with the J79 was the change to the air intakes. At high supersonic speeds, the volume of air coming into the intake was more than that needed by the engine. This could cause the air to "choke" at the intake. For the new engine to power the YF-104 to Mach 2, it required that the air entering the intake be slowed to below Mach 1. This had not been needed for the J65, which could not reach into that speed realm. To make use of the potential power of the J79, the YF-104 used a fixed geometry half-cone positioned in the air intake.

The use of these "center bodies" was considered classified, and covers were always put over them when the plane was photographed during its public unveiling in April 1956 (oddly, the covers were no longer used by

July). The air intake not only slowed the incoming air, but it had an internal slot which allowed some air to pass through the fuselage (internally bypassing the engine compressor) to help cool the 17-foot long engine and its afterburner. This flow of air exited through a secondary exhaust nozzle which also reduced aft drag.

The intake was a "*Rube Goldberg*" affair, according to George Andre: "*all kinds of mechanical linkages… as the inlet guide vanes and the first six stages of the compressor stator blades were variable and shifted in order to avoid compressor stalls such as those that plagued the J57s in the 100 and 102.*"

The YF-104 grew in combat weight with the new engine and expanded internal fuel capacity to almost 19,000 pounds. Four "hardpoints" under the wing and one under the center fuselage allowed for bombs and external fuel, which raised the gross weight to almost 29,000 pounds when all hardpoints were fully loaded.

First flight of the "Y" version was in February 1956, and the following April the YF-104A became the first jet-powered aircraft to exceed Mach 2 in level flight. It also demonstrated the ability to accelerate through Mach 1 while in a climb. Based on the service testing of the YF-104, production orders were placed for 146 F-104As in 1956.

Several additions were made to the plane, including a ventral fin (on the bottom of the fuselage) to improve longitudinal (directional) stability at high speeds and altitudes. The first 35 production models were also used for service testing and introduced the tip tanks and AIM-9 *Sidewinder* infrared-guided air-to-air missile.

The early testing revealed many problems with the engine, which would occasionally flame out for no apparent reason. The wide expanse of the dry lakebed at Edwards was often put to good use. However, during the extensive testing seventeen F-104s were lost to a wide variety of causes. Those that remained were brought up to the latest standards (including beefing up the airframe, which was stressed for 7.33 Gs) and eventually turned over to operational squadrons.

With such high landing speeds, and small tires and brakes on some *Century Series* aircraft, overrunning the runway was an expensive and potentially dangerous problem. To address this, two methods of arresting an airplane at military bases were developed. The first was the earlier barrier system, in which the nose gear encountered a two-foot high nylon web that stretched across the far end of the runway. This triggered a strong cable that would pop up and snag the main gear. This cable would usually be attached to a length of old anchor chain laid out along the side of the runway. Most often, the control tower could raise and lower the barrier. The early F-104 had small hooks built into the main landing gear doors to help catch the cable. The pilot was required to "punch-off" any pylon or centerline stores before encountering the wire, although tip tanks could remain attached during an arrested rollout.

The other arresting system was similar to that found on an aircraft carrier, with a cable suspended up from the runway about 5 inches with rubber donuts and usually connected to old B-52 brake drums for energy absorption. This system, which appeared after the A model, used a tail hook. It does not require any jettisoning, and is much more reliable. The F-104 was the first *Century Series* aircraft to have a tail hook that was pneumatically charged and extended by pulling a handle in the cockpit near the left knee. Canadians deployed the hook when taxiing in on icy surfaces to keep from skidding. To save on brakes and tires—and hopefully avoid the arrestor system—an 18-foot diameter drag chute was incorporated that reduced the landing roll by about 15 percent.

M-61 Gatling Gun

Some of the visionaries of the 1950s predicted the end of the era for the gun-equipped fighter. Accordingly, several of the *Century Series* were equipped only with air-to-air missiles. Nevertheless, "Kelly" Johnson, although known as an "early adopter" of technology, believed the gun still had a place. During the preliminary design stages, a revolutionary new cannon was considered—the General Electric 20-mm M-61 *Vulcan* (named for the Roman god of fire). It was decided to use a single gun of this new type in place of the two 30-mm cannon originally proposed.

The air-cooled M-61 (originally developed as the Model T-171) was mounted on the left side of the fuselage and was capable of firing up to 6000 rounds per minute. The six-foot long cannon weighed about 300 pounds and was fed by a 725-round container of ammunition—little more than 7 seconds worth of firing time. It was integrated with a K-19 fire-control system, an AN/APG-34 radar (with a range of about 20 miles), and a computing gunsight.

However, the development period of the M-61 was extended by many problems. The second XF-104 prototype (37787), which flew in October 1954, was equipped with the M-61 cannon and the AN/ASG-14T-1

Figure 10-13. The extraordinary sharp nose and the air intake spikes are obvious in this perspective of the XF-104A. USAF Photo.

fire control system for the airborne tests. The first few firings went well, but on the flight of 17 December 1954, as Tony LeVier started a gun run, he experienced an explosion followed by the J65 engine running rough. Unknown to Levier at the time, one of the 20mm rounds had exploded in the breech. The bolt was blown out of the rear of the gun, puncturing a hole in the fuel tank. Jet fuel filled the gun bay, leaked out through the gun bay doors, and was sucked into the air intake—eventually killing the engine.

For LeVier, it was important that he bring the plane home in one piece, if possible, so that the engineers could more quickly determine what had happened. Of course, gliding the XF-104 took a great deal of skill—not to mention the fact that the plane could have exploded at any time. LeVier made a successful dead-stick landing on the Rogers Dry Lake at Edwards AFB where the tests were being conducted.

A few months later, following some modifications, Lockheed pilot Herman "Fish" Salmon was conducting more firing tests at 50,000 feet when the gun again malfunctioned violently, causing the hatch that covered the downward firing ejection seat to be blown off and explosive decompression to take place in the cockpit as it lost pressurization. Salmon's pressure suit inflated and, as often happened under those conditions, the faceplate fogged over. Recalling the events of the previous December with LeVier, Salmon thought a similar problem had occurred and elected to eject—the first time the downward system was used. As it turned out his malfunction did not incapacitate the engine, and if he had stayed with the plane to a lower altitude, his faceplate might have cleared and he believed he could have saved the plane.

This was the first loss of many that would plague the *Starfighter* during its lifetime. To keep the M-61 tests moving forward, Lockheed quickly modified an F-94 to supplement the testing. The remedy for one of the M-61's problems was to purge the gun compartment of the gases produced by its firing using bleed air from the engine.

Another M-61 problem involved what to do with the spent shell casings and the links that joined them. Keeping them in the airplane meant that 'unfired' rounds that had been ejected were sitting amongst a heap of hot metal. The possibility that they could "cook-off" and take the plane down was considered. Likewise, ejecting them posed the problem that they could be sucked into the engine air intakes—with disastrous results. In the end the casings were retained, while the links were expelled into the slipstream. Eventually "link-less" ammunition was developed.

As the gun-carrying F-104A neared service introduction, the M-61's reliability was still questionable. Several catastrophic accidents resulted in the gun being omitted from the A series production aircraft as early as November 1957, and it was removed from those that had already been built. The *Starfighter* flew for more than six years, until 1964, with only the *Sidewinder* as its armament, when an improved version—the M61A1—finally restored it to operational use. Today the "Gatling gun" (in several calibers) is in common use in numerous fighter- and attack-type aircraft.

Downward Firing Ejection Seat

When the F-104 was in the design stages, the question of escaping the fighter at Mach 2 was a pivotal issue. The amount of propellant charge necessary to accelerate the seat and its passenger upward to avoid the vertical tail was considerable. Many injuries had resulted in other aircraft during ejection. As a result, it was decided that a downward-firing seat would require less force. Therefore, the F-104 was placed into production with that feature.

The seat functioned in a completely automated sequence to secure the pilot once the decision had been made to abandon the aircraft. First, the cockpit was depressurized and the control stick, between the pilot's legs, was retracted. The shoulder harness was pulled tight and the pilot's legs secured by a "stirrup" arrangement to keep them from being forced off the seat and broken by the force of the slipstream. The early versions consisted of metal spurs attached "cowboy style" to the flight boots. Upon entering the cockpit, the pilot would attach the spurs to a cable that would automatically pull his feet off the rudders and against the seat during the ejection sequence. While most pilots would wear the spurs only on the flight line, some wore them in other venues to show that they had "the right stuff." To complete the escape sequence, a hatch on the bottom of the plane was jettisoned and the seat fired. All this was accomplished in a few seconds—time was of the essence.

Extensive use of the seat, because of the questionable reliability of some of the early F-104's systems, revealed egress problems. The most obvious was with downward ejection within a few thousand feet of the ground. The pilot had to roll the plane over on its back (to eject away from the ground) to ensure having enough altitude for the complete sequence to function. Thus, low-altitude escape was problematical. Twenty-one pilots were killed trying to eject from the F-104, including Iven Kincheloe, in July 1958. He was a double Ace in Korea and had set an absolute altitude record of 126,200 feet in the experimental X-2 rocket plane in September 1956. As his F-104 was passing through 2,000 feet after takeoff he experienced a flameout. Rolling the plane inverted, he made a last transmission, *"Edwards, Mayday Seven Seventy-two, bailing out."* However, the chute was still unfurling when he hit the ground.

As a result, the downward-firing C-1 seat was replaced with the Lockheed C-2 upward-firing seat that used a small rocket engine rather than a single-impulse charge. However, the field replacement was difficult and time consuming. One obvious improvement in ejection capability was that it could be activated on the ground at speeds greater than 90 knots. A zero-time-delay lanyard was engaged by the pilot when operating at low altitudes that would cause immediate separation of the seat and opening of the parachute.

Performance

In May 1958, the F-104 set both the altitude (91,249 feet) and speed record (1,404 mph) while being flown by military pilots—the first time any one plane had held both. The time-to-climb record was also captured in December 1958 when an F-104A reached 82,000 feet

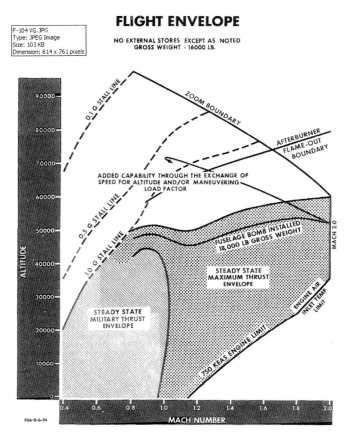

FLIGHT ENVELOPE

Figure 10-14 This V-G diagram from the F-104 Dash-1 manual illustrates some unusual performance aspects (such as "Zoom Boundary") that would not be found on most aircrafts. USAF Illustration.

just four minutes and 26 seconds after brake release. The plane could reach even higher altitudes, but these were the results of a "zoom" climb and could not be maintained in level flight. Its service ceiling (the altitude at which it could effectively maneuver and maintain level flight) was still an amazing 65,000 feet. Its rate of climb peaked at 60,000 fpm going through 35,000 feet.

For the first time the speed of a plane was limited by temperatures. Aerodynamic heating below 36,000 feet had adverse effects on the strength of the front frame of the engine, as measured and displayed as CIT (compressor inlet temp)—thus its sensitivity to the surrounding air temperatures. The Flight Manual (Dash-1) red-line limits included 750 knots indicated airspeed (KIAS) (true airspeed is dependent on altitude and temperature), Mach 2.0, or an engine inlet temperature of 100 degrees Centigrade. For emergency over-speed requirements, these restrictions could be ignored and a speed of Mach 2.2 was possible. George Andre: *"... for the altitude record flight, Mach 2.4 was used which trashed the engine."* The airframe had a maximum one-time limit of Mach 2.4 and a five-minute limit at Mach 2.2. The airframe on later models was stressed to Mach 2.8; however, the canopy limit was Mach 2.26 due to optical failures.

A rather novel method of advising the pilot when he was encountering a thermal limitation was an annunciator that flashed the word "SLOW" when the limiting temperature was sensed. The SLOW light was initiated by a temperature of 101 degrees centigrade as measured in the generator cooling air duct. Andre: *"Anther use for CIT, other than the SLOW light, was to reschedule the engine rpm. As the air got real hot, it became less dense, therefore the engine could be 'revved up' to a higher limit speed. So, at about 1.85 mach, it went into a phase called 'T2 reset', and the rpm would advance to about 104%. You could feel the effect of 'T2 reset' accelerating the plane at 1.8... the inlets were optimized for 2.0...where* [the] *F-104 generated the 'max excess' thrust. Therefore a variety of external stores and tanks could be mounted and still achieve 2.0."*

Because of its high thrust-to-weight ratio (.72), its ability to accelerate was impressive. From subsonic cruise to Mach 2 required less than three minutes at its optimum operating altitude of 35,000 feet. Pilots commented that they could literally feel the acceleration provided by the effect of the inlets as the plane passed through Mach 1.4. The F-104A exhibited its abilities as a point defense interceptor when, in operational configuration, it successfully engaged a target drone 150 miles from its base just 9 minutes after brake release.

The ability to operate at Mach 2 exacted high fuel consumption. Supplementing an internal capacity of 900 gallons, the *Starfighter* had wingtip tanks (340 gallons total) and two pylon-mounted tanks (390 gallons more) that could be dropped to leave the fighter in its trim maximum performance configuration.

Fuselage-mounted speed brakes could be used under almost all flight conditions to quickly dissipate energy. For landing, final approach was flown at 175 knots and 87-90% power, with touchdown at 155 knots, which was comparable to other *Century Series* aircraft. Of some importance is that the F-104 could be landed at its full combat weight without the need to jettison external stores.

As had been demonstrated during its early test flights, landing an F-104 following an engine failure could be accomplished, but was very demanding. The procedure called for the pilot to over-fly the intended touchdown point at 15,000 feet (AGL) and 260 KIAS. A single 360-degree turn was initiated as the descent rate approached 11,000 fpm.

Rolling out on final, the emergency release lowered the gear as the pilot crossed the threshold at 240 KIAS. Without power from the engine, there was no bleed air to enhance the effectiveness of the flaps—thus the higher approach speed. For flameout landing, the *Dash-1* said to start the landing flare at 300-500 feet AGL. While this procedure was practiced early in the operational period, the number of accidents that were caused by the inability to control the high sink rate reportedly led the Air Force to discontinue practicing the maneuver. Andre contends that: "*Flameout landings were never banned and we trained for them regularly, including my service with the Turkish and Greek air forces—not to mention the Luftwaffe. The F-104 had a ram air turbine (RAT) to be extended when needed. It furnished both hydraulic and electrical backup power. Very handy and is the first step in several emergencies.*"

In yet another use of the bleed air from the J79's compressors, it transferred the external fuel supply to the internal tankage. Positive pressure was maintained within the tanks to avoid their collapse from the rapid change in atmospheric compression when the plane performed high-speed descents.

The J79-3B (9,600-pounds of thrust and 14,000 in AB) was later replaced by the J79-19 (12,850 and 18,900, respectively) in some of the squadrons in 1967. The increase in power and efficiency was the result of an improved exhaust nozzle and higher ratio of the compressor stage. In operational (non-combat) use, the maximum power was typically limited to 90 percent of the rated thrust to assure a longer service life. The new engine provided longer range or loiter time; a typical mission was extended by ten minutes with internal fuel only. The Dash 19-equipped plane was capable of Mach 1.1 in level flight without AB (a functionality that is referred to in today's fighters as "super cruise") and

could maintain level flight at 73,000 feet at Mach 2 with the AB.

As most air-to-air combat takes place at subsonic speeds, the ability of the F-104 to maneuver in this realm was critical. Through its use of both leading- and trailing-edge flaps in rapid and limited extension, the plane could perform tight turns while using its excess thrust to maintain airspeed and altitude. These maneuvering flaps could be extended at speeds up to 540 knots (Mach 1 at altitude). However, its lack of wing area put it at a disadvantage to more traditional fighters in this flight region. Some tacticians believed that the F-104 was best employed as an interceptor—not a dogfighter.

It was acknowledged that the turning ability of the F-104 in subsonic flight was its weakest point. However, despite its lack of wing area, in simulated combat with other U.S. fighters of the era (including the Navy's new F-4), the F-104 was found to be "*superior to all other aircraft evaluated at altitudes below 20,000 ft.*" according to one Air Force report—despite the official stance that the age of the dogfight had passed. Tactics were developed to take advantage of the F-104's unmatched climb capability, especially those with the Dash 19 engine. It was important not to allow the F-104 to slow below Mach 1 and to use the vertical climb capability (which was unrivaled at the time).

More than 10,000 flight-hours were accumulated by 60 aircraft in a wide variety of climates ranging from the tropics to the arctic before the aircraft was declared operational.

Operational Use

Throughout its development, the Tactical Air Command had intended using the F-104 as a replacement for the F-100. However, its relatively short range and limited weapons-carrying ability worked against that role. The Air Force had originally planned to procure more than 700 F-104As, but this was scaled back to 170 when TAC decided that the plane did not have the range or carrying capacity. The competition for the tight defense dollar in the Eisenhower era was also a factor, especially following Sputnik in 1957, when many new missile programs came into being and others were expanded.

During that period, the Air Defense Command was experiencing problems in getting the Mach 2 F-106 into service. Although the F-104 was not designed as an all-weather interceptor, and lacked the range of either the F-102 or the follow-on F-106, its outstanding performance virtually demanded that it find a place in ADC. An additional shortcoming was that it initially did not have the avionics that allowed it to be linked to the SAGE intercept system that was being designed as the hallmark of the United States air defense network. Nevertheless, the first operational squadrons of the *Starfighter* were assigned to the 83rd Fighter Interceptor Squadron at Hamilton AFB in California in February 1958.

Despite the relative simplicity of its systems, the F-104 was a high-tech airplane and its J79 engine was state-of-the-art. Numerous engine problems, such as flameouts (the engine losing its combustion), caused several crashes and near crashes during the initial period and it was grounded in April 1958. The biggest problem related to the articulating exhaust nozzle. It was supposed to change its opening size based on throttle settings. However, it occasionally remained in the full open position following shutdown of the afterburner, which severely restricted the normal engine thrust. The early versions had only two positions, and thus the pilot was faced with limited speed variations of either flight up to Mach 1 or full afterburner power that would quickly accelerate the aircraft to Mach 2 (and beyond).

In an effort to remedy the problem the -3B engine was retrofitted. It had a thrust of 9,600-pounds and 14,800-pounds with afterburning. Despite modifications that returned the *Starfighter* to the air by July 1958, the plane continued to experience a high accident rate.

Because it had a very high wing loading (105 lbs/sq ft—the highest of all the *Century Series*), its ability to make tight turns was restricted. High angles-of-attack occasionally would cause the wing turbulence to blank out the airflow over the horizontal stabilator and the plane would pitch uncontrollably and enter a flat spin. This was recoverable only if significant altitude was available, otherwise the pilot earned a place in the coveted "*Caterpillar Club*"—an ever-enlarging fraternity of pilots who had to bail out of an aircraft and were thus saved by the thin silk strands produced by the caterpillar.

Pilots who transitioned to the *Starfighter* were divided in their assessment over the ease of that move.

Perhaps it depended more on the experience level of the individual, as some felt the change was easy while others felt it was "*difficult to learn to fly.*" In an effort to allow pilots to make a safer and more effective transition to the F-104, Lockheed developed the two-place trainer version designated the F-104B. It not only had a full dual set of cockpit controls and instrumentation, but it was fully combat-capable. With the exception of range (the second cockpit displaced some of the internal fuel capacity), the plane had the same Mach 2 performance as the single-seat A. One other noteworthy change was the addition of 25 percent more vertical fin.

In October 1960, 12 of the 83rd Fighter Interceptor Squadron's F-104As were shipped from Hamilton AFB to Taiwan when an international crisis occurred over the two small islands of Quemoy and Matsu off the coast of mainland China. They were all returned a few months later without firing a shot.

The F-104's service with ADC was relatively short. By 1960, sufficient numbers of F-101B *Voodoos* and F-106A *Delta Darts* were available, and the F-104As and Bs were transferred to National Guard squadrons.

One particular problem caused numerous losses as described by James C. Parham, Jr., who flew the F-104 as a member of the 157th Fighter Interceptor Squadron of the South Carolina Air National Guard: "*We lost 6 104s and two pilots because of engine stalls caused by a faulty Bendix fuel control. One of the pilots was our commander, Brigadier General Barnie B. McEntire, who was then on a mission to determine a possible replacement for the Bendix control.*" (McEntire was the first commander of the South Carolina ANG, and the first general officer to become qualified in the F-104.)

Stan Hood notes: "*McEntire lost his life as a direct result of an engine problem immediately after takeoff from Olmsted AFB, Pennsylvania, on 25 May 1961. McEntire was a superb flight leader who had told us younger pilots never to try to land the Starfighter gear up since your feet and legs were so close to the external*

Figure 10-15. The F-104A was a very futuristic looking airplane, shown here with a centerline store. USAF Photo.

skin of the aircraft. General McEntire and Col. Robert H. Morrell had just completed a meeting with the AMA (Air Materiel Area) people charged with resolving the ongoing problems of the J79-3B engine."

Hood recalls the events of that day: "*First, he notified Col. Morrell (number 2), 'Bob I have an engine problem'. He then began an attempt to restart the J79-3B engine (or to clear the compressor stall or cold shift) all of which are critical during the takeoff. During this time, he was positioning the aircraft away from the populated Harrisburg area, and over the Susquehanna River. When he got lined up with the river he had plenty of time to eject, according to a helicopter pilot who reported the F-104 as being at 2500 feet. The take-off (maneuvering) flaps were not in the extended position, causing the aircraft to approach the water... at a very high angle of attack and much higher airspeed (full fuel load), hence causing the aircraft to slam into the water and break up. McEntire was going to save that engine in order to help AF specialists at Olmstead resolve the flameout problem in the GE engine. I believe he thought he had extended the takeoff flaps when in fact he hadn't. The flaps had to be extended promptly due to the generator dropping off-line quickly after the engine RPM got below 60%.*" The name "Congaree ANG Base" was changed to "McEntire ANG Base" in 1961 in his honor.

Parham adds: "*Although limited in range with two Sidewinders and no drop tanks, the F-104 was the quintessential high altitude interceptor. The pilots had a love affair with the F-104. I always experienced a thrill walking out to the aircraft on the ramp—an 'other-worldly' creation. The cockpit was simple, compact, and comfortable. The canopy was straightforward, light and manually opened and closed. At Mach 2, it was quiet—and the long, flexible fuselage rippled ever so gently. Every flight was like a dream come true for a young pilot—I was a Second Lieutenant when I checked out in it! It was the most responsive aircraft that I have ever flown.*

"*In an occasional encounter with a Marine Crusader from the Beaufort Marine Air Station, we could slow down with the Crusader (whose wings tilted for carrier landings) by dropping trailing edge flaps (with their bleed-air boundary control), leading edge flaps, and landing gear—with a wing span of just [22] feet!*

"*Our squadron was deployed to Moron, Spain for approximately 8 months in 1962 during the 'Berlin/Cuban missile crises.' Our 104As were not equipped for air-to-air refueling so we took the wings off and put them inside C-124s for the trip over. While there we lost 4 aircraft (engine stalls from fuel control) and one of our pilots—he was in the front seat of the B model on the turn to final—the pilot in the back seat got out, but by that time the AC [aircraft] was too low and steeply banked for the front seat to get enough altitude. On another occasion, our test pilot, Captain Clifton 'Demi' McClure made a successful dead stick landing in one of the 104s when the engine stalled during a test flight over the base. In spite of this problem, the pilots (without exception) considered the 104 the greatest airplane they had ever flown—superb performance, responsive and straightforward, but demanded concentration.*"

Over the years, the F-104 acquired a faithful following of those who had mastered its idiosyncrasies, and it was given the moniker of "*Zipper*" for its obvious performance qualities.

Dudley Larsen flew the CF-104 as an exchange pilot to the Canadian Air Force from 1981 to 1983. He transitioned from the McDonnell F-4 *Phantom*. He found this an interesting shift, in that he was moving

Figure 10-16. Lockheed F-104A of the 83rd Fighter Interceptor Squadron at Taeyan Air Base, Taiwan, in September 1958, during the Quemoy Crisis (Operation Jonah Able). USAF Photo.

Figure 10-17. F-104 Starfighter's cockpit. USAF Photo.

back a generation: "*It was an easy transition because the plane was very honest to fly—it talked to you. It had a good feel when it settled in. The engines were the same as the F-4 (J79). Of course, the avionics were not as advanced as the F-4 but it was a very basic fighter… I am probably the only USAF pilot that has been qualified and mission ready in the F-104, MiG-21 and the F-4 Phantom. It would perform admirably in the visual multi-bogey ACM [air combat maneuvering] arena, as it was very fast and small. If you turned more than 30 degrees, you became a target [alluding to the F-104's high wing loading—poor turning ability]. The CF-104 would hold its own against the Rhino [F-4] and the proficiency of the pilot made a big difference.*"

The Canadian Air Force used the CF-104 with a reconnaissance pod and for nuclear attack, but not as an interceptor: "*The airplane was a superb low-level attack platform although limited in range. All-in-all, it was a good airplane in its environment (low and fast) and was great fun to fly. The MiG was also a good airplane in the visual turning BFM [Basic Fighter Maneuvers] world but was very limited in range. The Rhino [F-4] was a warhorse, not superb at any one role, but multi-purpose across the board and with a proficient pilot would hold its own in most environments.*

"*Flying out of Cold Lake, Canada, the CF-104 exhibited exceptional performance. On a cold winter day, the two-seater (which was lighter) could indicate 500 KIAS by the end of the 10k runway. Every one of those planes would still do mach 2—the Canadians had excellent maintenance.*"

"*The engine would not stand up to a bird strike or any foreign object damage. If you ran into a bird, you would probably have to leave the aircraft. We lost a number of aircraft and three pilots during my time with the Canadians, but none to mechanical problems or training deficiency.*

"*Because of its limited range, targets were typically within 90 to 165 miles into Eastern Europe—which was as far as you could go … and get back. The airplane was so stable at low altitude because of the high wing loading—you didn't have to spend a lot of time keeping the airplane on a heading.*

"*The ground mapping radar was really good as it allowed you to pick up ground features in miserable weather. We flew with hardcopy strip maps in our lap— 1:500,000 [scale] for navigation legs and 1:50,000 on target run. When you flew off one, you'd stick it down under your leg to get it out of the way, and move on to the next strip. "You'd cut and paste your maps for each mission. We had a set of turn radius templates for different airspeeds at 45 degrees of bank that allowed you to more easily define your ground track.*"

As for the MiG-21: "*It was a true sports car. We only flew it as an Aggressor [at Nellis] and it was a great training aid. In the visual environment, it would certainly handle the F-104 and the F-4. Against the new generation fighters (F-15, F-16 and F-18) we [the MiGs] would be*

Figure 10-18. Looking into the afterburner of the F-104's J79. USAF Photo.

Figure 10-19. The F-104 was a thing of beauty. U.S. Air Force Photo.

able to win on day one—but with a competent pilot in the new generation jets, it was a lot tougher the second day. The 'gee whiz' factor and no previous exposure to the MiG was a decider. The avionics of the new generation and exposure to the MiG made our job a lot tougher on day 2."

George Andre adds: "Regarding combat maneuvering, it is always fatal to play the other guy's game and rules. Keeping the 104 in its optimum performance envelope is the only way to survive. So fly in at 1.6 or better and fire and get the hell out is the answer."

Ed Carney writes: "I flew the Zipper for 3 years with the West German Navy from '79-'82 and loved it. Coming from the A-7E it was like transitioning to jets all over again. Crazy fast and light, and would outrace anything out there. Flying slow (defined as less than 450 kts) could be dicey if you tried to pull any G's. This jet can super cruise at sea level and can maintain its Q [i.e., maneuvering energy] while fighting, as long as the fight never gets too slow. The Europeans used it for many missions (recce, ground attack, nuc delivery, and obviously air-to-air, and it did ok at most and excelled at recce and air-to-air. With the smokeless J79s it was almost invisible and fast and could take gun camera photos of much more sophisticated fighters because their jocks relied too much on their systems and not enough on tactics. It has a nasty temper if abused and will kill you for a mistake. Most crashes in Europe were due to bird strikes, hitting the ground during maneuvering at low level, or takeoff and landing accidents. It demanded a skilled pilot and rewarded him with amazing performance, but was the least forgiving airplane I have ever flown. On the deck, plugging in the burner would shove you from 450 to 750 kts so fast it was almost scary. We were always pulling it back to keep from exceeding a speed or temp limit. In my opinion, along with the SR-71, it is Kelly Johnson's greatest creation."

Making it with TAC—F-104C

In an effort to make the F-104 more acceptable to TAC, a "strike" version of the F-104 was developed that became the "C" series. The reason for this was that the development of a Mach 2-capable fighter-bomber (the F-105) was experiencing its share of teething problems. The Air Force needed a nuclear delivery capability that was significantly faster than the F-100C then in service.

The primary modifications included the addition of an in-flight refueling probe that allowed the filling of both internal and external tanks to extend the range and loiter time. This probe was attached in a "fixed" position (it did not retract) on the left side of the fuselage but was easily removed. It could be retained for extended combat operations but reduced the high-speed performance.

The second change to the plane was the addition of two more wing hardpoints (for a total of six) and a new centerline pylon that could carry the 2000-pound Mk 28 or Mk 43 nuclear bomb (the B61 was added later), as well as conventional ordnance. Any of these could be delivered at speeds greater than Mach 1 using the M-2 bombing computer with a number of release options. These included the toss method (LABS) and low-level nuclear delivery (LADDS).

In March 1956, Lockheed received a contract to build 56 (later increased to 77) F-104Cs. Although equipped with an improved AN/ASG-14T-2 fire control system (which added a clear/night target acquisition capability), the F-104C (with IR-guiding

AIM-9s and a gun) was still not capable of all-weather missions. These versions became operational in late 1958 with TAC squadrons and, although intended primarily for nuclear capability, they could deliver conventional weapons to include air-to-ground unguided rockets in pods suspended beneath the wings.

With 5,800 pounds of internal fuel, the two tip tanks with 1,100 pounds each, and two additional under-wing tanks (2,400 pounds more), a typical B61 nuclear mission would provide for 2 hours of flight at about 500 knots. This would permit strike capability from bases in Western Europe to virtually all of the Warsaw Pact countries. At light weights, the F-104 would break ground at 170 knots; however, the full gross weight F-104C required 227 knots.

With the speeds at which the *Century Series* fighters could fly, it was vital for the pilot to have accurate positional information. Working in the confined cockpit environment, the pilot needed a navigation capability that did most of the tasks of continual positional plotting. The Position and Heading Indicator (PHI) provided the pilot with both vertical and horizontal situation information, a display of navigation data, and a built-in "dead reckoning" computer. It took information from either the TACAN receiver or the Litton LN-3 Inertial Navigation System (INS); the INS was self-contained and did not require input from ground stations, as does TACAN. Also unlike TACAN, the INS's independence of external signals meant it could not be jammed, and it emitted no electro-magnetic signals that could be detected and homed on by an adversary (although it could use available external signals, to include TACAN). However…

George Andre: "*The F-104G was the first airplane to use an INS, which became the primary over-water navigation system for all airliners. This system also furnished attitude data for the flight instruments and the autopilot. In the early days, it was very unreliable and often failed on the first turn after takeoff. We aborted dozens of test flights because of this. Its failure rate also was a causal factor on many accidents in the Luftwaffe because without it, the pilot had no attitude instruments, and in bad weather he was in deep trouble. Later, a backup attitude indicator was added.*"

One exercise that was occasionally performed with the F-104 was to intercept U-2 flights being conducted over the continental U.S. The high-flying spy plane (70,000 feet) had gained fame in 1960 by being shot down over the heart of Russia while performing a photo reconnaissance mission—something it had done some 21 times over a period of three years. During U-2 training flights, F-104s were dispatched to practice coordinated intercept profiles with the ground radar controller. Because of the high altitudes of these missions, the pilot was required to wear a standard pressure suit.

Recapturing the Altitude Record

The Soviets had regained the world altitude record for turbojet-powered aircraft in July 1959 with their Sukhoi T-43-1—the prototype of the Su-9. The Air Force sought to overturn that, but it would take some changes to the F-104 to top the 94,661 number by the 3% required by the FAI sanctioning body. However, the Navy stepped in with their new YF4H-1 and set a new mark of 98,561 feet—making yet another 3% increase that much more difficult.

The "C" series had been flying only little more than a year and used the J79-GE-7 engine (which would prove to be a very troublesome and deadly version). Its nominal thrust in AB was 15,800-pounds, but several modifications reportedly raised this to almost 18,000-pounds for the record attempt. These modifications were primarily to allow the engine to provide thrust in regions of the upper atmosphere whose environment would normally cause the engine to shut down. The AB fuel flow was increased by about 10 percent and the minimum fuel flow rate was reduced from 500-pounds per hour to 250-pounds, increasing the engine "shutdown" altitude and allowing for an over-speed and over-temperature condition to exist—maximum compressor face temperature was raised from 250 degrees F to 390 degrees. The high-speed compressor rpm was increased by about 3.5 percent. The "Top Reset" rpm was likewise increased to 104.5 percent and the engine flow bypass flaps were allowed to operate in the "open" position. To feed the air into the engine, the compression cones on the exterior of the inlet were lengthened to permit the higher Mach number entry speed. These changes also required fitting the larger "B" Series empennage.

The attempt was made on 14 December 1959, with Captain Joe Jordan as pilot of the F-104C (56-0885). Jordan followed a prescribed flight path that had been calculated to provide the greatest "zoom" capability. He accelerated to Mach 2.36 at 39,400 feet and then pitched up at 3.15-Gs to a 49.5-degree climb. The AB was shut down at 70,000 and the engine brought to idle going through 81,700 feet. The peak altitude of 103,395 feet was achieved only 105 seconds after initiating the pull-up. Perhaps the most delicate part of the flight was keeping the plane under control going "over-the-top" at an estimated 445 KTAS, as there was very little aerodynamic force available for the control surfaces. The recovery began as Jordan descended through 60,000 feet and was completed at 25,000 feet.

Jordon received the Harmon Trophy for 1959 for his efforts.

Nevertheless, the "C" series retained some of the liabilities of the basic F-104—principally the J79. Despite repeated attempts to remedy problems with the then "most powerful jet engine," forty accidents over a five-year period had now taken the lives of nine pilots and destroyed 24 aircraft. Another major year-long modification program called *"Project Seven Up"* began in May 1963 to improve the reliability and maintainability of the engine.

Training Astronauts

One of the more interesting adaptations of the *Starfighter* was the inclusion of a liquid-fuel rocket engine set above the J79's exhaust and extending out beneath the vertical tail. The wingspan was increased by two feet on each side and the intake cone was lengthened 20 inches to allow for a more adequate supply of air for speeds up to Mach 2.2.

Three aircraft designated "NF-104" each had a Rocketdyne AR2-3 6,000-pound thrust engine to augment the J79. Using the JP-4 that fueled the J79, the rocket engine used hydrogen peroxide as an oxidizer and allowed "zoom" flights to 120,000 feet during the early 1960s.

To provide for three-axis control in a region of the atmosphere too thin to allow the control surfaces to be effective, the NF-104 used a Reaction Control System

Figure 10-21. Chuck Yeager and the NF-104, 4 December 1963, one week before that fateful flight depicted in the movie "The Right Stuff." USAF Photo.

(RCS) powered by hydrogen peroxide. Composed of 12 small thrusters mounted to provide pitch, roll and yaw, it was similar to that used by the X-15.

The Air Force was eager to train pilots for their pending space flights in such advanced rocket ships as the X-20 *DynaSoar*. Boosted by a modified Titan ICBM, the X-20 was to have carried out military programs in Low Earth Orbit. The NF-104 was designed to allow the pilots to experience a few minutes of weightlessness while orienting the aircraft using the same type of RCS system as was being developed for the X-20.

From straight and level at 35,000 feet, the NF-104 was accelerated to Mach 2.2 and then put into a 3.5-G pull-up to an angle of about 70 degrees. The aircraft would continue through 75,000 feet, where the J79 would be shut down and the rocket motor would be fired until its fuel was exhausted. The pilot would essentially be in a weightless state for almost 90 seconds as he coasted over the top, using the RCS system to control the aircraft. When engine power was lost, the bleed air was no longer available to pressurize the cockpit. Thus, the cockpit was intentionally depressurized before the maneuver began to verify the pressure suit integrity.

It was on one of these flights that Chuck Yeager experienced another close brush with death. At the time, he was the Commandant of the Air Force Flight Test Center that was to use the unique aircraft. He had flown a flight earlier in the morning of 10 December 1963 to get a feel for the aircraft and had reached 108,700 feet. His objective in the second flight was to see how high he could get the aircraft—he wanted

Figure 10-20. The NF-104 going into the vertical plane. USAF Photo.

to set a new record. As he went over the top at 104,000 feet, Yeager attempted to lower the nose using the RCS. However, the nose failed to respond, as it had on the earlier flight, and the angle of attack continued to increase. Yeager knew the consequences of allowing the tail to become blanked by the wing and continued to use the thrusters until he exhausted the hydrogen peroxide fuel.

The plane fell off into a spin, and this was essentially a maneuver from which he could not recover. With the engine spooled down, and in flat vertical descent, there was not enough air moving through the engine to allow for an air start. There was no hydraulic power available because that too was operated off the engine. Yeager remained with the aircraft through thirteen turns before he determined that he was not going to be able to recover.

As he initiated the ejection sequence (the pressure suit was already inflated), the small rocket propelled the seat vertically from the plane. Yeager separated from the seat and the parachute began its opening sequence. However, the seat entangled with the shroud lines of the parachute. The small rocket motor that had propelled the seat was still emitting some molten residue and it began burning through some of the nylon risers. Yeager was momentarily alarmed at the possible consequences. Although the chute successfully completed its opening, the worst was yet to come. With the parachute retarding the fall of its passenger, the seat, which was slightly above Yeager, continued its accelerating fall—right onto his helmet.

The impact was severe enough to stun him temporarily. It broke the visor on the helmet and allowed the burning lava-like substance of the ejection motor to mix with the pure oxygen environment within the suit. The rubber seal around the helmet immediately ignited. Yeager relates, "*My head was engulfed in flames…I couldn't breathe!*" He immediately opened what was left of the visor, which shut off the flow of oxygen, but the fire had yet to burn itself out. He was still struggling to extinguish the flames and clear the smoke so he could breathe when he hit the ground—hard.

The area around his left eye was badly injured. Much of his face and hand were severely burned. Nevertheless, Yeager was released after little more than a month in the hospital and was able to continue his flying career.

Vietnam
As America ramped up its military involvement in Southeast Asia in 1965, interdiction by the North Vietnamese Air Force of missions being flown into

the North by both Navy and Air Force fighter-bombers became a problem. Although it was recognized that the F-104 represented one of the best air superiority fighters in the world at that time, its introduction into the region would require yet more logistics support, and so the move was initially not considered. However, as the North Vietnamese and the People's Republic of China escalated their own aggressive role in the air war using MiG-17s and -21s that decision was quickly reversed. In April 1965, twenty-four F-104s were flown to Taiwan. Following a one-week period of preparation, 14 of these F-104s were operated out of DaNang in South Vietnam with rotations back to Taiwan every two weeks.

Two primary missions were initially established. The first was to escort the Lockheed EC-121D *Warning Star*, the *College Eye Task Force's* radar warning aircraft (and military equivalent of the Lockheed *Constellation*). A typical sortie would consist of three flights of four F-104s, the EC-121, and two KC-135 tankers to provide aerial refueling, and the sortie lasted up to five hours.

The second role was as MiG Combat Air Patrol (CAP) to escort fighter-bombers into North Vietnam. These missions were typically of a much shorter duration, lasting upwards of 90 minutes. The arrival of the F-104 had an immediate effect on MiG operations. The North Vietnamese avoided engaging the F-104s, which were armed with the M-61 and four *Sidewinder* missiles. Only two contacts were recorded during the next several months and neither resulted in any weapons being fired. A third role, as a forward weather observer, was also occasionally provided.

With the F-104C in the combat theater and the MiG threat subdued, it was decided to use their capability against targets in the North as well as ground support in the South. Reports indicated that the aircraft was very effective and accurate, especially with its M-61 and ability to arrive quickly to a specified location. However, it still lacked load-carrying and all-weather capabilities, and was very susceptible to ground fire damage.

The first deployment was released by December 1965 for return to the United States. However, early in 1966, the high performance MiG-21 began to make its appearance. Although the F-4C was more than capable of handling the MiG-21; its "missile only" armament had already come into question, and it was in the process of being modified to carry the M-61 cannon. By June the F-104 had returned to Southeast Asia.

The F-104s provided escort for the heavily laden F-105s going into the North on low-level bombing missions. The F-104 was preferred over the F-4 because it could fly at the F-105's speed over a longer range. However, because the F-104s were not equipped with electronic countermeasures (ECM), they had to depend on the F-105s to warn them of radar "lock-on" from SAM sites. Although the MiGs avoided the F-104s two were lost to SAMs on the same mission, and it was decided not to operate them over the North so long as the MiG threat remained minimal.

The ground attack role was again implemented, but the F-104's inability to carry a large number of bombs made it less effective than the F-105 or the F-4. Thus, it was decided that the F-104 was not well suited for either close air support or strike force escort. By July 1967, the decision was made to withdraw the F-104 from combat operations in Vietnam.

Ron Darcey, a former F-104 pilot, made these observations: *"I had the good fortune to talk with Tony LeVier, who brought me up on why the Air Force (the bomber guys) didn't want the airplane. What I learned ... convinced me the airplane was poorly used throughout its service life in the USAF. Unfortunately the problem with most written material on the airplane is by people who are not pilots, do not understand aerodynamics and do not understand the realities of sitting in a single-place airplane that was designed as a clear air, air superiority fighter, not a strike platform. To better understand the 104 as an air-to-air fighter, one must first understand that while it does not turn well, that is not the way the guys with the 479th [at George AFB] flew it—fighting the airplane you play the vertical and few airplanes of the day will compete with it and (if well flown) will win most every time.*

"The 479 guys would ACM [Air Combat Maneuver] with all types of dissimilar fighters and if they played their turn and burn games would lose every time. If however they went vertical, and won, the other guys would go home; so...to keep the fight going they played the turning game, lost but [with] each engagement, learned a lot more about the airplane's capability and how not to fight. However, the guys they really trained with were Navy and Marine pilots flying the F-8. One of my Marine air officers who ACM'd with them commented: 'When the 104 guys went into the vertical you rarely had a chance unless they made a mistake, which was not often.'

"Of interest when deployed in Nam, several engagements occurred, one involving a MiG-19S

Figure 10-22. Two F-104A Starfighters (s/n 56-0769 and 56-0781) in flight with Lockheed RC-121D Warning Star. Note the Sidewinder missiles on the wings in place of the tip tanks. USAF Photo.

CHAPTER TEN

(Shenyang J-6) [and] *a flight of 104s flying an F-105 BARCAP* [which] *bounced the J-6… [the pilot] locked up but was refused [permission] to shoot as they approached Hanoi—to this day he feels he should have taken the shot. There is more to the story however, much of which tells how poorly the USAF ran the air war there.*

"Also of interest, when the 104 was deployed as MigCAP, BARCAP or escort, the MiGs usually stayed on the ground. On occasion MiGs from China would scramble, probably to test reaction time, and on several [instances] 104 pilots would respond, at Mach to run them back.

"The 104 was originally deployed to Nam, once the VNPAF began intercepting air strikes, as MiGCAP. When they flew these missions, the VNPAF stayed on the ground, as it wasn't their mission to go air-to-air. Another criticism was its range. On air superiority missions (Nam) the airplane was configured with a pair of AIM-9s [Sidewinders] on the wing tips, and drop tanks under the wing. That gave the airplane a range comparable to the F-4. But, when configured with a pair of 750-lb bombs [and] tip tanks, performance and range fell way off. Of course, what should be realized is that the 104 did fly missions up to 7 hours at a time when required—air refueling of course, a must for every mission for every airplane. What was (and still is) appalling with our military procurement policy on fighters is, if it can't carry a bomb, it ain't worth having. That was the Starfighter's swan song in the USAF."

Foreign Service

Because of its lack of "fit" into USAF operations, the F-104A was released to foreign governments early in its career. The F-104 was adopted by ten other NATO countries (including Canada) and by the Japanese, who flew more of them than the USAF. It also served with the air forces of Jordan, Taiwan, and Pakistan. It was built under license, as well as through "component" build-up kits. Because these foreign countries had such a large stake in the plane, the export versions evolved into a more capable aircraft with upgrades to its avionics and it served longer than those used by the United States.

The F-104G was built under license in Europe in 1960 and had the all-weather capability needed to operate in the severe European climate and provide for both interception and tactical delivery of conventional weapons. The "G" received the Litton LN-3 inertial navigation system that allowed for a display of the direction and distance to pre-selected targets. However, although once more being on the leading edge of technology, the aircraft's operational capability suffered from the LN-3's development problems.

With slightly increased fuel capacity and seven hard-points, the F-104G had a higher take-off weight, which necessitated larger wheels and brakes, as well as an increase in the size of the landing drag-chute from 16 to 18-feet in diameter. The Lockheed C-2 ejection seat was replaced with the British Martin-Baker Mk GQ7(F) in 1967. The Martin-Baker seat became popular because of its ability to allow safe escape even from speeds and altitudes of "zero-zero."

West Germany recorded an extraordinarily high accident rate in 1965 when they lost 26 *Starfighters*— at least half to "pilot error," according to Lt. General Werner Panitzki, then the Luftwaffe Inspector General. German pilots were flying 15 hours per month, which was not considered adequate proficiency in *any* fighter, let alone one as "hot" as the F-104. Additional pilot training and better maintenance improved their record in subsequent years.

George Andre: *"The accident rate in the Luftwaffe was horrendous and worst of all [European] users for several reasons: First, they operated in the world's worst weather and were hesitant to cancel for weather. Second, employment in the civilian market was very good and just as soon as a mechanic learned some skills and was useful, he got out and went to work for Mercedes, Volkswagen, Porsche or Messerschmitt and made lots more money. When I was flying with them, I usually had a two-striper for a crew chief, whereas in the USAF, it would have been a senior sergeant. Third, the ranking pilot would be the flight leader. They had some flying sergeants with lots of experience, but 'flight lead' would go to an officer— regardless of time in model. Finally, their air force lost a generation of good talented people in WWII. These men would have been the 1960s wing commanders, etc, but due to the losses, a level of management expertise had vanished. The airplane's nickname in the media soon became 'The Widowmaker.' Out of about 700 planes, they lost around 130 from my best memory. Most were fatal."*

The F-104F was a limited production two-seat trainer version developed for export, and was replaced by the TF-104G model in 1971. The F-104G itself remained in production until 1973, by which time 1,122 had been built.

The F-104J took to the skies in 1961 and remained the primary air defense fighter for Japan until it was replaced by the F-15J in 1986. By that time, about 15 percent of the fleet had been destroyed in accidents—a much improved record over that 25-year period than any other country.

The F-104S was the longest-lived and highest-performing model to operate. It was built by

Fiat in Italy and remained their first line of air defense and tactical air support for more than 40 years. It had nine pylons (to carry up to 7,500 pounds of external stores, vice the 4,000-pound loads of other '104s), and the out-of-sequence suffix "S" denoted that it was the AIM-7 "Sparrow" version. It was chosen in 1965 as an all-weather interceptor instead of several other very capable aircraft (including the McDonnell F-4 *Phantom II* and the French *Mirage III*). Its more fuel efficient engine, coupled with advanced avionics and missiles, allowed this *Starfighter* series to outperform aircraft designed a decade after it had left the U.S.' drawing boards.

The delivery of the last F-104S in March 1979 signaled the end of production in any country—a span of 23 years. However, its subsequent upgrades, which included frequency-hopping lookdown/shootdown fire control capabilities (to include all-aspect AIM-9L as well as AIM-7 missiles) for its interceptors, along with a new IFF, GPS and other advanced avionics, effectively improved it to third- and even fourth-generation levels.

Follow-on

While subsequent fighters continued to grow in size and weight, an Air Force study towards the end of the Vietnam War concluded that a new lightweight day fighter, like the F-104, was needed in the Air Force's inventory. "Kelly" Johnson attempted to improve on the F-104 with an "in-house" design known as the CL-1200 *Lancer*. Despite the reputation of the "Skunk Works," the CL-1200 never went beyond the mock-up stage.

Lockheed produced the Mach 3 A-12 *Blackbird* as a response to the CIA's request for a follow-on to the U-2 reconnaissance plane. This was subsequently developed into the SR-71 and the YF-12 interceptor, which first flew in August 1963. A YF-12A set both speed and altitude records in May 1965 of 80,258 feet and 2,070 mph with Pilot Colonel Robert Stephens and FCO (Fire Control Officer) Daniel Andre. Also in May 1965, the Air Force issued a production order for 83 F-12Bs, but with rising Southeast Asia War costs and a changing threat priority from bombers to ballistic missiles, the F-12 program was officially cancelled in 1968.

Lockheed would not produce another fighter until research began in 1973 on a stealth fighter, which became the F-117 "Nighthawk." In reality, the F-117 was not a fighter but a subsonic ground attack aircraft and had no armament with which to engage other aircraft. The reversion to the "old" numbering scheme for the project was an attempt by the United States to misdirect Soviet intelligence.

Variants

There were sixteen variations of the F-104, most of which were built for, or under license by foreign governments.

Table 10-1.

Lockheed F-104 Variants		
Type	Notable aspects	No.
XF-104	First two Prototypes	2
YF-104A	Service evaluation	17
F-104A	First operational variant	153
F-104B	Two place transition trainer — Combat capable, no M-61	23
F-104C	All-weather for TAC — additional pylons	77
F-104D	Two seat version of F-104C — Last model operated by USAF	21
F-104DJ	Built for the Japanese	206
F-104G	European C Mod w/ GE J79-11A 15,600 lbs— Upgraded FCS	1,127
TF-104G	Two-seat F-104G	220
RF-104G	Tactical Reconnaissance	189
CF-104	G version built by Canadair	200
CF-104D	Two-seat CF-104	38
F-104J	Japanese version of G Mod	210
F-104DJ	Japanese Two-seat	20
F-104N	Built for NASA as chase plane (not to be confused with NF-104).	3
F-104S	Italian built — Operational through 2004	245
NF-104	Rocketdyne AR2-3 astronaut trainer	(3)
	Total Build	**2,580**

Phase Out

Despite its unquestioned performance, the *Starfighter* never achieved the prominence or permanence that it might have found as an air-superiority day fighter in the United States. Development problems continually plagued many of its innovative technologies, which included the M-61 cannon and its J79 engine system. It gained a questionable reputation almost from the beginning as "a missile with a man in it," and being too hot for the average pilot to handle. (Of course, that label was applied to many aircraft that eventually found their niche.) Of the 2,580 aircraft built, a high percentage was lost due to a variety of operational accidents, leading to much criticism. However, most authorities agree that the problem was more due to mechanical failure and training deficiencies than to its Mach 2+ performance envelope.

Cost per unit varied with the series, but the F-104A was typical at $1.7 million. Like many of the *Century Series*, the price of an F-104 was about equally divided between its airframe, avionics, and engine. It was estimated that maintenance was $400 per hour—rather modest by today's standards.

From the time of its introduction in the late 1950s and through the mid-1960s, the F-104 was judged superior to practically every fighter of its day, provided it could freely use its speed and vertical maneuvering advantages. Most F-104 assets, transferred in and out of ADC and TAC during the 1960s (and with service in Southeast Asia and other contingencies along the way), wound up in the Air National Guard, the boneyard, or as drones—leaving only units in Texas (until 1967) and southern Florida (through 1969). The Puerto Rican Air Guard was the last unit to have F-104s, where they served until 1975.

Although it was operational for only 15 years as a fighter in the USAF inventory, the F-104 (in several incarnations) found unquestioned, though sometimes troubled, homes with several foreign air forces. Its F-104G tenure with the German Luftwaffe saw an exceptionally high accident rate that was induced more by inadequate pilot training and proficiency in the face of poor European weather than by technical deficiencies with the aircraft. Once this aspect was recognized and addressed, it went on to serve effectively for more than 20 years. Canadian CF-104s, many of which also operated in Europe (as nuclear strike fighters), had their own high loss rates.

On the other hand, and despite its own losses, Italy used and upgraded its F-104S fleet as multi-mission front-line aircraft for more than 35 years.

As of this writing, there are at least three airworthy *Starfighters* in civil registry.

"Kelly" Johnson's fighter achieved all that it was designed to do, but it had never been effectively employed in the role for which it was best suited—day point-defense interceptor.

Characteristics & Performance Data	XF-104 1-seat Prototype	F-104 1-seat Interceptor	F-104B 2-seat Trainer	NF-104 1-seat Astro Tng
Length (ft in)	49'2"	54'8"	54'8"	54'9"
Wing Span (ft in)	21'11"	21'9"	21'9"	26'9"
Height (ft in)	13'6"	13'6"	13'5"	13'6"
Wing Area (sq ft)	196	196.1	196.1	212.8
Engine	J65	J79	J79	J79-GE-3B AR2-3
– Mil Pwr /AB (lbs)	7,800/10,200	10,000/16,600	9,600/14,800	9,600/16,000 6,000
First Flight	Mar-54		Jan-57	
First Delivery (for op'ns)	N/A		Feb-58	
Empty Weight (lb)	11,500	14,000	13,727	13,500
Combat Weight (lb)	16,700	20,640	17,812	21,400
Max TO Weight (lb)	16,700	29,027	24,912	21,400
Max Speed, 40Kft (mph)	1,324	1,328	1,145	
Initial climb (ft/min)	35,000	48,000	64,500	
Service Ceiling (ft)	55,000	50,000	64,795	
Normal Range (sm)	695	420/1,080	460/1225	
Wing Loading lb/sq ft	85	105		
Thrust/Weight	0.61	.54 .76		

Table 10-02. Lockheed F-104 Specifications

Origin of Republic Aviation

There were many colorful and extraordinary characters who founded aviation companies during the early years. Alexander de Seversky (1894-1974), whose father was one of the first to own an airplane in Russia during the reign of Czar Nicholas II, stands out. The young de Seversky had already mastered the art of piloting by the age of 14 and earned an engineering degree from the Russian Naval Academy before going to sea during the First World War. At his request he was transferred to the Military School of Aeronautics, where he received a graduate degree in 1915 and served as a naval aviator. It was while on his first combat mission against a German destroyer that he was shot down and lost his left leg. Only by appealing directly to the Czar was de Seversky able to return to combat. He was subsequently forced down behind German lines but managed to escape. He ultimately completed 57 missions and shot down six confirmed enemy, making him the Russian Navy's leading "*Ace*." By 1918, he had been posted to the United States as an Assistant Naval Attaché to the Russian Naval Aviation Mission.

Following the Bolshevik Revolution, in 1918 de Seversky requested to remain in the United States, as he was an ardent anti-communist. He approached the War Department with an appeal to put his aviation experience to good use and was made a consulting engineer and test pilot. After the war ended he was an aide to General "Billy" Mitchell and assisted him in his efforts to prove the strategic value of air power. This close tie of friendship as well as common vision would remain with de Seversky long after death had taken General Mitchell.

One of de Seversky's first patents was issued in 1921 that involved air-to-air refueling—a capability that would dramatically extend the reach of air power—but not for more than 30 years into the future. Another of his innovations, developed in concert with the Sperry Gyroscope Company, was the gyroscopically stabilized bombsight. This innovation earned him what at the time was a very large sum of money—$50,000. De Seversky decided to use the money from the bombsight to start his own aviation company in 1923, the Seversky Aero

USAAC photo

Figure 11-01. Major Alexander de Seversky poses with his SEV-3XAR in 1934. This was a land-plane conversion of his record-breaking seaplane. PD.

Corporation. He joined the Army Air Corps Reserve in 1928 and was given the rank of Major; a title he would use proudly throughout the rest of his life.

Seversky's corporation built only component parts and instrumentation, and the business folded with the stock market crash of 1929. Nevertheless, he had gained the friendship of several influential and wealthy people during his travels and, with the help of investor Edward Moore and other associates, he founded Seversky Aircraft in 1931. Employing several Russian expatriates, including Michael Gregor and Alexander Kartveli, de Seversky set out to become a force in America's aviation industry.

The first airplane produced was an all-metal, single-engine three-place amphibian, the SEV-3, which would set several speed records between 1933 and 1939. Seversky, who continued to fly despite his handicap, set a world speed record for piston-engine amphibious airplanes and a transcontinental speed record in 1938. The SEV-3 was much more than a stodgy seaplane, as its lines and construction allowed the Seversky design team to engineer the basic structure of their first offering to the Army Air Corps—the SEV-1P. An enclosed cockpit monoplane with retractable gear, the Seversky P-35A, as it would be known, became the first of a long line of fighters. However, despite the efforts of the Seversky team, the company had been steadily losing money and was deeply in debt. At a rebellious board meeting in September 1939 Seversky was replaced by Wallace Kellett, and the company name changed to Republic Aviation in October.

Although the P-35 would not earn any substantial production contracts, its design (known internally as Army Project AP-4) was continually improved, moving to the P-41, and then the P-43 *Lancer* before finding success as the P-47 *Thunderbolt*. Ultimately, 15,686 P-47s would be built in several variants; the only American fighter to be manufactured in greater numbers was the North American P-51 *Mustang*.

De Seversky no longer had a direct relationship with Republic Aviation, but was a controversial figure for the remainder of his life. His 1942 book *Victory*

Through Air Power described the concepts of strategic bombing that would be the focus of the air war during WWII, and prophesied the direction of the postwar Strategic Air Command.

Design Foundation

As with virtually all of America's aviation companies in the mid-1940s, the jet engine was brought into the development process at Republic Aviation. In response to a September 1944 Army Air Forces requirement for a "day fighter," Alexander Kartveli, who was then the chief engineer, recognized that the jet engine centrifugal compressor designs did not allow for a reasonable fineness ratio and decided to work with the newly emerging axial flow technology. And, like all the other manufacturers, he too opted for the straight, relatively thick wing, as little was then known of the problem of compressibility. However, the speed defined in the specification was 600 mph with a combat radius of 700 miles. This was a tall order for the fuel-thirsty jet engines of the day.

Using the General Electric TG-180, which would become the J35 as the nomenclature became standardized, three prototypes of Republic's AP-43 were ordered in November 1944, to be known as the XP-84. With the war still raging in both Europe and the Pacific, there was no competitive bidding and a production order was placed for 85 P-84s by January 1945 with the plane still a "paper" design. The projected weight continued to grow during the engineering process, while the promised 4,000-pound thrust J35-GE-7 engine developed only 3,750 pounds in its first iteration. The initial XP-84 prototypes were thus overweight and underpowered—a typical problem for the day.

Making its first flight in February 1946, the XP-84A was a clean airplane, but the type would suffer from a variety of problems, such as the "control (stick) reversal." This phenomenon was caused by tip-tank oscillation that

limited its dive speed to .8 Mach. Structural deficiencies limited maneuvers to 5.5Gs because of buckling of the aluminum skin—"doubler plates" were installed at the wing roots to address this trouble. Nevertheless, the F-84 did set a new American speed record in September 1946 of 611 mph. The design underwent many changes before it achieved limited acceptance into operational squadrons as the F-84B in June 1947. Following Republic's use of the name *Thunderbolt* for the P-47, the F-84 was called the *Thunderjet*.

Like its predecessor (the P-47), the F-84, beginning with the C model, had underwing "hardpoints" for air-to-ground rockets for tactical air support—its primary use during the Korean War. It also found itself escorting B-29s on bombing runs over the North, but was not competitive with the MiG-15. It was not until the fifth iteration (F-84E) that the type reached its optimum capability. It was the first production fighter with an ejection seat, and the first fighter (the G model) with in-flight refueling, an autopilot, and qualified to carry a nuclear weapon (the Mk7).

Almost from the beginning Republic tried to interest the Air Force in a swept-wing version. In 1947 and again in 1948, Kartveli made proposals that were rejected by the Air Force, in part because the anticipated performance was no better than the F-86. Only when Republic indicated that as much as 60 percent of the new design would use existing F-84 tooling did the Air Force finally show interest and assigned the designation XF-96 to the project.

A fuselage from the last production F-84E was fitted with swept-wings and tail, and the aircraft made its first flight from Muroc in June 1950. The YF-96A was also fitted with a V-shaped forward windscreen that provided less drag than the more traditional flat plate. However, as was discovered with other fighters of the period that had initially employed that design, the pilot's forward visibility

Figure 11-02.
The Republic P-84 Thunderjet shows its clean lines. U.S. Army Photo.

was significantly impaired and the configuration was changed back.

The performance was good (693 mph at sea level) but not exceptional, and the project probably would have been cancelled had the Korean War not occurred at the end of June 1950. In an effort to avoid the funding restraints on new designs, the designation was changed back to F-84 with the suffix "F" in September 1950. Production began in early 1951 using the 7,200-pound thrust Armstrong-Siddeley *Sapphire* engine built by Curtiss-Wright under license as the J65. The more powerful engine also necessitated enlarging the air intake, using a more vertical oval configuration. In the end there was very little commonality in the tooling.

The second F-84F airframe was reconfigured with the air intakes in the wing root to make room in the nose for reconnaissance cameras. While this change created many new problems for the intake system that took a while to resolve, the knowledge would be used in Republic's next fighter—the F-105.

A New Design Takes Form

As the doctrine of strategic nuclear strike became more focused in the late 1940s, Kartveli took up the cause (no doubt with influence from his early mentor, Alexander de Seversky). Obviously, the interior targets of the Soviet Union would be the province of the newly designed B-47 and the 10-engine B-36. However, it was not hard to envision a supersonic fighter-bomber that could make the dash across the Eastern frontiers of the Iron Curtain in Europe to deliver an atomic payload on targets that were less than 500 miles from bases in West Germany, France, and England.

To do this would require an internal bomb bay to avoid the aerodynamic drag of external weapons. Kartveli and his team decided to use the F-84F layout as a foundation (knowing how frugal Congress was during this period), giving the new fighter-bomber the company designation AP-63-FBX (Advanced Project 63 Fighter Bomber Experimental). The mid-mounted wing had the same 45-degree sweep of the F-84F, but was much thinner (NACA 65A airfoil) and used leading edge flaps and large trailing edge fowler flaps to lower the landing speed.

To provide for internal weapons storage, the air intake was moved to the wing root. This would prove advantageous for several reasons. The availability of the nose for the photo equipment of a reconnaissance version was an obvious thought. However, this configuration would also allow for the large array of electronics that would ultimately be required for the complex navigation and weapon delivery that a supersonic fighter-bomber would have to perform in

Figure 11-03. The Republic YF-96A with its V-shaped forward windscreen. USAF Photo.

all-weather conditions. Problems with the wing root location for air intake at Mach 2 would prove difficult to overcome, however.

Initially the J71, with 14,000-pounds of thrust (in AB) to provide a speed of about 800 mph was considered. However, the projected combat weight of the design kept increasing, eventually reaching 28,000 pounds, and that continued to degrade the anticipated performance. The project was still an in-house funded effort, and Kartveli did not want to submit his proposal until he was quite sure he would have a design that would be hard for the Air Force to turn down.

Yet another redesign, the AP-64, saw the incorporation of the Pratt & Whitney J75—an engine that was also a paper project at this point. Nevertheless,

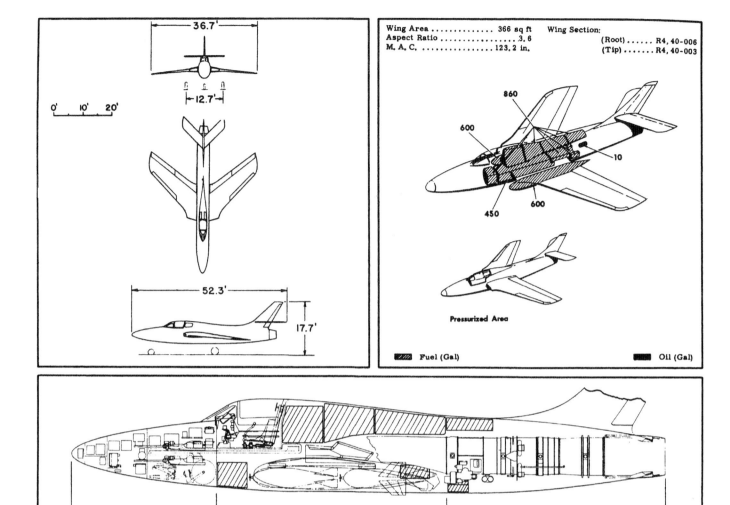

Figure 11-04. This December 1952 illustration of the proposed Republic F-105 shows the design lineage from the F-84F, but bears little resemblance to the final F-105 configuration. The machine guns are shown mounted in the nose as opposed to the wing root. The number and location of the various fuel tanks is also interesting. USAF Photo.

P&W was gaining a strong reputation, and their somewhat revolutionary J57 was just going through its test period and showing great promise. It was not a coincidence that Pratt & Whitney's next iteration of jet engine used the same numerals—reversed. The J75, like the J57, was a two-spool, axial-flow design that would provide 23,000 pounds of thrust in AB—almost twice that of the J57. In this iteration, the fuselage had grown more than ten feet over the initial AP-63, while the wingspan remained almost the same (actually reduced from 36.7 feet to 35 feet).

Armament initially consisted of four T-130 .60 caliber guns in the wing just outside the intake. Provisions for four hardpoints on the wing allowed for air-to-air and air-to-surface missiles then in development.

Initially the design called for "spoilerons" on the upper surface of the wing to perform roll control, but these were later supplemented by traditional ailerons for low speed control. All the control surfaces required hydraulic boosting.

Having spent three years working over the design, Republic formally submitted their proposal to the Air Force in May 1952—it would become a part of Weapon System WS-306A. Several changes were noted, including the switch to a single GE M-61 20mm Gatling gun then in the development stages. The incorporation of the revolutionary MA-8 Fire Control System was a prelude to the sophisticated electronics that would be a hallmark of the F-105 in the years to come. These avionics would also include the AN/APG-31 Radar system and K-19 gunsight. While the Air Force liked the overall concept, it was disappointed that the maximum speed was projected at only Mach 1. However, it gave approval for 199 aircraft. It would be more than a year before the mockup was ready for inspection in October 1953. However, with the end of the Korean War and some doubt as to Republic's ability

Figure 11-05. The first of two YF-105As (54-0098) with the less-powerful J57 engine. It did not have the small AB cooling inlet at the base of the vertical stabilizer. Note the obviously slimmer fuselage at the aft wing root as compared with the B model. USAF Photo.

to bring the project into production in a reasonable time, the order was cut to 15 aircraft by February 1954. A part of the pessimism was due to development problems with the J75.

A second part of the problem was that by August 1953 the Convair F-102 had confirmed that the "area rule" existed—the high drag of the forming supersonic shock wave required careful sculpting of the fuselage profile. It was also at this time that wind tunnel tests determined that a ventral fin would be required for enhanced directional stability. The horizontal stabilizer was "all moving" to incorporate the elevator function as a "stabilator" and, like the F-100, it was positioned low on the aft fuselage.

The design that finally emerged was a mid-wing arrangement that incorporated a sweep of 45 degrees. In keeping with its intended role of high-altitude cruise and low-attitude attack (the hi-lo-hi scenario), the wing area was kept small to provide a smoother ride in low level turbulence. While this aided in pilot comfort, it also reduced structural fatigue to ensure a longer airframe life. However, the relatively small wing area for a plane of its weight resulted in a wing loading (92 lbs/sq ft.) that was 50% greater than the F-100 and was exceeded only by the F-101 and F-104. However, its role was to be high-speed penetration for tactical delivery of nuclear weapons—"yank and bank" maneuvers were never intended as its strong point. It could carry 8,000 pounds in its internal bomb bay and another 4,000 pounds on its five external pylons. The "Toss-bombing" method of nuclear delivery was to be employed with either the Mk 28 or the Mk 43 weapon.

Probe and drogue refueling was a necessary capability initially designed into the F-105—the boom version would eventually follow. The ejection seat, designed by Republic, featured a small solid-fuel rocket-propelled catapult (ROCAT). The charge fired for about one-half second and produced 1,500 pounds of thrust to boost the pilot clear.

With the revelation of the "area rule" and development of the J75 lagging, the Air Force authorized Republic to complete the first two prototypes with the J57-P-25, which provided only 15,000 pounds of thrust in AB. This would allow some preliminary testing of the basic airframe as the engineers went back to the drawing board to incorporate the new "area rule" into a completely redesigned fuselage of aircraft number three. This airframe was not as far along in the manufacturing cycle as the first two and would be known as the F-105A. A full foot had to be added to the fuselage diameter just aft of the wing. The reworked airframe of prototype number three with the area rule incorporated the J75-P-19 with 16,100 pounds of thrust (dry) and 24,500 pounds in AB, and was designated the F-105B. As the project was being procured under the Cook-Craigie plan of development concurrency, the Air Force was again facing mounting re-tooling costs.

Flight Test

The first flight of the YF-105A (54-0098) occurred on 22 October 1955 at Edwards AFB, with Republic test pilot Russell M. "Rusty" Roth at the controls. Roth, a WWII P-38 combat veteran, had joined Republic in 1952 and was their Chief Test Pilot. He reportedly exceeded Mach 1 on this 45-minute flight, but the conditions of that event were not clearly defined to the public. However, the aircraft could not accelerate beyond Mach 1, confirming the obvious presence of transonic wave drag.

A major setback in the test program occurred on 16 December 1955, when the first prototype was executing some high-G maneuvers. During one run at 530 knots, while in a 5.5-G turn, the right main landing gear extended and was torn off by the force of the slipstream. Fortunately, Roth was able to maintain control and made a gear-up landing on the dry lakebed. Although the plane appeared in good condition as it sat on its belly in the sand, the landing had seriously damaged its internal structure and it would not fly again. On 28 January 1956 (43 days later) the second prototype (54-0099) took flight and the test program was able to continue.

Although 15 aircraft were procured in the initial build (with two being the J57-powered "A" series), the B series was the significant redesign, incorporating the area rule fuselage and the J75 engine. The "A" series can be easily distinguished by its elliptical air intake opening, rather than the forward-swept design that would be the hallmark of subsequent variants. Four of the fifteen were designated as YF-105B and the remainder as F-105Bs. The delay in the delivery, however, caused the Air Force to cancel the WS-306L reconnaissance program.

Although Republic apparently had the inside edge for the RF-105 reconnaissance version, some dedicated work by the Reconnaissance Group in the Pentagon saw that there were too many deficiencies as proposed for it to be a viable recce platform. Following some diligent work comparing systems and performance, the RF-4 (nomenclature successor to the F-110) was ultimately chosen. The three YRF-105B airframes planned for that program were completed as the JF-105 (the "J" prefix indicated a temporary modification). These were used in a variety of test programs and never became operational.

The first F-105B (54-0100) made its first one-hour flight on 26 May 1956, with Republic test pilot Henry G. "Hank" Beaird. However, the nose landing gear failed to extend at the completion of this flight and extensive repairs had to be made before further testing could continue. A month later Republic officially applied the name *Thunderchief* to the F-105. (Operationally, the plane would receive a somewhat less glamorous and more disparaging moniker.)

Following completion of the Category II tests in early 1957, the analysis revealed a plane with a lot of potential, but with several problems to overcome. The most significant was "poor acceleration" to reach its top speed. The YF-105B required nine minutes to transition from Mach 1 to Mach 1.95 (in AB) and consumed most of its fuel reserves during that period. It was determined that the air intake was "choking" at the higher Mach numbers; the excess air was interfering with the flow into the engine. The answer to the problem lay with using the same forward-swept "shark-like" design by NACA researcher Antonio Ferri as had been planned for the XF-103.

Coupled with that redesign was the ability to change the intake size to meter the airflow to match the Mach number. The variable air inlet (VAI) control system used an analog computer to manage the air flowing into the engine. At airspeeds below Mach 1.5, a duct plug or "ramp" in each intake would be fully open. As the speed increased the duct plug would move forward to restrict the air intake opening. Moreover, smaller "bleed doors," positioned just before the engine face, would open (based

Figure 11-06. Compare this photo of the F-105B with the previous one to note the larger diameter fuselage just aft of the wing and the AB cooling air intake at the base of the vertical fin. USAF Photo.

on Mach number and temperature) to allow excess air to "bleed off." Finally, "auxiliary air inlets" within the intake duct could be opened by negative differential pressure (if the landing gear was extended) to improve low-speed air flow. These doors were the cause of a second gear-up landing when the suction created by their failure kept the main gear from extending.

Another significant problem was aerodynamic flutter detected in the vertical stabilizer and rudder assembly. As with the F-100, this surface was enlarged. The tail was raised from 17.5-feet to 19.7-feet, and the chord and rudder area were increased as well. Overheating in the aft section of the afterburner due to insufficient airflow was addressed by adding a small air intake at the base of the rudder. It is interesting to compare the similarity of contours of the tail with that of earlier XF-103 designs.

The final innovation to the overall layout was the incorporation of speed brakes into the exhaust nozzle. Four hinged segments of the nozzle allowed the entire circular aft section to open in a "petal" arrangement. Depending on the aircraft configuration, two modes were available. If the landing gear were down, only the left and right "petals" were allowed to open, as the bottom petal would strike the ground during the landing flare, and the top petal would interfere with the drag-chute deployment. If the aircraft were in a "clean" configuration, as would be the case in a high-angle descent during a bombing run or in a dogfight, all four petals would provide for a high-drag configuration for rapid deceleration. All four segments opened slightly when in AB mode to allow for higher exhaust velocities.

Adverse yaw was a problem, but not as bad as with the F-100. A Stability-Augmentation system was employed as part of the autopilot and was activated by a push button on the autopilot control panel on the left console. The Dash-1 noted: "The *stab-aug* mode of operation improves control of the aircraft by damping oscillations about its pitch and yaw axis. Automatic

Figure 11-07. An F-105 taking on fuel with the boom from a Boeing KC-135. USAF Photo.

turn coordination is provided to counteract sideslip or skid. There is no evidence of *stab-aug* action at the control stick or rudder pedals except for the increased stability of the aircraft."

The high wing loading made for long take-offs and landings (up to 8000 feet), with the approach speed being as high as 230 mph at the maximum landing weight. Spin recovery was protracted but conventional, as it was with most of the *Century Series*. The F-105 employed a faired canopy unlike the more traditional "bubble" canopy of most of its contemporaries. This inhibited the pilot from effectively "*checking six.*"

Initial Operational Deployment

The first units of the B series were accepted by the USAF in May 1958 and were assigned to the 335th Tactical Fighter Squadron (4th Tactical Fighter Wing), which had transferred to Eglin AFB, Florida. With support of Command-wide resources, the unit performed Category II and III tests and the first squadron strength units were operational in January 1959.

Because of the accelerated manufacturing process there were many differences between the early production aircraft—this was true for virtually all the *Century Series*. Each "block" was defined by a specific "dash" number—thus there were four early aircraft built in the F-105B's "block 1," five aircraft in the F-105B-5 block, one as a B-6, nine as B-10, 18 as B-15, and 38 as F-105B-20. A total of 75 B-series aircraft were delivered to the USAF, with the B-20 block's production ending in late 1959.

Thus, the B-20 block comprised the largest single production group, and also had the J75-P-19W engine that produced 2,000-pounds more thrust in AB using de-mineralized water-injection. Most "B"s were passed to the Air Guard by 1964, but a few were retained for Instructor Pilot operations as late as 1970 at Nellis and McConnell.

With the advanced capabilities of such a high-tech aircraft came the problems of maintenance. The electronics and the hydraulics were a major concern during the early operational period. For each hour of flight the aircraft required 150 hours of maintenance. In an effort to achieve standardization—a critical factor for providing spares and maintenance training—a program called OPTIMIZE was initiated to modify them to the same standards. In fact, there was a period in 1960 when all the operational F-105s were grounded by a lack of spares. Despite the problems of bringing the airplane into full combat readiness, the potential that it offered appeared worth the cost.

Maximum speed of the F-105B, the first production variant destined for operational use, was Mach 2.15 (1,420 mph). This performance was highlighted in December 1959 by Brigadier General Joseph Moore (then 4th TFW commander) setting a world record of 1,216 mph over a 62-mile (100 km) closed course (a "closed course" is one where the plane completes the speed run after flying a circuitous pattern). Moore earned the 1959 Bendix trophy for his accomplishment. December 1959 also saw the last B models roll off the assembly line.

Despite its performance, the F-105 was not greeted enthusiastically by some pilots—it was big, heavy, and complex. However, the F-105 was the first Air Force plane not to have a loss in its first year of operation. When the pilot mastered the responsive and powerful craft, a bond was created that led to a long-term relationship.

Thunderbirds

Although the F-105 was big and not particularly maneuverable, it was capable of Mach 2, and the Air Force wanted to use its presence as a recruiting tool. One of the most effective recruiting tools since its inception has been the *Thunderbird Flight Demonstration Team*. The *T-Birds* had been flying the F-100C since 1956 and established a 25-minute crowd-pleasing routine. The Air Force felt it was time to provide a new look. With the F-105D filling out the critical operational needs, the B model was considered available for the team, as it was being transferred to ANG units.

The transition to the F-100 seven years earlier had been controversial because of its size and demanding flying characteristics. The switch to the F-105 also brought protest from some quarters because of its size and weight—nearly four tons heavier than the F-100 and twice the weight of the Grumman F11F being used by the Navy's *Blue Angels*. The F-105B had only a slightly better thrust-to-weight ratio over the F-100 (.74 as compared to .66) but a somewhat slower roll rate, and loops would require an extra 800 feet of altitude.

Early in 1964, nine F-105Bs were removed from service and sent back to Republic for modification. The changes included replacing the MA-8 FCS and the M-61 *Vulcan* gun with ballast and two 50 gallon tanks for the different color (red and blue) smoke tracking system. A small baggage area was provided in place of the Doppler navigation system. Provisions were made for gaseous oxygen in addition to the standard liquid O_2 by installing a storage bottle and associated plumbing.

Several structural enhancements were made, including a change to the flap operating speed. It was determined that some *T-Bird* flight profiles would require a "maneuvering flap" capability. Normally the flaps could be deployed at speeds no higher than 275 knots—normal flap operating speed. The new change allowed partial flap extension at up to 500 knots. The fuel system was modified for extended inverted flight. To improve the acceleration response, the speed-brake petals (which open slightly during AB operation and arm the AB ignition circuit), were modified to remain in that position for the duration of a performance. This reduced the normal five second delay in AB operation to less than two seconds. The main landing gear was upgraded to "D" specifications, and a spare drag chute was carried to allow for quick turn-around.

The final change was to the vertical fin of two aircraft. As the fin of the slot aircraft (No. 4) protrudes into the exhaust of the lead aircraft (No.1) in the diamond formation, stainless steel was used for the leading edge to protect it from the heat. The rudder itself was modified to allow full deflection to 18 degrees from the normal 8 degrees to achieve the "knife edge pass." Inside the cockpit, a small control panel called the "Show System" was installed. This allowed specific caution lights to be displayed that related to the plane's "demonstration role," as well as switches for the smoke and flap settings. The two solo aircraft had a switch that enabled the increased rudder deflection. The modifications were completed in time for the team to choreograph their 1964 show.

From the June 1964 article in *Fighter Weapons Newsletter*, Slot pilot Jerry Shockley provided these observations: "*The stability of the aircraft at high and low speeds is amazing; power response is great; flies good with stab aug in or out,... Low speed handling characteristics are very good (once you learn to use spoilers instead of ailerons). ... We are very pleased with the bird and have modified our show slightly from... the 100. ...We do go higher over the top—800 feet to be exact. And the solo's point rolls... pull stab aug and the point will stop as crisp as you'd want. .... Actual figures are 6500 to 7000 feet over the top for the diamond, 3000 feet for the solo slow speed Cuban.*"

With respect to the airspeeds, Shockley added: "*For the diamond, our average entry speed for looping maneuvers is 430 KIAS and our slowest speed over the top has been 65 KIAS (normal 110 to 130 KIAS). ... For the solos—fastest speed slightly over 600 depending on temp, (can't exceed Mach 1), for the opposing hi/lo speed pass and bomb burst vertical rolls. Slowest speed is on the slow speed Cuban—40 KIAS over the top. ... Entry speed for this maneuver is 275 KIAS.*"

Flight leader Paul Kauttu had the following comments: "*Its handling characteristics at both low and high speed were incredible. In close formation at 500 knots on the deck—even in choppy air—she was rock steady. She turned handily and by using the vertical could match the F-100 maneuver for maneuver... maybe a little better. Inverted flight capability was amazing. ... All the power you needed and more. Entry speeds at 400. Over the top, sometimes as low as 80 ... let 'er float ...*

and let 'er fall. The loops were very elliptical, allowing us to easily perform two consecutive loops at any show site ... double loop."

The team had completed six performances and were arriving for their air show at Hamilton AFB, California, on 9 May 1964. As a formation of three who had made a "smoke-on" low pass (100 feet), Captain Gene Devlin began a pull-up in preparation for landing. The aircraft broke in two behind the cockpit and Devlin was killed. It was determined that a structural "splice plate" at that point had failed.

Only six months earlier, at the end of 1963, the *Thud* had the lowest accident rate of any jet fighter in Air Force history—14.7 per 100,000 flying hours. Devlin's crash, and one a week later at Nellis AFB, which was the fifteenth F-105 accident in the intervening period, resulted in a grounding of all 500 F-105s, as the accident rate had soared to 33.7 per 100,000 flight hours. A modification program called Project BACKBONE reinforced the airframe of all early production F-105s. While there was some discussion of returning the *T-Birds* to the F-105 after the modification program was completed, the situation in SEA worked against that decision. The *Thunderbirds* completed the season by transitioning back to the F-100 (D variant).

F-105D—Nuclear Delivery

Although the F-105B was a very capable fighter-bomber, its MA-8 FCS lacked a full all-weather potential. Design began on the "D" series in late 1957 to provide for the larger AN ASG-19 "*Thunderstick*" FCS. The nose was extended 15 inches for the larger diameter R-14 *North American Search and Ranging Radar* (NASARR). As its name implied, this package was developed by the Autonetics Division of North American Aviation. Contained within this unit was the means to perform terrain following for low-level weapons delivery. This was a major leap in capability, as it essentially allowed the F-105 to navigate to a target without any visual references. An on-board computer compared the radar image with a set of predefined waypoints and provided a course line that allowed the pilot to determine his relative position.

This change also revised the primary flight display in the cockpit to incorporate the use of vertical "tapes" for both the airspeed and altitude readouts—combining seven related "round dial" instruments into the two rectangular presentations (similar in appearance to those incorporated in the F-106). Located on either side of the attitude indicator, these two instruments greatly eased the pilot's task of monitoring the flight conditions of his aircraft.

Figure 11-08. The wide array of electronics in the F-105 is apparent in this PR photo, along with the detail of the engine air intake. USAF Photo.

Figure 11-09.
The lines of the F-105D show the many changes from the initial configuration. The "area rule" contours are also quite apparent. USAF Photo.

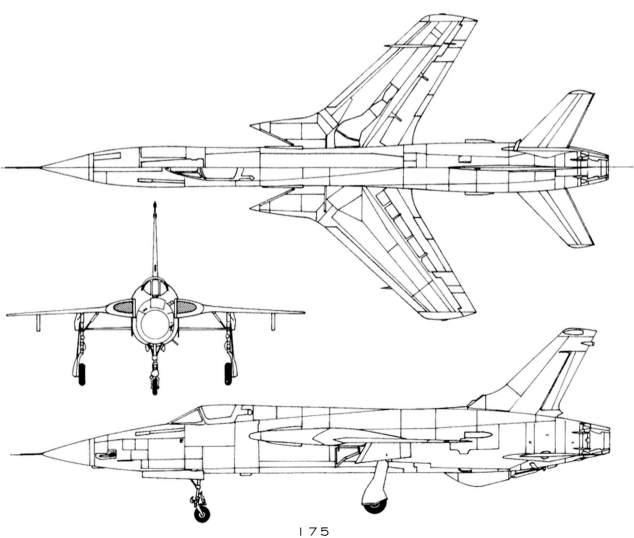

The redesigned fuselage now extended to over 64 feet, and an arrestor hook was built into the ventral fin to avoid overshoots for those runways so equipped. The empty weight had grown from 21,000 pounds for the A series to 27,500 pounds for the D. The maximum take-off weight escalated from 40,561 pounds for the A through 46,998 for the B, to 52,546 for the D. This required the landing gear, brakes, and some structural components of the fuselage to be "beefed up." Performance was maintained by using the P-19W version of the J75, which employed a water-methanol injection system to provide 26,500 pounds of thrust in AB—an increase of 2,000 pounds. This, in turn, required another "retuning" of the air intakes. Dry thrust was 14,300 pounds.

The "D" was unique for several reasons; perhaps one of the more significant was that the entire 12,000-pound weapons load could now be carried externally. With the internal bomb bay to be used for fuel, the plane could depart with a full ordnance and minimum fuel load, refuel in air, and take the maximum payload to the target.

The first flight of the D variant (58-1146) occurred in June 1959, with Republic test pilot Lin Hendrix, but by then the F-105 was several years late in achieving its promised capability. Category II tests at Eglin AFB were to begin in May 1960, but problems with the engine delayed that effort by six months. A fatigue test of some components in 1961 revealed a problem and the fleet was briefly grounded. Another grounding in June 1962 for engine failures (that resulted in two fatal accidents) added more problems to the already troubled airplane. There was talk about canceling the entire program.

A fly-off was staged between the F-105 and the F-101C in 1960 to determine if it really was as potent as had been advertised, but it was no contest. The new avionics allowed the F-105D to outperform the *Voodoo* in virtually every category of its combat role. Initial deliveries to TAC were completed by late 1961, but by then another contender had arrived on the scene: the Navy F4H-1. Given all the problems that had occurred, the projected production of 1,500 aircraft would be dramatically scaled back. Only seven Tactical Fighter Wings would be equipped with the F-105, while seven more would get the F-4C *Phantom II*.

As had occurred with previous models, production blocks resulted in configuration differences that began to cause problems with maintenance procedures and spares ordering. Another standardization program was undertaken between 1962 and 1964 that was called "*Project Look-Alike.*" This called for the inspection of the miles of wiring, as well as hydraulic and fuel lines. Problems with routing and securing these systems had resulted in chafing that eventually caused shorts and leaks that led to high maintenance and several accidents.

Replacement/rerouting were accomplished as required. As a part of the "makeover," it was decided to address the problem of water gaining entry into various nooks and crannies and creating serious electronic failures and other maintenance problems. This difficulty had not come to light until deployment to Europe, where seasonal weather was much more severe. Access panels were resealed and all the aircraft were painted with a silver lacquer to seal as much of the plane as possible. It apparently worked, as the failures noticeably decreased.

Overheating in the AB area of the fuselage had been a constant problem, so two additional air intakes to provide more cooling from outside air were provided on either side of the aft fuselage. Howard Plunkett comments: "*A 'constant problem' is a bit understated. Fuel leaks and overheating caused explosions and aircraft losses. Safety Pack II was the mod that installed the cooling scoops on the aft fuselage (among other things) during March - July 1965. It was probably the most significant mod to the F-105 and fixed the problem in time for combat deployments that year. The engineering problem and design deficiencies were defined during 'Project X' testing at Eglin.*"

While the name *Thunderchief* was appealing to Republic and its PR department, those who flew this heaviest fighter of its time, with a wing loading that guaranteed a high descent rate when the engine faltered … applied another name. Whether it was the sound of 50,000 pounds of metal uncontrollably im-

Figure 11-10. Here the F-105's retractable probe, used for in-flight refueling, is extended. The boom method was added to the last 135 D models, supplementing the "probe and drogue." USAF Photo.

pacting the earth, or the light-hearted shortening of the name of Howdy Doody's Indian rival, *Chief Thunderthud*, the airplane became known affectionately as the "*Thud*" by those who flew and maintained it.

With the delivery of the last F-105F in January 1965, the production line was closed after 833 aircraft.

Transition Training—F-105F

Unlike many of its contemporaries, the F-105 was envisioned as a weapon that would use advanced electronics to achieve operational capabilities that were futuristic to that point. As it evolved, the performance of the *Thud* coupled with the complexity of its avionics demanded more intense pilot training to use its capabilities effectively.

The first F-105Ds that went to the 4520th Combat Crew Training Wing at Nellis AFB, Nevada, arrived in September 1960. This transition program provided initial training in the F-100F to ensure that the pilots had a thorough mastery of high-performance jet operations before moving to the F-105 for a 45-hour curriculum. Most of the F-105 flight time related to using the high-tech R-14 NASARR for navigation and target acquisition. The first squadrons of F-105s became operational in May 1961, with their delivery to the 36th TFW at Bitburg AFB in Germany.

The F-105D was deployed to the 18th TFW in Kadena AFB, Okinawa, in late 1962 and the 8th TFW at Itazuke AFB, Japan, in early 1963. These actions reflected the growing involvement of the U.S. in military action in Southeast Asia.

From this early experience, it became obvious that a two-seat version of the F-105 was needed. However, a tandem version, the F-105C, had been planned by 1956, but was cancelled due to fiscal restraints, as was the F-105E in 1959. As the type became more prolific, and the mission more demanding, it was decided to proceed with a two-seat adaptation—the F-105F. The fuselage was again stretched 31 inches and the vertical fin made slightly taller to accommodate the new "fineness ratio." Unlike other two-seat variants, each pilot had his own "clamshell" canopy. First flown in July 1963, the F-105F was fully capable of performing the complete array of combat operations. This would prove very useful in the coming Southeast Asia War.

Vietnam

While the F-100 and the F-101 had been flying in Southeast Asia for several years, it was not until the "Gulf of Tonkin Resolution" of 7 August 1964 that the F-105 got the call. Eight aircraft of the 36th TFS that had been posted to Yokota AB, Japan, were sent to the Korat Royal Thai Air Base just two days later.

Figure 11-11. A later model F-105D cockpit layout illustrates the vertical tape primary flight display on either side of the attitude indicator. USAF Photo.

Their stated function was to provide Combat Air Patrol (CAP) for any pilots who went down in Laos; their real role was to support CIA operations in that area. Setting aside its sophisticated nuclear capability to deliver iron bombs in a conventional conflict, the *Thud* was also to become a hallmark of defense suppression in the SEA War.

Although the official U.S. government position at the time was that there were no combat operations out of Thailand, the first F-105 flak damage occurred on 14 August 1964. The pilot was 1Lt Dave Graben in F-105D 62-4371, who landed back at Korat. The plane was repaired and flew again until its demise over NVN on 21 September 1966. Although there were more problems yet to come for the *Thud*, this incident highlighted the fact that the aircraft could sustain a lot of damage and remain airborne and under control. Within six months more F-105s were sent to SEA, being based at both Korat and Takhli.

Several major operations were undertaken during the months that followed. However, it was not until February 1965 that the first F-105 raids into North Vietnam began with *Flaming Dart* and then *Rolling Thunder* in March. The objective was to demonstrate to the North a "measured" military response in opposition to their support of the insurgency in the South, and to force them to cease operations there. Some referred to the effort as "gradualism." However, as demonstrated many times through history, this type of effort more often motivates the enemy to become more committed to their cause.

Rolling Thunder would be the longest and most costly air campaign in American history, with more than one million sorties flown, a loss of more than 500 aircrew, and a probable two billion dollars expended. It was estimated that it cost America $10 for every $1 in damage to the North. One-fourth of the 300,000 tactical sorties were flown by *Thud* pilots—arguably the most dangerous missions of the war. Many military historians agree that *Rolling Thunder* was a tragic failure—a sharp contrast to the air operations over Iraq a quarter century later. While there was no lack of courage, skill and resourcefulness of the aircrews in *Rolling Thunder*, by contrast, the different Rules of Engagement during *Desert Storm* in 1990 and the more sophisticated "standoff" and precision-guided weapons available in the Persian Gulf War assured a successful outcome while minimizing losses.

The F-105 is inextricably linked with the air war against North Vietnam during the *Rolling Thunder* period of operations. A mountainous ridgeline (Tam Dao range) just northwest of the capital city of Hanoi was used as a waypoint and as a terrain-masking feature for air attacks in the vicinity of Hanoi. It was given the name "*Thud Ridge*" by the men who flew those missions. Colonel Jack Broughton, with his best-selling 1969 memoir *Thud Ridge*, made the geographical feature famous.

A typical target required a variety of aircraft to accomplish the mission. In addition to the F-105 fighter-bombers, there would be the pre- and post-strike RF-101 recce flights, F-100 flak suppression and fighter cover, KC-135 refueling tankers, stand-off EB-66 ECM, and later in the war, EC-121 AEW (airborne early warning) aircraft to provide a radar overview of the battlespace. This assemblage was referred to as the "strike package."

There was occasional confusion over the North with interference between strikes by the Navy and Air Force, whose control of air operations was separated into alternate three hour intervals. However, this did not work well. In December 1965, the north was divided into zones called "route packages". The supporting navigational charts and air defense measures that could be expected were provided to the pilots as "route packs," or RPs. There were six RP zones labeled RP-1 through RP-6 that ran from the border between the Vietnams toward the north—"six" being the Hanoi area, where the most extreme air defenses were found. Pilots referred to RP-6 as "going downtown." The expression resulted from the lyrics of "*Downtown*," a popular song of the day (by British songstress *Petula Clark*), which contained the line "*...everything's waiting for you... downtown!*" RP-6 was subsequently divided into two areas (RP-6A and RP-6B), essentially along the main rail line into China. Initially each service operated in all RPs at assigned times. In April 1966 RP-1, 5 and 6A were assigned to the Navy and RP-2, 3, 4 and 6B to the Air Force.

The effect of the 2 March 1965 mission was perhaps felt more deeply by the U.S.—when they reviewed the cost—than by the North Vietnamese. Three F-105s and two F-100s had been lost—four pilots were dead and one captured. Twenty million dollars of hardware and irreplaceable American lives had vanished. All of these losses were from ground fire—principally 37mm AAA. The Soviets and Chinese had supplied the North Vietnamese with thousands of these and larger caliber flak guns. Delivery of "iron bombs" using low-level attacks exposed the aircraft to anti-aircraft fire that would double in intensity within a few months. At this point surface-to-air missiles (the Soviet SAM-2) were not yet employed.

A month later, a railroad bridge was the target of another "strike package." F-105s escorted by F-100s dropped 300 750-pound bombs. Although they damaged the bridge, it was not destroyed. An F-101 and an F-100 were shot down by AAA. The next day another attack by an even larger force of 46 F-105s, some with *Bullpup* air-to-ground missiles, sought to complete the job. Bridges are difficult targets because their structure is not greatly affected by the shock wave of the explosive. Only a direct hit on a major support segment will drop the span. The use of the

Figure 11-12. The mix of ordnance the F-105 was capable of carrying was impressive. USAF Photo.

Figure 11-13. A complete load of sixteen 750-pound bombs is an impressive display of carrying capacity. This complement was rarely used in Vietnam. USAF Photo.

Navy-developed *Bullpup* was an attempt to use a guided weapon to achieve that result. However, the warhead of the AGM-12B *Bullpup* was only 250-pounds, and the guidance was pilot-directed by a "joy stick." An intense white flare in the aft end of the missile allowed the pilot to track the missile's path visually while providing course corrections via radio link, to direct it to the target. Although these missiles, propelled by a 30,000-pound thrust liquid fuel engine to Mach 2, allowed the explosive to be more accurately placed than a free fall bomb, they still were not precise enough to hit critical points reliably. In addition, the pilot remained exposed to defensive fire during the "*Bullpup's*" guidance time, while its relatively low explosive force required a "direct hit."

While the impact on the North by the U.S. offensive was severe, Ho Chi Minh recognized that the American people were divided in their opinion of the conduct and cost of the war. No American war (except for the Revolutionary War) had ever lasted longer than 45 months. As major American ground operations entered their fourth year, significant anti-war and racial protests spread throughout the United States. Ho Chi Minh believed that if the war could be protracted another two years, the American government would be forced

by its own people to end their participation. He was correct. For many Americans it was a war seemingly without end, and whose purpose was lost in political rhetoric and social division.

With respect to combat operations, it was discovered that the primary and secondary hydraulic systems of the F-105 were close enough together that they represented a vulnerable "single point of failure." If battle damage disabled both, the stabilator would usually move to the fully "up" position, causing the aircraft to nose down violently.

Republic responded with a mechanical lock that required the pilot to move the stick to neutralize the stabilator, then flip a switch to activate the lock, which clamped the stab in the neutral position. This allowed the aircraft to remain "somewhat" under control in a level attitude. This would (in theory) permit the pilot to fly to a more "friendly" location to eject. A better fix was the installation of a third hydraulic system that was located in a different portion of the airframe.

By mid-summer 1965, it was determined that Vietnam would be a long-term engagement and the silver paint gave way to a green and tan camouflage pattern with either white or gray underside. This paint scheme was later amended after the F-105 was withdrawn from SEA to have the green/tan on the bottom as well so that it would "blend" with the terrain when inverted. Even the national insignia was reduced in size and eventually became muted in color.

The F-105, because of its load-carrying capacity, all-weather capability (somewhat), and its ability to exit at high speed carried the burden of the air war in the North. Using Multiple Ejector Racks (MERs), the *Thud* could carry six M117 750-pound "general purpose" bombs on the centerline and four under each wing MER (inboard), and an additional bomb on the outer single pylon—however, this was not a usual load. Howard, Plunkett recalls: "*More typical were six 750s on the centerline MER, two 450 gal. tanks on inboards, and two ECM pods—or one pod and one Sidewinder, or two 750s on the outboards.*" Many other ordnance options were available, to include napalm canisters and 5-inch High Velocity Aircraft Rockets (HVARs). In addition to its M-61 *Vulcan* 20mm cannon, it could carry up to four *Sidewinders* and wing pylon fuel tanks, depending on the target and mission profile.

For *Thud* pilots, Vietnam became a war of survival. Loss rates of ten percent per mission assured that few would complete the 100-mission requirement (WWII Eighth Air Force bomber pilots were initially required to serve a tour of 25 missions). Although pilots had the prerogative to opt-out of combat at any time, the stigma and loss of integrity of such an action was unthinkable to the typical fighter pilot. To ease the pilot into combat operations, the first few flights were typically flown into the RP-1 (low threat) area.

With the high attrition rate, the availability of F-105 pilots became critical. Pilots who had not chosen, or been selected for fighter assignments during their early training and who had been assigned to SAC or one of the other flying Major Commands, found themselves being re-assigned to TAC. An 80-hour course was designed to transition these pilots to jet fighters.

Following his first tour in Vietnam in the F-100, Craig Colter attended the Test Pilot School at Edwards AFB and eventually found his way back to Vietnam flying interdiction missions in the F-105. Colter recalls the F-105 with a short smile: "*It was a BIG airplane, very stable and honest—especially compared to the F-100. I only had a couple of flights in the F-105F [two-seat] before flying the D model, but then lots of practice on the range dropping bombs after that. The*

Figure 11-14. The coveted "North Vietnam 100 Mission" patch. USAF Museum Photo.

cockpit was comfortable and well laid-out. The new instrument tapes were easy to read and you could set 'bugs' that would readily catch your eye to keep you aware of the required airspeed and altitude for the drop. We all loved the airplane—though not as capable as the F-4 [which Colter flew after his Vietnam tour]. *No, it wasn't a very maneuverable airplane with its high wing loading—not as bad as the F-104, but it wasn't designed to be. It got you in and out fast.*"

A combat mission would typically start with a 3 AM wake-up to achieve a time-over-target ("ToT") of 7 AM. While the average mission required three-plus hours of flight time, an equal amount was devoted to both the pre-flight and post-flight briefing. During the preflight brief on the mission, the wing leader would present the target and the plan for attack. Coulter: "*He would try to set it up so each aircraft would approach from different points of the compass to confuse the AAA, but weather and other unexpected events could change our plans en route. The anticipated location of the AAA (lots of 23mm and 37mm) was important and would influence the track-in to the target.*"

A typical 3.5-hour mission consisted of three parts. The first was the minimum fuel departure to permit the maximum load of ordnance, followed by the first aerial refueling at about five AM. These refuelings were particularly difficult because, at its maximum weight of 52,000-pounds, the F-105D could only make it to about 15,000 feet. Coulter: "*This meant that the link-up with the tanker often had to be accomplished at the worst possible altitude—in turbulent IFR [instrument] conditions in bad weather, and occasionally in thunderstorms.*" The tankers for the F-105 were the KC-135s with the boom, rather than the KB-50 "probe and drogue," although some *Thuds* were equipped for both. "*If the weather was good, refueling was a piece of cake.*"

The second part of the mission was the attack on the target: "*At the target we would roll inverted at about 350 knots and pull to the desired dive angle which could be 10, 30, or 45 degrees. Dive angle dictated the roll-in altitude, with steeper angles requiring higher altitudes. We even did some bombing from a level attitude. The 'pipper' would be placed short of the target and offset for forecast winds. The airspeed would build as the aircraft came down the 'chute,' and the very difficult trick was to pickle the bombs as the* airspeed, altitude and sight picture all were at the proper values. This was before GPS could give you that readout so we were guessing a lot. The bombs would be 'pickled' at about 3-5,000 feet; again depending on dive angle and various other conditions—the intensity of the ground threat being one of them.

"An average pilot could place his bombs within 200 feet of the aim point. I felt that I was not performing well if I couldn't put bombs within 100 feet. At this point in the war, we often worked with F-4 'fast mover FACS' [Forward Air Controllers]. They would spot the target with single white phosphorous 2.75-inch rockets from a 19-tube LAU dispenser.

"We would bottom-out at about 2,000 feet and exit the area as quickly as possible. You usually didn't have to go into burner to get a decent speed out of the Thud. On the way out, the warm humid air would reveal the location of the shock-wave forming a condensation fog around the rear part of the canopy and you could watch it walk its way forward as you accelerated to 700 knots.

"The third part of the mission was joining up and looking each other over. On more than one occasion, I thought I had been hit as the AAA was so intense. Then the second hook-up with the tanker and the return to base."

A part of Colter's period in SEA was during the bombing halt up North, when the ROE were changed so that targets were restricted to the Laotian part of the infamous Ho Chi Minh trail. Colter: "On night missions, you could see the truck headlights lined up for miles on the North Vietnam side of the border entering Laos where they would turn them off. We couldn't touch them until they crossed but by then they were a lot harder to see. I never felt we were really very effective in terms of stopping the flow of supply to the South by hitting the supply lines in a thick jungle. We should have been hitting the depots in Hanoi and Haiphong as we finally did in the closing months. I supported the war because I felt it was a part of something bigger—stopping the spread of communism."

Wild Weasels

The first U.S. aircraft lost to a North Vietnamese surface-to-air missile was an F-4C in 24 July 1965. A retaliation raid on 27 July on two SAM sites near Hanoi by 48 F-105s was, according to Hobson's *Vietnam Air Losses*, "... one of the blackest days of the war for the USAF". The NVA missiles and AAA fire decimated the mission with four planes shot down, and two lost to a mid-air. Three pilots were killed, two captured, and only one was rescued.

This galvanized the U.S. into creating tactics, countermeasures, and weapons to mitigate the risk of the Soviet supplied SA-2 *Guideline*—the *Wild Weasel*.

Using a hunter-killer concept, a lead aircraft (initially the F-100F) carried electronic warning equipment that could determine when aircraft were being tracked by the SAM radar and provide direction to that location. The "hunter" would mark the site with rockets, and then the "killer" part of the team (the F-105) would attack with heavier ordnance. It was later determined that cluster bombs (CBU-24s) were more effective than rockets. The CBU-24 contained 665 tennis ball size "bomblets" that were scattered over a large area. They could be set to explode in the air as well as on contact. It proved to be a very effective weapon for lightly armored installations typical of the SAM and AAA batteries.

It was apparent that the United States was up against the most difficult air defenses ever put into operation. The Soviets recognized that the Vietnam War presented them with an opportunity to measure America's full spectrum of air power—from the perspective of a limited conventional war. They supplied weapons, techniques, tactics and intelligence to the North Vietnamese... and observed the results.

It was also obvious that going head-to-head against the Americans in the air was not a wise strategy for the North. Instead, using their small force of MiG fighters, to include a few of the Mach 2 MiG-21s, allowed the North to keep the U.S. off balance. Just enough interception probability was presented to cause the Americans to supply "cover" for all of their missions—providing more targets for their SAMs. But the big losses for the Americans would be at the hands of simple, less expensive AAA

Figure 11-15. The CBU-24 Cluster Bomb Unit on an F-105 Wild Weasel. USAF Photo.

weapons. An added plus for the NVA was that the presence of MiGs often caused the F-105s to jettison their bombs in order to engage the MiGs—who could then simply exit the battlespace, as their mission had been accomplished.

To apply its air defense strategy, the Soviets created a three-tier system: intense medium caliber (23mm and 37mm) AAA by the hundreds at each site, effective to 5,000 feet; heavier, radar-directed cannon (from 57mm to 100mm), useful to 20,000 feet; and the SAM-2 missiles that could reach targets up to 60,000 feet. This required a variety of radars: SON-4 (NATO *Whiff*) and SON-9 (NATO *Fire Can*) for the heavy AAA; P-12/P18 (NATO *Spoon Rest*) for target acquisition, and SNR-75 (*Fan Song*) for missile track. It was variously estimated that the NVA had (at the height of the conflict) over 4,400 AAA, 150 SAM sites (6 missiles per site), and 70 MiGs.

The reliance on radar was both a blessing and a curse for the NVA. The electronic emissions of their sites allowed detection and location to be accurately plotted with the right equipment. Because the SAM relied on radar, it was possible to "jam" the signals to inhibit the launch or deflect the missile's path. Getting that right equipment into the cockpit and learning how to use it in a tactical situation was the problem for the Americans.

Ed Rock notes that the F-105 was later equipped with the QRC-160-1 (renamed the AN/ALQ-71) noise jammer, which was "...*intended to deny accurate azimuth information on the intended target while the Air Force 160-1 denied range and, when used in formation, azimuth information. Generally, many pilots were not pleased with external ECM pods because the pods were often unreliable, occupied a weapons station and caused increased drag. However, they were quite effective and significantly improved survivability and mission effectiveness.*

"*The jamming was not as effective as it should have been when the formation spacing was not maintained or one or more of the jamming pods in the formation was not functioning properly. If all of the pods worked and if the proper formation was maintained it was unlikely that any of the aircraft in the formation would be shot down by a SAM-2!*"

With respect to "hunter-killer" teams, initial efforts to equip the "hunter" had been made with the F-100F in the fall of 1965 and, after a rocky start, the evolving system showed promise. It quickly became obvious that, to alleviate the differences in performance, both members of the team should be flying the same type of aircraft. In January 1966, it was decided that the two-seat F-105F would be modified to replace the F-100F.

The aircraft, designated the F-105F WW-III (a part of "*Project Wild Weasel III*"), initially had the same ATI equipment installed as in the F-100F. These included the Radar Homing And Warning (RHAW) system that monitored the various radar frequencies. Several small bulges and antennas began to appear on the fuselage of the F-105 to accommodate these. Training was moved from Eglin AFB to Nellis AFB (*Willie Weasel College*) and was much more sophisticated than the earlier F-100 crews had received.

By May 1966, five F-105F *Wild Weasel* aircraft had arrived in Korat to perform the initial "Iron Hand" missions (as they were code-named), which were flown within days. The first confirmed successful strike was recorded on 6 June with a typical operation consisting of two F-105 WW-IIIs and two F-105Ds.

Ed Rock: "*These missions were the most hazardous of the war because they* [the *Wild Weasel*s] *had to arrive in the target area before the strike force and stay until all strike aircraft had struck their target thus being exposed to enemy fire (MiGs, AAA and SAMs) longer than any others. The strike force was in and out as fast as possible while the Weasel had to hang around for extended periods of time.*

"*My first combat mission on 11 July 1966...was unremarkable except it was the first time I had seen the Radar Homing And Warning gear light up like a Christmas tree from all the radars trying to track and destroy us with real bullets and real missiles. In addition, each radar made its own particular sound. The SAM radar had a very distinctive aural signature that sounded like a rattlesnake about to strike. The lights and noise were enough to scare the hell out of you.*"

The Navy-developed AGM-45 *Shrike* missile was adopted by the Air Force and proved a valuable asset. Referred to as an "anti-radiation" missile (ARM), it used the airframe and propulsion of the AIM-7 *Sparrow* air-to-air missile with a special guidance package that could home-in on radar emissions. The 390-pound *Shrike* allowed the attack aircraft to avoid overflying the target by launching up to 10 miles away—resulting in a flight time of less than a minute. However, there were several problems with the early variants of the *Shrike*. The type of guidance package had to be "tuned" to one of several radar bandwidths employed. The launch azimuth had to be within about 3 degrees of the target to assure a good track. The small fragmentation warhead (about 150 pounds) did not provide for much damage. These problems resulted in a "kill" rate of only 25 percent, and typically required an "overhead" strike following the initial *Shrike* attack to destroy the rest of the complex.

By July 1966 eleven F-105F WW-IIIs were in operation, but within a month five had been lost to enemy action. The loss rate virtually guaranteed that no pilot could complete a 100-mission tour as a *Weasel*. Several tactics were employed, such as "terrain masking," in which ridge lines were used to conceal the approach, while a set of maneuvers were practiced that would help the pilots dodge incoming SAMs.

Rock comments on one flight in March 1967 flown by pilot Merlyn Dethlefsen and EWO Mike Gilroy: "*Despite being damaged by AAA their actions resulted in rendering ineffective the enemy defensive SAM and AAA sites in the target area and enabled the ensuing fighter-bombers to strike successfully the important industrial target without loss or damage to* [those aircraft]." Dethlefsen was awarded the Medal of Honor and Gilroy the Air Force Cross for this mission.

A second Medal of Honor was awarded just a few weeks later in April 1967 to Major Leo K. Thorsness, with EWO Capt. Harold E. Johnson in the back seat. After successfully disabling two SAM sites, Thorsness observed a MiG-17 that appeared to be after the parachutes of an F-105 crew who had been shot down. He destroyed it with his 20mm gun. He

was shot down by a MiG-21 on 30 April 1967 and spent the rest of the war as a POW.

Continued improvements in each of the components within the *Wild Weasel* system were coupled with a major enhancement to the *Shrike*. Using the Navy *Standard Missile* that was a surface-to-air weapon, and installing the *Shrike* guidance system, the much larger (1,350-pound) weapon could deliver a 220-pound warhead to a distance of 60 miles. The development of the AGM-78 was completed, and it was made available to operational units in SEA in less than a year. The AGM-78 cost $200,000, as opposed to the $7,000 for the *Shrike*. By the summer of 1967, six F-105F WW-IIIs had been modified with a special launch rail to handle the much larger AGM-78.

As aircraft losses to radar-directed defenses began to mount, by 1967 the ECM pod was made mandatory for all flights going North. But with the problems noted by aircrew, it was decided to make the pod (now having been improved and designated the ALQ-101) an integral part of the F-105F WW-III and call the new variant the F-105G. Westinghouse Electric, working with Republic Aviation, literally split the pod lengthwise and mounted it on each side of the lower fuselage, parallel with the bomb bay doors, creating the ALQ-105. There were 64 "F"s converted to "G"s, with the first SEA service in December 1969 using in-house conversions (really re-designations) at Takhli. Most of the conversion work was done at the depot at Sacramento through December 1972. Some early "G"s lacked the ALQ-105 pods attached to the fuselage sides.

Figure 11-16. A Shrike missile can be seen on the outer F-105D pylon with an AGM-78 on the inner pylon. Note the fuel tank on the left wing. USAF Photo.

Figure 11-17 Republic F-105G in flight on 5 May 1970. External stores include QRC-380 blisters, AGM-45 Shrike and AGM-78B Standard ARM (Anti-Radiation Missile). USAF Photo.

Greater Bombing Accuracy

When the war moved into the monsoon season of 1965, upward of 90% of the missions were being cancelled for low ceilings and visibilities for extended periods. It was obvious that a more effective method of delivering bombs to the target was needed to keep the pressure on the North Vietnamese.

Beginning in July 1965, the Navy's A-6 *Intruder* was having notable success with night and poor weather strikes because of its apparently superior bombing system—a capability that was lacking in USAF fighter-bombers (it would be several years before the third generation F-111 would make its appearance in SEA). While the Air Force had moved to Mach 2 nuclear delivery with its *Century Series*, the Navy had addressed the needs of conventional delivery in a more modest less-than-Mach 1 airframe.

Although speed was the F-105's strong point in the nuclear delivery role, it employed less sophisticated technology that did not provide the precision needed to hit small targets with iron bombs. Even in good visual conditions, it took much piloting skill to deliver bombs to within a 200-foot radius of the intended target.

Thus, the F-105D had arrived in SEA with its two methods of delivery using Republic's "Thunderstick-Fire-Control" system, consisting of a ground-mapping radar, Doppler navigator, and analog toss-bomb and air-data computers. These allowed for Blind Target Identification Point (BTIP) and Blind Laydown (BLD), which achieved circular error averages (CEAs) of 1,313 feet and 884 feet, respectively—under ideal weather conditions and with no enemy defenses. These were unacceptable for conventional ordnance and neither proved effective.

To address this problem, the Air Force decided to use radar in several different modes. The first and perhaps the most obvious was the use of the "*pathfinder*" missions, where Douglas EB-66B *Destroyers* led small formations of 4 to 12 F-105Ds on top of the overcast—usually above 15,000 feet. Called *synchronous radar bombing* (or *buddy bombing*), it used the EB-66 navigator and his K-5 radar bombing navigation system to detect the target and send a signal tone to the F-105s at the designated point to drop their ordnance. These missions officially began in February 1966, but were effective primarily against "area" targets, as the CEA was about one-eighth mile. (The technique had been pioneered in the later stages of WWII over Europe with formations of the Boeing B-17 *Flying Fortress*).

Howard Plunkett notes: "*A total of 82 radar strikes were flown in February, dropping approximately 95 percent of all bombs delivered on North Vietnam by the Air Force during the month. … Bad weather over North Vietnam during March 1966, forced the continued use of pathfinder bombing.*"

It was determined that the *Thud* could improve the accuracy of its own delivery system if some components were slightly modified and tweaked to the limits of their sensitivity. The project was originally called *Northscope*, and involved modifications to the radar to increase the sweep speed and expand the scope presentation by a factor of two. This allowed a longer time for the EWO to get greater resolution of the target. It was expected that an accuracy of 750-feet could be achieved. Another change was the ability of the "back seat" to toggle the release of the bombs. A camera was mounted in the cockpit to record the action, both for review of technique and for preliminary bomb damage assessment (BDA).

As the request for this specialized capability came from General John D. Ryan, then-Commander of PACAF (Pacific Air Force), the group was informally (and somewhat derisively) known as "*Ryan's Raiders.*" A training program was established for 25 *Thud* pilots to qualify them for all-weather combat missions in SEA.

These changes were completed to four F-105Ds by April 1967 and an initial group of eight pilots was chosen—four for the "front seat" and four for the "back seat." This required that each pilot become competent as B/N and Electronic Warfare Officer (EWO). Although all the pilots would eventually move to the front seat, this arrangement was not popular with the pilots—but they would have a thorough understanding of all the systems. Because these aircraft retained their *Wild Weasel* III RHAW electronics they were doubly capable. Beginning in late April 1967, missions were flown into the very heart of the North (RP-5 and RP-6) with two losses by the end of the first month of operation—one attributed to equipment failure. Flying at 500 feet and 450 knots in the black of night left little margin for error. As the program expanded, the back seat was eventually occupied by the traditional EWO, who needed to get Bombadier/Navigator (B/N) training to be qualified for all the tasks.

The group flew 415 missions under the designation of *Commando Probe* and then *Commando Nail* before it returned exclusively to its former *Wild Weasel* mission. While the modifications permitted almost unrestricted use of USAF air power on a 24-hour basis—with *Pathfinder* missions during the day and *Commando Nail* at night—the results were not impressive.

In yet another effort to improve the bombing results, the Air Force established a radar site in northern Laos, only 12 miles from the border of North Vietnam and 125 miles from Hanoi. It used existing MSQ-77 *Sky Spot* radar—originally designed to record the accuracy of Strategic Air Command bombing in training exercises stateside. These radars had been installed in South Vietnam and Thailand, and could position the *Thuds* accurately, out to 196 miles (into Route Pack 3) to produce effective results.

Identified as Lima Site 85 (LS-85), it included a TACAN navigation transmitter and was operational in October 1967. The first mission, referred to as *Commando Club*, was flown in November. The F-105s carried 27 ALQ-71 ECM pods, and the aircraft were separated by 1500 feet to provide optimum signal jamming. As they neared the target, they closed formation to within 500 feet to get the best bombing accuracy from the flight. Plunkett picks up the story: "*... the NVN were employing a new tactic called track-on-jam that directed the SAM to the source of the jamming signal. Thirteen SAMs were fired and two scored hits downing the F-105s. The strike force jettisoned their bombs and exited. From this point forward only single flights were permitted in* high threat areas and the formation spacing was maintained for most effective countermeasures.

"*In an evaluation of Commando Nail and Commando Club operations, it was found that over the 600 missions flown against 70 targets with 3.594 bombs dropped, the average CEP was 3,300 feet. ... Subsequent improvements included modifications developed by Republic Aviation to six aircraft resulted in better bombing accuracy. These changes included removal of the rear cockpit control stick and installation of a blind bombing pedestal control that provided, among other aspects, better scope resolution.... Spares and reliability continued to be a problem in keeping the aircraft combat ready.*"

The LS-85 radar station in Laos was subsequently attacked by four Soviet built AN-2 fabric covered biplanes in January 1968 in a raid that did little damage. One of the attackers was shot down by a UH-1 helicopter with an AK-47 rifle. Another crashed during its getaway. However, in a surprise commando raid in March 1968, the NVA attacked and destroyed the *Commando Club* radar in Laos, killing or capturing the eleven-man contingent.

Accuracy, as tracked by the 388th TFW, showed an average CEP (middle of all bombs dropped) of 1600 feet and a CEA (average of all bombs dropped) of 3900 feet. Individual results varied from 19,250 feet to 167 feet.

The concept of improving the navigation capability to permit bombing operations at night and bad weather was continued in yet another program called *Thunderstick II.* Using the ITT AN/ARN-92 Long Range Navigation (LORAN) coupled with the F-105's Doppler radar system, now designated the APN-131, the radar image presented to the pilot was significantly improved. It was expected that the Circular Error Probable (CEP) could be improved to ±50 feet from altitudes as high as 15,000 feet. This modification never found its way into combat because the F-105D was withdrawn from Vietnam before the program became operational.

Another adaptation was to equip ten F-105Gs with the Hallicrafter QRC-128, which could effectively "jam" the communications signals between the ground controller and the MiG pilots. As the Soviet system was predicated on closely controlled intercepts under the direction of the ground "controller," this approach appeared to have merit. For this mission, the equipment replaced the rear ejection seat and its occupant—these missions would be flown by the pilot alone. However, rather than a high-power transmitter, the QRC-128 simply recorded the transmissions and played them back on the same frequency but slightly time shifted. This made the communication between the MiG pilot and "controller" virtually unintelligible. The remainder of the F-105's capability was retained so that it could fully participate in a strike mission while "jamming" the NVA communications. The aircraft, identified by a one-foot square blade antenna immediately behind the second cockpit, were referred to as "*Combat Martins*."

It has been reported that the Martin F-105s flew only one mission. The National Security Agency (NSA), which is responsible for "signals intelligence" (SIGINT), immediately detected the jamming and directed the Air Force not to interfere with the communications, as they were in the process of monitoring and evaluating the Soviet system. They apparently did not want the Soviets to develop a response to the jamming that would disrupt the larger strategic implication.

However, Plunkett offers the following: "... *the main reason they weren't used had more to do with timing than ... the NSA* [which Plunkett says he has found no evidence to support]. *On 1 April 1968, when the Combat Martin's were being delivered to SEA, the bombing of the North was restricted to RP-1. MiGs weren't considered a threat this far south and so the jamming equipment was removed and stored. The planes were 'F's but without the rear seat they couldn't be used as Weasels. Also, by this time 'F's were considered a scarce resource and were restricted from low-altitude strafing missions. These restrictions caused the 388 TFW to complain about having the birds in their inventory since they caused scheduling problems. Most of their Combat Martin birds were swapped with 'D's from Kadena.*"

With the bombing halt of 1 November 1968 as decreed by President Johnson, most missions to RP-5 and RP-6 ceased for almost three years, as the United States again sought diplomatic means to end the conflict. Most F-105s were withdrawn from SEA, being replaced by the McDonnell F-4 *Phantom*. The F-105G *Weasels* were supplemented and then replaced by the F-4C *Advanced Wild Weasel*. F-105Gs stayed at Korat in the 17th Wild Weasal Squadron (WWS) until October 1974.

When the bombing was resumed by President Nixon in the spring of 1972, in a final desperate action to force the North Vietnamese government to serious negotiations,

the air defenses of the North had been significantly strengthened. *Operation Linebacker* began in May 1972 and ran into October. *Linebacker II* flew its operations from 18 to 29 December 1972. The F-105Gs flew almost constantly during that period, with some aircrews flying four missions a day. Despite the enhanced ECM efforts, a fourfold increase in SAM sites enabled the downing of 15 B-52s during the period. Many of the SA-2s were reportedly fired at the bomber formations in volleys using visual guidance (without radar) and proximity fuses to find their target.

While the official function of the *Wild Weasel* is "Suppression of Enemy Air Defenses" (SEAD), the phrase "*Wild Weasel*" is universally recognized as representing one of the most hazardous operations of the Vietnam War. As noted, two members were awarded the Medal of Honor for their efforts. As for the overall effectiveness of the *Wild Weasel* program, General William Momyer notes in his book *Air Power In Three Wars* that the North Vietnamese fired 18 SA-2 missiles for every aircraft they brought down in 1965. This increased to 32 in 1966 and 50 in 1967. By 1968, it took 107 launches to down one American plane and 87 during the Linebacker Operation in 1972. Thirty-one F-105s were lost to SAMs. Of the 3,322 aircraft downed during the war, only 90 were from MiGs and 205 from SAMs.

With the availability of the F-4 *Phantom* in the interdiction role, the F-105D was gradually phased out of the Vietnam War, with the last combat mission flown on 6 October 1970. Losses (according to Chris Hobson's book *Vietnam Air Losses*) amounted to 397 F-105s (almost half the production). Of these, 61 were from operational accidents, 23 to MiGs, 31 to SAMS, and the remainder went down to AAA.

Although its primary mission was to deliver ordnance to ground targets, the F-105 was credited with downing 27½ MiGs; all but three by cannon—those three were by AIM-9 *Sidewinders*.

Figure 11-18. Lined up for departure, these F-105s begin the take-off roll. USAF Photo.

Variants

Table 11-01

Republic F-105 Variations

Type	Notes	No. Built
YF-105A	J57 engine	2
YF-105B	J75 engine	4
JF-105B	Cancelled YRF-105B	3
F-105B	27 May 1958 achieved 1,420 mph	71
F-105C	Two place cancelled	0
F-105D	15 inches longer 1,390 mph	610 *1959-1964*
F-105E	Two place cancelled	0
F-105F	Two place	143 *1963-1965*
F-105G	Modified F-105F	61
Total Build		**833**

Phase Out

By January 1971, most of the surviving F-105s were transferred to Reserve units and the Air Guard. The Air Force retained the F-105G *Wild Weasel* until mid-1980. The Reserve units retired their mounts by March 1984. Like the F-106, no other country opted to purchase the expensive ($2.14 million per copy) and complex ($1,000 per hour to operate) fighter-bomber.

The Air Force had proposed to build more F-105s when Vietnam began to ramp-up in 1965, but then-Defense Secretary Robert McNamara had been enamored with the Navy's F4H-1 *Phantom*, which represented a "multi-role" fighter that appealed to him. He was quoted as saying *"the F-105 has only single mission capability, fails to meet criteria for integrative enhancement of flexible force structure, and is non-cost-effective."*

Characteristics & Performance Data	YF-105A 1-seat Prototype	F-105B 1-seat Nuclear Attack	F-105D 1-seat All-Wx	F-105F 2-seat Tng/Combat
Length (ft in)	61'5"	64'3"		69'7"
Wing Span (ft in)	34'11"			
Height (ft in)	17'6"	19'8"		20'2"
Wing Area (sq ft)	385			
Engine	J57-P-25	J75-P-3/P-19	J75-P-19W	
– Mil Pwr /AB (lbs)	10,200/15,000	16,470/23,500	17,200/26,500	
First Flight	Oct-55	May-56	Jun-59	Jun-63
First Delivery (for op'ns)	N/A	Ma3y-57	Sep-60	Dec-63
Empty Weight (lb)	21,010		27,500	
Gross Weight (lb)	28,966		48,400	
Combat Weight (lb)	40,561		35,637	
Max TO Weight			52,542	54,027
Internal Fuel (gal)	850	1160		
(w/Drop Tanks) (gal)	2500		3100	
Max Speed (mph)	857 @ 36K		1420 @ 38K	1386 @ 38K
Initial climb (ft/min)	32,000	34,000	34,500	
Combat Ceiling (ft)	50,000	49,000	48,000	
Normal Range (sm)	1,000	690	780	740
Max Range/DT (sm)	2,700	2000	2200	

Table 11-02. Republic F-105 Specifications.

Origin of General Dynamics

We begin this chapter with a continuation of the Consolidated Vultee/Convair genealogy that started in the F-102 chapter. Consolidated Vultee Aircraft had made a name for itself during World War II by producing thousands of B-24s and PBYs. In 1946 Ruben Fleet, its primary founder, resigned from the board, ending another pioneering era. The Consolidated Vultee name continued to fade in the late 1940s as the company became known by the contraction "Convair."

Floyd B. Odlum, a wealthy investor who was described as *"possibly the only man in the United States who made a great fortune out of the Depression,"* had been buying up the stock in the company, and by 1947 was the majority stockholder. Odlum, whose second wife, Jacqueline Cochran, had been good friends with Amelia Earhart, was the principal backer of several of Earhart's flying adventures in the 1930s. In 1954, Odlum was the prime instigator in a merger between Consolidated and the Electric Boat Company, which made submarines, and the company became known as General Dynamics. The Convair division continued to operate as an independent company for several decades, but was increasingly referred to as "General Dynamics".

F-102B Redesign

In the early stages of the F-102's development, both Convair and the Air Force recognized that it was not going to be able to achieve the goals that had been set for it. This became painfully obvious when the first YF-102 flew in October 1953 and was unable to achieve Mach 1.

However, with the transonic drag problem aptly handled by the redesign of the fuselage (to incorporate the "area rule"), the F-102A in December 1954 was finally on its way into production. Convair and the Air Force again looked forward to the follow-on, the F-102B—*the ultimate interceptor*, as they had termed it. In November 1955, the Air Force moved ahead by issuing a contract for its development. Convair addressed several issues to ensure that the new iteration would truly live up to its expectation—Mach 2 interceptions out to 430 miles and to altitudes of 70,000 feet. This was considered critical, as there had been some indications that the Soviets were producing a large number of *Badger*, *Bison* and *Bear* bombers and there was a perceived "bomber gap," where the U.S. would be significantly behind in quantity. However, some of the funding that should have been applied to the F-102B was used for the changes to the F-102A, resulting in a slow start for the F-102B effort.

The fuselage for the F-102B was redesigned and stretched another two feet (to over 70 feet). This not only allowed full advantage of the "area rule," but it did away with the aerodynamic bulges to the aft end that were the hallmark of the F-102—and a constant reminder of a costly design mistake. The "conically cambered" wing (a more pronounced leading edge cuff) of the F-102A was included, and the wing area was increased from 661 to 695 square feet. The first production series had outer-wing boundary layer fences as on the F-102A. These were replaced on subsequent models with leading edge slots.

The forward canopy windscreen was similar to the F-102A, having a sharp edge at the most forward point that was covered by a steel strip. This somewhat limited the pilot's forward vision and would not have been acceptable had the plane been designed as a "dogfighter" rather than a high-speed missile platform.

Pratt & Whitney had moved beyond the J57 that powered the F-102, and the result was the J75. The availability of this new powerplant increased the thrust to 15,000-pounds dry and 23,500-pounds in afterburner. The air intakes were enlarged to accommodate the J75's need for significantly more volume of air and to handle the shock wave that accompanied its using a variable geometry duct. The intake path was also shortened, with the inlet moved well behind the cockpit. Even the position lights retracted automatically when the plane went Mach 1 (this feature was later disabled as an unnecessary complication). With these changes and a truncated vertical fin that no longer reflected the delta shape, the F-102B was easily distinguished from its earlier cousin.

The lower aft part of the vertical fin contained the speed brakes as well as a drag chute within clamshell doors. With a maximum weight five tons heavier than the F-102A (42,750 vs. 31,500-pounds) the landing gear was beefed up, and the nose wheel was now a dual assembly. Also included was the capability for aerial refueling from a boom. The mock-up completed an Air Force review in early 1956. With all of the changes, the F-102B was in fact a completely new airframe. In consideration of this, its designation was changed on 17 June 1956 to F-106.

An interesting feature of the F-106 exhaust nozzle was its "idle thrust reduce." This significantly reduced the exhaust flow when the

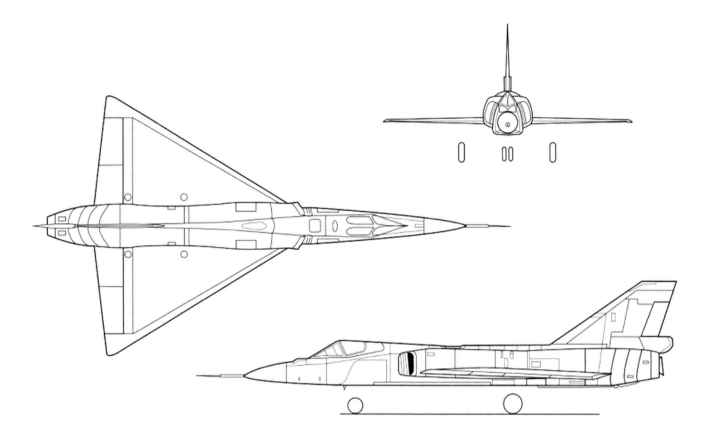

Figure 12-01 The abbreviated vertical fin and the air intake locations differentiate the F-106 from its F-102 cousin. NASA Dryden Illustration.

aircraft was taxiing—thus avoiding possible damage to surrounding aircraft and facilities due to its powerful engine, and also wear and heating of the brakes and tires.

The F-106 retained the internal three-bay storage area for air-to-air weapons—the same complement as the F-102A. The bay was almost a third the length of the aircraft and, unlike the F-102, did not have provisions for the 24 FFAR. The center bay was available for a single MB-1 *Genie* nuclear air-to-air unguided rocket (which was redesignated the AIR-2A in 1962). Despite the nuclear "two-man rule," the single-seat F-106A aircraft were flown so armed. The two outer bays each held two improved AIM-4 *Falcon* missiles, one of which one was radar-guided (AIM-4F) and the other a heat seeker (the AIM-4G).

Flight Test

The first prototype F-106 (56-0451) flew on 26 December 1956 and did not carry an X or Y prefix—perhaps because it was initially to be the F-102B. The pilot was the same Richard Johnson who had first flown the YF-102. This flight was cut short after only 20 minutes by engine frequency resonances and speed brakes that failed to retract. Despite the apparent improvements, the initial performance of the F-106 did not measure up.

Problems with the J75-P1 engine and the electronics plagued the early models, and the F-106 was in danger of being canceled. The next group of twelve aircraft had the J75-P9 engine and were able to reach Mach 1.9 and 57,000-feet. However, it was not until the air intake was increased in size and the duct lips were tapered (a change that had worked for the F-100) that the acceleration was improved. However, it was the switch to the J75-P17 that finally brought the F-106 into its own so far as performance went. The reliability improvements and the 17,200-pound thrust of the new engine coupled with the redesigned intake system turned the airplane into a winner. However, the damage had been done. The protracted development cycle caused the Air Force to rework the F-101 into an interim interceptor, which took a big chunk of the allocated money from the F-106 production run.

To permit extended range operations, the F-106 had provisions for two underwing pylons. Either a pair of subsonic 350-gallon tanks or 250-gallon supersonic tanks could be carried. The latter were so effectively designed that the aircraft was capable of over Mach 2 with them installed (later tanks were larger).

Figure 12-02. Note the lack of wing fences on the F-106 and the boom refueling access (dark area) between the vertical fin and the canopy. USAF Photo.

Figure 12-03. An early version of the F-106 instrument panel reveals the use of the round dial gauges for the primary flight display. The top of the dual-grip yoke is visible in the lower portion of the photo. The upper segment of the large Tactical Situation Display (TSD) with a moving map is also evident. USAF Photo.

The needed improvements also resulted in a change in designation to F-106A, and finally cleared the plane for production. However, the delay allowed another milestone in military history to occur in August 1957. The Soviet Union announced it had successfully tested an intercontinental ballistic missile (ICBM)—followed a few weeks later by the launch of the first of several *Sputnik* earth satellites. This heightened a perceived deficiency in America's defense posture. The alleged "*bomber gap*" became the "*missile gap.*"

With the hindsight of a half-century, neither of these perceived gaps represented a military advantage for the Soviets. While there was a decided "lead" by the Soviets in the development of the ICBM, its existence, as with the bomber gap, was an advantage only in the political realm. Of course, the U.S. Congress, for a variety of reasons, could not allow a "perceived gap" to exist, and it was transfixed on the missile gap from 1958 on. Thus, for the F-106, its production numbers would dwindle, as missile funding took dollars that had been previously allocated to its production. At $4.7 million per aircraft cost was also a major factor.

A catchy name was applied as the plane became operational—the "*Delta Dart*." However, the men who flew it quickly assigned a more terse and less alluring alias "*the Six*."

Cockpit Layout

Because the F-106 interceptor was a single-pilot operation, the layout and workload sequence were very important. To help facilitate this, a *dual-grip* yoke allowed the pilot to fly with either hand, and each "grip" provided selected intercept functions. Daniel R. "Doc" Zoerb comments: "*The right stick*

Figure 12-04. The new flight display instrumentation is shown in the two rectangular boxes on either side of the circular (black/white) attitude indicator in the center. The two segments of the well-used (chipped paint) control stick are also apparent. USAF Photo.

grip was used to fly the airplane and incorporated standard features such as weapons-firing trigger and trim, and additionally, a mic switch enabling radio transmissions when the left hand was not on the throttle grip. The left stick grip controlled the radar/IRST, with radar elevation wheel and a trigger which, together with movement of the grip—right and left—controlled the radar or IRST field of regard, generation of a non-scanning pre-lock mode ['spot-lighting' the target] and generation of a range gate necessary to command a radar lock-on [in range as well as angle] or IR system lock-on [in angle only] to the target. When not employing the radar, the left grip could be locked and used to fly the airplane if desired."

Zoerb continues: "*Cockpit layout was typical for the early 60's, relatively small, and accommodated a multitude of switches and indicators reflecting the lack of automation and HOTAS found in more modern fighters.* [HOTAS—Hands-on-Throttle-and-Stick is the placement of critical buttons and switches that allows the pilot to access various functions while keeping his hand on the primary flight control—the 'stick'].

"*Setting up the cockpit for an intercept and conducting the intercept required hand-eye movement that ranged throughout the cockpit from left side-panel to front panel to right side-panel. The number of switch settings and*

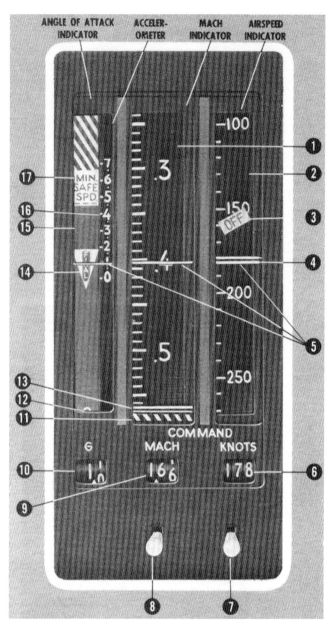

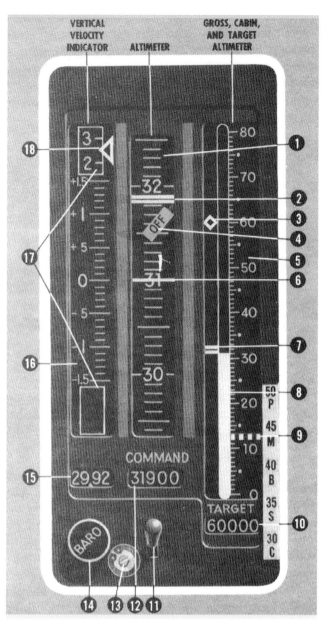

Figure 12-05. The F-106 pitch and speed data display. Note that the data can be interpolated directly from the vertical tape or read as digits beneath. The display shows 178 kts and Mach 1.66 (obviously not correct speed relationships!) with 1-G of acceleration (i.e., the aircraft is "at rest" vertically). (The callout numbers around the periphery are from the Dash-1 manual and are not identified here.) USAF Photo.

Figure 12-06. On the right side are the altitude reference data showing the current altitude of 31,000 feet with a vertical velocity of 2,300 feet per minute. (The callout numbers around the periphery are from the Dash-1 manual and are not identified here.) USAF Photo.

changes to those settings along with the attendant head movement required much proficiency and a tolerance for spatial disorientation during night or weather operations. Below the instrument panel, between your knees, was a large Tactical Situation Display with a moving map...great piece of gear for maintaining orientation. Upgrade of the primary and secondary flight instruments from standard multiple round-dials to the vertical tape configuration was a major leap forward—still, a busy cockpit requiring lots of flying time to remain proficient."

As noted by Zoerb, one of the many improvements to the F-106 was the incorporation of a more advanced primary flight display. Virtually all military aircraft prior to the 1960s were equipped with traditional round dial displays to provide flight performance data to the pilot. This included such primary performance indicators as airspeed, altitude, and rate-of-climb/descent, plus several engine gauges. However, this required the pilot to scan, interpret, and respond to a wide variety of separate instruments. With the complexity of aircraft such as the F-106, this presented the pilot with a significant mental workload, as he had to move his eyes to several locations to determine a given flight condition.

To ease the "scan" burden, several of the flight displays were changed from the round dial to a vertical tape. Two such arrangements, called *Integrated Instrument Displays* (IID)—one to the left of the attitude indicator and one to the right—provided information previously obtained from seven different instruments. (This same "tapes" approach had been used for the F105 a few years earlier.)

By re-grouping the data, the pilot has immediate access not only to the analogue display, but also to a digital readout directly beneath, as shown in the accompanying figures. There were several other pieces of information also embedded in the display. The later production numbers came with the IID, while many of the earlier aircraft were modified to incorporate it.

MA-1 Fire Control System

The Hughes MA-1 Fire Control System was an integral part of the F-106 and its data-link with the Semi-Automatic Ground Environment (SAGE) system. The MA-1 included the first use of a digital computer in a fighter, along with a cathode ray tube (CRT) that allowed the pilot to view his position on a moving map called a *Tactical Situation Display* (TSD). As with the F-102 and F-101B, the SAGE system (by way of the controller on the ground) could "fly" the F-106 (via its autopilot) to a point where the onboard radar could pick-up the target; the pilot would then lock onto the target and complete the intercept mission. The MA-1 was the weak link in the total weapons system and underwent many modifications during its lifetime.

Along with the incorporation of an Infrared Search and Track (IRST) subsystem and fast-tuning magnetron options (as with the F-101B/F), other such "mods" are best described by Mark Foxwell, veteran F-106 pilot with multiple assignments to the USAF Interceptor Weapons School (IWS)—ADC/ADCOM's "post-graduate" school for FIS *Weapons Training Officers*, but which also pioneered tactics and technical upgrades to both interceptors and their control environment. Mark Foxwell: "*I was the F-106 computer and data link instructor at IWS from 1970 to 1974. I worked directly with Hughes Aircraft and made several trips to their plant in Culver City to work on defining and testing upgrades to the [MA-1] fire control system. Later on, I came back as both an instructor and eventually as the last IWS Commander, so I was up on all the latest changes until the early 1980s.*

"*The F-106 was the first aircraft in the Air Force to receive a programmable digital computer; the computer 'ran' the rest of the systems. The upgrade from the original*

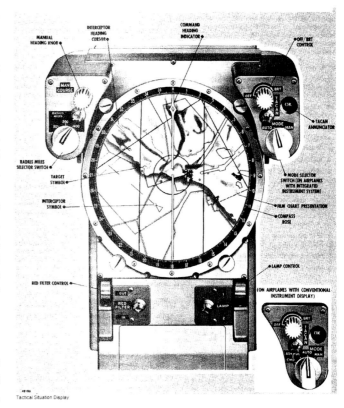

Figure 12-07. The Tactical Situation Display (TSD) presented target returns in azimuth and range selectable from 5 nm (nautical miles), 10 nm, 20 nm and 40 nm. (There was some ground-mapping capability at 80 nm.) USAF Illustration.

analog computer was complete in the latter half of the 1960s. But the basic radar was always the same and was not updated. The rest of the avionics, communication, navigation (except for the UHF radio), were unchanged.

"*The new digital computer was not only more reliable, but added great flexibility. It interfaced with the radar, the FCS, the TACAN, the data-link and the autopilot with inputs from the pitot-static system and altimeter. That meant that all of these analog systems had to have their outputs converted to digital and their feedback from the computer converted back to analog. BUT, the computer had a crude 'inertial' system that kept track of location and was automatically updated by TACAN when it was received. It also navigated to the target, either by CC (close control) from data-link like the 101 and 102, or by MCC (modified close control) where data-link from SAGE would input the target location and velocity vectors and the computer would solve the intercept geometry without direction from the ground. The computer was essential for firing the Genie and the AIM-4F (radar) and AIM-4G (IR) missiles and, later, the 20mm Gatling gun. We could modify what the computer did with digital 'tape' updates and did so many times. IWS would create the change requirements; Hughes would reprogram and send us a new 'tape.' IWS would flight-test the changes and then send them to the field with tactical instructions*

Figure 12-08. An F-106 fires an ATR-2A *Genie* air-to-air training rocket from its weapons bay. Note the aircraft's slimmer supersonic drop tanks. USAF Photo.

on how to use the new features. As far as the pilot was concerned, radar operation was a raw display on an analog B-scope just like the 101 and 102, but was helped by computer-generated overlays with target info, navigation/intercept guidance, and firing solutions.

"But an important upgrade was a more reliable UHF radio… The original tube technology UHF radio (and TACAN, too, I think) was very unreliable and failed a lot. The data-link receiver was a separate UHF receiver-only. If the voice UHF failed, we could still complete a combat mission by following Dolly, CC or MCC. But without data-link and no UHF voice, we were down to detecting and intercepting targets autonomously (which we practiced a lot). We could change the frequency on the data-link receiver and use it as a backup UHF voice receiver and often did when the voice radio quit. The new 'solid-state' UHF (and TACAN, too, I think) were very reliable."

Zoerb describes the radar/data-link functions: *"Fighter-sized targets were typically not detectable outside of 20 nm, and bomber-sized targets rarely outside 30 nm, thus 40 nm was normally selected for an intercept. The azimuth scan [of the antenna] was 60 degrees either side of center until the B-sweep was commanded with the trigger on the left stick grip.*

"At that point, the B-sweep slewed with left/right movement of the left stick grip—the goal was to center the desired target return in the very narrow B-sweep, then generate a range gate using the second detent on the left stick grip trigger, placing the range gate over the target return and releasing the trigger to complete

the lock-on. After lock-on, the radar would track and provide steering guidance (small dot in a larger circle) to the selected weapons parameters.

"As the firing point was approached, assuming the right stick grip trigger was depressed, the launch sequence would begin—missile bay doors open, missile rails extended into the airstream, and missiles would fire. Following the missile firing pulse, the rails would retract and the doors would close…and you became an ace…simple."

Because of the possibility that the target might employ sensors that could detect the tracking radar of the F-106 and employ defensive countermeasures to defeat the intercept, a back-up capability was later added—Infrared Search and Track (IRST). The pilot could select the IRST mode and search for, acquire and track his quarry passively, i.e., without producing any electronic emissions. One of the problems with this form of intercept is that the IR system could only locate the relative angle-bearing (in azimuth and elevation) of the target, but not provide a direct range indication (although range indication could be estimated, based on selected overtake speed and observed increases in the target's IR signal). Thus, the IRST subsystem would still allow the interceptor to move in on the quarry without being electronically discovered—although, depending on the intercept mode and mission ROE, this could require visual acquisition. It should also be understood that not all intercepts involved a "kill" intent. An unidentified intruder might be a civilian aircraft off course. It could be a Soviet ferret flight that remained outside the territorial airspace of the U.S. and the objective would then be to identify and "shadow" it. There were also situations that would require the interceptor to proceed to a holding point and await further instructions.

Zoerb explains: *"The IRST used a C-scope display of azimuth and IR intensity, along with an aural tone that indicated detection of a heat source. IR lock-on was similar to the radar process using the left stick grip and the resultant steering cue was pure-pursuit (vice lead-collision steering for the radar [with a range lock-on])."*

Foxwell explains how the IRST (on all the *Century Series* interceptors) could help when their radars were faced with deception (vice noise) jamming: *"...A good range gate stealer, and we saw many during IWS training against SAC and Navy targets, was best handled by using the IR Search and Track system to track the target and then slave the radar to the IRSTS, which meant that the radar would always see the target even if the range gate stealer broke your automatic radar tracking. We could fire in IRSTS either with the radar tracking the target or with the radar super-searching the target (rapidly scanning the target at the azimuth of the IR source)."*

The Speed Record

The performance of the F-106 was quite phenomenal for its time—rivaling or exceeding all the *Century Series*. As was the custom, each country and each branch of service wanted the "bragging rights" of having "the fastest" aircraft. With the arrival of the F-106 into operational squadrons, the Air Force set out to break what was then the current world speed record of 1491 mph. That record had been set just two months earlier in October 1959 by the USSR with the Ye-152-1 (a specially modified MiG-21) flown by Colonel Georgii Mosolov. To confuse the issue a bit, the Soviets later identified the plane as the Ye-166 and Ye-66.

Figure 12-09. The Soviet Ye-152-1 used to set the world speed record in 1959. Soviet Air Force Photo.

On 15 December 1959, Major Joseph W. Rogers flew the F-106 to a speed of 1,526 mph (Mach 2.31) at an altitude of 40,500 feet. What makes this so impressive is that this record for a single-engine turbojet has stood for more than 50 years. The maximum speed for the F-106A was listed at Mach 2.5, but several pilots reported Mach readings as high as 2.85. There was no published temperature or Mach limit as there was with the F-104.

The Soviets claimed to have beaten the F-106A record in 1962 with the Ye-152-1, as Colonel Molosov reportedly attained 1,665 mph. However, the Fédération Aéronautique International (FAI), the international organization that sanctions and recognizes aviation records, never accepted that record.

Operational Use

The F-106A was initially assigned to Air Defense Command units (first the 539th FIS at McGuire AFB, New Jersey) starting in May 1959, and they were considered "operational" by October of that year. Operational units typically maintained a "quick response" capability, in which several interceptors were on 5-minute alert and could be "scrambled" (ordered airborne) in that time following the sound of the klaxon horn. Many problems surfaced during the F-106's first year with the ADC squadrons. In one instance a canopy was inadvertently released in flight, which caused the entire fleet to be grounded for a short period.

To ferret out American radar frequencies and intercept capabilities, the Soviets would frequently send out their long-range Tu-95 turboprop *Bear* bomber. These would often fly to the east coast of the United States just outside the territorial waters. They would then continue down to Cuba to land and refuel before returning to the USSR. F-106s would be dispatched to intercept and "escort" the Soviet planes.

Daniel Zoerb and William Rutledge relate a typical intercept using the SAGE system data-link. Note the *Multiservice Tactical Brevity Code*, such as "Judy" and "Dolly," used by American military (and NATO) to convey complex information with a few words.

Rutledge: *"On either training missions or actual air defense scrambles, we would take-off under control of the normal ATC [air traffic control] agencies and be handed over to the GCI controller, so the timing of initial voice contact depended on the air traffic control structure and our position in it. We would perform weapons system and data-link checks and, if all was normal, begin receiving data-link commands to the intercept or holding point.*

"If it was 'manual' control, without the data-link being active, the controls were all by voice. Once we checked in with the controller, he told us what altitude, heading, and airspeed to fly until we got radar contact on the target. If the

Figure 12-10. A Tu-95 Bear is intercepted and "escorted" by an F-106. USAF Photo.

data-link was active and accurate, and *we had indicators on our instruments that displayed the recommended flight parameters and we were directed to 'follow Dolly.'"*

Zoerb: *"Data-link commands included type of intercept (forward quarter/stern intercept), intercept objective (ID, kill, shadow, etc), target heading, fighter altitude, heading and airspeed commands ('bugs' on the appropriate instruments), and a small target designation circle on the radar scope indicating where, in azimuth and range, the target should appear (or azimuth-only for an IR intercept). The data-link greatly reduced the amount of radio communications required and increased effectiveness in a communications jamming environment (although data-link could also be jammed)."*

The pilot could "couple" his autopilot to the data-link to relieve himself of the navigation chores, but he would still be required to maintain the selected airspeed, initiate the radar (or IR) track, to arm and fire the missiles, and to break away and/or initiate a reattack until the intercept results were known.

Rutledge: *"When we had a radar lock-on to the target, we called 'Judy'* [brevity code for: 'the aircrew has radar/visual contact on the correct target, has taken control of the intercept, and only requires situation awareness information. Controller will minimize radio transmissions]. *At that time, the MA-1 fire control system*

gave us steering commands and sequenced signals to the weapon that was selected to prep it for firing. We had to have the weapon selected and armed and the trigger squeezed to launch the weapon (or simulate launch during training)."

Zoerb: *"During training, the AIM-4 missile rails with test missiles would be extended in firing position* [and] *recording relevant parameters and intercept data for maintenance purposes and for pilot de-briefing.*

"If the mission was ID, there were selectable, radar-driven steering cues that, if followed, would place the interceptor about 500 feet abeam and above/below the target to facilitate identification in poor weather. Bad-weather, night intercepts were the biggest challenge and periodically, pilots were required to demonstrate intercept proficiency flying under a hood in the back seat of the F-106B."

During the intercept process, Rutledge notes: *"The work load was pretty high! You had to fly the aircraft—maintaining heading, altitude, and airspeed. Plus, 'fly' the radar by selecting desired modes and by using the radar control handle—a 'stick' handle on the flight control stick to the left of the actual flight stick (giving the appearance of a yoke), to set the scan altitude and operate the 'range gate' to activate the lock-on feature. As the terminal phase of the intercept was reached, the* pilot began to 'steer the dot' to the intercept point, hold down the launch trigger, and monitor the progress of signals to the weapons prior to launch. 'Steering the dot' was simply flying a small circle displayed on the radar screen to an even smaller dot that was displayed when the radar was locked onto the target.

"You could take over the intercept at any time by calling 'Judy.' Without radar contact, however, it would have been foolish to have done so. Practically, most of us did not call 'Judy' until the MA-1 had a solid lock on to the target. Nominal ranges for detection and lock-on to a fighter-sized target would have been 35-40 miles at high altitude, but much less at lower altitude, particularly if the target was below the interceptor. Bomber-sized targets were detected much farther out. The radar was a pulse radar rather than pulse Doppler, so it would detect the ground more readily than a small aircraft. That created significant problems when looking down on a low-altitude target, and required the pilot to finesse the elevation control on the radar 'stick' to paint the target just below the ground return on the scope." (The low-altitude intercept, especially over land, was where addition of the IRST subsystem could greatly aid target acquisition day or night—at least in relatively favorable weather. At the same time, sharp "pings" and well-defined "spikes" on the IR scan display needed to be separated from more ambiguous signals from other "hot spots" in the area.)

As to the accuracy and reliability of the system, Rutledge responds: "Very accurate, not very reliable. Neither the MA-1 nor the SAGE systems were reliable by today's standards, because of the very old electronic technology involved (vacuum tubes rather than transistors and diodes, etc). For their time, however, they were incredibly advanced. Like little girls, 'when they were good, they were very, very good, and when they were bad, they were horrid.' At least 50 percent of the time or more, a pilot flew with some degradation of the MA-1. As noted elsewhere, however, the airframe and engine were very reliable, so if we wanted to get flying time, we flew."

Zoerb: "In its day, the data-link and connectivity to the SAGE system provided enormous improvements to air defense effectiveness through precise voice and non-voice intercept communications. Automation enabled large numbers of threats to be intercepted while maintaining a reasonable controller workload. Although primitive by today's standards, the Hughes MA-1A radar was very capable versus the design threat. The IR Search and Track sub-system was a huge advantage, providing independent ability to acquire/track without alerting the target. Versus large, non-maneuvering targets the AIM-4, both IR and radar variants were effective fired in pairs, and the Genie would likely have been a 'crowd-pleaser' versus large bomber formations. Airframe speed and endurance/range,

coupled with advanced avionics and weapons made the F-106 a formidable air defense interceptor throughout the '60s and '70s."

Rutledge: "In my three years and almost 800 hours of flying the Six and sitting alert, I had active scrambles only twice—once out of Dover AFB. The first time was for an airliner, which was identified before the intercept was completed. The second was out of Tyndall AFB on a 65,000+ foot U-2 (I assume it had to be a U-2, very high and very slow) on a heading that indicated he had been over Cuba. Interestingly, I got the Six to 62,300 feet with only 1.55 mach before I started the 'snap-up'. The relative low airspeed (I would have preferred 1.8+) was because one of the vari-ramps didn't extend and I was getting 'stall-buzz' when the shock wave inside the inlet got all the way back to the face of the compressor, so I had to throttle back."

Zoerb adds: "Snap-up intercepts were used to engage high-altitude, fast targets above about 50,000 feet. Using best time to climb, then near-unloaded acceleration to max mach at around 35-40,000 feet, pitch was then increased to around 60 degrees, IR/Radar acquisition and a weapons firing solution achieved. A severely nose-high, low airspeed recovery/break-away followed and occasionally an engine re-start [the engine could experience a "flame-out" at these high altitudes].

"Early F-106 pilots wore pressure suits for these intercepts, but by the time I flew it, we didn't wear them and were restricted to 55,000 feet. Low airspeeds at apogee, with engine roll-backs usually caused a decay in normal cabin pressure, but the emergency cabin pressure system-would activate and rapidly generate about 25,000 feet cabin pressure (brute force). It wasn't uncommon for 3 or 4 F-106s to be vectored in a trail chain separated by 4-5 miles for head-on-intercepts against priority hi-fast targets-in an effort to maximize the number of firing opportunities and probability of killing the target."

The pilot workload was high. Dick Stultz, who spent 3,300 hours in the cockpit of the F-106, recalls: "The F-106, as a single-seat fighter, was considered the most heavily tasked cockpit. Although the official Air Force history reports that the airplane was flown by the computer—the computer was actually unable to move the throttles, move the gear, select weapons, arm, unlock, fire the trigger, or even lock onto a target, let alone employ ECM, ECCM, or Infrared systems."

Ultimately, the plane was flown by 15 ADC units (including one training unit) from bases in Alaska, Iceland and, for short periods, West Germany and South Korea. It was the only operational *Century Series* not to see combat in Vietnam—nor, along with the Republic F-105, to see service with any other country (although Convair made a valiant effort to make foreign sales).

Only 277 of an anticipated 1000 were built when production ended in the summer of 1961. Funding was so tight and the airplane's capabilities so needed that all of the 35 test articles were brought up to combat specification and assigned to operational squadrons.

F-106B Two-Seat

A two-seat variant was also built, with the first order submitted in August 1956. While these were initially intended to be transition trainers with the designation TF-106A, it became apparent that they must also fill a full combat role and the designation was changed to F-106B.

Recognizing the significance of the area rule and the impact that changing the cross-section had on the sonic pressure wave, the F-106B was designed from the start with a tandem cockpit. This reduced the internal fuel capacity and required rearranging some of the avionics, but the overall length and width of the fuselage remained the same as the F-106A. The F-106B also carried the same complement of weaponry (i.e., the *Genie* as well as *Falcons*). Although initially powered by the J75-P-9, all were eventually upgraded to the P-17.

The first flight of the F-106B (57-2507) was in April 1958, and the first eight aircraft completed were temporarily designated JF-106B for flight test. Although deliveries began in February 1959, they were not declared operational until July 1960 because of a variety of problems. Typically each squadron operated two F-106Bs for use in transition and proficiency training and for flight checks.

Ejection Seat Upgrades

Among the shortcomings of the F-106 was its ejection seat. The first model fitted was built by Weber Aircraft Corporation and was similar to that used in the F-102. It was a relatively simple design that used a gas cartridge (about the size and propellant of a 37mm shell) that literally blew the seat out of the aircraft. The high G-force imposed by the sharp impulse was a distinct drawback, often causing spinal compression and occasionally permanent injury to the pilot. There was concern, however, that this conventional type of seat would expose the pilot to excessive windblast and high-G force deceleration at supersonic speeds (reference George Smith's supersonic F-100 bailout), and that a safer and more sophisticated seat was needed.

Convair stepped in and designed what was called the bobsled, or "B" seat. If the Weber seat was simple, the Convair seat was at the other end of the spectrum. When the pilot elected to eject, he raised the ejection handle to activate five separate actions to secure his body to the seat and jettison the canopy. Squeezing the ejection handle trigger began his exit, as it fired the vertical thruster and, in sequence, a set of rotational thrusters designed to turn the seat backwards 90 degrees as it left the plane. This avoided the windblast impinging directly on the pilot and positioned him for positive G-force deceleration. The sequence then called for gas-operated stabilizers to extend horizontally behind the seat, the attachment bolts to be severed, and finally, a small rocket motor fired to propel the seat clear of the tall vertical stabilizer.

Figure 12-11. The clean lines of the Delta Dart were maintained with the two-seat F-106B and are apparent even with the external fuel tanks. USAF Photo.

Figure 12-12. In this test of the F-106 ejection seat, the 90-degree rotation is apparent as the rocket begins to accelerate the seat upwards and the stabilizers are extended. USAF Photo.

Although the seat was apparently well tested (15 sled tests, 11 dummy airborne ejections, and one human ejection in 1961), the first few emergency uses resulted in fatalities and pilots quickly built a distrust of their "safety" system. The Air Force finally responded by awarding Weber a contract for a new simpler "zero-zero" system. The prevailing wisdom was that low altitude ejections were far more prevalent. The new seat proved successful and all F-106s were retrofitted.

Dennis Geesaman had the rare opportunity to experience the ejection sequence over the Gulf of Mexico in 1981: "*A misty hydraulic leak (very flammable in those days) met with an arc or spark in the wheel well, and caused a flash fire/explosion that blew the right gear down when I was going about Mach 1. I got it semi-under control and slowed before I ejected. All electronics were gone (so no communications), the aileron torque tube was severed (no aileron), one mangled right gear was down and the other two would not come down, and the trim went out at full nose down (the standard trim at Mach, but very heavy once slowed). I flew north on the whiskey compass and followed the coast to Tyndall AFB, and ejected heading south over the Gulf.*

"*There were two ejection handles on the* [Weber] *seat just outside the thighs (similar in configuration in all the USAF aircraft I flew). By grabbing the side thigh handles it also helped you assume a proper ejection position. The sequence was initiated when the handles were raised, and an exposed trigger squeezed to complete the canopy release and seat firing.*

"*All emergency items worked as advertised and I flew again four days later, but I had recurring back problems throughout my 21-year high-G career. In 1997 it was X-rayed and they found an old fracture in a vertebra that had healed on its own—guess where that came from.*"

Project Six Shooter

By the late 1960s, when the experience of "missiles only" fighters had proven problematic in Vietnam, it was proposed that an M-61 20mm cannon pod be made available that could be installed in the F-106A's center weapons bay (displacing the *Genie*). The F-106 had proven that its low wing loading (52 lbs/sq ft) made it a "somewhat" competitive dogfighter. This was done as a part of *Project Six Shooter*, which also included a semi-bubble canopy for greater pilot visibility.

The gunsight development for this project was conducted at Tyndall AFB, Florida, and managed by two visiting Air Force Academy instructors. They essentially "cracked" the MA-1's software code to insert their own software for the M-61 "Vulcan": instead of using the F-4's lead-collision optical sight (LCOS) logic, which calculated the guns' aimpoint based on ballistics, target position and the fighter's G-loads, it projected the bullets' flight path in relation to the target's (changing) position so that the F-106 pilot could adjust his own maneuvers to superimpose the

Figure 12-13. The center position in the F-106 weapons bay was modified to accept the M-61 20mm Vulcan cannon. Two *Falcon* missiles are seen flanking the M-61 cannon pod. USAF Photo.

bullets' projected impact point onto the target before shooting. The appropriate analogy was to adjust the aim of a garden hose to have its water stream land on the "target" plants, regardless of any breeze effects; in other words, instead of calculating the guns' aimpoint, it would be determined empirically by where the bullets would actually be landing at the target's range and angle-off.

Two F-106As prototyped *Project Six Shooter* during 1969. The project was quite successful, and was eventually incorporated into those F-106As that had the "vertical tape" instrumentation (about 178 remaining aircraft); the other ("Round Eye") F-106As and the two-seat F-106Bs remained unmodified. (F-106 pilot comments attest to the need for this gun, gunsight and "bubble" canopy reconfiguration if F-106s were to be used in overseas contingency operations, as was being considered at the time.)

Pilotless Landing

Perhaps one of the oddest occurrences involving an F-106 occurred on 2 February 1970. Three F-106s were engaging in mock combat among themselves when one, piloted by Captain Gary Faust, attempted to execute a maneuver at about 40,000 feet that caused his plane to enter a flat spin. Typically, this is an unrecoverable condition in most aircraft. After having gone through the appropriate procedures to attempt to recover, Captain Faust ejected at 15,000 feet. When he did, apparently the change in the center of gravity (and/or aerodynamic conditions) caused

the F-106 to recover from the spin and enter a shallow flat glide (the engine was at idle power). As he had set the trim for "take-off" during the procedure to recover, the aircraft assumed a 175-knot descent (which is about its published landing speed). It made a soft touchdown on the snow-covered ground and slid to a stop.

A local sheriff saw the plane land and went to the aid of the pilot—whom he thought was still inside. He was surprised to find the canopy and the seat missing but the engine still running. As he stood near the plane, the heat from the engine caused the ground to thaw and the plane would occasionally inch forward. He called the Air Force to ask how to shut down the engine but was told to let it run out of fuel. The plane had so little damage that it was returned to service and later put on display at the Air Force Museum.

Reflections

Bill Rutledge, who would attain the rank of Brigadier General, was commissioned a Second Lieutenant on 19 December 1969 from the ROTC program at the University of Kentucky. He went directly to pilot training in Class 71-05 at Craig AFB, Alabama, graduating in January 1971. Rutledge was then posted directly to the F-106 school at Tyndall AFB, Florida, since the requirement to check out in the F-102 prior to taking on the F-106 had been deleted just a few months prior. Rutledge, who represents a later generation that transitioned to the F-106, recalls: "... *we all checked out*

Figure 12-14. F-106 58-0787 sits in a cornfield where it landed without its pilot. Note the effect of the exhaust on the snow as the engine remained running after it landed. USAF Photo.

in the T-33 and did some basic ground control intercepts (naturally voice only and visual only since the T-33 had no radar or data-link) to familiarize us with the interactions between interceptors and GCI controllers. The F-106 was, therefore, the first fighter I flew and Hemingway was right—what a beauty." (Rutledge is referring to the famous quote by Ernest Hemmingway. The noted author wrote: "*You love a lot of things if you live around them, but there isn't any woman and there isn't any horse, nor any before nor any after, that is as lovely as a great airplane, and men who love them are faithful to them even though they leave them for others.*")

"*I began F-106 CCTS in May 1971 and graduated in October the same year and was assigned to the 95th Fighter Interceptor Squadron at Dover AFB, Delaware, from October '71 to October '72. The Six was extremely clean at low angle-of-attack, and, with low wing loading, airspeed bleed-off was very slow at one G. When the AOA was increased, however, the airspeed bleed-off was dramatic, a factor that could be either good or bad in a dogfight with another-type fighter.*

"*An unrecoverable flat spin could occur due to the Six's strong adverse yaw at high AOA. A minimum of 200 hours in type was required to begin to check out in Air Combat Maneuvering against other fighters.*" Rutledge concurs that this may have been the attribute that caused the flat spin experienced by Captain Gary Faust over Montana a few years earlier.

"*All training prior to that time was in the intercept role and operation of the complex radar system. The low reliability of the radar system in the Six resulted in us having to take frequent cross-country flights just to make the squadron's quota of flying hours (not enough aircraft with operational radars for home base intercept training!). While the radar was fickle and unreliable, the airframe/ engine/flight control systems were very reliable.*

"*The cleanness of the aircraft and the efficient design of the external tanks made going supersonic unnoticeable and the aircraft would just continue to accelerate. It differed, in this respect, from the F-102 because of the much more pronounced 'coke bottle' or area rule effect of the Six.*

"*The 'Wedge' windscreen had a central metal ridge and flat plate sides. There was a saying that the Six was a 'Mach 2 airplane with a Mach 6 windscreen.' Many of us had old windscreen halves made into coffee tables when the internal wiring necessary for defog failed. Landing with the defog failed in a crosswind could be interesting, too.*

"*Since the Six was designed for very high altitude intercepts of the Soviet Bear, caution led the designers to provide an oxygen system that provided 100% oxygen, under pressure, all the time if the mask was on—instead*

of being a blend of ambient air and oxygen that increased in oxygen content as higher altitudes were reached. The pressure-necessitated 'reverse breathing' in which air was taken in when the pilot relaxed and had to be forced out with chest/diaphragm action. The 100% oxygen would also be absorbed into the tissues of the middle ear and pilots would frequently wake at night with painful ear blocks if they had not performed the 'valsalva maneuver' [equalizing the pressure in the ears] enough after the flight and before going to sleep. Most of the time, a valsalva would clear the problem. The first few attempts at radio calls were also difficult, and somewhat amusing, since the pilot was fighting the pressure of the system just to talk.*

"*The Six had the capability for data-link control [during intercepts] and ILS [Instrument Landing System] approaches. The pilot could couple the autopilot to either and the aircraft would fly itself except for throttle adjustments. The autopilot was notoriously unreliable, however, and I never coupled it with an ILS except once in training and you can be sure I had my hand on the disconnect switch in case of stray electrons.*"

Rutledge was transferred back to Tyndall and assigned to the Interceptor Weapons School's Southern Air Defense detachment. Prior to the Cuban Revolution in 1959, the air defense network in the Gulf of Mexico had been all but disbanded. Two incidents caused a reversal of that decision. In October 1969 Cuban Air Force pilot Lieutenant Eduardo Guerra Jimenez decided to defect to the United States with his MiG-17. Guerra surprised not only the Cuban hierarchy but the Americans as well by landing at Homestead AFB, Florida, where *Air Force One* (Boeing 707) was waiting for (then) U.S. President Richard Nixon, who was vacationing at his Key Biscayne home.

"*The second incident was an International Sugar Cane Conference in New Orleans. The Cubans, not invited of course, flew an AN-24 COKE (two-engine turboprop transport) into New Orleans in 1971, and landed without being detected or intercepted. In response to this vulnerability (and concurrent with some F-106 squadrons being deactivated!), a small air defense network was established in the Gulf. Alert detachments were established at Homestead, Tyndall, and New Orleans, and a radar site was activated at Dauphin Island near Mobile.*"

Rutledge indicates that there was no time or temperature limit on staying in AB: "*It was only limited by the amount of fuel in the tanks, and it burned a hell of a lot really fast in that J75 (a great engine!). Interestingly, for the scramble on the U-2 over the Gulf of Mexico, I lit the burner for takeoff and came out at 62,300 feet. The fuel load was 14,500 pounds full and I had only 1800 pounds when I terminated AB. Seems I had forgotten to check my fuel in the excitement of the live intercept. My* buddy Roger Estes, who was scrambled with me that day, had all the airspeed in the world (1.85+) but no fire control system. I had the radar but not as much airspeed as I would have liked. Such was flying the Six."

As for keeping "current," Rutledge often intercepted B-57s, "... with enhanced electronic countermeasure equipment, and some B-52s. Unfortunately, the B-58 was retired before I got into the Six, so no attempts on them."

Although Rutledge never carried a "live" Genie, "I did fire an ATR-2A, which was a Genie with the warhead removed and ballast and tracking equipment installed. It was amazing, an 832-pound rocket with a 35,000-pound thrust rocket motor. When that rocket motor fired, there was an instant contrail out in front of my aircraft. I never had a conscious sensation of seeing the actual rocket fly-out. The standard load for an F-106 was four AIM-4 Falcons (two G models-heat seeking; and two F models-radar guided) and a Genie. Obviously, this load was simulated for training and may not have included the Genie, depending on the DEFCON level. We controlled the armament switches in the cockpit. Contrary to popular belief, the SAGE guys did not control the selection of our armament, and we could always override their commands, even when coupled with the Dolly. Obviously, if it was a non-nuke stern shot, we would use the G model Falcons (IR guided) and if it was a face shot, we'd use the radar-guided F models. The Genie could be used for either.

"Primary weapon was the Genie—a nuclear air-to-air rocket. The fire control system would calculate a launch point and heading to effect proper launch, set the time of flight before detonation, and automatically launch the AIR-2A Genie given that the pilot had switches properly set. The pilot then did one of several escape maneuvers, depending on altitude to keep himself out of the fireball and overpressure shock wave.

"If the system was working properly, and we normally knew that before starting an intercept, we had a lot of confidence that the intercept would be successful, particularly if it was a Genie shot. The Falcon was something else entirely. The missiles actually guided very well indeed, but the contact (vice proximity) fuses meant that the leading edge of the missile fins had to strike a part of the target for the warhead to be activated. And the warhead itself wasn't much, just five pounds, so even if the missile tracked very well, it had to hit the target in a vulnerable spot to have a good chance at a kill. With the Genie, close was good enough and it didn't have to be very close!

"Desired speed for a normal intercept depended on the altitude and target speed. At low altitude, we looked for 1.2 times the target speed for stern intercepts (the only kind we could do at low altitude). At high altitudes,

for really high targets, we were commanded to VmaxP, or maximum-practical-speed, which was somewhere over 1.8 Mach. Mach .93 was a good speed in the 30-45,000 foot range, and was the speed we used for cross-country cruise."

Zoerb recalls: "We fired the [practice] Genie against high-speed, high altitude drones, most challenging of which was the Bomarc at about 70,000 feet and mach 2.5. The experience of feeling the weapons bay doors open, the 'clunk' as the 850 pound rocket fell from the bay, and the audible (even in the cockpit) roar as the rocket motor lit was quite an experience, as was the speed and smoke trail that allowed you to maintain visual contact with the rocket til the spotting charge exploded. As I recall, the distance to the target at rocket launch… was about 7 or 8 nm at high altitude. The Genie accelerated to twice the launch mach (~1.5 mach) in a two-second rocket motor burn…a real bullet! The challenge of acquiring and locking the radar to the target was a real trick.

"Most of us used the IRST to get an early IR track and steer out the geometry, then switch to the radar which was slaved to the IR line of sight, and generate a range gate at 30 nm…the maximum range at which a gate could be generated. As the target return appeared in the B-sweep at about 40 nm, we would turn the trigger (left grip) loose to allow the gate to lock the target as it flew into 30 nm. From that point till the weapons launch cycle began was just a few seconds, during which time it was required to steer a 2-mil steering dot into the exact center of a steering circle which collapsed from a full screen circle to an 8-mil circle at launch…no yaw allowed. The tight launch tolerances reflected the ballistic nature of the rocket and the need to precisely place the nuclear warhead within a lethal radius of the target or group of targets. Believe even a small nuclear warhead detonating in the vicinity of any type aircraft would have a negative effect on electronics; if close enough, on structural integrity of the target; or on the desire of enemy aircrew to continue the mission. The effects on friendly fighters, unaware of the Genie launch, would have also been unpleasant, with at least temporary blindness being the biggest fear (we carried an eye patch in the survival vest in hopes of preserving sight in at least one eye)."

Although the F-106 was built as a bomber interceptor, there was contingency training for the dogfight scenario, as Rutledge notes: "When a pilot reached 200 hours in type, he was evaluated for ACM (Air Combat Maneuvering) training, which consisted of a total of 12 sorties. The first six were 1-versus-1 (or BFM—Basic Fighter Maneuvers) with the IP; and sorties 6-12 were 2-versus-2 with your IP as your wingman/flight lead against two other guys in your squadron. The tactics package was called Six Pack (cute, huh?) and was loosely styled after the Navy's 'Loose Deuce' (?) tactics, in which the fighters were employed in a two-ship, rather than four-ship, formation. At the time, TAC was still using 'Fluid Four,' based on the Korean War tactics, in which only the four-ship lead and #3 actively maneuvered against the bogeys, while #2 and #4 were simply trying to keep up with Lead and Three, and in fact, were wasted in terms of either offensive or defensive capability. Their nominal job was to cover Lead and Three's six o'clock, but the aggressive maneuvering and full attention required to stay in an extended formation made that job a joke. They were essentially MiG bait while Lead and Three tried to become aces...."

Rutledge: "*Some time post-Vietnam (I transitioned from the Six to the F-4 in 1974 and the change had taken place), TAC saw the wisdom of the two-ship package from an economy and maneuverability standpoint and adopted tactics that employed the two-ship as the 'standard' dogfight formation, even though they might be part of a four-ship for navigation and patrol before engaging.*"

Zoerb: *The big delta wing enabled excellent instantaneous turn performance, but the penalty in drag (amongst other things), created a disadvantage in sustained maneuvering/turn performance. Cockpit visibility was restricted in a narrow forward band and in a significant rearward area aft of the cockpit/wing line. The weapons suite was designed to counter bomber-type threats and not well adapted to fighter-versus-fighter combat. Although the IRST was adequate for rapid acquisition and track, the radar was difficult to employ in dynamic, close range situations. The AIM-4 could only be employed at relatively short ranges and within limited angles off the longitudinal axis of the threat. AIM-4s had no proximity fuse, requiring contact to detonate, further limiting effectiveness in close-in, dynamic fighter engagements.*"

Rutledge: "*The limitations of the Six in close-in dogfights led to a couple of significant modifications, one before I left the Six and one after. First, the original canopy had a six-inch wide steel beam down the middle directly over the pilot's head with two Plexiglas side panels for visibility to the left and right. This arrangement was OK for intercepting Bears, but was lousy for ACM, in which you frequently want to point your lift vector, and therefore the top of your aircraft, at an adversary that you would also like to be able to see. As the Six was increasingly used for ACM and dissimilar ACM with TAC adversaries, the fix for this problem was to install a 'bubble' canopy, which didn't have the metal bar. It was similar to the canopy on the F-4, F-15, and other fighters in that it was a single piece of Plexiglas formed to the correct shape. The first time I flew a Six with the bubble canopy, I thought I was going to fall out of the thing. I got used to it rapidly! What an improvement.*

"*The second limitation the Six had in close-in maneuvering was the armament. The difficulty of locking the radar onto a moving target, the long prep time required to fire a Falcon, and the fact that you almost had to hit the enemy pilot in the heart to down his jet, made the Six questionable in a dogfight despite its low wing loading and very good maneuverability. If you could get behind him but couldn't kill him, what good were you? The fix was a gun! After all, missiles would destroy the enemy fighters before we got into gun range, wouldn't they? We know the answer is 'Not Exactly.' So the Six was retrofitted with an M-61 20mm Gatling gun identical (except for the external fairing) to the one retrofitted to the F-4C/D. The two interior weapons bay doors were modified and the gun was mounted in the rear of the weapons bay where the Genie would have been loaded.*"

Zoerb provides additional details: "*The gun was fired through a fairing in the weapons bay doors and, partly because of the installation and length of the fuselage ahead of the muzzle, was canted downward about 3 degrees. The downward cant increased the lead necessary to achieve a valid gun tracking solution to an extent that a highly maneuvering/high-g target would sometimes disappear under the nose of the airplane...unhandy. The 'snap-shot' gunsight and HUD was added when the gun was installed, but required much practice to master. The gun gave the F-106 its only viable dogfight weapon. Dogfight advantages of speed and great instantaneous turn performance were offset by a large visual signature, low sustained maneuvering performance, somewhat limited visibility and much head-in-the-cockpit 'switchology,' a fire-control*

Figure 12-15. The original Mercury Astronauts pose by one of the F-106B aircraft they used to maintain flight proficiency during their training. NASA Photo.

system with limited rapid acquisition/track capability, and weapons not optimized for dogfighting. In spite of these significant disadvantages, many of us were able to do very well in training against much more capable adversaries… the airplane counts, but the aviator may count more. Use speed, altitude and the airplane's one, big turn to achieve success, then leave quickly. If it worked, you were the hero…if not, you re-defined fight-center and adversaries were lined up awaiting their turn at you."

Zoerb: "The airplane was a true pleasure to fly, but required that the pilot pay attention to subtle and not-so-subtle signs that the airplane was unhappy. Failure to pay attention during heavy maneuvering could/did result in violent departures from controlled flight. Strong proficiency was required to employ the airplane to its optimum. When the new canopy was added, eliminating the flat-sided canopy and longitudinal overhead beam, the bulged canopy increased noise levels at higher mach numbers, but improved visibility. A very stable, steady, fuel efficient jet at high altitudes and mach numbers, with optimum cruise mach of 0.92, and ability to perform snap-up intercepts against targets at altitudes over 65,000 feet. Clean and fast, it was one of the only airplanes capable of catching an F-111 at very low altitudes.

"However, aero trim changes at high mach/high Q required almost full forward stick pressure to keep from climbing; very uncomfortable since any significant deceleration would result in a severe downward pitching moment. Another distraction was termed the 'G tuck,' which was experienced during deceleration from super- to subsonic when G's suddenly increased by 3 or 4 as the aero trim shifted and elevons became more effective. There were several instances in which pieces of wingtip were shed as the airplane experienced a sudden over-G while decelerating."

Mark Foxwell: "The F-106 was the love of my Air Force career, even more so than my combat missions in the F-105 and the great fun I had flying the F-16 in Germany…[I]t had some incredibly great advantages. I always thought that its tremendous speed, range, endurance and maneuverability were its greatest assets. It was very clean carrying all ordnance internally and its supersonic external drop tanks were truly capable of easily flying to mach 1.8 or more. I recently visited the 27 Fighter Squadron at Langley, flying the F-22. They touted the Raptor's supercruise capability, where they use AB to take it well supersonic and then cruise supersonic in military. Well I/we did that routinely on the Six; I would take it in full AB to 49,000 and Mach 1.5, then go to full mil and cruise supersonic for 500 miles or more. The optimum best range was achieved at 41.000 at mach 0.93! It would fly unrefueled for 3:20; I once flew from Colorado Springs [Colorado] to Loring [Maine] and had to hold at Loring for a SAC exercise before landing!

"The F-106 was optimized for its job of anti-Soviet bomber defense more than anything in its day. I don't know what features the F-12 would have had. [Primarily the AN/ASG-18 look-down/shoot-down fire control radar and three AIM-47 long-range Falcons—but no gun.] The F-15 and F-16 had/have greater firepower and radar and computer capabilities as does the F-22. But these fighters are not optimized for the Strategic Air Defense mission and the F-106 could match or exceed them in speed, range and endurance. I think the 106's speed and range gave us the ability to '…get there the firstest with the mostest,' which of course is how Cold Wars were won."

Variants

Table 12-01

Convair F-106 Variants

Type	Notes	No. Built
F-106A	The "Ultimate Interceptor"	277
F-106B	2-seat trainer combat capable	63
QF-106A	Target drones (converted form F-106A)	(194)
	Total Build	**340**

Phase Out

Consideration had been given to a supplemental build, but by December 1961, the Navy's F-4 Phantom II had taken root in the Air Force (under the prodding of the Secretary of Defense Robert McNamara, and known briefly as the F-110). A fly-off competition (Project High Speed) had been held between the two aircraft, in which the F-106 reportedly was able to hold its own in maneuvers against the then F4H-1 (later the F-4B). However, the F-4's APQ-72 fire control system outperformed the MA-1 with a 25 percent greater contact range and, especially, in the area of reliability. Thus, the F-4 Phantom II became the multipurpose fighter of choice for the 1960s. ADC, with its emphasis on anti-bomber missiles, would move through the decade with only the F-102, F-101B and F-106 as its primary interceptors, but with the progressive ECCM improvements to counter the evolving ECM threat from still-active Soviet bombers.

From 1972 to 1974 six ANG FISs got F-106s from the Active force, and both the Guard and a smaller number of regular Air Force FISs operated the F-106 concurrently until it was fully retired from air defense operations. The last two Active units, the 5th FIS at Minot AFB, North Dakota, and the 49th FIS at Griffis AFB, New York, retired their F-106s after 25 and 19 years' operations, respectively; the last two Air Guard units, the 101st FIS at Otis AFB, Massachusetts, and the 119th FIS at Atlantic City, New Jersey, retired theirs in 1988. Meanwhile, with air defense operations under the Tactical Air Command (since ADCOM inactivation in 1980) and focused primarily on Air Sovereignty operations, the F-106s (like F-101Bs before them) were selectively replaced by F-4s and early F-16s and F-15s, as TAC continued to modernize its fighter force.

Dennis Geesaman flew the F106A for 7 years and about 1450 hours and the F-15 for 12 years and 1850 hours: "*At the beginning of flying the F-15, I thought of it as a similar aircraft (basic handling feel and missions were similar) but that it did everything much better--bigger engines to sustain energy, a more powerful 'look-down' radar, and effective air-to-air weapons.*"

Because of its high-speed performance 194 F-106As were modified under a program called *Pacer Six* to serve as QF-106A target drones (like several earlier fighter and interceptor types). They were operated as Full Scale Aerial Targets (FSAT) out of White Sands, New Mexico, and Eglin Gulf test range in Florida.

NASA used two F-106s as chase planes, but it is believed that there are none in flyable condition at the time of this writing. Its 29 years on operational status was the longest serving of the *Century Series* fighters in the U.S. inventory.

Although the F-106 chalked up the best Air Force safety record for single-engine turbo-jet fighters, more than one-third were eventually lost to accidents.

Characteristics & Performance Data	F-106A 1-seat Interceptor	F-106B 2-seat Tng/Combat
Length (ft in)	70'8"	
Wing Span (ft in)	38'3"	
Height (ft in)	20'3"	
Wing Area (sq ft)	697.8	
Engine	J57-P-17	
– Mil Pwr /AB (lbs)	17,200/24,500	
First Flight	Dec-56	Apr-58
First Delivery (for op'ns)	May-59	Jul-60
Empty Weight (lb)	23,646	24,861
Gross Weight (lb)	35,500	37,522
Combat Weight (lb)	38,700	41,831
Max TO Weight	41,831	42,720
Internal Fuel (gal)	1440	1200
(w/Drop Tanks) (gal)	2100	1660
Max Speed (mph)	1,525 @ 40 K	1,315 @35K
Initial climb (ft/min)	42,800	42,000
Combat Ceiling (ft)	57,000	52,700
Normal Range (sm)	575	470
Max Range/DT (sm)	1,800	1,550

Table 12-02. Convair F-106 Specifications.

Figure 12-16. A QF-106 takes off. USAF Photo..

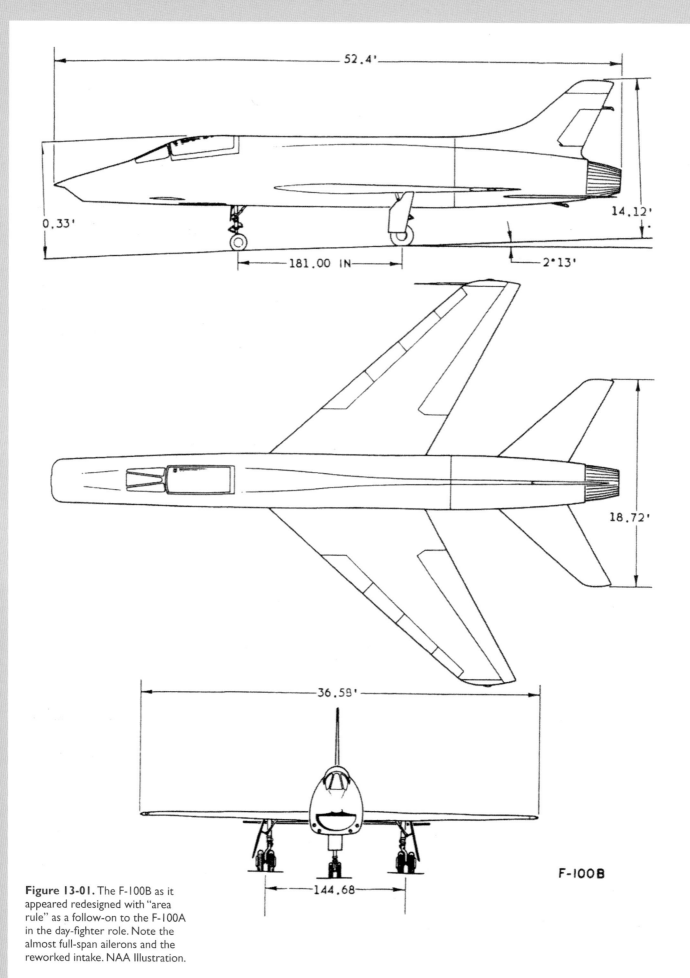

Figure 13-01. The F-100B as it appeared redesigned with "area rule" as a follow-on to the F-100A in the day-fighter role. Note the almost full-span ailerons and the reworked intake. NAA Illustration.

F-100B

Design Origin

Even before the start of the flight tests for North American Aviation's F-100 in May 1953, the NAA design team began to evaluate revelations coming from NACA's Langley Research Center. Aerodynamicist Richard Whitcomb had put forth the concept of the "area rule," and information being released to the aviation industry by NACA would have a profound effect on the shape of future high-speed aircraft. Coming too late to affect the initial design of the F-100, NAA embarked on its next-generation fighter with an in-house study that would produce a design to compete for several Air Force requirements. The Air Force encouraged this with a letter of authorization in March 1953.

A rework of the F-100 was undertaken using the designation "F-100B" (the A model was already an established variant), although that was not an official Air Force designation. The objective was to incorporate the "area rule" and to achieve major weight savings for an improved "day fighter" that would reach production by 1955—succeeding the F-100A.

Although the first flight of the YF-100 exceeded Mach 1, and NAA was encouraged, subsequent testing uncovered some notable problems (that would only get worse). Lt. Col. Pete Everest was able to establish a new world speed record in October 1953 of 755 mph. As events unfolded, the delta-wing YF-102 interceptor, flown that same month, failed to exceed Mach 1 in level flight and would have to undergo a major "area rule" redesign to achieve its ultimate performance. The F-100 compared well against the subsequent F-102A design, whose empty weight was 1,300-pounds heavier—the result of the large radar and internal weapons bay. Each powered by the Pratt & Whitney J57, the F-100 ultimately attained 864 mph, while the "area-ruled" F-102A achieved only 825 mph.

In a foreshadowing of events to come, NAA explored the possibility of an all-weather version that could be brought to production quickly. A large radar antenna was designed into the nose with the intake immediately under it—a similar modification had been done to the F-86, resulting in the F-86D. An existing F-100 fuselage was used as the basis for a mock-up, recognizing that, at the higher Mach numbers the plane was expected to operate, special considerations had to be made for the airflow into the engine. A radical sweptback variable–area intake duct was configured. However, it was eventually decided that a full F-100 redesign was needed to include the area rule.

The objective of the major make-over was two-fold: incorporate the "area rule" and continue to rework the

Figure 13-02. Using the basic fuselage of the F-100, a mock-up of the F-100B began to take shape in a modification reminiscent of the F-86D. USAF Photo.

air intake to allow the nose to accommodate radar for both an interceptor and fighter-bomber variant. NAA assigned the in-house designation of NAA-212 to the project in October 1953. The same 45-degree sweep and wing area as the YF-100 was initially specified, but with the extended chord to provide for the wing flaps that would eventually appear on the F-100D. Automatically actuated leading-edge slats provided for low-speed high angle-of-attack performance with "spoiler-slot deflectors" (both above and below the wing) for roll control. The use of this odd control surface arrangement was an attempt to avoid the adverse yaw problem that plagued the F-100 throughout its life.

In addition, the wing thickness was reduced to 5 percent from the 7 percent of the F-100A. However, this required that the landing gear retract into the fuselage. The mid-wing location required the stabilator to be positioned, as it had with the F-100, low on the aft end of the fuselage to avoid wing turbulence.

Defining the Role

At this time, the NAA design team was confronted with three variations of the F-100B—day-fighter, all-weather interceptor, and fighter-bomber. Each placed specific demands on the airframe and the trade-offs were challenging. To achieve the high performance maneuverability needed for the day-fighter, a higher thrust-to-weight ratio was needed. However, the added hardpoints, drop tanks, and structural enhancements (to permit a load factor of 8.67 Gs) for handling low-level turbulence for the nuclear delivery fighter-bomber added weight, as did the large radar for the all-weather version.

When the F-102 program went into redesign to incorporate the "area rule," NAA realized that they had an opportunity to pursue the all-weather interceptor as it had successfully done with the F-86D and follow-on F-86L. Following that path, there would be no guns on the all-weather design, which was at times referred to as the F-100BI—with the "I" defining the "interceptor" variant. Hardpoints on the wing were configured for drop tanks and a heated leading edge provided anti-icing to accommodate the all-weather environment. However, this design process was cut short by the need for the gun on the day-fighter; the guided missiles of the day (the *Falcon* and *Sidewinder*) had yet to prove themselves and were not considered viable options for the maneuvering dogfight. Even the use of the new six-barrel M-61 "Vulcan" (aka "Gatling Gun") being incorporated into the F-104 was thought to be a high-risk item. Therefore, the design proceeded with four M-39 20mm cannon. The answer to the growing weight problem was to increase the engine power. The decision was made to go with the Pratt & Whitney J75, which had almost 50% more thrust than the J57.

By January 1954, the Air Force had expressed little interest in the day-fighter project, as Lockheed

Figure 13-03. The third prototype F-107A shows the vertical wedge-shaped splitter in the middle of the intake and the ramp doors within the duct. USAF Photo.

Figure 13-04. Because of the positioning of the air intake, the more traditional clamshell canopy could not be used—thus the vertical movement of the canopy. USAF Photo.

was nearing flight-test with its own lightweight day-fighter, the F-104. Convair was completing its sweeping design changes for its F-102A and had an even more advanced version (which would eventually become the F-106) that would move the delta-wing planforms to even higher performance levels. NAA management realized that the only opportunity for the F-100B lay in competing for the nuclear fighter-bomber role, as the Republic F-105 was still in its design stage. Republic had faltered with its F-103, and there were some reservations about their ability to move the F-105 project along; eventually it too would undergo a major fuselage redesign to incorporate the "area rule."

In June 1954, NAA's rework of its F-100B into a fighter-bomber was encouraged with a development contract for 33 F-100Bs. (SAC then dominated the Air Force strategy and purchasing, and nuclear delivery was where the contract dollars were flowing.) The Low Altitude Bombing System (LABS) was incorporated, along with a number of other features needed to address the navigation and survivability aspects of this mission. A few weeks later, the Air Force decided to formally designate the NAA F-100B project as the F-107A—there would be neither an XF-107 nor YF-107. However, within another month (August 1954) the number of pre-production aircraft was cut to nine.

As the design continued to change, the nose air intake issue resurfaced. If NAA ran the air duct under

the cockpit, it would restrict the space available for the cannon. In addition, the NAA engineers were not excited about the complications of opening bomb bay doors at Mach 2. The decision was made to carry the nuclear weapon in a depression in the bottom of the fuselage and to put the air intake *above* the fuselage—a unique arrangement that was unparalleled in any aircraft to that point. Using a "Variable Area Inlet Duct," the amount of air fed to the jet engine was automatically controlled based on the Mach number and angle-of-attack in a manner similar to most other *Century Series*. The first two prototypes (55-5118 and 55-5119) provided for only two settings of a movable ramp, while the third (55-5120) was continuously variable.

An all-moving vertical fin (no separate hinged rudder) was another innovation that had not appeared on any previous *Century Series* aircraft. In an effort to reduce the landing speed, "boundary layer control" was designed into the inboard flaps using air from the engine compressor, as was done with the F-104. (Both of these features found their way into the large nuclear attack aircraft NAA would subsequently build for the Navy, the A-5 *Vigilante*.) A retractable probe provided for in-flight refueling.

By late 1955, the Air Force realized that it needed to keep Republic Aviation as a viable supplier despite concerns over the stability of the company, and was therefore committed to the F-105 nuclear fighter-bomber program. As a result, the Air Force

Figure 13-05. This view of the F-107A highlights the rather short flap span and large vertical rudder. The flat expanse and desolation of Rogers Dry Lake at Edwards is apparent. USAF Photo.

reduced the initial F-107A purchase to only three prototypes by the end of February 1956. Although North American Aviation continued forward with the F-107A towards Category I testing, at this point it would have required a major problem in the F-105 program for it to move into production.

Flight Test

The first flight of the F-107A (serial 55-5118) occurred at Edwards AFB on 10 September 1956, piloted by J. Robert Baker. Mach 1.03 was attained and Baker reported good handling characteristics. On landing, the drag chute failed to deploy; however, the aircraft sustained only minor damage and made its second flight three days later. On a subsequent flight in November 1956, the F-107A reached Mach 2. At the higher Mach numbers there were problems with "tuning" the intake as had occurred with virtually all

the *Century Series*. Later, more in-depth evaluation found some unsuitable flying qualities.

The second F-107A (55-5119) flew for the first time in November 1956, and it tested the four 20mm cannon and the separation characteristics of the external nuclear payload. In February 1957, test pilot Al White demonstrated a successful delivery of a nuclear "shape" at China Lake at Mach 1.87.

The third aircraft (55-5120) flew in December 1956 and explored the performance limits. However, the automated variable inlet duct system became a chronic problem; thus the maximum altitude for sustained flight was limited to 51,000 feet.

It was not until March 1957 that the Air Force made the final decision to cancel the F-107. Two of the three prototypes were turned over to NACA for high-speed research—the variable intake on the third F-107A (55-5120) being one of the prime

NORTH AMERICAN F-107 ULTRA SABRE

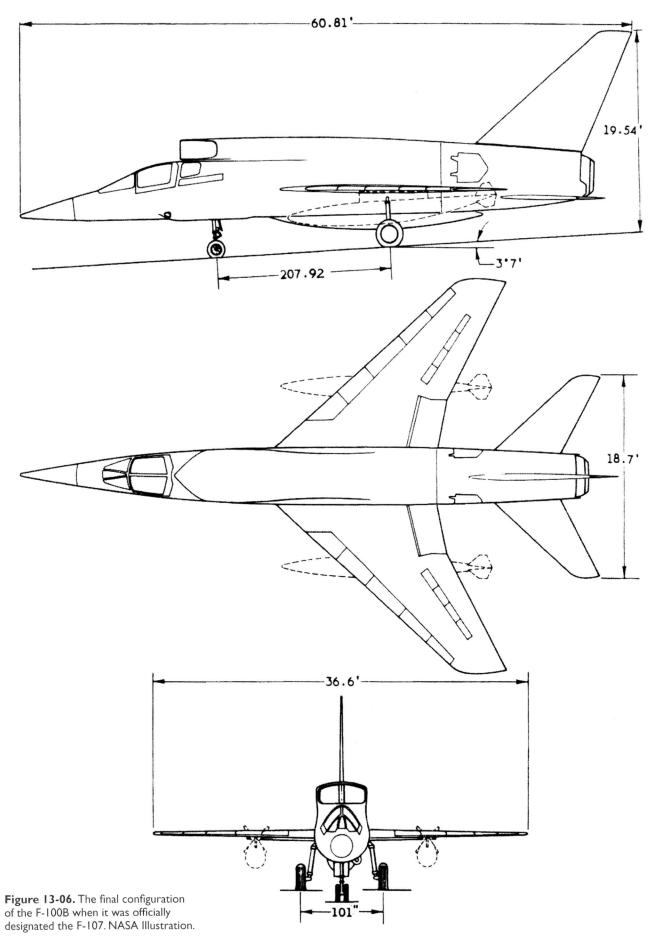

Figure 13-06. The final configuration of the F-100B when it was officially designated the F-107. NASA Illustration.

investigation points. However, the variable-area inlet duct proved a constant source of mechanical problems, and it was eventually made a fixed intake that limited the top speed to Mach 1.2.

A second area of interest to NACA and the Air Force was the evaluation of a "side-stick" installed on the right side of the F-107A cockpit in addition to the traditional center position. The North American Aviation X-15 rocket plane, then in the final stages of design, would use a "hand-controller" that cradled the pilot's right arm so that the high acceleration forces imparted by the rocket engine would not cause unintended control input. The traditional center stick was for use after burnout of the rocket engine.

Ultimate Disposition

The first prototype (55-5118) had so many problems that NACA eventually grounded it and used it as a spares donor for the other two. The third plane, which was turned over to NACA in February 1958 for the variable duct research and side-stick evaluation, completed forty flights before an incident ended its flying days. Test Pilot Scott Crossfield, who was preparing to fly the X-15, was piloting 55-5120 during a take-off when he encountered control problems. The plane ground looped, blowing both main tires, and a small brake fire resulted. Although the airplane was not badly damaged, it was decided not to invest in repairs. Crossfield indicated that the desired attributes of the side stick had been demonstrated and that no further testing was needed. The plane was cut up for use as a fire-fighting training form.

Airframe 55-5118 was acquired by the Pima Air Museum in Tucson, Arizona, and 55-5119 can be seen at the Air Force Museum in Dayton, Ohio.

Characteristics & Performance Data	F-107 1-Seat Fighter
Length (ft in)	61'10"
Wing Span (ft in)	36'7"
Height (ft in)	19'8"
Wing Area (sq ft)	376
Engine	YJ75-P-9
– Mil Pwr /AB (lbs)	17,200/24,500
First Flight	Sep-56
First Delivery (for op'ns)	N/A
Empty Weight (lb)	22,696
Gross Weight (lb)	39,755
Max TO Weight	41,537
Internal Fuel (gal)	1260
Max Speed (mph)	1295 @ 36K
Initial climb (ft/min)	40,000
Combat Ceiling (ft)	53,200
Normal Range (sm)	790
Max Range/DT (sm)	2400

Table 13-01 North American F-107 Specifications.

Figure 13-07.
In September 1959, the number three plane (55-5120) was involved in a dramatic ground loop that resulted in little damage, but a spectacular set of tracks in the sand at Edwards. The incident ended flights of the F-107A. NASA Photo.

Design Origin

The role of the fighter and its various permutations underwent a series of changes in the decade of the 1950s. The "new" Department of Defense was trying to determine how each of the services fit into the ever-changing paradigm of conflict as defined by the nuclear weapon and the politics of the Cold War. The strategic bomber continued its ascendancy under the tight control of General Curtis LeMay. This situation would only get more complex as the perceived requirements continued to drive technology and the costs to extremes.

A series of "studies" undertaken during the early 1950s revealed a schism in the strategy of air defense. The traditionalist looked to the single-place, highly maneuverable fighter and the rapid-fire cannon. The visionaries perceived the integration of radar and the air-to-air guided missile as the last gasp of the manned aircraft before being replaced by the surface-to-air missile.

As the F-103 project was moving towards its premature death in 1955 (the Air Force had grown discontented with Republic's lack of progress), a new proposal for a "Long-Range Interceptor, Experimental" (LRI-X) was generated in July 1955. Within a few months its published specifications called for an interceptor with more than twice the range of the F-106—which had yet to fly. There were new and disturbing implications with availability of the "Super" (the hydrogen bomb) in the Soviet arsenal. Some planners believed that the bomber had to be stopped well before it could approach America because of the possible development of "stand-off" missiles—air-to-surface missiles that could be launched by the bomber hundreds of miles from their targets (which indeed materialized).

This required the prospective interceptor carry a much more powerful radar, as the ground-based SAGE system (then just coming into operation) could not provide the required "over-the-horizon" coverage. In addition, the transition was then taking place where the bomber would no longer proceed at high altitude to its target, as it was too easily detected by radar—it would approach the U.S. at low altitude, below radar coverage. From its perch at 60,000 feet, the ideal interceptor would be able to "look down" at potential targets and discriminate them amid the ground clutter. The Infrared Search and Track system (IRST) that was then being developed was also specified. A two-man crew and three air-to-air missiles (the advanced AIM-47 *Falcon*) with active radar on a rotary launcher within an internal weapons bay were specified. These requirements dictated a large fuel load and two engines. The aircraft's size would more than double that of the F-106.

Design studies were sought from North American, Lockheed, and Northrop; missing from this list were Republic and Convair. The NAA project was labeled NA-236, and this was initially pursued during 1956, but canceled by the Air Force little more than six months later. The project was resurrected in April 1957, as the Air Force continued to redefine the role and to understand the level of technology that had to be achieved. With the designation F-108, WS-202A finally achieved some programmatic stability and North American Aviation proceeded with this new design under the NA-257 label. Two prototypes and 480 aircraft were initially defined as part of the bid package for production planning.

As the cost estimates of such an advanced fighter were revealed during the summer of 1957, it was thought that, by combining some of its R&D aspects with those of a new long-range supersonic bomber (then in the study stage), economies of scale might be realized. Both would need to *cruise* at supersonic speeds (as opposed to the "dash" capability of the current *Century Series*). This would require a much more fuel-efficient engine (the YJ93)—the bomber would simply use a larger number of those engines. The materials to allow the structure to sustain flight beyond Mach 2 would require similar

Figure 14-01. North American Aviation's SM-64 Navaho provided a good basis for supersonic aerodynamics. USAF Photo.

Figure 14-02.
The canard arrangement on an early NAA F-108 design. USAF Illustration.

investigation. The supersonic aerodynamics involving compression or "shock wave" lift would also provide symbiotic relationships. The target date for first flight of the fighter was 1961.

With Boeing deeply into its B-52 and the KC-135 projects, Republic struggling with the F-105 (and the virtually dead F-103), and Lockheed getting the F-104 into production, it was recognized that NAA might be the only available contractor for both the new fighter and the giant supersonic bomber. It was also obvious that NAA was probably not going to get a production contract for the F-107.

North American was not without some precedents in getting the F-108 contract; they were well into the development of a Mach 3 unmanned cruise missile called the *Navaho* that was launched on the back of a ballistic missile. (However, with the imminent success of the ICBM, that project was cancelled in 1957.) They were also developing a Mach 2 carrier-based bomber that would ultimately share much of its form with the F-108.

To this was added the possible expansion of the F-108 mission to include escort for the new bomber (which would become the B-70). As 1957 ended, NAA had a very extensive set of projects to address. However, events in the Soviet Union would play a major part in disrupting these plans. The launch of the Sputnik satellites in late 1957 placed new emphasis on the Intercontinental Ballistic Missile (ICBM)—abruptly signaling the end of the dominance of the manned bomber—and funding shifted rather rapidly to missile programs. Thus, the escort assignment was a short-lived role that was eliminated by the Air Force before the end of 1958; many had felt this was not a realistic capability in any case.

Refining the Features

Meanwhile, a delta wing with three vertical stabilizers appeared on the first iteration of the F-108 design that included a canard arrangement. However, the final configurations provided for a two-phased (cranked) sweep to the leading edge—40 degrees and 58 degrees—coupled with a 4-degree anhedral of the outer wing. A single vertical stabilizer was an "all-moving" unit similar to the F-107 (no separate rudder). A ventral fin extended when the landing gear retracted. The IRST system was built into the leading edge of the wing. NAA planned to use honeycomb stainless steel in much of the structure.

The General Electric YJ93 was a derivative of the J79 that powered the Navy A-5; it provided 20,000-pounds of thrust dry and 30,000 in AB. An alternative engine was also proposed in the P&W J58, which ultimately powered the A-12/SR-71/YF-12.

The exceptionally large internal fuel load (7,100 gallons) allowed for a range of over 1,000 miles, and in-flight refueling was to be available. One of the scenarios for the intercept role was to fly out to a position along the periphery of the U.S. border during periods of high DEFCON levels and "hold" in a large racetrack pattern for an indefinite period. A KC-135 would provide periodic refueling. As with the SR-71 the fuel was JP-7, a complex hydrocarbon blend with very low freezing temperature and with special high-temperature combustion additives.

Each of the two-man crew was enclosed in an escape module that encapsulated him for "ejection" at extreme speeds and altitudes. (A similar module was used in the B-70.) The second crewmember was the "Weapons Systems Officer" (WSO), who sat in tandem and did not have any aircraft controls.

Figure 14-03. Artist renditions gave some excitement to otherwise lifeless drawings. USAF Illustration

The fire control system was to be the AN/ASG-18 built by Hughes. It was unique for its time, in that it was the first system that allowed for target discrimination through the use of pulse Doppler radar. Although it could only engage a single target at a time, the electronic package, which still used vacuum tubes, was a massive one-ton unit. The tracking scenario had the F-108 find the target and launch the long-range missile while still up to 300 miles distant. The missile would activate its own radar and pick-up the target at about 100 miles and proceed to intercept and destroy it using terminal homing. This would allow the F-108 to be immediately redirected to a second target without having to wait for the first to actually be destroyed, as was the case with the early radar-guided *Falcon*.

The aircraft had a projected empty weight of 51,000 pounds with a maximum gross weight of 102,000 pounds, thus providing a thrust-to-weight ratio of .56 at its combat weight. However, its wing area of 1865 sq ft resulted in a wing loading of only 55.9 lbs/sq ft—among the best of the *Century Series*.

The mockup was reviewed by the Air Force in January 1959 and the name *Rapier* was applied to the fighter a few months later. (The name was the result of a contest held among ADC's enlisted ranks.)

Figure 14-04. The final design of the F-108 shared much of its lines with the Navy A-5 Vigilante. U.S. Navy Photo.

Figure 14-05. The NAA F-108 shows its elegance and unusual wing design. NAA Illustration.

Cancellation

The budget squeeze and the encroaching ballistic missile technology spelled doom for the F-108. After $150 million had been spent, the program was formally cancelled in September 1959. The Soviet bomber threat did not exist to the extent prophesied—as determined by the U-2 overflights of the late 1950s. As planned, however, much of the money expended was also applicable to the B-70 project, which continued and produced two flying prototypes before it too would be cancelled in the mid-1960s. Ultimately, the Navy A-5 was successfully put into production with some of the technology and design features paid for by the F-108 program.

Moreover, the capability to operate at Mach 3 and 75,000 feet was effectively demonstrated with a 'black" project known as *Oxcart* (Lockheed's A-12 for the CIA), which was being developed concurrently. It would spawn a fighter variant known as the YF-12, which would also be cancelled, though after completing its initial flight test program.

The Hughes AN/ASG-18 Fire Control System and radar found its way into the Lockheed YF-12. The long-range AIM-47 missile would fall by the wayside, succeeded by the AIM-54 *Phoenix* missile. The J93 continued in development and powered the B-70. NAA kept a minimal design team on the F-108 project for several months as it lobbied for its restoration—which did not occur.

Characteristics & Performance Data (Estimated)	F-108 2-Seat Interceptor
Length (ft in)	89'2"
Wing Span (ft in)	57'5"
Height (ft in)	22'1"
Wing Area (sq ft)	1865
Engine	(2) J93-GE-3AR
– Mil Pwr /AB (lbs)	20,900/30,000
First Flight	N/A
First Delivery (for op'ns)	N/A
Empty Weight (lb)	50,907
Gross Weight (lb)	76,118
Max TO Weight (lb)	102,533
Max Speed (mph)	1980 @ 76,000
Initial climb (ft/min)	18,000
Combat Ceiling (ft)	80,000
Normal Range (sm)	1020
Max Range/DT (sm)	

Table 14-01. NAA F-108 Specifications.

Origin of Bell Aircraft

Lawrence Dale "Larry" Bell (1894-1956) joined his older brother Grover and exhibition pilot Lincoln Beachey as a mechanic in 1912. When Grover Bell was killed in a plane crash in 1913 Larry wanted to quit aviation, but his friends convinced him to remain in the fledgling industry. He went to work for the Glenn L. Martin Company and ultimately became the Martin Company's general manager.

Bell left Martin in 1928 to join Consolidated Aircraft in Buffalo, New York, eventually becoming vice president and general manager. When Consolidated relocated to San Diego in 1935 Bell remained in Buffalo to start his own company, Bell Aircraft Corporation. His first military contract was the development of the YFM-1 *Airacuda* that made its first flight in 1937. An unconventional interceptor powered by two pusher engines, only 13 Airacudas were produced, and ultimately scrapped as useless.

Bell Aircraft subsequently built the P-39 *Airacobra*, which first flew in 1938. Not competitive against the Japanese *Zero* in the South Pacific, the P-39 found a home as an export to the Soviet Union for the ground attack role in the Lend-Lease program. The Bell P-59 *Airacomet* fighter was America's first jet-powered aircraft, which saw only limited production towards the end of the war. Bell is perhaps best known for building the X-1 research aircraft that Chuck Yeager took through the "sound barrier" in 1947.

The company branched off into helicopters in 1941, with the Bell Model 30 making its first flight in 1943. It evolved into the Bell 47 (made famous for its Medevac role in Korea by the TV series "MASH"). With Larry Bell's death in 1956, the company was subsequently purchased by Textron.

Vertical Take-off Concept

Aircraft designations were occasionally applied by manufacturers to designs not yet acknowledged by the Air Force. This was the case with the F-109, which was adopted by Bell Aircraft, but had also been previously used to designate a variant of the Convair F-106.

The Bell F-109 design was a continuation of the vertical take-off and landing (VTOL) paradigm that had begun in the late 1940s by the Navy. They had defined two programs at that time; the first resulted in the Convair XFY-1 and Lockheed XFV-1 in the early 1950s. These were powered by the massive Allison XT-40 turboprop that delivered 4,500 shaft horsepower (the equivalent of 17,000 pounds of thrust). The idea was to be able to allow small ships to provide their own "fighter" protection.

Figure 15-01. The Convair XFY-1, unlike its competitor, the Lockheed XFV-1, successfully achieved the transition from vertical to horizontal flight and back during its flight test. U.S. Navy Photo.

Figure 15-02. The Ryan X-13 demonstrated vertical take-off and landing with a pure jet powerplant. USAF Photo.

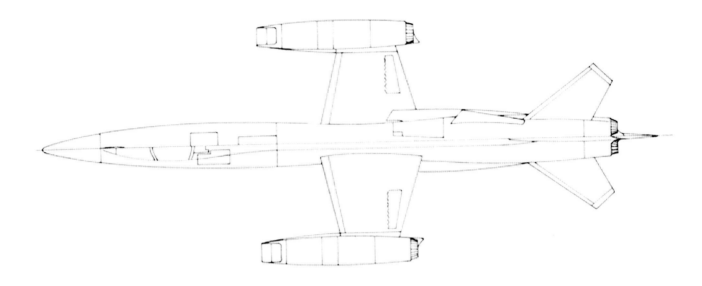

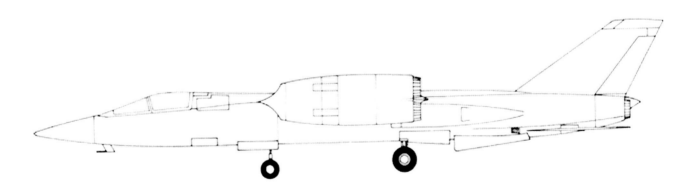

Figure 15-03. The Bell F-109 three-view. USAF Illustration.

Although both flew successfully, only the Convair XFY-1 demonstrated the transition from vertical take-off to horizontal flight and back again. It was determined that the skill level for the pilot to effect the transitions was considerable. Looking back over their shoulder, the task of maneuvering with respect to a solid runway was daunting and the thought of achieving a landing on a pitching deck was beyond reason. The project was abandoned by 1956.

The second and somewhat parallel effort (in concert with the Air Force) was undertaken by Ryan Aircraft to develop a pure jet for vertical take-off. This produced the X-13, which successfully demonstrated vertical take-off, transition to horizontal flight, and vertical landing. To avoid having the difficult task of looking backward during the landing, the X-13 hooked on to a vertically raised platform. The platform had a simple short length of steel cable that the pilot could snag with a hook that extended from the nose. The Rolls-Royce Avon turbojet provided 10,000-pounds of thrust, which was more than adequate for the very light weight 7,000-pound aircraft. Flight tests from December 1955 through to April 1957 demonstrated that the Ryan vertical platform technique was more easily mastered. The platform was mounted on a truck and, after landing, it could be lowered to the horizontal position for transport. However, the project moved no further towards an operational aircraft.

Bell D-198 Design

While these efforts concentrated on using the same thrust vector for both vertical and horizontal flight, a joint 1955 request by the Navy and the Air Force sought to investigate the ability to change the thrust vector, and the Bell D-198 was result. Of course, the performance expectation was ramped up from the 400 knots of the previous XFV-1 and XFY-1 prototypes to Mach 2. The multi-service role (it also carried the unauthorized Navy designation XF3L) was as a fighter-bomber and interceptor.

The essential concept for the D-198 was to use eight small General Electric J85 engines of 2,600-pounds thrust each (3,850-pounds with AB) in three different locations. The engine was only 18 inches in diameter and less than 4 feet long. The initial versions were designed to power the McDonnell ADM-20 *Quail*, a small decoy that was carried by the B-52 and launched when attack by surface-to-air missiles was imminent. When GE realized that they had created the highest thrust-to-weight ratio of any production turbojet, they re-engineered it for a longer life (the Quail was a missile that was expected to fly for only a few hours) and began to market it generally for lightweight manned aircraft.

For the D-198, two engines (with AB) were mounted in nacelles at the tip of each wing. They could be rotated 90 degrees from the horizontal

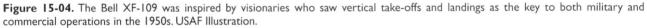

Figure 15-04. The Bell XF-109 was inspired by visionaries who saw vertical take-offs and landings as the key to both military and commercial operations in the 1950s. USAF Illustration.

Figure 15-05
Bell proceeded as far as a mock-up, but the project was cancelled before work on the prototype was begun. USAF Illustration

Figure 15-06.
The EWR VJ-101 fighter used much of the preliminary design work of the F-109 and achieved Mach 1 before the program was canceled.

to assist in vertical take-off, and an additional 10 degrees (90 to100 degrees) allowed modest rearward maneuvering. Two additional J85s without ABs were mounted vertically within the fuselage behind the cockpit. Together with the four engines on the pylons, these two engines provided the power necessary to lift the 24,000-pound fighter vertically off the ground. The remaining two engines (with ABs) were located in the conventional position in the fuselage and were fed by lateral intakes to provide only horizontal thrust. The area-ruled fuselage provided for a single pilot.

After rising to an appropriate altitude, the thrust from the horizontal engines would be increased from idle to accelerate the aircraft forward. The wing-mounted engines would then rotate to move their thrust vector horizontal. As sufficient speed was attained to allow the lift generated by the two small wing surfaces to support the weight of the aircraft, the two vertically mounted engines in the forward fuselage would be shut down and their intake and exhaust openings covered to provide appropriate streamlining.

Flight control about all three axes during the vertical transition was to be supplied by bleed air from the engine compressors through four variable-exit nozzles. The throttles controlled vertical rate. Armed with two M-39 20mm cannon in the fuselage and an internal weapons bay, the D-198 optimistically also had eight hardpoints on its short wings for ordnance.

The D-198's performance was to be competitive with its more conventional contemporaries. A top speed of Mach 2.5 for up to 30 minutes and a maximum service ceiling in excess of 50,000 feet were expected. One of its indeterminate requirements was the ability to operate from "unprepared" fields. The ingestion of debris kicked up by the exhaust and the rapid erosion of unprotected ground were a serious concern, as even hard surface runways could be damaged by the exhaust. Moreover, there were no indications that "rolling" take-offs were considered for gross weights in excess of the vertical capability.

Inter-service rivalry impeded the project, and the Navy dropped its support before the mock-up was unveiled in December 1960. The Air Force cancelled the program in April 1961 before any work had started on the prototypes.

Much of the preliminary design work was then used by the German consortium Entwicklungsring Süd (EWR, composed of Heinkel, Messerschmitt and

Figure 15-07. Lockheed Martin's comprehensive F-35 program includes a STOVL variant, currently under development and test as the F-35B. USAF Photo.

Bölkow) that formed in 1959 to build the vertical EWR VJ-101 Mach 2 fighter. The "VJ" was an abbreviation for *"Versuchsjäger"*—"experimental fighter." It had an almost identical configuration to the D-198. Three prototypes were built, and one attained Mach 1.04 in a test flight in 1964 before the program was cancelled in 1968.

The Hawker Siddeley *Harrier* GR.1/GR.3 and its derivative, the McDonnell Douglas AV-8A *Harrier*, went on to become the first operational "jump jet" (as they were often called). Using a single engine and vectored thrust nozzles, the aircraft first flew in 1967 and was capable of Mach .9. The AV-8A entered service with the U.S. Marine Corps in 1971 and proved successful in several shipborne and land-based expeditionary scenarios. In 1979, the USMC began upgrading their AV-8As to an AV-8C configuration designed to extend their Harriers' operational life and improve their VTOL performance. They were replaced in the mid-1980s when McDonnell Douglas' second-generation vertical/short take-off and landing (V/STOL) AV-8B became operational with a new composite wing, lift improvement devices, modified intakes, redesigned exhaust nozzles, and other UK *Harrier II* features. Despite a relatively high accident rate, the AV-8B has remained in active USMC service, along with its short-deck carriers and other such small-platform ships, through the present day (2011).

The contemporary Lockheed Martin F-35B *Lightning II* is being developed as a variation of the conventional F-35 production fighter but with a "Short Take-Off Vertical Landing" (STOVL) capability. Derived from the X-35 Joint Strike Fighter (JSF)

Characteristics & Performance Data (Estimated)	F-109 2-Seat Interceptor
Length (ft in)	62
Wing Span (ft in)	23'9"
Height (ft in)	12'9"
Wing Area (sq ft)	194
Engine	(8) J85-GE-5
– Mil Pwr /AB (lbs)	2,600/3,850 ea
First Flight	N/A
First Delivery (for op'ns)	N/A
Empty Weight (lb)	13,800
Gross Weight (lb)	23,900
Max TO Weight (lb)	N/A
Max Speed (mph)	1,500
Initial climb (ft/min)	30,000
Combat Ceiling (ft)	60,000
Normal Range (sm)	1.382
Max Range/DT (sm)	N/A

Table 15-01. Bell XF-109 Specifications.

program, this version has a primary role as "ground attack." Like the Harrier, when configured with external ordnance it cannot make a vertical take-off, but must use a "short" runway. As of this writing (June 2011) there remain serious issues with implementing the design and cancellation is a possibility—perhaps again postponing the vision of a vertical take-off supersonic fighter.

As the U.S. Air Force entered the decade of the 1960s, it had responded to the expected nuclear threat posed by the Soviet Union with a stable of specialized aircraft whose roles had some degree of overlap—the *Century Series*. Each represented a cross-section of the technology of the period, driven by the military and political climate of the day. A decade later, the Air Force entered the 1970s bloodied by a conflict that defied even the traditional definition of a "conventional war." The use of the *Century Series* in a "limited war" dominated by guerilla and insurgency tactics did not allow effective use of their technology. Strafing jungle trails and dropping iron bombs amid intense ground defenses was not an efficient or cost-effective use of these assets in terms of decisive effects upon the enemy—although, so far as friendly forces were concerned, they saved countless lives.

America found air combat over North Vietnam significantly different from that experienced in Korea. With air defenses radically more effective and strict politically imposed rules of engagement, the Air Force was unable to duplicate the mastery of the skies that had been the hallmark of "MiG Alley" in Korea. The SAM threat kept missions at low altitude, where thousands of low-tech AAA weapons made the environment treacherous. The MiG threat, although minimal, required an expensive and frustrating response capability. The NVAF intercept tactics allowed them to strike at will when they held an advantage and disappear quickly to avoid engagement. Although the U.S. still held the upper hand in "kills" by a final 2-to-1 ratio. that was not an acceptable number to claim "air supremacy."

A top-level belief in the dominance of technology over ACM skills had allowed the tactics and training of Air Force fighter pilots to degrade to the point that the outdated MiG-17 and MiG-21 became threats that were difficult to deal with during the early stages of the war in SEA. Only after recognition of the situation did the Navy "Top Gun" (1969) and the Air Force "Red Flag" (1975) combat simulation programs re-establish air-to-air combat as a priority. Likewise, the poor performance of the first-generation air-to-air missiles—a lack of ability to use them in a close-in "knife fight" or permission to use them "beyond visual range" (BVR)—brought the gun back to the fighter and the bubble canopy back to the design (F-15, F-16). Half a century later, both 5th-generation USAF fighters (F-22 and F-35) are so equipped. "Smart

bombs" and unmanned remotely piloted systems (RPSs) have allowed "stand-off" destruction of key facilities with pinpoint accuracy—avoiding most SAMs and low-tech AAA.

Partly from changed threats and partly from budget constraints, the Air Defense doctrine has changed since the *Century Series* first flew. The SAGE and BUIC systems are now gone; the DEW line is dismantled—replaced by the North Warning System, which is largely unmanned. NORAD functions have been moved out of Cheyenne Mountain, though that facility is maintained on a backup readiness status in case of emergency. The Strategic Arms Limitations Treaty has significantly diminished the fleets of manned bombers on both sides of the once "Iron Curtain." The Soviet Union disintegrated into 15 separate states, the largest of which—Russia—is closely monitored by intelligence satellites to guard against any possible "surprise" attack. Meanwhile, the F-15 and F-16, plus the F-22—all with lookdown/shootdown FCSs and armament—continue to stand alert to provide for interception of "unknown" targets detected by the radar facilities, and now the threat of internal terrorist actions. Electronic systems, stealth, and a "networked" battlespace that allows aircraft systems to communicate between each other and Airborne Warning and Control System (AWACS)'s mobile "radars in the sky" have enlarged the concept of "situational awareness" and C3I beyond anything realizable a few decades past. Similarly, the E-8 Joint Surveillance and Attack Radar System (JSTARS) performs analogous functions in support of the ground battle.

The technology-versus-pilot skills controversy of more than 50 years ago is still relevant today, though based on moving points of capability, friction, or overlap. Unmanned Aerial Vehicles (UAVs, aka Remotely Piloted Systems, or RPSs) have made steady inroads into the fighter pilot's domain, but they relieve him of routine tasks and save him (and now her) from excessive risks, and hence costly losses; with reduced forces, the manned aircraft can concentrate on the joint mission support that has largely replaced the "service competition" of yesteryear. The *Predator* UAV is able to stay aloft for over 24 hours and carry a variety of electronic sensors, lasers, and GPS-guided smart weapons. Using video and data-links, they can be directed, almost undetected, by ground-based "pilots" sitting in a darkened room, thousands of miles from the action, via satellite links against images on digitally produced color displays. The

Global Hawk can provide intelligence, surveillance and reconnaissance (ISR) products from even larger areas, from higher altitudes and during even longer missions.

Is there a "legacy lesson" to be learned from the *Century Series*—that the manned fighter still has a place in America's "arsenal of democracy"? Certainly; the U.S. (and its true allies) will always need cutting-edge systems and a select few to operate them on behalf of all. But, as each new "fighter generation" evolves (manned and not), their capabilities will combine different "edges of the performance envelope" with both on-board and remote networked sensors, C2, and secure links to connect them. This, along with tactics to enhance "situation awareness" and support of joint-force operations and flexibility in their employment will be the key to sustained air superiority. Likewise, policies to improve stability in their acquisition and control of costs are equally fundamental to being able to afford these extremely high tech weapons.

Figure 16-01. The fifth generation F-22 *Raptor* incorporates all of the advances in aerodynamics, stealth technology, and avionics needed to achieve a 21st century air superiority fighter. With unbelievable maneuverability, thanks to thrust vectoring it also doubles in the ground attack role, and provides for electronic warfare. It cost about $160 million.

AAA Antiaircraft Artillery

AB Afterburner

AB Air Base

ABCCC Airborne Battlefield Command and Control
    Center

ACM Air Combat Maneuvering

ADC Air Defense Command

ADCOM Aerospace Defense Command (1968)

ADF Automatic Direction Finder

ADWC Air Defense Weapons Center

AEC Atomic Energy Commission

AFB Air Force Base

AGL Above Ground Level

AIM Airborne Interceptor Missile

ANG Air National Guard

AOA Angle-of-Attack

ARDC Air Research and Development Command

ARPANET Advanced Research Projects Network

ATI Applied Technologies Inc.

AWACS Airborne Warning and Control System

BCM Basic Combat Flight Maneuvers

BDA Bomb Damage Assessment

BUIC Backup Interceptor Control

CAF Canadian Armed Forces; Canadian Air Forse

CCC Command, Control and Communication (C³)

CCTS Combat Crew Training Squadron

CFB Canadian Forces Base

CNAF Chinese Nationalist Air Force (also ROCAF)

CRT Cathode Ray Tube

DASH-1 Operator's Flight Manual (Tech Order)

DEFCON Defense Conditions

DEW Distant Early Warning

DoD Department of Defense (Formerly the War
    Department)

ECM Electronic Countermeasures

EWO Electronic Warfare Officer

FAC Forward Air Controller

FCS Fire Control System

FFAR Folding Fin Aerial Rocket

FIS Fighter Interceptor Squadron

GAR Guided Airborne Rocket

GCI Ground Control Intercept

GE General Electric Corp

G-LOC G-induced Loss of Consciousness

GPS Global Positioning System

HOTAS Hands-on-Throttle-and-Stick

HVAR High Velocity Aircraft Rocket

IBM International Business Machines

ICBM Intercontinental Ballistic Missile

IFF Identification Friend or Foe

INS Inertial Navigation System

IP Instructor Pilot

IR Infrared

IRST Infrared Search and Track

IWS Interceptor Weapons School

KIAS Knots Indicated Air Speed

KT Kiloton

LABS Low-Altitude Bombing System

LADD Low Angle Drogue Delivery

LASL Los Alamos Scientific Laboratory (Later
    LANL "National Laboratory")

MIT Massachusetts Institute of Technology

MSL Mean Sea Level

MX Material Experimental

NAA North American Aviation

NACA National Advisory Committee for Aeronautics

NASA National Aeronautics and Space Administration

NATO North Atlantic Treaty Organization

NORAD North American Air Defense Command (later "...Aerospace...")

NVA North Vietnamese Army

NVAF North Vietnamese Air Force

NVN North Vietnam

OTS Officer Training School

P & W Pratt & Whitney

PACAF Pacific Air Forces

POW Prisoner of War

PRC People's Republic of China

PRF Pulse Repetition Frequency

QRA Quick Reaction Alert

QRC "Quick Reaction Capability" equipments (usually ECM/ECCM), to meet urgent combat needs

R & D Research and Development

RCAF Royal Canadian Air Force

Recce Reconnaissance (USAF)

RFP Request for Proposal

RHAW Radar Homing and Warning

RIO Radar Intercept Officers

RO Radar Officer

ROC Republic of China

ROCAF Republic of China Air Force

RP Route Pack (North Vietnam)

RPS Remotely Piloted System

RTAFB Royal Thai Air Force Base

RTU Replacement Training Unit

RVN Republic of Vietnam (also Vietnam)

SAC Strategic Air Command

SAGE Semi-Automatic Ground Environment

SAM Surface to Air Missile

SARH Semi-Active Radar Homing

SEA Southeast Asia

SEATO Southeast Asia Treaty Organization

T-1 Pressure Suit

T-4 Sage Air Defense Tactics Program (1968-on)

TAC Tactical Air Command

TACAN Tactical Air Navigation

TDY Temporary Duty (USAF)

TFS Tactical Fighter Squadron

TFW Tactical Fighter WIng

TNF Theater Nuclear Forces

ToT Time-over-Target

TRS Tactical Reconnaissance Squadron

TRW Tactical Reconnaissance Wing

TSD Tactical Situation Display

UAV Unmanned Aerial Vehicle

USAAF U.S. Army Air Forces

USAF United States Air Force

V-G diagram Velocity and G-loading graph

Vmax Maximum (Interceptor) Speed (SAGE)

Vmaxp Maximum Practical (Interceptor) Speed (SAGE)

Vmc Maneuverable Cruise (Interceptor) Speed (SAG)

Vmc Minimum Controllable Speed (Test)

Vmin Minimum (Interceptor) Speed(SAGE)

Vso Power-off stall speed

WR Warning Receiver

WS Weapon System

WW Wild Weasal

WWI World War One

WWII World War Two

WWW Wild Weasal Squadron

YGBSM A phrase of sarcastic mock disbelief!

Anderton, David, Republic F-105: Thunderchief, Osprey Publishing Limited, Long Acre, London, 1983

Archer, Robert D., The Republic F-105, Aero Publishers Inc., Fallbrook, CA, 1969

Belyakov, R.A., Marmain, J., MIG, Naval Institute Press, Annapolis, MD, 1994

Bonds, Ray, The Vietnam War, Crown Publishes Inc., New York, NY, 1979

Boyne, Walter J, Handleman, Philip, Air Combat Reader, Fall River Press, New York, NY, 1999

Boyne, Walter J, Beyond The Wild Blue, St. Martin's Press, New York, NY, 1997

Budiansky, Stephen, Air Power, Penguin Group, New York, NY, 2004

Byrnes, Donn A, A Boy Who Loved Airplanes, Sage Mesa Publications, Albuquerque, NM, 2010

Byrnes, Donn A, Air Superiority Blue—The F-15, Sage Mesa Publications, Los Lunas, NM, 2007

Chant, Christopher, Taylor, Michael J.H., The World's Greatest Aircraft, Chartwell Books Inc., Edison, NJ, 2003

Childerhose, R.J., The F-86 Sabre, Aero Publishers Inc., New York, NY, 1965

Clancy, Tom, Skunk Works, Little, Brown and Company, 1994

Coram, Robert, BOYD, Back Bay Books, New York, NY, 2002

Cross, James, Punching Out, St Martin's Griffin, New York, NY, 2011

Davies, Steve, Dildy, Doug, F-15 Eagle Engaged, Osprey Publishing, 2007

Davis, Larry, Menard, David, Republic: F-105 Thunderchief, Specialty Press Publishers, North Branch, MN, 1998

De Seversky, Alexander P, Victory Through Air Power, Simon and Schuster, New York, NY, 1942

Drendel, Lou, Aircraft of the Vietnam War, Aero Publishers Inc., New York, NY, 1980

Franks, Norman, Aircraft vs. Aircraft, Macmillan Publishing Co., New York, NY, 1986

Gordon, Doug, Tactical Reconnaissance in the Cold War: 1945 to Korea, Cuba, Vietnam and the Iron Curtain, Pen and Sword, London, UK, 2006

Greene, Michael P, US Air Power: Key to Deterrence, US Air force, Maxwell AFB, AL, 1985

Hallion, Richard P, Test Pilots, Double Day and Company Inc., Garden City, NY, 1981

Hansen, Chuck, U.S. Nuclear Weapons, AeroFax Inc, Arlington, TX, 1988

Heinemann, Edward H, Combat Aircraft Designer, United States Naval Institute, Annapolis, MD, 1980

Higham, Robin, Flying American Combat Aircraft, Stackpole Books, Mechanicsburg, PA, 2005

Hobson, Chris, Vietnam Air Losses, Midland Publishing, England, 2001

Hoover, Bob, Forever Flying, Pocket Books, New York, NY, 1996

Hurt, H.H. Jr., Aerodynamics for Naval Aviators, Naval Air Systems Command, 1986

Jackson, Robert, Air War Over Korea, Charles Scribner's Sons, New York, NY, 1973

Jenkins, Dennis R, Landis, Tony R, Experimental & Prototype: U.S. Air Force Jet Fighters, Specialty Press Publishers, North Branch, MN, 2008

Johnson, Clarence L, Smith, Maggie, Kelly: More Than My Share of It All, Smithsonian Institution Press, Washington D.C., 1987

Jones, Lloyd S, U.S. Fighters, Aero Publishers, Fallbrook, CA, 1975

LeMay, Curtis E, Kantor, MacKinlay, Mission with LeMay, Doubleday and Company Inc., Garden City, NY, 1965

Lopez, Donald S., Fighter Pilot's Heaven, Smithsonian Institution Press, Washington D.C., 1995

Nichols, John B, Tillman Barrett, On Yankee Station: The Naval Air War over Vietnam, United States Naval Institute, Annapolis, MD, 1987

Pace, Steve, Skunk Works, Motor Books International, Osceola, WI, 1992

Peacock, Lindsay, North American F-86 Sabre, Gallery Books, London, UK, 1991

Peebles, Curtis, Dark Eagles, Presidio, Novato, CA, 1995

Pisano, Dominick A, Van Der Linden, F Robert, Winter, Frank H, Chuck Yeager and the Bell X-1, Smithsonian Institution Press, Washington D.C, 2006

Redding, Robert, Yenne, Bill, Boeing, Planemaker to the World, Thunder Bay Press, San Diego, CA, 1983

Rendall, Ivan , Rolling Thunder, The Free Press, New York, NY, 1997

Rock, Edward T., First In, Last Out: Stories by the Wild Weasels, Author House, Bloomington, AL, 2005

Sherwood, John Darrell, Fast Movers, The Free Press, New York, NY, 1999

Thomason, Tommy H, U.S. Naval Air Superiority, Specialty Press Publishers, North Branch, MN, 2007

Upton, Jim, Lockheed F-104: Starfighter, Specialty Press Publishers, North Branch, MN, 2003

W. Howard Plunkett, Rolling Thunder Radar Bombing, Air Power History, Spring/Summer 2006

W. Howard Plunkett, When the Thunderbirds Flew the Thunderchiefs, Air Power History, Fall 2009

Walpole, Nigel, Voodoo Warriors: The Story of the McDonnell Voodoo Fast Jets, Pen and Sword Aviation, Great Britain, 2007

Wegg, John, General Dynamics Aircraft and their Predecessors , Naval Institute Press, Annapolis, MD, 1990

Winchester, Jim, Modern Military Aircraft, Amber Books, London, UK, 2010

Wolfe, Tom, The Right Stuff, Picador, New York, NY, 1979

Wooldridge, E.T. Jr., The P-80 Shooting Star, Smithsonian Institution Press, Washington D.C, 1979

Yeager, Chuck, Janos, Leo, Yeager, Bantam Books, 1985

Yeager, Chuck, Wings, Thomasson-Grant, , 1984

Yenne, Bill, Convair Deltas: From Sea Dart to Hustler, Specialty Press Publishers, North Branch, MN, 2009

Referenced Web Links:

von Wodtke, Carl (Editor), Aviation History Magazine, http://www.historynet.com/y-interview-with-frank-k-pete-everest-who-flew-a-bell-x-2-to-record-speed-of-mach-3.htm

http://www.bmtflightphotos.af.mil/index.asp

http://en.wikipedia.org/wiki

http://www.ejectionsite.com

http://www.nationalmuseum.af.mil/index.asp

http://www.flightglobal.com/pdfarchive/index.html

http://www.history.army.mil/acquisition/research/fa_oh_intro.html

http://www.joebaugher.com/usaf_fighters

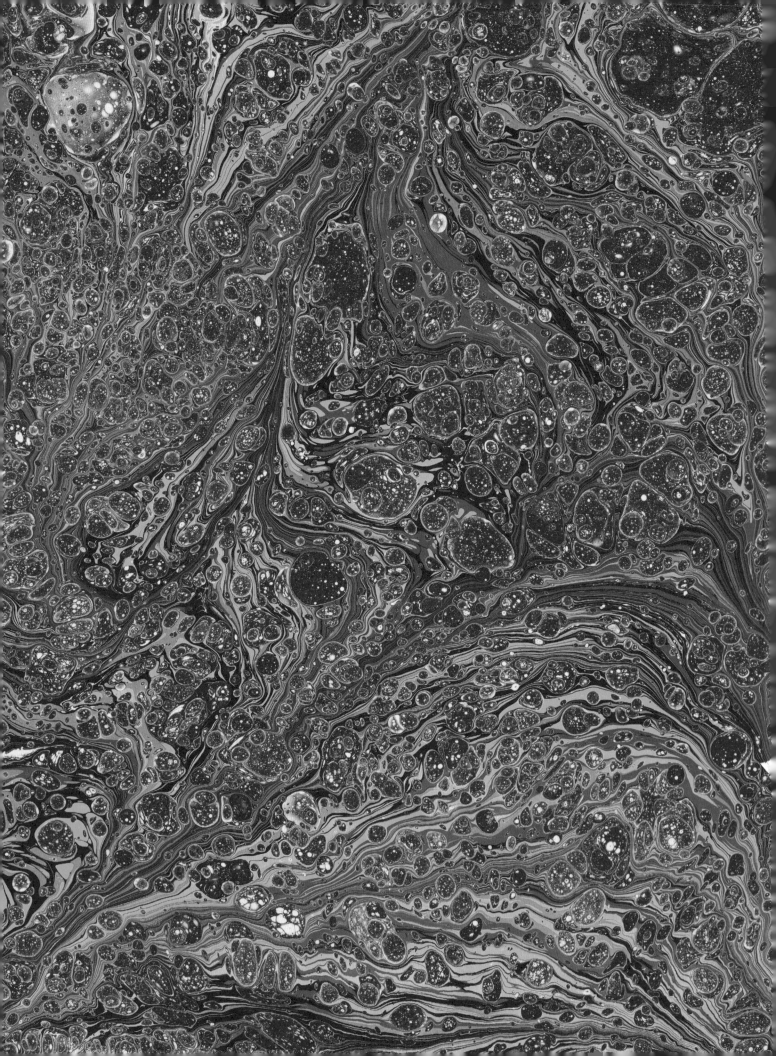